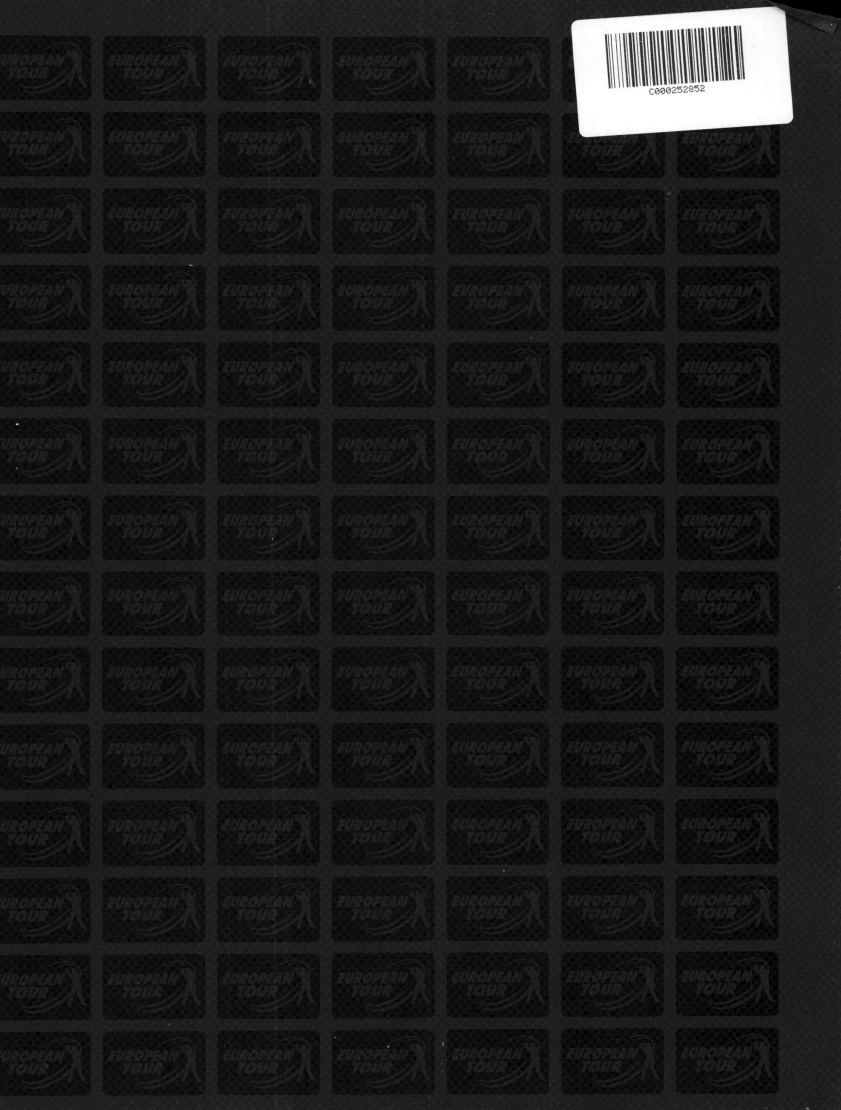

The European Tour
Yearbook 2001

OFFICIAL  PUBLICATION

PGA Golf de Catalunya, Girona, Spain: The 9th hole from behind the green

Introduction from The European Tour

Executive Editor
Mitchell Platts

Production Editor
Vanessa O'Brien

Editorial Consultants
Chris Plumridge
Gordon Simpson

Picture Editors
Stephen Munday
Andrew Redington

Art Director
Tim Leney
TC Communications Plc

Produced By
London Print & Design Plc

The European Tour Yearbook 2001
is published by
The PGA European Tour,
Wentworth Drive, Virgina Water,
Surrey GU25 4LX.

Distributed through Aurum Press Ltd.
25 Bedford Avenue
London WC1B 3AT

Colour reproduction through Essex Colour.

Printing and binding by Mohn Media.
© PGA European Tour.

ISBN 1 85410 778 X

This millennium edition of the European Tour Yearbook provides ample evidence of the spectacular growth of the game highlighting as it does the achievements of the world's finest golfers in the international arena and the competitiveness of all players on the European Tour, European Challenge Tour and European Seniors Tour.

We congratulate Lee Westwood in finishing Number One in the Volvo Order of Merit, and acknowledge that in so doing he was compelled to parry the considerable thrusts made by Darren Clarke, Ernie Els, Michael Campbell, Thomas Björn, and, of course, Colin Montgomerie whose accomplishment in leading the Volvo Order of Merit for seven successive seasons from 1993 to 1999 might never be equalled.

Lee's achievement in winning five Volvo Order of Merit titles in addition to the Cisco World Match Play Championship, so emulating Severiano Ballesteros (1986), Nick Faldo (1992) and Colin Montgomerie (1999) in winning six times in a single season on the European Tour International Schedule, was one of many outstanding performances by European Tour Members in the first year of the new millennium and this included Darren's superb success in the WGC - Andersen Consulting Match Play. We also congratulate Ian Poulter in becoming the 2000 Sir Henry Cotton Rookie of the Year.

Henrik Stenson and David Higgins decided their enthralling encounter for leading honours in the European Challenge Tour Rankings at the 2nd Cuba Challenge Tour Grand Final, with Henrik finishing Number One, and we congratulate the 15 leading players for securing their cards to compete on the 2001 European Tour International Schedule.

Australia's Noel Ratcliffe ended England's Tommy Horton's four year reign as Number One player on the European Seniors Tour but it came down to the last putt of the concluding tournament in Abu Dhabi before he could celebrate as he finished a mere 1,639 euro (£953) ahead of America's John Grace followed by Ireland's Denis O'Sullivan, Tommy Horton, Australia's Ian Stanley, Brazil's Priscillo Diniz and Scotland's David Huish on what is a truly international Tour.

There has been a steady growth pattern for all three Tours over the years. We had 35 host nations in the year 2000, and we will target to increase this number by orderly progress in the forthcoming years. That is the future. For now please reflect on the events of the millennium year which took the game to a new level, and enjoy this Yearbook which reviews another superb season in the history of the Tour.

KENNETH D SCHOFIELD CBE
Executive Director, The European Tour

WINNING COUNTS.

PGA EUROPEAN TOUR BALL COUNT		
Up to and including the Scottish PGA Championship		
Titleist	3,334	74%
Maxfli	391	9%
Spalding	394	9%
All others	357	8%

WIN COUNTS			
Up to August 28th 2000			
	Worldwide	PGA European	US PGA
Titleist	108 (57%)	22 (73%)	21 (58%)
Bridgestone	21 (11%)	0 (0%)	1 (3%)
Nike	16 (9%)	2 (7%)	7 (19%)
Callaway	16 (9%)	1 (3%)	1 (3%)
Maxfli	13 (7%)	4 (13%)	2 (6%)
All others	15 (8%)	1 (3%)	4 (11%)

Ask Sergio, José Maria or Davis Love. Ask Duval, Westwood or Clarke. In golf, success is all-important. And if that's what counts on the world's professional Tours, our statistics prove that Titleist is the ball that counts the most. This season, like every season, the #1 ball in golf is winning more titles and more tournament counts than any other ball. Twenty two out of 30 wins on the European Tour, for example, compared to just four for the nearest competitor. And week-in, week-out on the European Tour, seven out of ten players trust their game to the advanced golf ball technology of Titleist. So if you're serious about your game, look no further for the ball you can really count on.

Source: Sports Marketing Surveys Ltd (Europe) Darrell Survey (US)

Titleist
#1 ball in golf.®

Titleist, St. Ives, Cambs PE27 3LU
www.titleist.co.uk

Contents

Westwood and Upwards

*E*ven a casual glance in Lee John Westwood's direction confirms instantly the impression that here is a man whose lineage surely is rooted in that richest of traditions, the English yeoman.

While his modern-day battles may be restricted to this or that golf course it does not require too vivid an imagination to picture Westwood in another time standing firm at Agincourt, Flanders Field or perhaps Waterloo. Broad of thigh and wide of shoulder he is the walking epitome of the solidly dependable Englishman, forever bearing out those yeomanly qualities of staunchness, courage and loyalty.

Lee and Laurae Westwood

Yet if it always was going to take someone very special to replace Colin Montgomerie at the epicentre of European golf the irony of Westwood is that while his game at times is fit to dance with the sporting gods, it is his unblinkered, unfazed, bloke-next-door approach to life, the universe and everything that otherwise marks him out from the herd.

Of course he knows that he is one of the most blessed players of his generation but it is his refusal to allow his feet to leave the ground and his abiding loyalty and commitment to his family and old friends back in the uncomplicated northern English town of Worksop that most warmly charms public and critics alike.

As the European game's Number One player he is clearly confirmed as a major global star, a fact happily illustrated by an earning power that is now equal to the Gross National Product of at least a few small nations. Yet despite the obvious trappings of serious wealth, his cars, his splendid new home set in 60 acres of finest Worksop real estate, the private plane and the adulation that sweeps over him wherever he plays, Westwood remains cheerily unaffected.

Well, cheerily unaffected by everything except any discernible decline in his ability to play exquisitely the game he has pursued obsessively ever since his grandparents bought him a half set of clubs when he was 13 years old, his father suddenly left to wonder what had happened to the happy afternoons they had spent together on a river bank.

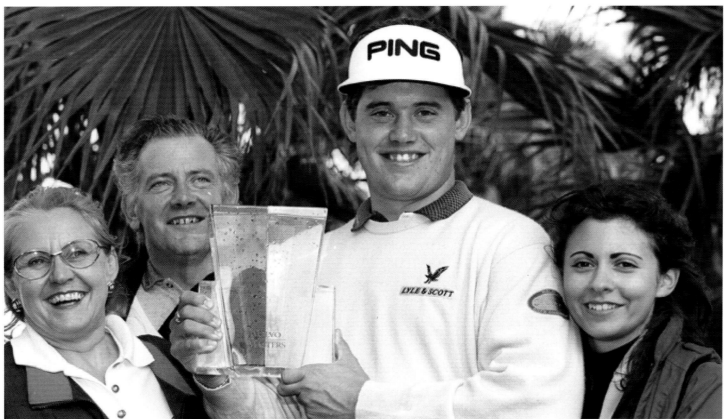

Family celebration: Parents Trish and John with Lee and Laurae

Such a bleak moment arrived in the spring of 2000 during the Benson and Hedges International Open at The De Vere Belfry. That week Westwood was out of sorts, frustrated with his form, or lack of it, and ready, it seemed, to retreat for a while. He said he was no longer enjoying the game that had so captivated him 14 years earlier and that if it was not for the fact that there were some big events coming up he would dearly love to toss his clubs into the garage and enjoy a month or so away from the circuit.

Yes, it was a moan but it was a sincere and honest one. Instead of taking a holiday, however, he travelled 48 hours later to Hamburg for the Deutsche Bank-SAP Open TPC of Europe. It was a glittering field that assembled at Güt Kaden with no-one glittering more than World Number One Tiger Woods but at the end of the tournament it was a rejuvenated Westwood who stepped forward to accept the trophy. Just as swiftly as it had deserted him, his form had returned and over the rest of the season he fed voraciously off the confidence that welled within his sturdy chest. After Germany he won another four Volvo Order of Merit tournaments, emerging triumphant at the Compaq European Grand Prix, the Smurfit European Open, the Volvo Scandinavian Masters and the Belgacom Open. Just to emphasise his class in 2000 he also won the Cisco World Match Play Championship title at Wentworth Club and, furthermore, he had won in January the Dimension Data Pro-Am on the Southern Africa Tour.

And when push came to extremely nervous shove during the WGC-American Express Championship at Valderrama it was Westwood who rose above every rival but one to finish second and secure his European Number One title. He had entered this final tournament 100,800 euro (£63,000) adrift of close friend and ISM stable-mate Darren Clarke but when Westwood seized his moment, Clarke very gracefully seized his own, stepping forward to admit: "Lee's been more consistent than me this season so I think he deserves the Number One title more. I'm disappointed for me but I'm really pleased for him."

Westwood was helped in this remarkable surge forward by the fact that for the first time since turning professional in 1993 he suddenly could see distant greens clearly, his sight problems having been remedied by lazer surgery earlier in the year. Until this operation the extraordinary truth was that Westwood had to rely on his caddie to tell him just what he was aiming at on a distant and dramatically blurred horizon.

Helped also by sports psychologist Bob Rotella whose book 'Golf Is Not A Game Of Perfect' was read with an enthusiasm he admits he had previously only bestowed on 'Tootles The Taxi-Driver'. His wife, Laurae, read 'Perfect' also and suggested he arrange to see Rotella to discuss ways in which he might further improve an already burgeoning game.

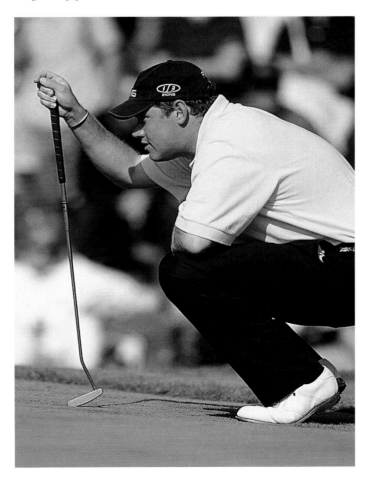

The advice, when it came, was unorthodox, Westwood discovering to his embarrassment that he should congratulate himself on any decent shot, even, quite literally, patting himself on that broad back. After initial misgivings he entered into the spirit of this mind-game, discovering to his surprised delight that it worked. As his elf-esteem escalated, so too did his success rate.

No-one was the slightest bit surprised. His old club captain Tony Coupland is, like everyone else at Worksop Golf Club, thrilled at what their best known member is currently achieving. It is, however, no more than they expected to witness.

Coupland was junior organiser when Westwood first began to hint that here just might be a special player. This was back in the mid-eighties and the club had just revolutionised their junior section so that lads like Lee were actually encouraged to come along, to play and to take advantage of free coaching once they made it into the junior squad. This was radical stuff.

"In all honesty it was easy to spot that Lee might be something out of the ordinary," Coupland said. "I'll give you just one example. When he was 13 he was playing for the club in the Notts Junior Cup

Final, a competition which we'd never won. He was out in the last singles match which he had to win to half everything and take us into a play-off. He was small even for 13 and the lad he was playing was 18-years-old and towered over him. But Lee won his match and then won the title for us at the first extra hole. "That was a clincher for me because it proved he not only had a decent swing and so on but that he had the right attitude and determination. Now despite all his success he remains the same, down to earth lad, the life and soul of any party, that I've always known."

Now Westwood's target is to move ever onward and upward. It promises to be an exciting ride. "Greg Norman was my hero when I was growing up, still is really. I just love the way he plays the game. He's aggressive all the time, really goes for it, and that is the way I like to see golf played. We should never lose sight of the fact that we are entertainers and I think that is the way the public want to view the game. They want some excitement. And, to be honest, so do I."

Bill Elliott

II

Global Pilgrimage

Lee Westwood

When the venerable John Jacobs decided in 1971 to broaden the horizons of tournament golf not even he could have imagined the breathtaking appeal it would achieve because of such prescience. What the then Director-General assumed would be a unification and creation of European events to form a co-ordinated circuit has since grown into a global structure that has transformed the face of golf.

It now touches 24 countries annually from Australia to the United States and inspires interest and enthusiasm wherever it performs to such an extent that golfers of international class are now beginning to emerge from nations which hitherto held no perceived pedigree within the sport. There is almost a missionary zeal to this pilgrimage which knows no limits and seeks new opportunities with every year that passes.

The fruits of such activity are self-evident, none more so than during the the season which has launched the new Millennium and underlined the consistent rite of succession by which the European Tour International Schedule gathers strength and endures through its brightest stars. The sheer openness for the battle to top the 2000 Volvo Order of Merit, held by Colin Montgomerie for an unprecedented seven years, illustrates that point.

First, New Zealander Michael Campbell made the running until Ulsterman Darren Clarke took control for 21 weeks following his WGC-Andersen Consulting Match Play triumph over Tiger Woods at La Costa and Spa in Carlsbad, California. Then the mighty South African Ernie Els grabbed the helm briefly only to be nudged gently aside by Lee Westwood, who himself was then displaced by Clarke in the full knowledge that this precious prize would not be decided until the very last event particularly with Thomas Björn and Montgomerie still within reach

That, indeed, was the case with Westwood passing Clarke on the final day of the 2000 season to finish Number One ahead of his friend and rival.

Darren Clarke

Roger Chapman

Other evidence of the progressive health of the European Tour International Schedule could be found in the procession of 13 first-time winners who made up an eventual cast of champions from 17 countries that included Argentina, Australia, Canada, Denmark, England, Fiji, Holland, Ireland, Italy, New Zealand, Northern Ireland, Scotland, South Africa, Spain, Sweden, Taiwan and the United States.

Moreover those newcomers to the winners's circle were not all fresh-faced recruits in the first flush of their careers because Roger Chapman, at the age of 40, offered inarguable proof that it is never too late to become a champion. It had taken him 19 years including a re-visit to the European Tour Qualifying School for him to score his first victory as he captured the Brazil Rio de Janeiro 500 Years Open at Itanhangá. Nor was he the only seasoned campaigner to have both patience and persistence rewarded. Jamie Spence, aged 37, ended an eight-year wait since his last win to earn the Moroccan Open Méditel at Golf D'Amelkis in Marrakech and Josè Coceres, 36, from Argentina, scored his second victory in six years with the Dubai Desert Classic at the Dubai Creek Golf and Yacht Club.

Padraig Harrington

In a sense their personal triumphs serve to show that not all the enthralling drama takes place solely among the top of the bill performers, but that every success contains its own saga of effort and self-belief. Gary Orr for example had been a consistent campaigner for the past decade without ever topping a finishing list. Yet, at the age of 32, the Scottish professional's outlook and prospects changed when he eagled the last hole at Le Meridien Penina to win the Algarve Portuguese Open and then took the Victor Chandler British Masters later in the season at Woburn.

Niclas Fasth, from Sweden, made in 1999 his fourth visit to the Tour School, before finding the confidence to become a first time winner and Madeira Island Open champion at Santo da Serra. Rolf Muntz made an additional piece of history when he became the first Dutch professional to win a Tour event as he took the Qatar Masters at Doha Golf Club.

Curiously enough the list of first-time winners for 2000 was launched by New Zealand's Michael Campbell who, although being a major figure on Tour for several seasons, had never quite clinched a title until the Johnnie Walker Classic at The Westin Resort Ta Shee in Taiwan then made up for lost time by taking the Heineken Classic at The Vines Resort in Perth and the Linde German Masters at Gut Lärchenhof in Cologne. Anthony Wall from Sunningdale, playing in his fourth full season on Tour, became a new winner with a cool-headed performance in the Alfred Dunhill Championship at Houghton Golf Club in Johannesburg .

Other new faces included Taiwan's Yeh Wei-tze (Benson and Hedges Malaysian Open at Templer Park Golf and Country Club, Kuala Lumpur), Australia's Lucas Parsons (Greg Norman Holden International at The Lakes Golf Club in Sydney), Englishman Brian Davis (Peugeot Open de España at PGA Golf de Catalunya in Girona), Denmark's Steen Tinning (The Celtic Manor Resort Wales Open at the Celtic Manor Resort in Newport), Italy's Massimo Scarpa (Buzzgolf.com North West of Ireland Open at the Slieve Russell Hotel Golf and Country Club in County Cavan), England's Ian Poulter (Italian Open at Is Molas in Sardinia) and Canada's Mike Weir (WGC-American Express Championship at Club de Golf, Valderrama).

For sheer heroic resilience Irishman Padraig Harrington's victory in the Brazil Sao Paulo 500 Years Open at Sao Paulo Golf Club stands as a shining example to others because only a week earlier he had lost a play-off to Chapman yet still summoned the tenacity to keep on trying. Moreover, he was to earn admiration and praise from the world of sport in general for the dignified manner in which he accepted disqualification when leading the Benson and Hedges International Open at The De Vere Belfry later in the season following a scorecard mix-up. Even so, his ill fortune took nothing away from the brilliant efforts of José Maria Olazábal, the eventual winner, who scored a last round 66 to take the title for the second time in his career, and, happily, Harrington returned to the winner's podium at the BBVA Open Turespaña Masters Comunidad de Madrid later in the season at Club de Campo in Madrid.

Ernie Els

One key aspect of the European Tour International Schedule's prestige is the manner in which its key figures perform in all arenas, particularly the major championships which were dominated in 2000 by the phenomenal exploits of Tiger Woods, who not only completed the Grand Slam of four major titles but also captured three of them - the US Open (Pebble Beach), the Open Championship (St Andrews) and the US PGA Championship (Valhalla) to become the first golfer since Ben Hogan in 1953 to accomplish the feat.

The only major championship to elude him was the Masters Tournament at Augusta National which went to Fiji's Vijay Singh, who honed his craft on the European Tour and continues to return for regular appearances throughout the season. But it was the additional strength of European Tour presence in all these Championships that again underlined its importance on the world stage.

Els, besides winning the Standard Life Loch Lomond title, struck superb if frustrating consistency by finishing runner-up in the Masters Tournament, the US Open and the Open Championship. Björn shared second place with him at St Andrews then went on to finish third in the US PGA Championship - as well as winning the BMW International Open at Golfclub München Nord-Eichenried. Miguel Angel Jiménez also maintained a defiant presence in the US Open with a share of second place as Harrington finished joint fifth with Westwood and Nick Faldo made a welcome return in seventh place.

The collective impact of the European Tour International Schedule players was equally apparent in the US PGA Championship at Valhalla with American Bob May, the 1999 Victor Chandler British Masters winner, finishing second with Björn third, Olazábal fourth and Clarke ninth. Moreover Welsh professional Phillip Price went on to share second place in the WGC-NEC Invitational at Akron, Ohio, behind - guess who? - Woods.

Of course, Clarke had shown early evidence of the European Factor when he scored that decisive 4 and 3 victory over Woods in California and was to regain that winning touch later in the season when he successfully defended The Compass Group English Open at the Marriott Forest of Arden Hotel in Warwickshire. Clarke belongs to that select group of campaigners who can erupt without warning into commanding action and therefore can never be counted out. Among that number is Sweden's Mathias Grönberg, who triumphed in the Mercedes-Benz - SA Open Championship at Randpark Golf Club in Johannesburg, fellow countryman Pierre Fulke who became Scottish PGA champion at the Gleneagles Hotel, then took his game to a new level by winning the Volvo Masters, Argentina's Eduardo Romero (Canon European Masters in Crans-sur-Sierre, Switzerland), South Africa's Retief Goosen (Trophée Lancôme at Saint-Nom-La-Bretèche near Paris) Sweden's Patrik Sjöland (Murphy's Irish Open at Ballybunion) and Australia's Stephen Leaney (TNT Dutch Open at the Noordwijkse Golf Club).

Phillip Price

Colin Montgomerie

It is somewhat ironic that the most successful season so far in the remarkable career of Westwood should have started on such a low note that verged on despair as the Tour was reaching the halfway mark and he languished in 33rd position in the Volvo Order of Merit. He confessed to not knowing what was wrong with his game but hoped that just a couple of good rounds might put things right.

Sure enough, they came during the Deutsche Bank - SAP Open TPC of Europe, at Gut Kaden in Hamburg, which not only earned him the title but in which he overtook defending champion Woods in the process. Indeed the familiar battle lines looked to have been drawn a week later when Montgomerie sprang into action with his third successive victory in the Volvo PGA Championship at Wentworth Club to accompany his earlier win in the Novotel Perrier Open de France at Le Golf National in Paris and thus move into a menacing position for the defence of his Volvo Order of Merit title.

What happened next was quite astounding as Westwood embarked on a phenomenal winning streak by taking the Compaq European Grand Prix at De Vere Slaley Hall in Northumberland, the Smurfit European Open at The K Club, near Dublin, the Volvo Scandinavian Masters at Kungsängen in Stockholm, the Belgacom Open at Royal Zoute in Belgium and the Cisco World Match Play Championship title at the 38th hole of a rain-delayed final in which defending champion Montgomerie was his victim.

Thomas Björn

Michael Campbell

In the inevitable ebb and flow of fortune that is part of every player's season, there were other moments to savour too - Miguel Angel Martin linking with Jiménez and Olazábal in Spain's successful defence of the Alfred Dunhill Cup and Seve Ballesteros leading his Continental Europe team to a thrilling 13½ to 12½ victory over Great Britain and Ireland in the inaugural Eurobet Seve Ballesteros Trophy at Sunningdale.

The inspiring Spaniard scored a 2 and 1 win over Montgomerie in the last day singles while Bernhard Langer played his part with a 4 and 3 triumph over fellow former Masters Tournament champion Ian Woosnam, and Sergio Garcia birdied the last two holes to snatch a half-point from Clarke. It offered more evidence of the rich and varied feast of golf in all its forms that now challenges the entire ensemble on the European Tour International Schedule and pushes them to beyond limits they never knew existed. Come to think of it, that canny John Jacobs knew what he was doing all those years ago.

Michael McDonnell

Arise Sir Michael

THE WESTIN RESORT TA SHEE, TAIWAN

*T*he renaissance of Michael Campbell was always felt by those who knew him well to be only just around the corner, and he more than justified that support by winning the Johnnie Walker Classic with a performance that smacked of class and character.

Those two words - class and character - had become closely associated with Campbell in the summer of 1995. Where better to make an international name for yourself than on the West Course

at Wentworth Club and the Old Course at St Andrews. For that year Campbell came within a whisker of winning the Volvo PGA Championship and the Open Championship. At Wentworth, he finished eagle-birdie-birdie-birdie to come up one shot shy of winner Bernhard Langer and little more than a month later he led the Open entering the final round only to be edged out by one shot as John Daly claimed the title in a play-off. Still, Michael Campbell had arrived.

Ernie Els

This, then, was another triumph for the burgeoning European Challenge Tour. Campbell had moved on from being Rookie of the Year on the 1993 Australasian Order of Merit to win back-to-back tournaments on the 1994 European Challenge Tour and graduate to the European Tour. The strongly built, amiable Maori from Wellington, the leading amateur in New Zealand in 1992, had been encouraged by his father at the age of ten to play golf and now, not too many years later, he had the world at his feet.

Maoris, so it is written, believe all living things are descended from the gods, and the gods are embodied in certain brooks, mountains and rivers. "I came from a mountain called Taranaki," said the great-great-great-great grandson of Sir John Logan Campbell, the first mayor of Auckland. "It's where I get my strength still."

Michael Campbell would need that strength. Suddenly those golfing gods, in that vindictive manner that only they possess, looked unkindly down on the young man even as praise from the great golfers of the world was still ringing in his ears.

You see Campbell had bucked up the courage at a golf banquet to talk with Greg Norman. "G'day," I said. "My name's Michael Campbell. Can I play with you tomorrow." Norman told Campbell to meet him on the tee the next day. He did, and there to greet him was not only Norman but also one Jack Nicklaus. " I found him to be a talented, aggressive, impressive young golfer," said Nicklaus afterwards. "He's a very good ball-striker and a fine young man. I think he has a great future ahead of him." Norman weighed in: "Potentially, Michael's the best young player I've ever played with. Raymond Floyd, another practice round partner, declared: "I think he's the brightest young player out there, without a doubt."

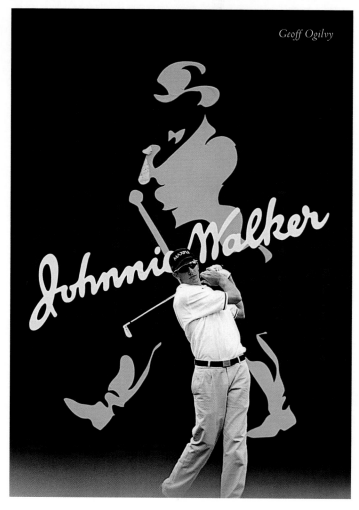

Geoff Ogilvy

Shot of the Week

Played by Tiger Woods at the 16th hole. His tee shot ended right by a tree from which any mere mortal would have simply chipped the ball back into play. Woods took a full swing knowing that the club shaft would crash into the tree trunk just after a moment of impact. The club was knocked from his hands, but the ball found the sanctuary of the green. Tiger made his four and a third round of 70 kept him in the hunt.

Then the star dimmed. At the start of 1996, he picked up a golf club to practise. Suddenly he could no longer swing it because his left wrist was so painful. He tried acupuncture, exercise and medication, none of which seemed to work, and it was only that strength of character, fuelled by positive thoughts, that enabled him to get back to the first tee. But the magic had deserted him.

Campbell plunged down the Volvo Order of Merit from fifth (1995) to 120th (1996) and to 133rd in 1997 when he was compelled to return to the European Tour Qualifying School. He immediately regained his card, but one top ten finish in 1998 was some way from confirming that Floyd, Nicklaus and Norman possessed the same talent for spotting a star of the future as they did for hitting a seven iron 'dead' when it mattered.

What is more, Ernie Els and Tiger Woods had now arrived centre-stage and Campbell was simply part of the supporting cast when these two new giants of the game teed-up in the Johnnie Walker Classic - the first event on the 2000 European Tour International Schedule - at The Westin Resort Ta Shee in Taiwan.

Campbell's opening 66, however, emphasised he was anything but stage struck. He shared the lead with Jeremy Robinson and Johan Skold, one ahead of American Ryder Cup player Jim Furyk, and stayed there alongside Els, who fashioned a second round 67, at the halfway stage.

Jim Furyk

Campbell spread-eagled the field with outward 33 in the third round, making birdies at the third, sixth and ninth, as a strong wind played havoc. He shot 69 to Els's 73 as the young Australian Geoff Ogilvy (68) moved into second place, three shots behind, but Els and now Woods (70) were just one shot further back. "This is definitely the best looking leaderboard I have ever seen my name on," said Ogilvy. Campbell mused: "I'd like to be ten ahead of Tiger!"

In fact Campbell pretty much had his wish after only a handful or so holes at the start of the final round. He birdied the first two holes and made another at the sixth. Defending champion Woods, seeking his fifth tournament victory in a row, dropped two shots at the sixth and another three at the eighth. Els and Ogilvy, however, remained as threats and after 14 holes they shared the lead with Campbell. Then Campbell birdied the 15th from 12 feet, Els bogeyed the 16th and with a closing 70 to Ogilvy's 68 the golfing gods decreed that the New Zealander should win by one shot. "Finally, the monkey's off my back," said Campbell. "It's just unbelievable. It's been a long, frustrating four years. After such a great year in 1995, when I was so near so many times, this is a great feeling."

So, without doubt, Nicklaus and Norman are good judges of talent, and character, after all

Mitchell Platts

Michael Campbell

The Course

The Westin Resort Ta Shee made history by hosting the first event to be co-sanctioned by the European, Australasian and Asia Tours. The course is long on the scorecard, but does not play quite as long because the fairways can be really fast. Even so it is a tough course where par is a virtue when the wind blows in certain directions.

Eduardo Romero

THE WESTIN RESORT TA SHEE, TAIWAN, 11-14 NOVEMBER 1999, PAR 72, 7150 YARDS, 6538 METRES

Pos.	Name		Rd1	Rd2	Rd3	Rd4	Total	Par	Prize Money Euro	£	Pos.	Name		Rd1	Rd2	Rd3	Rd4	Total	Par	Prize Money Euro	£
1	Michael CAMPBELL	NZ	66	71	69	70	276	-12	207728.00	133329.91		Marcus WHEELHOUSE	NZ	72	69	72	76	289	1	9721.86	6239.96
2	Geoff OGILVY	Aus	70	71	68	68	277	-11	138475.00	88879.97		Wayne SMITH	Aus	72	73	69	75	289	1	9721.86	6239.96
3	Ernie ELS	SA	70	67	73	68	278	-10	78009.00	50069.96		Soren HANSEN	Den	70	75	70	74	289	1	9721.86	6239.96
4	Vijay SINGH	Fiji	71	72	68	68	279	-9	62320.00	40000.00		Lucas PARSONS	Aus	73	71	75	70	289	1	9721.86	6239.96
5	Peter SENIOR	Aus	67	72	74	67	280	-8	52785.00	33879.97	39	Eduardo ROMERO	Arg	72	74	72	72	290	2	7977.00	5120.03
6	Tiger WOODS	USA	68	72	70	71	281	-7	43624.00	28000.00		Klas ERIKSSON	Swe	71	73	74	72	290	2	7977.00	5120.03
7	Frank NOBILO	NZ	72	71	70	69	282	-6	34276.00	22000.00		Jean-Francois REMSEY	Fr	73	73	70	74	290	2	7977.00	5120.03
	Phillip PRICE	Wal	68	72	75	67	282	-6	3427.00	22000.00		Paul GOW	Aus	74	72	72	72	290	2	7977.00	5120.03
9	Richard BACKWELL	Aus	72	70	73	68	283	-5	25219.00	16186.78		Hennie OTTO	SA	73	71	71	75	290	2	7977.00	5120.03
	Steen TINNING	Den	69	71	72	71	283	-5	25219.00	16186.78		Christian PENA	USA	73	73	75	69	290	2	7977.00	5120.03
	Angel CABRERA	Arg	70	71	69	73	283	-5	25219.00	16186.78		David PARK	Wal	74	72	70	74	290	2	7977.00	5120.03
12	Nick FALDO	Eng	72	72	69	70	283	-5	20191.67	12959.99	46	Wayne RILEY	Aus	73	73	71	74	291	3	6606.00	4240.05
	Peter O'MALLEY	Aus	72	70	70	72	284	-4	20191.67	12959.99		David McKENZIE	Aus	73	72	76	70	291	3	6606.00	4240.05
	Prayad MARKSAENG	Thai	71	70	73	70	284	-4	20191.67	12959.99		Robin BYRD	USA	70	76	71	74	291	3	6606.00	4240.05
15	Kenny DRUCE	Aus	75	70	70	70	285	-3	17948.00	11519.90		Terry PRICE	Aus	74	68	72	77	291	3	6606.00	4240.05
	Roger WESSELS	SA	69	73	72	71	285	-3	17948.00	11519.90	50	Danny CHIA	Mal	71	74	78	69	292	4	5484.20	3520.03
17	Kyi Hia HAN	Myan	74	71	69	72	286	-2	15134.86	9714.29		Roger WINCHESTER	Eng	71	74	77	70	292	4	5484.20	3520.03
	Jeev Mikha SINGH	Ind	71	74	71	70	286	-2	15134.86	9714.29		James KINGSTON	SA	73	72	74	73	292	4	5484.20	3520.03
	Andrew PITTS	USA	69	72	73	72	286	-2	15134.86	9714.29		Wen Teh LU	Taiwan	71	75	74	72	292	4	5484.20	3520.03
	Chawalit PLAPHOL	Thai	74	72	70	70	286	-2	15134.86	9714.29		Jean Louis GUEPY	Fr	71	74	76	71	292	4	5484.20	3520.03
	Felix CASAS	Phil	71	74	70	71	286	-2	15134.86	9714.29	55	Paul NILBRINK	Swe	70	74	73	76	293	5	4487.00	2879.97
	Peter LONARD	Aus	69	73	70	74	286	-2	15134.86	9714.29		Ter-Chang WANG	Taiwan	74	71	75	73	293	5	4487.00	2879.97
	Koichi NOGAMI	Jpn	72	68	76	70	286	-2	15134.86	9714.29		Amandeep JOHL	Ind	71	70	79	73	293	5	4487.00	2879.97
24	Jim FURYK	USA	67	73	78	69	287	-1	13087.00	8399.87	58	Soren KJELDSEN	Den	75	71	76	73	295	7	3926.00	2519.90
	Nick O'HERN	Aus	67	71	77	72	287	-1	13087.00	8399.87		Gregory HANRAHAN	USA	73	70	77	75	295	7	3926.00	2519.90
	Bradley KING	Aus	70	71	75	71	287	-1	13087.00	8399.87	60	Johan SKOLD	Swe	66	73	77	81	297	7	3739.00	2399.87
27	Marten OLANDER	Swe	68	70	76	74	288	0	11591.60	7440.05	61	Mark McNULTY	Zim	74	71	76	77	298	8	3552.50	2280.17
	Wook-Soon KANG	Rep. Kor	73	72	72	71	288	0	11591.60	7440.05		Tim ELLIOTT	Aus	74	72	75	77	298	8	3552.50	2280.17
	Simon YATES	Eng	72	74	73	69	288	0	11591.60	7440.05	63	Greig HUTCHEON	Scot	73	73	75	78	299	9	3365.00	2159.82
	Jeremy ROBINSON	Eng	66	78	73	71	288	0	11591.60	7440.05	64	Maarten LAFEBER	Hol	73	72	78	77	300	10	3241.00	2080.23
	Robert ALLENBY	Aus	70	72	76	70	288	0	11591.60	7440.05	65	Eric CARLBERG	Swe	70	72	77	82	301	11	2493.00	1600.13
32	Sandy LYLE	Scot	72	71	76	70	289	1	9721.86	6239.96		Rodrigo CUELLO	Phil	72	74	78	77	301	11	2493.00	1600.13
	Andre STOLZ	Aus	70	76	70	73	289	1	9721.86	6239.96	67	Tatsuhiko ICHIHARA	Jpn	73	72	73	84	302	12	1867.00	1198.33
	Shane TAIT	Aus	71	72	72	74	289	1	9721.86	6239.96											

Father and Son

HOUGHTON GOLF CLUB, JOHANNESBURG, SOUTH AFRICA

Whenever London taxi driver, Tom Wall, flicked the 'off duty' switch on his mini-cab, he invariably sought refuge on the golf course, where he indulged his obsessive passion for the game.

For the past two decades, that obsessive nature has been shared by his son, Anthony, in whose childish hands he first placed a golf club at the age of four, while dreaming that, one day, the same youngster would develop and mature into a champion in the professional game.

Such dreams are usually fanciful, but not in the case of Tom and Anthony Wall. Father and son shared the identical ambitions and worked for twenty years with unbridled enthusiasm to achieve their common objective. Month after month, year after year, Tom Wall

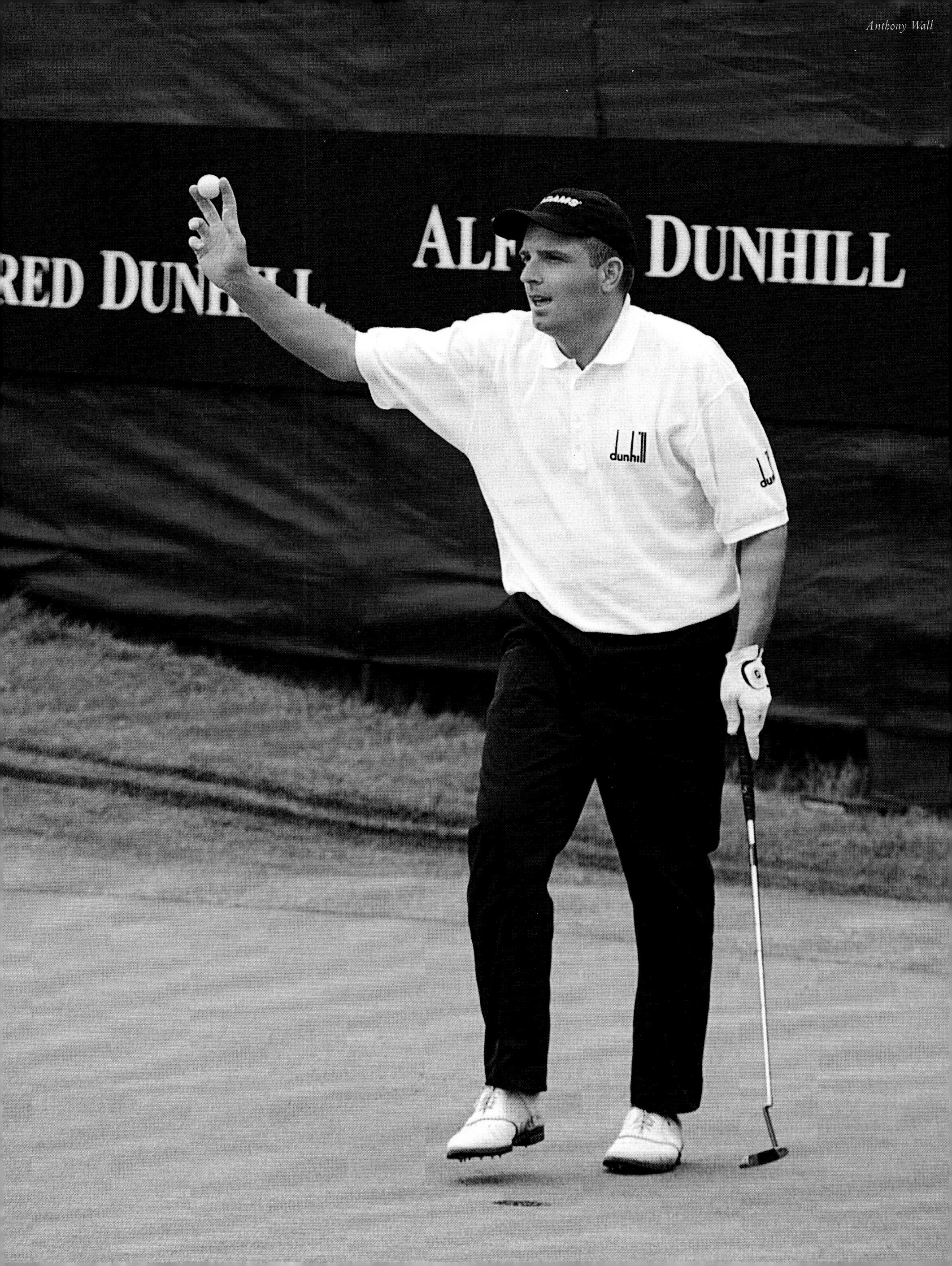

Anthony Wall

The Course

Houghton, a long, scenic, parkland course, was in immaculate condition leading up to the tournament, despite unseasonably heavy rain. The fact that it stood up to the test under severe problems was a tribute to the work of the staff, who had the greens in perfect shape.

would spend endless days on the practice range as mentor, coach, father, friend and confidant to young Anthony.

In the circumstances, only a cynic with a heart of granite could fail to be moved by the sight of their warm, emotional embrace on the 18th green at the conclusion of the Alfred Dunhill Championship at Houghton GC. Anthony had won his first title on the European Tour and the sense of achievement and fulfilment radiated in their contented faces.

For both men, it was the realisation of the dream they had nurtured through years of sacrifice and honest sweat and toil. Nothing tugs the heart strings like the bond between a parent and offspring on reaching the pinnacle of achievement. Just ask Earl and Tiger Woods.

Father paced the 18th like a restless tiger in its cage as his 24-year old-son pitched to four feet and sank the winning four foot putt. Relief was followed by a few tears as the pair hugged, and as Anthony was announced the new champion with a 12 under par total of 204 in the rain-shortened tournament.

Even at the subsequent press conference the pair were inseparable, sitting side by side with the Alfred Dunhill trophy gleaming between them on the table. Pride was etched in their faces as Anthony paid tribute to the role played by his father.

Celebration time for father and son

Retief Goosen

overcame testicular cancer to win on the US Tour in 1998, shot the low round of the week, a superb seven under par 65, to lead by two on ten under par.

The inclement weather prompted the tournament officials to take a Saturday decision to curtail the championship to 54 holes, a move supported by the sponsors and the European and Southern African Tours.

Dodds maintained his lead until the back nine but slipped back into a tie for fifth place. Orr, chasing his maiden victory on the European Tour, became a threat, as did the vastly improved and newly-married Welshman, Phillip Price, who set the clubhouse target with a closing 67 for 206, ten under par.

However, the moment that the Wall family had planned with such meticulous precision finally arrived on a bright day when the rains relented. Anthony showed control and composure under pressure to birdie five holes coming home. His inward 31 for a 68 secured the title, leaving Orr (70) and Price to share the runner-up position with Retief Goosen in fourth.

Gordon Simpson

"Ever since my dad started me off at the age of four this has been my dream - to get on the European Tour and then win tournaments. I always play well when dad is around. He has coached me since day one and for him to be here to witness this moment is great. Not only is he my dad, he is also one of my closest friends."

The compliment was reciprocated as Tom Wall observed: "This means everything to me. The greatest feeling I've ever had. I tried to plan this since Anthony was a little kid and to have this feeling is indescribable. Every day of our lives we've worked for this. We worked so hard you wouldn't believe it."

It was in November that Anthony, while playing in Australia, had invited Tom to join him for the start of the new millennium on the European Tour's International Schedule. Two weeks in the heat of South Africa sounded like a pleasant way to launch the 2000 campaign.

After the first round, which had been delayed by five and a half hours due to an overnight deluge, Wall lay one stroke off the pace set by a trio of Englishmen, Brian Davis, Paul Broadhurst and Peter Baker, on 68, four under par. The first round could not be completed until Friday lunchtime, but the fact that play was possible at all was due to the remarkable condition of the Houghton greens.

Wall trudged back into the incessant rain on Friday afternoon and proceeded to shoot a 67 to muscle his way into contention on 136, eight under par, a score he shared with Scotsman, Gary Orr.

Leading the way was 40-year-old Trevor Dodds from one of South Africa's neighbouring countries, Namibia. Dodds, who successfully

Shot of the Week

Anthony Wall's four iron second to the 496 yards, par four 14th on the final day. The toughest hole at Houghton, he had birdied it the previous day and proceeded to drill a superb shot 230 yards uphill to 18 feet to set up a crucial birdie.

Gone fishing! Greg Owen in splendid isolation

HOUGHTON GOLF CLUB, JOHANNESBURG, SOUTH AFRICA 13-16 JANUARY 2000, PAR 72, 7309 YARDS, 6683 METRES

Pos.	Name		Rd1	Rd2	Rd3	Rd4	Total	Par	Prize Money Euro	£
1	Anthony WALL	Eng	69	67	68		204	-12	125927.20	79100.00
2	Phillip PRICE	Wal	72	67	67		206	-10	73431.00	46125.00
	Gary ORR	Scot	69	67	70		206	-10	73431.00	46125.00
4	Retief GOOSEN	SA	72	69	66		207	-9	39163.20	24600.00
5	David FROST	SA	71	68	69		208	-8	24341.68	15290.00
	Tjaart VAN DER WALT	SA	72	68	68		208	-8	24341.68	15290.00
	Paul MCGINLEY	Ire	73	66	69		208	-8	24341.68	15290.00
	Trevor DODDS	Nam	69	65	74		208	-8	24341.68	15290.00
	David LYNN	Eng	71	71	66		208	-8	24341.68	15290.00
10	Jeev Milkha SINGH	Ind	69	70	70		209	-7	13989.70	8787.50
	Brian DAVIS	Eng	68	74	67		209	-7	13989.70	8787.50
	Anders HANSEN	Den	71	72	66		209	-7	13989.70	8787.50
	Nic HENNING	SA	71	68	70		209	-7	13989.70	8787.50
14	Bernhard LANGER	Ger	70	69	71		210	-6	11283.30	7087.50
	Malcolm MACKENZIE	Eng	72	71	67		210	-6	11283.30	7087.50
	Peter BAKER	Eng	68	70	72		210	-6	11283.30	7087.50
	Mathias GRÖNBERG	Swe	72	69	69		210	-6	11283.30	7087.50
18	Ricardo GONZALEZ	Arg	70	68	73		211	-5	9950.00	6250.00
	Fabrice TARNAUD	Fr	72	71	68		211	-5	9950.00	6250.00
	Desmond TERBLANCHE	SA	69	70	72		211	-5	9950.00	6250.00
21	Paul BROADHURST	Eng	68	70	74		212	-4	9233.60	5800.00
22	Peter FOWLER	Aus	72	70	71		213	-3	7522.20	4725.00
	Raphaël JACQUELIN	Fr	74	68	71		213	-3	7522.20	4725.00
	Maarten LAFEBER	Hol	71	70	72		213	-3	7522.20	4725.00
	Steve WEBSTER	Eng	70	69	74		213	-3	7522.20	4725.00
	Tom GILLIS	USA	71	69	73		213	-3	7522.20	4725.00
	John SENDEN	Aus	70	73	70		213	-3	7522.20	4725.00
	Dean VAN STADEN	SA	73	72	68		213	-3	7522.20	4725.00
	Greig HUTCHEON	Scot	73	71	69		213	-3	7522.20	4725.00
	Ian POULTER	Eng	74	69	70		213	-3	7522.20	4725.00
	Soren HANSEN	Den	71	71	71		213	-3	7522.20	4725.00
	Jonathan LOMAS	Eng	72	72	69		213	-3	7522.20	4725.00
	Ignacio GARRIDO	Sp	71	71	71		213	-3	7522.20	4725.00
	Bobby LINCOLN	SA	71	71	71		213	-3	7522.20	4725.00
	Peter LONARD	Aus	74	71	68		213	-3	7522.20	4725.00
36	Mark MCNULTY	Zim	74	71	69		214	-2	5651.60	3550.00
	Mark MURLESS	SA	75	68	71		214	-2	5651.60	3550.00
	Desvonde BOTES	SA	72	69	73		214	-2	5651.60	3550.00
	Justin HOBDAY	SA	69	74	71		214	-2	5651.60	3550.00
	André CRUSE	SA	71	74	69		214	-2	5651.60	3550.00
	Stephen GALLACHER	Scot	71	74	69		214	-2	5651.60	3550.00
	Nico VAN RENSBURG	SA	70	75	69		214	-2	5651.60	3550.00
43	Wayne RILEY	Aus	70	72	73		215	-1	4298.40	2700.00
	David HOWELL	Eng	72	71	72		215	-1	4298.40	2700.00
	Brenden PAPPAS	SA	73	70	72		215	-1	4298.40	2700.00
	Marco GORTANA	SA	69	74	72		215	-1	4298.40	2700.00
	Wallie COETSEE	SA	71	73	71		215	-1	4298.40	2700.00
	Paul EALES	Eng	72	72	71		215	-1	4298.40	2700.00
	Scott ROWE	USA	75	69	71		215	-1	4298.40	2700.00
	Niclas FASTH	Swe	72	71	72		215	-1	4298.40	2700.00
	Daren LEE	Eng	74	68	73		215	-1	4298.40	2700.00
	Robert BILBO JNR	SA	76	68	71		215	-1	4298.40	2700.00
53	Philip GOLDING	Eng	69	73	74		216	0	3024.80	1900.00
	Per NYMAN	Swe	72	72	72		216	0	3024.80	1900.00
	John MASHEGO	SA	73	71	72		216	0	3024.80	1900.00
	Ian GARBUTT	Eng	74	69	73		216	0	3024.80	1900.00
	James KINGSTON	SA	71	73	72		216	0	3024.80	1900.00
	Clinton WHITELAW	SA	70	75	71		216	0	3024.80	1900.00
59	Darren FICHARDT	SA	71	71	75		217	1	2348.20	1475.00
	Knud STORGAARD	Den	73	71	73		217	1	2348.20	1475.00
	Justin ROSE	Eng	76	69	72		217	1	2348.20	1475.00
	Adilson DA SILVA	Bra	72	72	73		217	1	2348.20	1475.00
	John MELLOR	Eng	70	72	75		217	1	2348.20	1475.00
	Bradley DAVISON	SA	71	74	72		217	1	2348.20	1475.00
65	Rudi SAILER	Aut	72	72	74		218	2	1270.76	798.22
	Kevin CARISSIMI	USA	71	74	73		218	2	1270.76	798.22
	Noel MAART	SA	73	72	73		218	2	1270.76	798.22
	Chris WILLIAMS	Eng	73	69	76		218	2	1270.76	798.22
	Robin BYRD	USA	75	70	73		218	2	1270.76	798.22
	Bafana HLOPHE	SA	73	72	73		218	2	1270.76	798.22
	Marc CAYEUX	Zim	70	71	77		218	2	1270.76	798.22
	Thomas GÖGELE	Ger	74	70	74		218	2	1270.76	798.22
	Bradley DREDGE	Wal	75	69	74		218	2	1270.76	798.22
	Alan MICHELL	SA	75	68	75		218	2	1270.76	798.22
75	Gavin LEVENSON	SA	75	70	74		219	3	1162.50	730.21
	Ronnie MCCANN	USA	69	74	76		219	3	1162.50	730.21
	Didier DE VOOGHT	Bel	75	70	74		219	3	1162.50	730.21
	Alastair FORSYTH	Scot	71	74	74		219	3	1162.50	730.21
79	Wayne BRADLEY	SA	71	73	75		220	4	1155.00	725.50
80	André BOSSERT	Swi	72	73	76		221	5	1150.50	722.68
	Robbie STEWART	SA	71	73	77		221	5	1150.50	722.68

Tight Lies²™
SPIN CONTROL

D R I V E R

STRAIGHTER IS BETTER.™

"There are a lot of players who don't use a driver because it's too hard to control. The Tight Lies₍®₎² Driver gives those golfers exactly the club they need."

Hank Haney
Former PGA Teacher of the Year

Call 01483 239 333 or visit your nearest golf professional or retailer.

TEEING OFF WITH A 3 WOOD? HIT STRAIGHTER AND LONGER WITH THE NEW TIGHT LIES₍®₎² DRIVER

DRIVER DISTANCE. FAIRWAY WOOD CONTROL.

SPIN CONTROL TECHNOLOGY DESIGNED TO HELP YOU HIT CONSISTENTLY STRAIGHTER SHOTS

HEEL-WEIGHTED SOLEPLATE
Moves the center of gravity toward the heel, making it easier to square the clubface on impact for greater accuracy.

DRAW-BIASED CLUBFACE
Its unique face curvature helps control ball spin to produce straighter drives.

HITTING EASE ADVANTAGE

PATENTED "UPSIDE-DOWN" CLUB HEAD DESIGN
Lowers center of gravity and increases effective hitting area to help you get the ball airborne more easily without sacrificing distance.

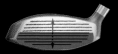

Available in 8.5°, 9.5° and 10.5° lofts.

◢ADAMSGOLF®

The Claxon Sounds

RANDPARK GOLF CLUB, JOHANNESBURG, SOUTH AFRICA

*W*hen Mathias Grönberg won the Smurfit European Open at The K Club in 1998, it was by a whopping ten shot margin. Three years earlier, the Swede landed his first title on the European Tour, capturing the Canon European Masters in Switzerland by a comfortable two shots after once again leading from the front.

This begged a fairly pertinent question in Grönberg's mind...namely, could he also win a tournament when the heat of battle was intense and he had to attack the leaders rather than defend a substantial lead?

The answer arrived in the most emphatic manner possible at Randpark Golf Club in Johannesburg when the affable Swede

with the ruddy complexion captured the Mercedes-Benz - SA Open Championship title.

Grönberg had seemed no more than a possible outside bet to become only the fifth European golfer to lay claim to the second oldest Open Championship in the world (the inaugural tournament was played in 1893, 33 years after the inception of the British version at Prestwick).

Going into the final day, he lay five shots behind South African leader, Darren Fischardt, and his title prospects had not improved greatly after seven holes when two birdies and back-to-back bogeys had left him with limited hope and only a few straws to clutch.

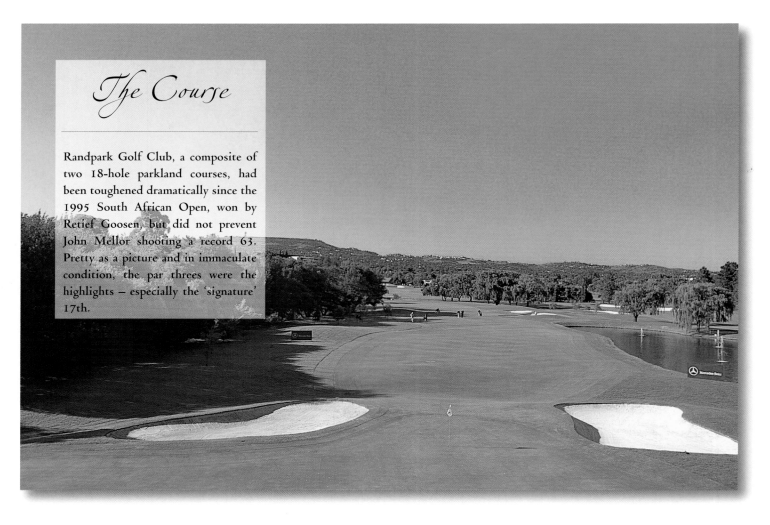

The Course

Randpark Golf Club, a composite of two 18-hole parkland courses, had been toughened dramatically since the 1995 South African Open, won by Retief Goosen, but did not prevent John Mellor shooting a record 63. Pretty as a picture and in immaculate condition, the par threes were the highlights – especially the 'signature' 17th.

Camouflage!

Then fate intervened. The klaxon sounded, heralding a lengthy delay while a violent electrical storm passed overhead. While most of the field cursed, it proved to be a blessing in disguise for the man from Stockholm.

"The break came at a very convenient time for me" he later recalled. "Things were not going well. I had just holed a vital putt on the seventh to prevent me bogeying three holes in a row. I was glad to hear the hooter sound!"

Grönberg and his wife, Tara, retired to the sanctuary of the Players' Lounge at Randpark to review the day's events. At The K Club, Grönberg had bemoaned the fact that Tara - then his girlfriend - had been at her home in New Jersey in America and could not make the journey to Ireland to share in the greatest moment in his career. This time he wanted to win in her presence.

"I always regretted that she couldn't be there" he said. "She had to watch on television but it wasn't the same. Now Tara was by my side and I was determined to win a title with her looking on.

"We sat down and talked about my bogeys and Tara told me to relax, gather my thoughts and come out after the rain delay feeling positive and strong and to play the best golf I could. That's exactly what I did."

Nick Price with his gallery

Two and three quarter hours later, Grönberg returned to the course with the new mental approach recommended by his wife. The policy paid off handsomely. He proceeded to conjure up his most telling stroke of the week - a 55 yards sand wedge from deep, tangly rough at the eighth which set up a birdie four. He didn't take a backward glance after that.

A further four birdies brought him into the clubhouse with a closing round of 67 and a 72 hole total of 274, 14 under par. In the Media Centre, Nick Price witnessed the drama on television and, having completed his tournament with a 67 for 13 under, commented ruefully: "Well, at least I can go for a nice cold beer now!"

Equally frustrated was Argentina's Ricardo Gonzalez, who struck two majestic blows to the final hole and left himself with a five foot putt for an eagle which would have elevated him from 12 under to 14 under. He mis-read the putt and a resulting birdie gave him a 68 and a finishing position alongside Price.

Earlier, South African Tjaart Van Der Walt had shot 66 to set the target of 276, 12 under par, while Frenchman Jean-Francois Remesy buried his head in his hands after watching a birdie putt for 13 under slide narrowly past.

Shot of the Week

Mathias Grönberg called it himself – his 55 yards sand wedge from a buried lie in thick rough at the eighth on the last day. He had just returned from the storm break and the shot to eight feet set up the first of five birdies in the closing eleven holes which secured the title.

As darkness descended on Randpark, Grönberg dashed to the 18th green and was being 'miked up' for a television interview as the final group approached the last. Only Fichardt, the joint halfway leader and outright pace-setter after 54 holes, could catch the Swede, but he was still 100 yards short of the green in two, requiring an eagle three to force a play-off.

The young local prospect fired his wedge straight at the flag and the ball sucked back down the slope, coming to a halt just two inches to the side of the hole. Grönberg's expression was a comic study in sheer anxiety as his eyes bulged in disbelief, turning to relief as he recognised that victory was his.

The Grönbergs embraced happily and Mathias declared: "This is the first time Tara has been with me when I've won and it is very, very special to have her here watching and cheering me on. I could not see her for the last few holes as I was concentrating so hard...but I knew she was there. That was all that mattered."

Gordon Simpson

Darren Fichardt

RANDPARK GOLF CLUB, JOHANNESBURG, SOUTH AFRICA 20-23 JANUARY 2000, PAR 72, 6982 YARDS, 6386 METRES

Pos.	Name		Rd1	Rd2	Rd3	Rd4	Total	Par	Prize Money Euro	£
1	Mathias GRÖNBERG	Swe	70	70	67	67	274	-14	156784.00	97049.83
2	Nick PRICE	Zim	72	69	67	67	275	-13	77167.67	47767.05
	Darren FICHARDT	SA	68	67	67	73	275	-13	77167.67	47767.05
	Ricardo GONZALEZ	Arg	75	66	68	66	275	-13	77167.67	47767.05
5	Jean-Francois REMESY	Fr	68	70	69	69	276	-12	30245.20	18721.88
	Tjaart VAN DER WALT	SA	71	70	69	66	276	-12	30245.20	18721.88
	John MELLOR	Eng	72	72	63	69	276	-12	30245.20	18721.88
	Retief GOOSEN	SA	68	71	68	69	276	-12	30245.20	18721.88
	Ashley ROESTOFF	SA	69	69	69	69	276	-12	30245.20	18721.88
10	Bernhard LANGER	Ger	74	69	68	66	277	-11	17927.67	11097.29
	Greg OWEN	Eng	66	72	69	70	277	-11	17927.67	11097.29
	Lee WESTWOOD	Eng	69	68	72	68	277	-11	17927.67	11097.29
13	Steen TINNING	Den	71	73	69	65	278	-10	14752.00	9131.54
	Paul EALES	Eng	66	69	69	74	278	-10	14752.00	9131.54
	Christopher HANELL	Swe	71	70	69	68	278	-10	14752.00	9131.54
16	Brian DAVIS	Eng	70	73	70	66	279	-9	13197.00	8168.99
	Thomas LEVET	Fr	74	66	68	71	279	-9	13197.00	8168.99
	Gary ORR	Scot	70	73	66	70	279	-9	13197.00	8168.99
19	Sven STRÜVER	Ger	74	68	70	68	280	-8	11391.40	7051.32
	Richard GREEN	Aus	68	73	73	66	280	-8	11391.40	7051.32
	Bradford VAUGHAN	SA	71	73	66	70	280	-8	11391.40	7051.32
	Donald GAMMON	SA	68	68	72	72	280	-8	11391.40	7051.32
	Desmond TERBLANCHE	SA	66	72	65	77	280	-8	11391.40	7051.32
24	Ian WOOSNAM	Wal	70	66	74	71	281	-7	10270.50	6357.47
	Mark MCNULTY	Zim	72	69	71	69	281	-7	10270.50	6357.47
26	Steve WEBSTER	Eng	68	75	72	67	282	-6	8973.29	5554.50
	Wallie COETSEE	SA	65	71	71	75	282	-6	8973.29	5554.50
	Jaco OLVER (AM)	SA	72	72	70	68	282	-6		
	Geoff OGILVY	Aus	69	73	70	70	282	-6	8973.29	5554.50
	Simon YATES	Scot	71	71	70	70	282	-6	8973.29	5554.50
	Peter LONARD	Aus	69	75	70	68	282	-6	8973.29	5554.50
	Markus BRIER	Aut	72	70	69	71	282	-6	8973.29	5554.50
	Stephen GALLACHER	Scot	69	72	70	71	282	-6	8973.29	5554.50
34	Anthony WALL	Eng	70	71	72	70	283	-5	7838.67	4852.16
	Hennie OTTO	SA	72	71	69	71	283	-5	7838.67	4852.16
	Jean HUGO	SA	70	73	68	72	283	-5	7838.67	4852.16
37	Tony JOHNSTONE	Zim	68	73	69	74	284	-4	6946.17	4299.70
	Jeev Milkha SINGH	Ind	70	71	69	74	284	-4	6946.17	4299.70

Pos.	Name		Rd1	Rd2	Rd3	Rd4	Total	Par	Prize Money Euro	£
	Desvonde BOTES	SA	72	70	70	72	284	-4	6946.17	4299.70
	Justin ROSE	Eng	72	72	69	71	284	-4	6946.17	4299.70
	Fredrik LINDGREN	Swe	73	70	70	71	284	-4	6946.17	4299.70
	Nico VAN RENSBURG	SA	68	72	73	71	284	-4	6946.17	4299.70
43	Bruce VAUGHAN	USA	69	74	71	71	285	-3	5755.17	3562.47
	Maarten LAFEBER	Hol	69	74	72	70	285	-3	5755.17	3562.47
	Paul BROADHURST	Eng	71	71	71	72	285	-3	5755.17	3562.47
	Jonathan LOMAS	Eng	69	71	72	73	285	-3	5755.17	3562.47
	Jarmo SANDELIN	Swe	71	72	70	72	285	-3	5755.17	3562.47
	Clinton WHITELAW	SA	74	70	69	72	285	-3	5755.17	3562.47
49	Andrew MCLARDY	SA	72	70	72	72	286	-2	4267.11	2641.36
	Chris WILLIAMS	Eng	72	72	72	70	286	-2	4267.11	2641.36
	Nicolas VANHOOTEGEM	Bel	71	72	74	69	286	-2	4267.11	2641.36
	Wayne BRADLEY	SA	69	73	72	72	286	-2	4267.11	2641.36
	James KINGSTON	SA	75	69	72	70	286	-2	4267.11	2641.36
	Andrew MCKENNA	Scot	73	71	73	69	286	-2	4267.11	2641.36
	Adilson DA SILVA	Bra	71	72	73	70	286	-2	4267.11	2641.36
	Craig KAMPS	SA	73	71	74	68	286	-2	4267.11	2641.36
	Trevor MOORE	SA	69	72	75	70	286	-2	4267.11	2641.36
58	Greig HUTCHEON	Scot	72	71	74	70	287	-1	3076.20	1904.18
	Keith HORNE	SA	70	72	71	74	287	-1	3076.20	1904.18
	Phillip PRICE	Wal	69	75	72	71	287	-1	3076.20	1904.18
	Derek CRAWFORD	Scot	72	71	73	71	287	-1	3076.20	1904.18
	Steve VAN VUUREN	SA	73	68	71	75	287	-1	3076.20	1904.18
63	John SENDEN	Aus	69	73	70	76	288	0	2679.00	1658.31
	Trevor IMMELMAN	SA	68	74	73	73	288	0	2679.00	1658.31
	Ronnie MCCANN	USA	71	72	74	71	288	0	2679.00	1658.31
66	Per NYMAN	Swe	74	69	72	74	289	1	2431.00	1504.80
	Emanuele CANONICA	It	75	69	71	74	289	1	2431.00	1504.80
68	Didier DE VOOGHT	Bel	73	70	73	76	292	4	2283.00	1413.18
69	David HOWELL	Eng	71	72	77	73	293	5	2083.67	1289.80
	Deane PAPPAS	SA	71	72	75	75	293	5	2083.67	1289.80
	Doug McGUIGAN	SA	70	74	76	73	293	5	2083.67	1289.80
72	Ian PALMER	SA	71	72	80	72	295	7	1984.00	1228.10
	Brett LIDDLE	SA	72	71	77	75	295	7	1984.00	1228.10
74	James LOUGHNANE	Ire	72	69	80	75	296	8	1984.00	1228.10
75	Raphaël JACQUELIN	Fr	70	73	75	79	297	9	1984.00	1228.10

Vintage Stuff at The Vines

THE VINES RESORT, PERTH, AUSTRALIA

Traditionally it is hot at The Vines for the annual Heineken Classic - perfect you might agree for an event sponsored by one of the world's best known companies selling ice cold beer - and the golf usually matches the weather too. Now the event is co-sanctioned by the European Tour and the Australasian Tour, and the fields, as a result, are of a high quality, it was probably no surprise that in-form New Zealander Michael Campbell, appropriately a member of both the Australasian and European Tours, should

produce a record-breaking performance to add the first Heineken title of the new millennium to his Johnnie Walker Classic victory. At The Vines he won by a whopping six shots.

In a week when the temperatures soared beyond the 110 degrees fahrenheit mark, Campbell's golf was so hot that his 20 under par 268 winning total in the blistering strength-sapping conditions broke the previous 72-hole record set by Miguel Angel Martin in

Michael Campbell salutes victory

1997 by five shots. Martin's total had been an incredible score. Campbell's was outstanding, his play over the weekend considered by the player himself as the best of his career. Yet it was only in the closing stages of play, punctuated dramatically by a fierce electrical storm that had everyone scurrying to the clubhouse for safety, that the 29-year-old Campbell, whose Scottish connections can be traced back to his great-great-great-great grandfather, managed to edge out former Heineken winner Thomas Björn, the Danish Ryder Cup star now based in London again after a year in Dubai.

Campbell first made the international headlines when he nearly won the 1995 Open Championship at St Andrews. Maybe he was not quite ready to win a major then, although he only missed out on a play-off with eventual winner John Daly and Italian Costantino Rocca, by a shot. He recalled that in the last round that year his mind had wandered too much as he thought what the implications of winning the Open title would be, not least in making him financially stable for the following ten years.

He may not have had the mental strength then that he has now but back in 1995 he felt he was ready to conquer the world, only to see his hopes and aspirations come crashing down around him. A wrist injury proved so damaging that he lost both his Australasian and European Tour cards and, for a time, was in no-man's land relying on invitations and on competing on the European Challenge Tour.

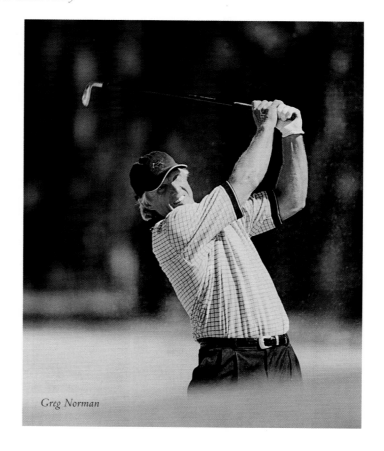

Greg Norman

Coltart celebrates

During two tough years, when he dropped out of the international scene, he learned so much about himself that he can now appreciate the good times even more.

Happily married to Julie, with an infant son Thomas, and based for the European summer in East Sheen, London, Campbell used the start of the new millennium to propel himself towards the threshold of golfing greatness. Towards the end of 1999 he had won the Johnnie Walker Classic impressively from a quality field that included World No 1 Tiger Woods. Indeed, he gave Woods his only defeat in eight consecutive starts which had given him a further massive confidence boost.

After Christmas, when he headed for New Zealand, the week before Perth, to try to win his own national Championship for the first time, he had not lost his touch. Cheered on by over 50 family members in the enthusiastic crowd, he got the job done there and, after his triumph at The Vines, he found himself heading both the Australasian and European money lists. Indeed with four events still to be played Down Under after Perth he had made more money than anyone else in an Australasian season and was insisting his goal was to become first to make a million before the summer circuit was over.

The Course

The Vines, which is regularly included in the list of Australia's top courses, has hosted the Heineken for the past eight years and has provided an interesting and at times demanding challenge especially when the wind is blowing. Designed by Perth-based Graham Marsh and Ross Watson in the attractive Swan Valley, noted for producing some of the country's finest wines, the course is set in pleasant rolling countryside. Interested spectators at times can see the remarkably tame kangaroos. Always in excellent condition - this year was no exception - it demands shrewd course management to miss the carefully -sited fairway bunkers and a deft touch with the putter on the undulating greens. The venue remains a popular one with the players although Open Champion Paul Lawrie, suffering from blistered hands and feet, found the heat this time just too oppressive.

Shot of the Week

For many Gary Emerson's hole in one with a two-iron at the 208 yards fourth hole in a second round 70 merited consideration. It was his seventh ace of his career but a more significant shot was the one played by eventual winner Michael Campbell at the par five 15th on the final day. He was battling with Thomas Björn coming down the final stretch when he stepped into a greenside bunker and holed out for a birdie that gave him a three-shot cushion with three to play.

Campbell's bunker play has been admired before. In the 1995 Open Championship he conjured up a recovery from the Road Hole bunker that helped him to lead with a round to go. His timely trap recovery at The Vines helped him land the first prize of 199,613 euro (£121,767) and moved him to the 407,341 euro (£250,000) mark at the top of the Volvo Order of Merit sending a message to Colin Montgomerie that he is after the Scot's No. 1 spot in Europe.

What had turned things round for him? Campbell had nothing but praise for US-based coach Jonathan Yarwood to whom he switched over two years earlier after a long relationship with Mal Tongue in New Zealand; for Australian Dale Richardson, whom he described as his chiropractor, physiotherapist, dietician and fitness instructor; and for Belgian-based psychologist Jos Vanstiphout, who is helped him handle the mental side. His is a most effective team.

Campbell, after opening rounds of 68 and 69, set up his stunning victory with a third round 65 but even then was only two clear of Björn playing the 15th on the final day. He had just holed a bunker shot for a birdie to stretch his lead to three when the storm hit but when they returned to the course he wrapped it all up expertly to beat Björn with Alastair Forsyth, who had led the 1999 European Tour Qualifying School, a most creditable third ahead of fourth - placed Ernie Els.

Maybe Greg Norman, who finished joint seventh after having birdied the last three holes on the second day to make the cut, summed it all up best when he said: "Michael deserved this win. He has a great game, a great attitude and he's great for golf."

Renton Laidlaw

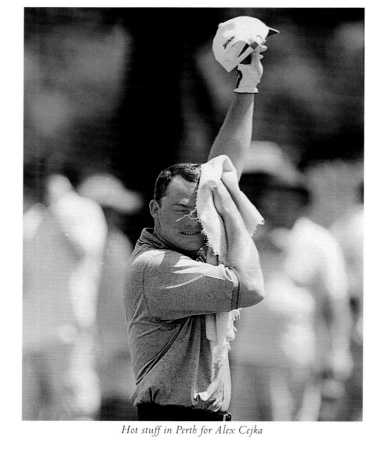

Hot stuff in Perth for Alex Cejka

THE VINES RESORT, PERTH, AUSTRALIA, 27-30 JANUARY 2000, PAR 72, 7101 YARDS, 6493 METRES

Pos.	Name		Rd1	Rd2	Rd3	Rd4	Total	Par	Prize Money Euro	£
1	Michael CAMPBELL	NZ	68	69	65	66	268	-20	199613.22	121767.35
2	Thomas BJÖRN	Den	68	68	68	70	274	-14	113118.03	69003.86
3	Alastair FORSYTH	Scot	72	68	68	67	275	-13	74853.63	45661.95
4	Ernie ELS	SA	72	69	68	67	276	-12	53235.10	32474.29
5	Stephen LEANEY	Aus	70	69	69	71	279	-9	44364.34	27062.98
6	Greg TURNER	NZ	74	69	67	70	280	-8	39928.97	24357.33
7	Greg NORMAN	Aus	73	71	69	68	281	-7	29943.56	18266.06
	David SMAIL	NZ	70	70	69	72	281	-7	29943.56	18266.06
	Shane TAIT	Aus	72	71	68	70	281	-7	29943.56	18266.06
	Paul GOW	Aus	71	69	70	71	281	-7	29943.56	18266.06
	Johan SKOLD	Swe	71	67	70	73	281	-7	29943.56	18266.06
12	Christopher D GRAY	Aus	67	74	71	70	282	-6	22176.91	13528.28
13	Peter SENIOR	Aus	71	72	69	71	283	-5	18854.76	11501.71
	Markus BRIER	Aut	72	67	71	73	283	-5	18854.76	11501.71
	Patrik SJÖLAND	Swe	69	71	71	72	283	-5	18854.76	11501.71
16	Neil KERRY	Aus	74	69	72	69	284	-4	15191.97	9267.35
	Brett OGLE	Aus	72	69	69	74	284	-4	15191.97	9267.35
18	Mike CLAYTON	Aus	69	70	76	70	285	-3	11764.97	7176.83
	Craig PARRY	Aus	70	71	72	72	285	-3	11764.97	7176.83
	Alex CEJKA	Ger	72	66	70	77	285	-3	11764.97	7176.83
	Peter O'MALLEY	Aus	68	71	69	77	285	-3	11764.97	7176.83
	Paul MCGINLEY	Ire	71	70	70	74	285	-3	11764.97	7176.83
	John BICKERTON	Eng	69	76	69	71	285	-3	11764.97	7176.83
	Stephen GALLACHER	Scot	73	71	71	70	285	-3	11764.97	7176.83
25	Raphaël JACQUELIN	Fr	71	72	72	71	286	-2	8220.21	5014.46
	Sven STRÜVER	Ger	69	72	75	70	286	-2	8220.21	5014.46
	Anders HANSEN	Den	71	70	75	70	286	-2	8220.21	5014.46
	Paul DEVENPORT	NZ	72	70	75	69	286	-2	8220.21	5014.46
	John SENDEN	Aus	70	75	71	70	286	-2	8220.21	5014.46
	Gary EVANS	Eng	73	70	70	73	286	-2	8220.21	5014.46
	Andrew COLTART	Scot	71	73	71	71	286	-2	8220.21	5014.46
	Christopher HANELL	Swe	74	69	70	73	286	-2	8220.21	5014.46
33	Wayne RILEY	Aus	73	68	71	75	287	-1	6211.64	3789.20
	Soren KJELDSEN	Den	75	69	71	72	287	-1	6211.64	3789.20
	Grant DODD	Aus	73	70	74	70	287	-1	6211.64	3789.20
	Steen TINNING	Den	70	74	73	70	287	-1	6211.64	3789.20
	Wayne SMITH	Aus	67	73	74	73	287	-1	6211.64	3789.20
38	Jeev Milkha SINGH	Ind	70	72	71	75	288	0	4656.62	2840.61
	Tim ELLIOTT	Aus	71	74	73	70	288	0	4656.62	2840.61
	Rodney PAMPLING	Aus	69	75	72	72	288	0	4656.62	2840.61
	Knud STORGAARD	Den	73	68	76	71	288	0	4656.62	2840.61
	Soren HANSEN	Den	72	73	71	72	288	0	4656.62	2840.61
	Jonathan LOMAS	Eng	71	71	69	77	288	0	4656.62	2840.61
	Van PHILLIPS	Eng	73	72	72	71	288	0	4656.62	2840.61
	Gary SIMPSON	SA	75	67	73	73	288	0	4656.62	2840.61
	Brett RUMFORD	Aus	71	74	69	74	288	0	4656.62	2840.61
47	Greig HUTCHEON	Scot	72	71	73	73	289	1	3329.17	2030.85
	Geoff OGILVY	Aus	67	74	71	77	289	1	3329.17	2030.85
	Paul MOLONEY	Aus	74	71	71	73	289	1	3329.17	2030.85
50	Roger CHAPMAN	Eng	70	72	74	74	290	2	2625.41	1601.54
	Kyi Hla HAN	Myan	70	73	73	74	290	2	2625.41	1601.54
	Scott LAYCOCK	Aus	72	72	74	72	290	2	2625.41	1601.54
	Gavin COLES	Aus	71	72	71	76	290	2	2625.41	1601.54
	Roger WESSELS	SA	74	71	72	73	290	2	2625.41	1601.54
55	Tony MILLS	Aus	74	70	73	74	291	3	2391.53	1458.87
	Bradley KING	Aus	70	73	78	70	291	3	2391.53	1458.87
	Jarmo SANDELIN	Swe	72	72	71	76	291	3	2391.53	1458.87
58	Mark ALLEN	Aus	71	72	74	75	292	4	2307.24	1407.45
	Marcus CAIN	Aus	73	69	71	79	292	4	2307.24	1407.45
	Peter BAKER	Eng	72	72	73	75	292	4	2307.24	1407.45
	Paul LAWRIE	Scot	70	73	78	71	292	4	2307.24	1407.45
	Jim BENEPE	USA	74	71	72	75	292	4	2307.24	1407.45
63	Euan WALTERS	Aus	72	72	72	78	293	5	2244.02	1368.89
64	Peter FOWLER	Aus	73	71	76	74	294	6	2201.89	1343.19
	Gary EMERSON	Eng	75	70	74	75	294	6	2201.89	1343.19
	Chris GAUNT	Aus	73	70	75	76	294	6	2201.89	1343.19
67	Jarrod MOSELEY	Aus	72	73	74	76	295	7	2159.74	1317.48
68	Anthony WALL	Eng	75	70	73	79	297	9	2138.68	1304.63
69	Terry PRICE	Aus	73	72	82	71	298	10	2117.60	1291.77

Only the finest...

Charles Church's diverse range of new and forthcoming developments comprise a variety of homes, from one bedroom apartments to six bedroom luxury homes.

Prices from £112,500 – £1.5m.

For further details on developments in:

• Berkshire • Hampshire • London • Surrey

Call 01276 808080

• Gloucestershire • Oxfordshire
• Warwickshire • West Midlands

Call 01926 310000

• Buckinghamshire • Essex • Hertfordshire

Call 01707 662662

• Kent • London • Sussex

Call 01737 228500

www.charles-church.co.uk

CHARLES CHURCH

DESIGNING MODERN CLASSICS

Home Town Boy

THE LAKES GOLF CLUB, SYDNEY, AUSTRALIA

The similarity between the careers of close friends Michael Campbell and Lucas Parsons is remarkable. Both have suffered dramatic slumps in the early professional careers, both have had to cope with off-course personal problems and both are on the comeback trail. Just like Campbell and, indeed, helped by his advice and encouragement, Parsons made it to the big-time at last with his impressive win in the Greg Norman Holden International, the richest event on the Australasian Tour and, for the first time, a co-sanctioned tournament with the European Tour this year.

Parsons had won three titles Down-Under between 1993 and 1995 but the former Australian and New Zealand Amateur champion, then lost his game and his Tour cards and, like, Campbell had to rely for a time on invitations to play. Last year he competed on the European Challenge Tour, won twice and earned his European Tour card again. Now he is realising his potential and rounds of 70, 66, 70 and 67 for a commendable 19 under par 273 winning total in the at times blustery wind at The Lakes underlined that.

Staying admirably focused he effectively held off the respective challenges of "veteran" Peter Senior, Per-Ulrik Johansson, Andrew Coltart and 1999 Compaq European Grand Prix winner David Park to land the 243,118 euro (£146,456) first prize and move in to second place behind Campbell in both the Australasian money list and the Volvo Order of Merit.

As he played the last there was a tremendous reception for the home town boy not least from Campbell who, having missed the cut himself when going for three straight wins in three weeks, had walked the last four holes with his friend and was by the 18th green to meet and congratulate him.

Campbell's influence on Parsons has been not inconsiderable although the New Zealander is always quick to insist he has done very little. Whatever Campbell says, however, is contradicted by Parsons who, when the money was tight and things were really tough for him, was offered a room in the New Zealander's London home on the most advantageous terms.

Parsons said: "Cambo (Campbell's nickname in Australia) has been the one who has stuck by me over the past five years and has a lot to do with this victory. I had a long chat with him before the event began and picked his brains. He told me to stay in the present. If I started thinking about a three foot putt on the last green for first prize I had to immediately turn my thoughts to the trees or the birds to bring me back to where I was. In golf at this level you have to forget the bad shot and get on with it, but it is just as important not to get ahead of yourself too. That is what I tried to do all week and it worked. Coming to the last green knowing I had won was a very emotional moment."

His friendship with Campbell also encouraged Parsons to loose weight. He has shed the pounds dramatically and is fitter now that he has ever been. "I go to the gym four of five times a week and yesterday went swimming for an hour at Bondi, an advantage if you live in Sydney." He told us on Friday: "Tiger has set an example, if you want to beat him, you have to match him for fitness. You cannot do it if you are a couple of stones overweight. Anyway being physically fit keeps you mentally sharp."

Lucas Parsons

The Course

There are still those who say the old Lakes course laid out in 1928 was better than the new one forced on the Club in 1968 when the Sydney City authorities decreed that some of the original holes must go to make way for a super highway to the nearby Kingsford-Smith International Airport. Still, the replacement course, designed by Bob Hagge and toughened up in more recent years by Jack Newton and his architectural team, has many challenging holes to remember especially on the back nine where the vast expanse of water was once used to supply the city. After the turn the course is more open and becomes a monster when the wind gets up. Although he won the 1980 Australian Open here The Lakes has never been a particular favourite of Greg Norman's who once ran up an 11 at the 14th where the second shot is played over water. A regular venue for professional and amateur Championships over the years The Lakes must always be handled with a great deal of patience.

Bernhard Langer

Yet there were others who played a significant part in Parsons' success, not least former Australasian Tour employee Mark Williams, who had caddied for Roger Mackay a few years earlier when he won at The Lakes and who was on the Sydneysider's bag this time. And, of course, there was the help he received from Greg Norman, whose inspirational influence had been so important over the years. "As far as I am concerned he is the elite of Australian golf and I am proud to be a winner of his tournament," said Parsons.

It would have made it even more satisfying for Parsons had he beaten Norman down the stretch but, having trouble with his putting and clearly not having much fun on the course, The Shark, missing his regular caddie Tony Navarro, who had returned home because of illness in the family, had bowed out at half-way for the second successive year but only for the third time in 25 years of competing in Australian events. "My head just was not in it", said Norman, who announced he had been proud to accept the invitation to carry the Olympic Torch across the Sydney Harbour Bridge. "They asked whether I could be classified as a fast, medium or slow runner," he said with a smile. "You know I might just savour the moment and slow down to a walk at one point!"

Bernhard Langer, who had lost out the previous year in bizarre circumstances to Michael Long, never really threatened and neither did long-hitting John Daly who, wisely with so much water around, left the driver out of his bag. Still he drew the galleries, made the cut and was most appreciative of good friend Norman's support and invitation. The two-time major title winner, whose own career has been a dramatically emotional roller-coaster, produced one of the most amusing answers of the week to a question about his own fitness, his eating habits and his drinking. "I once went on a six-

Watch the Birdies!

Shot of the Week

Last year on the European Tour there were no fewer than 29 holes in one including one by Dane Soren Hansen in the German Open at Sporting Club, Berlin. The Copenhagen-based 25-year-old was quickly off the mark again this year when he aced the tough 209 yards par three 15th on the second day - a shot that helped him finish joint 21st behind winner Lucas Parsons. Using a mid-iron for his tee shot at a hole that was one of the most difficult all week, Hanson judged it to a nicety dropping the ball on the front edge to let it meander down the hill and into the cup. Perhaps winner Lucas Parson's deft chip to save par at the 16th on the final day was a candidate or Peter Senior's superb wood to the par five 17th on the third day which earned him an eagle, but Hansen's ace was a shot of quality.

Bernhard Langer

month workout programme. People said I would feel great but, hell, I threw up every time. Working out is not for me. I wouldn't last if I worked out regularly and anyway I can get an edge over the keep-fit brigade by practising when they are in the gym."

Andrew Coltart, putting left hand below right for the first time, covered eight holes in eight-under-par at one stage and remained in contention throughout as did Park who impressed on his first visit to Sydney. Craig Parry, a former winner at The Lakes, threatened then fell away as did joint first round leader Dutchman Maarten Lafeber, who sold shares in himself to finance his career. Swede Per-Ulrik Johansson threatened throughout but José Maria Olazábal, after an excellent third round 66 on his 34th birthday, could not produce the figures on the final day when it was left to the often underrated Senior to mount the most serious challenge.

After wins by amateurs Aaron Baddeley in the Australian Open and Brett Rumford in the Players' Championship, two more amateurs made their mark in Greg's event. Scott Gardiner, who has an Aboriginal background, finished a creditable eighth but 19-year-old Adam Scott, who had just left UNLV (the University of Las Vegas) and is coached by Butch Harmon, had the round of the week - a record second round 63 that included six birdies in a row from the eighth and then a 25 foot eagle at the 14th. His smile that day was only marginally less wide than that of winner Lucas Parsons when he ran in his 20-foot winner at the last on Sunday.

Renton Laidlaw

THE LAKES GOLF CLUB, SYDNEY, AUSTRALIA, 3-6 FEBRUARY 2000, PAR 73, 6904 YARDS, 6315 METRES

Pos.	Name		Rd1	Rd2	Rd3	Rd4	Total	Par	Prize Money Euro	£
1	Lucas PARSONS	Aus	70	66	70	67	273	-19	243118.26	146456.78
2	Peter SENIOR	Aus	67	70	71	69	277	-15	137771.72	82995.01
3	Per-Ulrik JOHANSSON	Swe	71	68	71	69	279	-13	78002.63	46989.54
	Andrew COLTART	Scot	67	68	73	71	279	-13	78002.63	46989.54
5	David PARK	Wal	68	65	73	74	280	-12	54033.41	32550.25
6	Anders HANSEN	Den	68	71	72	70	281	-11	45923.91	27665.01
	Wayne SMITH	Aus	74	67	67	73	281	-11	45923.91	27665.01
8	José Maria OLAZÁBAL	Sp	72	70	66	74	282	-10	34782.97	20953.60
	Ian GARBUTT	Eng	71	71	69	71	282	-10	34782.97	20953.60
	Phillip PRICE	Wal	72	70	70	70	282	-10	34782.97	20953.60
	Gary ORR	Scot	78	65	72	67	282	-10	34782.97	20953.60
	Scott GARDINER (AM)	Aus	75	69	68	70	282	-10		
12	Craig PARRY	Aus	71	72	66	74	283	-9	23975.64	14443.16
	Brett OGLE	Aus	73	71	68	71	283	-9	23975.64	14443.16
	Roger WESSELS	SA	72	70	71	70	283	-9	23975.64	14443.16
	Christopher HANELL	Swe	71	66	75	71	283	-9	23975.64	14443.16
16	Lian-Wei ZHANG	PRC	68	73	71	72	284	-8	16598.82	9999.29
	Craig HAINLINE	USA	71	70	71	72	284	-8	16598.82	9999.29
	Peter O'MALLEY	Aus	72	70	69	73	284	-8	16598.82	9999.29
	Gary EVANS	Eng	71	71	69	73	284	-8	16598.82	9999.29
	Retief GOOSEN	SA	70	72	71	71	284	-8	16598.82	9999.29
21	Andrew BONHOMME	Aus	72	74	68	71	285	-7	12991.89	7826.44
	Grant DODD	Aus	69	71	71	74	285	-7	12991.89	7826.44
	Stuart APPLEBY	Aus	73	69	75	68	285	-7	12991.89	7826.44
	Andrew MCLARDY	SA	71	66	75	73	285	-7	12991.89	7826.44
	Soren HANSEN	Den	70	70	73	72	285	-7	12991.89	7826.44
	Nicolas VANHOOTEGEM	Bel	75	68	73	69	285	-7	12991.89	7826.44
	Aaron BADDELEY (AM)	Aus	71	73	72	69	285	-7		
27	Rodger DAVIS	Aus	75	67	71	73	286	-6	9825.72	5919.11
	Bernhard LANGER	Ger	71	72	71	72	286	-6	9825.72	5919.11
	Nick O'HERN	Aus	70	74	68	74	286	-6	9825.72	5919.11
	Paul MCGINLEY	Ire	71	74	67	74	286	-6	9825.72	5919.11
31	Wayne RILEY	Aus	71	70	73	73	287	-5	7994.02	4815.67
	Shane TAIT	Aus	68	72	72	75	287	-5	7994.02	4815.67
	Scott LAYCOCK	Aus	78	68	70	71	287	-5	7994.02	4815.67
	Paul BROADHURST	Eng	72	74	69	72	287	-5	7994.02	4815.67
	Jarrod MOSELEY	Aus	69	71	73	74	287	-5	7994.02	4815.67
	Bob ESTES	USA	74	72	70	71	287	-5	7994.02	4815.67
37	Steen TINNING	Den	71	70	73	74	288	-4	6749.36	4065.88
	Massimo SCARPA	It	73	73	69	73	288	-4	6749.36	4065.88

Pos.	Name		Rd1	Rd2	Rd3	Rd4	Total	Par	Prize Money Euro	£
	Jarmo SANDELIN	Swe	73	71	73	71	288	-4	6749.36	4065.88
	Adam SCOTT (AM)	Aus	75	63	72	78	288	-4		
40	Robert WILLIS	Aus	73	71	71	74	289	-3	5402.06	3254.25
	Kenny DRUCE	Aus	72	72	72	73	289	-3	5402.06	3254.25
	Justin ROSE	Eng	76	69	70	74	289	-3	5402.06	3254.25
	Matthew LANE	NZ	73	71	73	72	289	-3	5402.06	3254.25
	Thomas GÖGELE	Ger	76	68	72	73	289	-3	5402.06	3254.25
	John DALY	USA	73	70	74	72	289	-3	5402.06	3254.25
	Brett RUMFORD	Aus	69	69	77	74	289	-3	5402.06	3254.25
47	Robert STEPHENS	Aus	73	73	69	75	290	-2	3519.04	2119.90
	Patrick JANSON	USA	75	71	73	71	290	-2	3519.04	2119.90
	Tom GILLIS	USA	73	73	72	72	290	-2	3519.04	2119.90
	David MCKENZIE	Aus	73	72	74	71	290	-2	3519.04	2119.90
	Paul GOW	Aus	72	74	70	74	290	-2	3519.04	2119.90
	Justin COOPER	Aus	76	67	71	76	290	-2	3519.04	2119.90
	Alex CEJKA	Ger	73	68	73	76	290	-2	3519.04	2119.90
	Van PHILLIPS	Eng	71	73	71	75	290	-2	3519.04	2119.90
55	Ross MCFARLANE	Eng	69	77	73	72	291	-1	2887.09	1739.21
	Søren KJELDSEN	Den	73	73	69	76	291	-1	2887.09	1739.21
	Matthew ECOB	Aus	74	72	71	74	291	-1	2887.09	1739.21
	Christopher D GRAY	Aus	71	72	71	77	291	-1	2887.09	1739.21
	Peter LONARD	Aus	69	71	77	74	291	-1	2887.09	1739.21
60	Stuart BOUVIER	Aus	70	73	71	78	292	0	2758.77	1661.91
	Stephen ALLAN	Aus	72	72	69	79	292	0	2758.77	1661.91
	Raymond RUSSELL	Scot	75	71	74	72	292	0	2758.77	1661.91
	David CARTER	Eng	70	71	70	81	292	0	2758.77	1661.91
	Daniel CHOPRA	Swe	74	69	74	75	292	0	2758.77	1661.91
65	Maarten LAFEBER	Hol	66	74	74	79	293	1	2668.95	1607.80
	Philip GOLDING	Eng	68	75	73	77	293	1	2668.95	1607.80
67	Gavin COLES	Aus	74	71	75	74	294	2	2604.79	1569.15
	Martyn ROBERTS	Wal	72	73	74	75	294	2	2604.79	1569.15
	Alastair FORSYTH	Scot	76	69	73	76	294	2	2604.79	1569.15
70	Andre STOLZ	Aus	72	72	71	80	295	3	2527.80	1522.77
	Peter BAKER	Eng	69	74	71	81	295	3	2527.80	1522.77
	Terry PRICE	Aus	74	70	74	77	295	3	2527.80	1522.77
73	Benoit TEILLERIA	Fr	74	70	74	78	296	4	2476.49	1491.86
74	Greig HUTCHEON	Scot	74	70	76	77	297	5	2437.99	1468.67
	Mike FERGUSON	Aus	71	75	73	78	297	5	2437.99	1468.67
76	Sven STRÜVER	Ger	73	68	76	81	298	6	2399.49	1445.48
77	Gary EMERSON	Eng	66	77	77	79	299	7	2373.83	1430.02

Oyez! Oh Yeh!!

TEMPLER PARK GOLF & COUNTRY CLUB,
KUALA LUMPUR, MALAYSIA

The 2000 edition of the Asian PGA Media Guide describes Yeh Wei-tze thus: "Hard working professional, speaks little English but has one of the friendliest faces on Tour."

Correct on all three counts. But that succinct biographical assessment can now be augmented by two vital statistics: First Asian winner of a European Tour title since 1983 and only the second Taiwanese golfer to win a European event since 1971.

There is also a hidden connection between the two paragraphs namely - Liang Huan Lu, more familiarly, and affectionately, known to golfing enthusiasts the world over as 'Mr Lu'.

It was Mr Lu who became the first golfer from Taiwan (then Formosa) to win on the European Tour almost three decades ago. He appeared from nowhere, complete with trademark 'pork pie' hat, to chase Lee Trevino all the way for the Open Championship at

Patrik Sjöland

Royal Birkdale in 1971, eventually missing out by a single stroke.

One week later he proved that performance was no fluke by winning the French Open title at Biarritz to rubber-stamp his arrival on the world golf stage.

Since then, not a great deal has been seen or heard in Europe of the popular Mr Lu. However, his name was to re-emerge significantly at the 2000 Benson & Hedges Malaysian Open, presented by Carlsberg, at Templer Park Golf & Country Club near Kuala Lumpur.

It just so happened that Mr Lu is the friend and mentor of Yeh - and it was the teacher's help and advice which enabled the pupil to shine brightly as the newest star in Taiwanese golf with a one stroke victory over Ireland's Padraig Harrington, Craig Hainline of American and South African Des Terblanche.

Yeh shot rounds of 74, 68, 67 and 69 to win with the ten under par aggregate of 278. He was besieged beneath a sea of smiling faces, jabbering away excitedly in Mandarin. However Yeh's thoughts turned first and foremost to Mr Lu.

He explained: "Mr Lu taught me four or five years ago and I learned a lot from him. I learned many things from from Mr Lu but he taught me how important it was to enjoy the game - not just win, win, win.

"You must have fun in golf and then you can move up. That is why I always smile when I play the game."

Per-Ulrik Johansson

There was no wider smile than the one worn by Yeh after a tense climax to a superb co-sanctioned tournament at Templer Park. He spent an eternity waiting to tee off at the fiendishly tricky par three 17th, where he missed the green but played a delicate chip to two feet for a tap-in par.

Then, recognising that he had a three-stroke lead over the field at the last, he let his guard down mentally. He knew a double bogey six would almost certainly allow him to prevail. A sloppy double bogey is what he took to triumph by just a solitary stroke.

He said: "When I stood on the 17th tee I was very, very nervous. I thought if I put the ball in the bunker I might lose so I was nervous. Fortunately I played to the edge of the bunker and made a beautiful chip and I still had a chance to win.

"On the 18th I knew if I made a double bogey I would still win so I played safe. Even though my third was over the green I still made it. But the 17th was the most nervous I've been. The chip was about five metres and I hit it close. The bottom line at the 18th was a double bogey and it was enough.

"Honestly I can't believe it at all. I never thought I could win. This is the most glorious moment in my career because it is my first time to win a professional tournament."

Shot of the Week

The delicate sand wedge from fluffy rough played by Yeh Wei-tze at the 71st hole. He had stood nervously on the tee for almost ten minutes and missed the green. He could have lost the title there, but held his nerve and chipped close for a tap-in par.

The Course

A spectacular feature of Templer Park is Bukit Takun, a million year old limestone rock formation which towers over the course and can be viewed from every hole. The two nines were reversed for the tournament, providing a stiff finish with a long par three over water followed by a tough par four selected by Bernhard Langer as the best on the course.

Indian Open champion, Arjun Atwal, who was educated in New York and resides in Calcutta, led the tournament for the first two rounds with a 65 and 70. Nico Van Rensburg, twice a winner on the Asian PGA Tour in Kuala Lumpur, had the chance of a hat-trick when he moved into second at halfway on 136 after emulating Atwal's 65.

Thailand's Thongchai Jaidee, who cut an interesting figure in his adapted basketball shoes on the course, moved ahead after 54 holes with a 68 but was unable to stay with the hot pace on a final day which saw Harrington appear the main threat to Yeh.

For most of the final afternoon the Irish Ryder Cup player - who finished runner-up no fewer than five times in 1999 - led or shared the lead but he allowed his concentration to wander over the homeward stretch with bogeys at the 15th, 17th and 18th.

Harrington said: "It was a weak finish. I lost my focus coming down the stretch. I am disappointed but it's better than the last two weeks when I missed the cut. I would love to say I'm tired of finishing second, but if I finished third I would want to finish second!"

Hainline and Terblanche shot 67 and 68 respectively to finish strongly, while Van Rensburg reached the last needing a birdie to tie Yeh. He bogeyed, and the title went to Taiwan. Yeh smiled broadly, and back in Taiwan, Mr Lu was surely doing the same.

Gordon Simpson

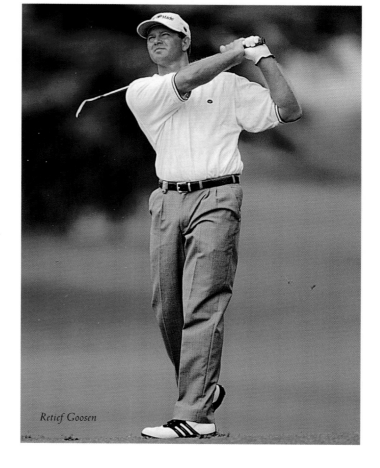

Retief Goosen

TEMPLER PARK GOLF & COUNTRY CLUB, KUALA LUMPUR, MALAYSIA, 10-13 February 2000,
PAR 72, 7176 YARDS, 6561 METRES

Pos.	Name		Rd1	Rd2	Rd3	Rd4	Total	Par	Prize Money Euro	£	Pos.	Name		Rd1	Rd2	Rd3	Rd4	Total	Par	Prize Money Euro	£
1	Wei-tze YEH	Tai	74	68	67	69	278	-10	136514.23	83720.24		John BICKERTON	Eng	72	71	73	70	286	-2	6677.79	4095.30
2	Padraig HARRINGTON	Ire	68	69	72	70	279	-9	62917.70	38585.61	36	Søren KJELDSEN	Den	72	72	72	71	287	-1	5917.02	3628.74
	Craig HAINLINE	USA	71	72	69	67	279	-9	62917.70	38585.61		Greig HUTCHEON	Scot	72	67	69	79	287	-1	5917.02	3628.74
	Desmond TERBLANCHE	SA	71	71	69	68	279	-9	62917.70	38585.61		Andrew MCLARDY	SA	72	73	72	70	287	-1	5917.02	3628.74
5	Jeev Milkha SINGH	Ind	68	72	70	70	280	-8	27471.91	16847.73		Thomas LEVET	Fr	70	71	73	73	287	-1	5917.02	3628.74
	Lian-Wei ZHANG	PRC	66	71	75	68	280	-8	27471.91	16847.73		Jim RUTLEDGE	Can	73	71	73	70	287	-1	5917.02	3628.74
	Retief GOOSEN	SA	68	74	67	71	280	-8	27471.91	16847.73		Massimo FLORIOLI	It	71	72	71	73	287	-1	5917.02	3628.74
	Nico VAN RENSBURG	SA	71	65	71	73	280	-8	27471.91	16847.73		Robert COLES	Eng	73	71	73	70	287	-1	5917.02	3628.74
9	Arjun ATWAL	Ind	65	70	75	71	281	-7	17877.87	10963.98	43	Steen TINNING	Den	67	70	71	80	288	0	4902.68	3006.67
	Per-Ulrik JOHANSSON	Swe	71	71	68	71	281	-7	17877.87	10963.98		Anthony KANG	R.Kor	73	72	74	69	288	0	4902.68	3006.67
11	Wayne RILEY	Aus	72	71	67	72	282	-6	13795.12	8460.15		Johan SKOLD	Swe	77	68	73	70	288	0	4902.68	3006.67
	Soren HANSEN	Den	71	67	74	70	282	-6	13795.12	8460.15		Scott TAYLOR	USA	69	73	71	75	288	0	4902.68	3006.67
	Mathias GRÖNBERG	Swe	73	72	67	70	282	-6	13795.12	8460.15		Periasamy GUNASAGARAN	Mal	72	71	68	77	288	0	4902.68	3006.67
	Jim PAYNE	Eng	72	68	69	73	282	-6	13795.12	8460.15	48	Andrew RAITT	Eng	70	70	76	73	289	1	4310.97	2643.79
	Ted PURDY	USA	67	72	76	67	282	-6	13795.12	8460.15		David LYNN	Eng	75	69	73	72	289	1	4310.97	2643.79
16	Bernhard LANGER	Ger	73	71	70	69	283	-5	10626.50	6516.93	50	Per G NYMAN	Swe	72	71	75	72	290	2	3867.20	2371.64
	Sammy DANIELS	SA	72	71	70	70	283	-5	10626.50	6516.93		Grant HAMERTON	Eng	73	72	70	75	290	2	3867.20	2371.64
	Thammanoon SRIROJ	Thai	68	72	73	70	283	-5	10626.50	6516.93		Adrian PERCEY	Wal	71	74	69	76	290	2	3867.20	2371.64
	Joakim HAEGGMAN	Swe	70	69	75	69	283	-5	10626.50	6516.93		Tatsuhiko ICHIHARA	Jpn	72	72	74	72	290	2	3867.20	2371.64
	Zaw MOE	Myan	75	68	71	69	283	-5	10626.50	6516.93	54	Andrew PITTS	USA	71	70	75	75	291	3	3507.95	2151.32
	David PARK	Wal	70	72	72	69	283	-5	10626.50	6516.93		Hendrik BUHRMANN	SA	70	72	76	73	291	3	3507.95	2151.32
	Gerry NORQUIST	USA	71	68	72	72	283	-5	10626.50	6516.93		Satoshi OIDE	Jpn	71	71	73	76	291	3	3507.95	2151.32
23	Taimur HUSSAIN	Pak	72	68	68	76	284	-4	8748.74	5365.35		Simon DYSON	Eng	70	70	76	75	291	3	3507.95	2151.32
	Ian POULTER	Eng	71	70	70	73	284	-4	8748.74	5365.35	58	Amandeep JOHL	Ind	72	72	75	73	292	4	3254.37	1995.81
	Gary EMERSON	Eng	72	72	71	69	284	-4	8748.74	5365.35		Taku YAMANAKA	Jpn	72	69	75	76	292	4	3254.37	1995.81
	Patrik SJÖLAND	Swe	70	71	68	75	284	-4	8748.74	5365.35	60	Peter TERAVAINEN	USA	73	71	75	74	293	5	3057.13	1874.85
	Ter-Chang WANG	Tai	72	71	72	69	284	-4	8748.74	5365.35		Massimo SCARPA	It	68	74	69	82	293	5	3057.13	1874.85
	Prayad MARKSAENG	Thai	71	71	71	71	284	-4	8748.74	5365.35		Andrew BUTTERFIELD	Eng	68	75	72	78	293	5	3057.13	1874.85
29	Kyi Hla HAN	Myan	75	68	74	68	285	-3	7370.92	4520.37	63	Andrew COLTART	Scot	72	73	77	73	295	7	2958.52	1814.38
	Mark MOULAND	Wal	67	74	72	72	285	-3	7370.92	4520.37	64	Ian HUTCHINGS	SA	69	72	76	79	296	8	2810.59	1723.65
	Jyoti RANDHAWA	Ind	72	72	69	72	285	-3	7370.92	4520.37		Boonchu RUANGKIT	Thai	72	74	80	74	296	8	2810.59	1723.65
	Gregory HANRAHAN	USA	74	70	68	73	285	-3	7370.92	4520.37	66	Soushi TAJIMA	Jpn	72	73	71	81	297	9	1267.93	777.58
	Thongchai JAIDEE	Thai	67	71	68	79	285	-3	7370.92	4520.37	67	Christian PENA	USA	72	73	74	79	298	10	1264.93	775.75
34	Alex CEJKA	Ger	74	66	74	72	286	-2	6677.79	4095.30											

DELIVERING TOUR QUALITY TURF AT THE WENTWORTH CLUB

Championship courses all over the world choose Toro turf equipment and irrigation systems to help maintain optimum turf playing conditions. As the official supplier of PGA European Tour Courses and events, we are passionate about golf — and healthy turf. For over 85 years, Toro has provided innovative, high-quality solutions to golf courses, parks, and individual lawns throughout the world. To help grow and maintain your turf, choose Toro as your official supplier.

TORO TOTAL SOLUTIONS

Sir Henry would Approve

LA MERIDIEN PENINA, ALGARVE, PORTUGAL

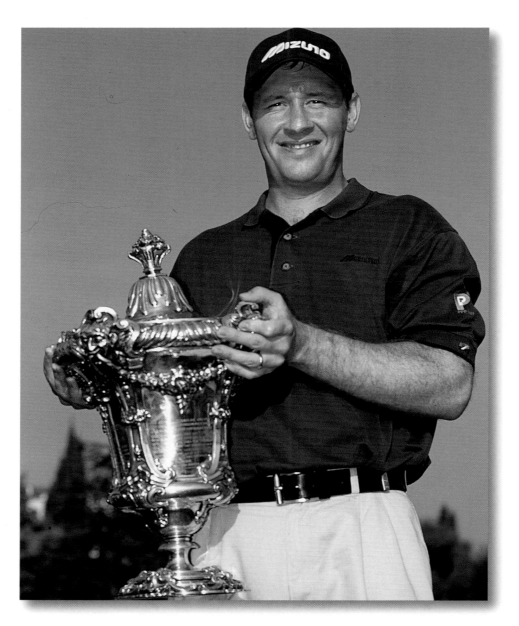

Sir Henry would have approved. On the course he so lovingly designed it was entirely fitting that Scotland's Gary Orr, the 1993 Sir Henry Cotton Rookie of the Year, should win his maiden European Tour title and he did so in style. A magnificent eagle three on the final hole at Le Meridien Penina swept him ahead of Welshman Phillip Price by a single shot and brought Orr the title he must have thought may never come.

Three times in the past two years, Orr had been denied at the last gasp, first by Colin Montgomerie in the 1998 Volvo PGA Championship, then by Lee Westwood in the TNT Dutch Open last year and then, by Anthony Wall in the 2000 Alfred Dunhill Championship. Inevitably, when his time came, Orr got his own back, stealing victory from the grasp of Price on the final hole.

Paul McGinley

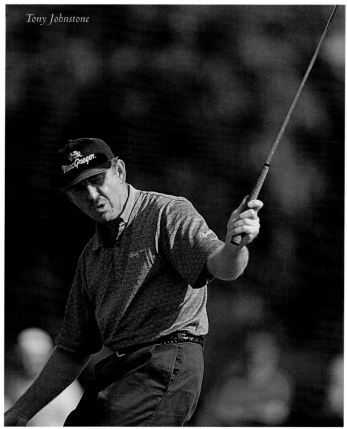

Tony Johnstone

After drawing level with Price, the 1994 champion, with a birdie on the 14th, Orr looked to have squandered his chance of victory after hooking his tee shot on the 17th and making bogey. Price had played a superb five wood from the right rough to within 15 feet but his putt for birdie stopped in the jaws of the hole. With just a one stroke lead playing the last, Price again found the rough with his tee shot and could do no better than a par five. Orr, however, rose to the occasion, splitting the fairway with his drive and then hitting a perfect two iron 220 yards to 12 feet before stroking the ball home to claim the Algarve Portuguese Open title with a 13 under par total of 275.

"It's a dream to do something like that - to win with an eagle on the last," said Orr. "Winning is what everyone works for. It's not easy sometimes when things don't work out but you've got to keep plugging away."

Orr was starting to earn an unenviable reputation as the perennial runner-up, always the bridesmaid but never the bride, and when he dropped three shots in the first six holes of the third round after taking the halfway lead it looked as if another title was slipping through his fingers. But, after undertaking a regime of weight training through the winter months, the 32-year-old emerged a stronger player both physically and mentally. On this occasion Orr fought back from his poor start, rolling in a birdie putt on the 11th and then four more birdies in the closing five holes for a round of 70 to share the third round lead with Price. Those nine holes on Saturday showed much about his grit and determination and when the tournament came down to the wire on the Sunday it came as no surprise that Orr rose to the challenge to claim his debut victory at the 203rd attempt.

Orr said: "It's a psychological barrier. Until you've won you don't know what your capable of. I always felt I had the game to win. I just had to take my chance when it came along. That putt on 18 - I wasn't going to leave it short. When you get an opportunity like that you've got to take it."

With Penina basking in glorious sunshine, Price set the early pace, opening with a four under par 68 to share the lead with last year's runner-up John Bickerton with Orr a shot adrift. Orr then stepped up a gear with a second round 67 to open up a two shot advantage but Price hit back in the third round with a course record 65, equalled by Brian Davis on the Sunday, to move alongside Orr and two clear of Ireland's Paul McGinley.

The golf on the final day was breathtaking as the final group shared ten birdies in the opening nine holes. Price got the ball rolling as he stroked in six single putts in the first seven holes for an outward half of 31, four under par. Orr held on with an eagle three on the fifth, followed by a birdie on the following hole to reach the turn one shot adrift. McGinley was also making up ground but his hopes faded with a bogey on the ninth and then two more dropped shots on the 13th and 14th.

Although the two leaders struggled around the turn, both dropping shots at the tenth and 12th, Orr regained his composure with a birdie on the 14th to draw level and set up the dramatic finale.

"Gary played the last perfectly so he deserved to win," said Price. "An eagle on the last is tough to beat. I had a very good front nine, holed some good putts, but ran into trouble in the middle. I'm disappointed but this is one of my favourite tournaments. I would love to win it again but will have to wait until next year."

But this was Orr's week and as the dust settled and the cheers faded, the pervading feeling on this golden Sunday was that Sir Henry Cotton, too, was watching down and adding his seal of approval.

Roddy Williams

The Course

Penina is a course moulded in the image of Sir Henry Cotton. In designing this course on the Algarve, Cotton created a fascinating examination of a golfers skill with every club in the bag required. The magnificent tree-lined layout, with its narrow fairways and subtly-contoured greens, has stood the test of time. For the first time in three years, following extensive work on the course, preferred lies were not in use, paving the way for Phillip Price to set a new course record of 65 in the third round, equalled by Brian Davis on the final day.

Phillip Price

Jamie Spence

LE MERIDIEN PENINA, ALGARVE, PORTUGAL, 17-20 FEBRUARY 2000, PAR 72, 6798 YARDS, 6217 METRES

Pos.	Name		Rd1	Rd2	Rd3	Rd4	Total	Par	Prize Money Euro	£
1	Gary ORR	Scot	69	67	70	69	275	-13	166600.00	103030.30
2	Phillip PRICE	Wal	68	73	65	70	276	-12	111000.00	68645.64
3	Tony JOHNSTONE	Zim	72	70	68	69	279	-9	51666.67	31952.18
	Brian DAVIS	Eng	73	68	73	65	279	-9	51666.67	31952.18
	Paul MCGINLEY	Ire	70	72	67	70	279	-9	51666.67	31952.18
6	Wayne RILEY	Aus	70	70	71	69	280	-8	30000.00	18552.88
	Richard S JOHNSON	Swe	73	70	69	68	280	-8	30000.00	18552.88
	Greg OWEN	Eng	72	71	68	69	280	-8	30000.00	18552.88
9	Ian WOOSNAM	Wal	74	72	69	66	281	-7	21200.00	13110.70
	Emanuele CANONICA	It	73	69	70	69	281	-7	21200.00	13110.70
11	Andrew OLDCORN	Scot	77	68	67	70	282	-6	17233.33	10657.59
	Paul BROADHURST	Eng	76	68	69	69	282	-6	17233.33	10657.59
	Joakim HAEGGMAN	Swe	72	71	71	68	282	-6	17233.33	10657.59
14	Malcolm MACKENZIE	Eng	74	70	69	70	283	-5	14400.00	8905.38
	Anthony WALL	Eng	71	72	72	68	283	-5	14400.00	8905.38
	Carl SUNESON	Sp	74	69	70	70	283	-5	14400.00	8905.38
	Niclas FASTH	Swe	72	70	70	71	283	-5	14400.00	8905.38
18	Ian POULTER	Eng	71	74	70	69	284	-4	12050.00	7452.07
	Peter MITCHELL	Eng	72	70	71	71	284	-4	12050.00	7452.07
	Olivier EDMOND	Fr	71	72	70	71	284	-4	12050.00	7452.07
	Michael JONZON	Swe	76	69	71	68	284	-4	12050.00	7452.07
	John BICKERTON	Eng	68	70	73	73	284	-4	12050.00	7452.07
23	Barry LANE	Eng	72	70	72	71	285	-3	11000.00	6802.72
24	Domingo HOSPITAL	Sp	72	71	72	71	286	-2	10100.00	6246.13
	Grant HAMERTON	Eng	72	72	70	72	286	-2	10100.00	6246.13
	Bradley DREDGE	Wal	73	71	71	71	286	-2	10100.00	6246.13
	Robert COLES	Eng	73	72	73	68	286	-2	10100.00	6246.13
	Benoit TEILLERIA	Fr	71	73	69	73	286	-2	10100.00	6246.13
29	Anders FORSBRAND	Swe	72	74	69	72	287	-1	8600.00	5318.49
	Jamie SPENCE	Eng	72	68	77	70	287	-1	8600.00	5318.49
	Fredrik LINDGREN	Swe	73	72	71	71	287	-1	8600.00	5318.49
	Paul EALES	Eng	72	74	71	70	287	-1	8600.00	5318.49
	Van PHILLIPS	Eng	71	71	72	73	287	-1	8600.00	5318.49
34	Anders HANSEN	Den	71	72	71	74	288	0	7300.00	4514.53
	Peter BAKER	Eng	72	71	73	72	288	0	7300.00	4514.53
	Max ANGLERT	Swe	72	71	75	70	288	0	7300.00	4514.53
	Stephen GALLACHER	Scot	73	72	70	73	288	0	7300.00	4514.53
	Alastair FORSYTH	Scot	71	71	73	73	288	0	7300.00	4514.53
39	Roger CHAPMAN	Eng	73	73	77	66	289	1	6400.00	3957.95
	Eamonn DARCY	Ire	73	73	72	71	289	1	6400.00	3957.95
	Francisco CEA	Sp	73	73	70	73	289	1	6400.00	3957.95
	Ivo GINER	Sp	71	70	75	73	289	1	6400.00	3957.95
43	Mark MOULAND	Wal	72	73	68	77	290	2	5600.00	3463.20
	Soren KJELDSEN	Den	70	72	75	73	290	2	5600.00	3463.20
	Philip GOLDING	Eng	74	73	70	73	290	2	5600.00	3463.20
	Simon WAKEFIELD	Eng	75	71	74	70	290	2	5600.00	3463.20
47	Nick LUDWELL	Eng	70	73	76	72	291	3	5000.00	3092.15
	Andrew RAITT	Eng	74	71	77	69	291	3	5000.00	3092.15
49	Gordon BRAND JNR.	Scot	75	70	73	74	292	4	4400.00	2721.09
	Miguel Angel MARTIN	Sp	70	73	73	76	292	4	4400.00	2721.09
	Thomas GÖGELE	Ger	72	73	76	71	292	4	4400.00	2721.09
	David PARK	Wal	74	74	73	71	292	4	4400.00	2721.09
53	Mats LANNER	Swe	77	71	74	71	293	5	3600.00	2226.35
	Kevin CARISSIMI	USA	73	72	74	74	293	5	3600.00	2226.35
	Russell CLAYDON	Eng	69	76	75	73	293	5	3600.00	2226.35
	Didier DE VOOGHT	Bel	70	72	77	74	293	5	3600.00	2226.35
57	Roger WINCHESTER	Eng	73	74	71	76	294	6	2900.00	1793.44
	Per NYMAN	Swe	77	69	72	76	294	6	2900.00	1793.44
	David LYNN	Eng	70	75	76	73	294	6	2900.00	1793.44
	Iain PYMAN	Eng	76	69	73	76	294	6	2900.00	1793.44
	Rodolfo GONZALEZ	Arg	71	73	75	75	294	6	2900.00	1793.44
62	Scott ROWE	USA	70	77	76	72	295	7	2500.00	1546.07
	Stephen FIELD	Eng	70	75	76	74	295	7	2500.00	1546.07
	Matthew BLACKEY	Eng	72	74	76	73	295	7	2500.00	1546.07
65	Gary MURPHY	Ire	73	75	74	74	296	8	2110.00	1304.89
	Greig HUTCHEON	Scot	72	75	74	75	296	8	2110.00	1304.89
	Paul AFFLECK	Wal	72	74	77	73	296	8	2110.00	1304.89
	Jonathan LOMAS	Eng	73	73	74	76	296	8	2110.00	1304.89
	Ola ELIASSON	Swe	72	73	77	74	296	8	2110.00	1304.89
70	Justin ROSE	Eng	72	71	77	77	297	9	1632.33	1009.48
	Gary EMERSON	Eng	74	73	74	76	297	9	1632.33	1009.48
	Ignacio GARRIDO	Sp	70	74	75	78	297	9	1632.33	1009.48
73	José RIVERO	Sp	74	74	74	76	298	10	1494.00	923.93
74	Ross MCFARLANE	Eng	75	73	77	76	301	13	1491.00	922.08
75	Elliot BOULT	NZ	74	74	79	77	304	16	1488.00	920.22

PROQUIP

Our total commitment to research, development and quality ensures each garment is designed to provide consistent protection - whatever the conditions. Today's golfer seeks a combination of high performance, advanced technological fabric and quality design and styling. Proquip clothing more than meets the challenge.

Perfect for birdies, eagles, cats & dogs

The Proquip name assures you of water and windproof protection combined with warmth. Our garments also provide full freedom of movement, maximum breathability, minimum movement noise and complete comfort during intensive sporting activity. Truly, *Winning Weatherwear™* in more ways than one.

Winning Weatherwear™
Part of Caledonian Golf Group

Call Sales on 01620 892219
for your nearest stockist.

Driving out the Demons

LA COSTA RESORT & SPA, CARLSBAD, CALIFORNIA, USA

No-one ever doubted Darren Clarke's ability. Certainly not Andrew 'Chubby' Chandler, who gambled on launching his sports management business on the strength of that conviction in August, 1990. Certainly not his peers and friends; players of the calibre of Colin Montgomerie and Lee Westwood.

So it was one of life's great anomalies that, during a decade on the European Tour, the strapping Ulsterman from Dungannon had captured only five titles compared to Montgomerie's 22 in 13 seasons and Westwood's haul of nine in just six years. The word 'underachiever' sprang readily to the minds of many of those inside the game.

The theory advanced more than once was that within his amiable frame lurked a volcanic, brittle character with a tendancy to get down on himself if things went slightly off the intended path. Clarke himself would often concur with that assessment - but not at La Costa Resort & Spa in Carlsbad, California, in February.

In one triumphant week, Clarke drove out the demons of uncertainty in his own mind when he overpowered, out-manoeuvred, out-thought and ultimately outclassed six of the greatest golfers of a generation to land the WGC-Andersen Consulting Match Play.

It was a monumental effort by Clarke, a bon viveur with a penchant for fast cars, a glass of beer and a large cigar, who knew by the end of that special week that no-one could question his suspect temperament again.

All but one of the leading 64 players on the Official World Golf Ranking attended the second visit to La Costa. Clarke, ranked No.19 at the time, drew a tough customer to start with in Paul Azinger, a former US PGA champion and a tournament winner in 2000.

Azinger, the world No.46, was dispatched 2 and 1. Next up was Mark O'Meara, the 1998 Masters and Open champion. The world's No.14 went out by a 5 and 4 margin. Fellow European Ryder Cup player, Thomas Björn (No.35) was next to fall by one hole.

If the draw seemed particularly tough in the early stages, it looked positively brutal in the latter parts. However, Clarke was undaunted by the sight of Hal Sutton, who had beaten him 4 and 2 in the Ryder Cup at Brookline. Sutton, ranked No.11, won three of the first four holes but was caught and overtaken 2 and 1.

At that juncture, it appeared clear that for Clarke to become the first European winner of a World Golf Championship event, he would in all probability have to take out the two top ranked players on the planet. He did - and with considerable style.

Few could have predicted the ease with which the affable Irishman picked off David Duval, the world's No.2, in the semi-final by a 4 and 2 margin, leaving him eyeball to eyeball with the undisputed No.1 on the planet, Tiger Woods.

David Duval

Darren Clarke and Tiger Woods: rivals and great friends

Shot of the Week

Not the best shot Darren Clarke hit all week but the most critical. Three down after four to Hal Sutton in the third round, his drive was heading towards trouble when it hit an overhead cable, allowing Clarke to 'reload'. This time he found the fairway, won the hole and never looked back when he would have been four down, and probably out.

If anything the 36-hole final was even more comprehensive as Clarke extinguished any lingering doubts along with his Saturday evening cigar butt and proceeded to beat Woods 4 and 3 with a magnificent display of golf. Whereas often his mind had seemed fragile, this time he played with a serenity and conviction.

As he pocketed the $1 million first prize Clarke revealed that his first victory on American soil, against a 'Who's Who' of golfing greats, was an exhilarating feeling. He said: "To come over to America and play as well as I have done is fantastic. To play as solid as I did against Tiger, the best player in the world, is a great feeling.

"I've had the potential these past few years but never actually finished jobs off. A lot of opportunities to win tournaments slipped through my fingers but this is certainly very gratifying, especially against the No.1 player in the world. This victory will hopefully be a stepping stone and I can go on and improve."

Clarke endeared himself to the American media with a genuine charm offensive. His wry responses to whether he owned a gym - "Yes we have one in the garage - gathering dust!" - met with howls of laughter from the assembled press corps.

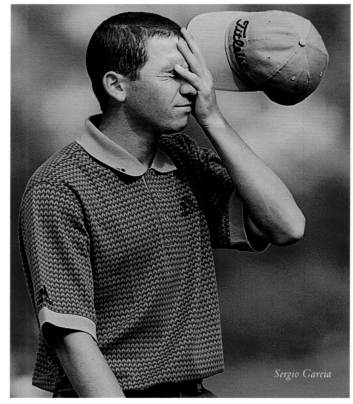

Sergio Garcia

The Course

La Costa Resort & Spa played much longer than in 1999 due to an unusual amount of rain prior to the event. The wetness toughened the course with cool and rainy weather in the early part of the week. The rough was also longer which made it essential to stay on the straight and narrow.

Tiger Woods

Woods, as ever, was magnanimous in defeat. He said: "Darren just flat out-played me. He played beautifully. I am not surprised. He played like that all week and he has the ability to play great golf."

Overall it was a wonderful week for the European Tour. Eight of the 1999 Ryder Cup side reached the second round with three other Tour members, Ernie Els, Retief Goosen and Björn, making it past the initial phase.

Paul Lawrie furthered his growing reputation by reaching the quarter-finals, only to be edged out by Woods on the final green having been two up with six to play. At the same stage, Miguel Angel Jimenéz bowed out 3 and 2 to Davis Love III. Sergio Garcia, who reached the third round, was outstanding against Canadian Mike Weir before falling to Duval 2 and 1.

Duval went on to beat Love 5 and 4 in the Consolation Match for third and fourth place, but it was Clarke who went home to Europe with the spoils, richer by $1 million but, more importantly, richer in experience at the uppermost levels in the game. For 'underachiever', read 'achiever'. No-one deserves the accolade more. It was left to Woods to leave the final message-pinned to Darren's locker: "Congrats Again. Be Proud."

Gordon Simpson

LA COSTA RESORT & SPA, CARLSBAD, CA, USA, 23-27 FEBRUARY 2000, PAR 72, 7022 YARDS, 6423 METRES

WINNER
DARREN CLARKE
4 & 3

THE CONSOLATION MATCH
DAVID DUVAL beat
DAVIS LOVE III
5 & 4

Woods 5 & 4 — Clarke 4 & 2

Left half of draw:

1 Tiger Woods
64 Michael Campbell — Woods 5 & 4
Woods 1 hole
32 Retief Goosen
33 Stewart Cink — Goosen 3 & 2
Woods 4 & 3
16 Justin Leonard
49 Fred Funk — Leonard 6 & 5
Maruyama 1 hole
17 John Huston
48 Shigeki Maruyama — Maruyama 1 hole
Woods 1 hole
8 Nick Price
57 Mark Calcavecchia — Calcavecchia 2 & 1
Calcavecchia 4 & 3
25 José Maria Olazábal
40 Craig Parry — Olazábal 1 hole
Lawrie at 3rd extra hole
9 Phil Mickelson
56 Billy Mayfair — Mayfair at 2nd extra hole
Lawrie 3 & 2
24 Chris Perry
41 Paul Lawrie — Lawrie 1 hole

4 Davis Love III
61 Olin Brown — Love III 2 & 1
Love III 3 & 2
29 Steve Elkington
36 Jeff Sluman — Sluman 2 & 1
Love III 3 & 2
13 Jim Furyk
52 Rocco Mediate — Furyk 2 & 1
Furyk 2 & 1
20 Jeff Maggert
45 Bob Tway — Tway 6 & 5
Love III 3 & 2
5 Ernie Els
60 Bernard Langer — Els 2 & 1
Estes 1 hole
28 Bob Estes
37 Steve Pate — Estes at 2nd extra hole
Jiménez 2 & 1
12 Tom Lehman
53 Andrew Magee — Lehman 6 & 4
Jiménez 4 & 3
21 Miguel Angel Jiménez
44 Brent Geiberger — Jiménez at 1st extra hole

Right half of draw:

David Duval 2
Angel Cabrera 63 — Duval 4 & 3
Duval 2 & 1
Tim Herron 31
Dudley Hart 34 — Herron 2 & 1
Duval 2 & 1
Sergio Garcia 15
Loren Roberts 50 — Garcia at 2nd extra hole
Garcia 7 & 6
Carlos Franco 18
Mike Weir 47 — Weir 4 & 3
Duval 5 & 4
Lee Westwood 7
Brandt Jobe 58 — Westwood 2 & 1
Hoch 1 hole
Stewart Appleby 26
Scott Hoch 39 — Hoch 1 hole
Hoch 2 & 1
Jesper Parnevik 10
Padraig Harrington 55 — Parnevik 2 & 1
Parnevik at 1st extra hole
Fred Couples 23
Joe Ozaki 42 — Ozaki 1 hole

Colin Montgomerie 3
Dennis Paulson 62 — Montgomerie 2 & 1
Björn at 5th extra hole
Glen Day 30
Thomas Björn 35 — Björn 1 hole
Clarke 1 hole
Mark O'Meara 14
Greg Norman 51 — O'Meara 1 hole
Clarke 5 & 4
Darren Clarke 19
Paul Azinger 46 — Clarke 2 & 1
Clarke 1 hole
Vijay Singh 6
Duffy Waldorf 59 — Waldorf 2 & 1
Waldorf 2 & 1
Steve Stricker 27
Lee Janzen 38 — Stricker 2 & 1
Sutton 2 & 1
Hal Sutton 11
Ted Tryba 54 — Sutton 4 & 3
Sutton 1 hole
David Toms 22
Brian Watts 43 — Toms 1 hole

PRIZE MONEY
Champion €1,015,227
Runner-Up €507,613
Third Place €406,901
Fourth Place €304,568
Quarter Finalists €152,2847
Third Round €76,142
Second Round €50,761
First Round €25,380

Hero's Welcome

DUBAI CREEK GOLF & YACHT CLUB, DUBAI

*T*he cheers when they pierced the early evening chill of this Arabian night came from the heart.

Long after the giant coffee pot had been lifted and a cheque for 230,742 euro (£141,610) banked, José Coceres walked into The Creek's state-of-the-art clubhouse to a hero's welcome.

The chorus of approval was for more than that afforded to the latest winner of the Dubai Desert Classic. The noise also recognised the heart warming story behind this generous son of Argentina.

For Coceres was born so far on the wrong side of the tracks it was a day's walk to the nearest station.

Coceres shared his story for the first time after the third round when he built a five-shot lead over England's Jamie Spence. It was difficult for all those listening to prevent their eyes turning into casual water. Few could imagine the poverty José endured during his upbringing among ten brothers and sisters.

José Cóceres

Paul Lawrie

The home in Chaco, 700 miles north of Buenos Aires close to the borders with Paraguay and Brazil, had precious little furniture and just two bedrooms - one for his parents and the other for the siblings. "Sometimes we slept five or six to a bed which was good when it was freezing, but not very good when it was warm," he said.

But across the road from where the Coceres clan made the most of the little they had, was a golf course to which José was for ever attracted.

He would be a regular visitor to the caddie shack and started carrying for the better off at an early age.

Coceres had aspirations beyond and at the age of 13 he was handed his first club. It was made purely from the wood of a branch his brothers stripped from a tree. The balls he used were as hard as rock... because that was exactly what they were.

About 200 miles across the border with Paraguay a certain Carlos Franco was enduring a similar upbringing in a home of many people and with dirt floors, but only later would the two strike up a friendship and rivalry. As teenagers they went independently in pursuit of their dreams even though most around believed they were contained in a pipe. José was 25 when he finally persuaded an acquaintance to sponsor his quest for a European Tour card and ironically, considering the triumph in the desert, the $45,000 he

On the tee . . . Ian Woosnam

The Course

Many players found themselves up The Creek without a paddle the previous year with tight fairways and penal rough. Underfoot conditions were not as severe in 2000, but the course was playing arguably tougher because of something no greenkeeper has control over. The severe wind proved the toughest to conquer and the last two holes, backing on to the water, provided no end of casualties. A quality leaderboard for a quality course, however.

received, was repaid with the proceeds of a hole-in-one at the 1992 Dubai Desert Classic.

Wealth beyond his wildest dreams started to trickle in starting in the mid-90's, but José never once forgot his roots. "I feel lucky to be where I am considering where I come from," he said.

José had already assumed control of the family's finances, such as they were, following his father's tragic death in a motor accident, but not just his nearest and dearest have benefited from his generosity. "Whenever I have the chance I go to the really poor neighbours in Buenos Aires because I came from a place like that," he said.

The 36-year-old leaves food, clothes, shoes and books for poor children, most of whom have never heard of the game one of their own is now famous for. "When I go home I like to help the people because I am not one to forget the past," he added.

Coceres now owns three houses in his country's capital - one for himself and the others for the rest of the family, which includes two other golfers.

The breakthrough in Europe came at the 1994 Heineken Open Catalonia and Coceres has never once been outside the top 70 in the last seven years.

Paul McGinley

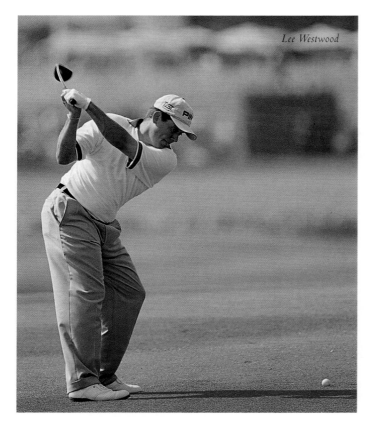

Lee Westwood

There have been disappointments to go with the glory and among the biggest was finishing second in the Argentine Open last year when he so wanted a home win for his many followers.

José remembered them in Dubai when he pulled out his nation's flag from his bag after completing the eighth worldwide win of his career. The latest came courtesy of some outstanding golf in all departments and against formidable opposition because Open champion Paul Lawrie, Lee Westwood and former World Cup winner Paul McGinley were among those waiting for any error.

When it came on the last hole of the last round, it was too late for anybody to do anything about it. José could afford the luxury of a double bogey and still beat McGinley and Swede Patrik Sjöland by two shots with Lawrie and Westwood among those in joint fourth.

It was a popular triumph among the many ex-pats who filled the Dubai Creek clubhouse afterwards as the cheers recognised. Thousands of miles away there would be other celebrations - another batch of food and clothing parcels would soon be on their way to children in desperate need of them.

Martin Hardy

Shot of the Week

Peter Downie, head professional at Dubai Creek, gave his own members something to enthuse over when he aced the 186 yards 16th hole in the first round. That shot ensured the Scots-born pro made the halfway cut, and although he finished last of the qualifiers, it was a moment to savour.

DUBAI CREEK GOLF & YACHT CLUB, DUBAI, 2-5 MARCH, 2000, PAR 72, 6853 YARDS, 6267 METRES

Pos.	Name		Rd1	Rd2	Rd3	Rd4	Total	Par	Prize Money Euro	£
1	José COCERES	Arg	64	69	68	73	274	-14	230742.17	141610.00
2	Paul MCGINLEY	Ire	67	72	70	67	276	-12	120218.61	73780.00
	Patrik SJÖLAND	Swe	71	72	66	67	276	-12	120218.61	73780.00
4	Jamie SPENCE	Eng	70	67	69	72	278	-10	54500.03	33447.50
	Paul LAWRIE	Scot	66	75	69	68	278	-10	54500.03	33447.50
	Lee WESTWOOD	Eng	64	75	68	71	278	-10	54500.03	33447.50
	Stephen GALLACHER	Scot	69	74	68	67	278	-10	54500.03	33447.50
8	Russell CLAYDON	Eng	70	73	64	72	279	-9	34625.18	21250.00
9	Paul AFFLECK	Wal	67	71	70	72	280	-8	29362.15	18020.00
	Alastair FORSYTH	Scot	68	72	70	70	280	-8	29362.15	18020.00
11	José RIVERO	Sp	66	72	74	69	281	-7	24653.13	15130.00
	Ross MCFARLANE	Eng	70	75	68	68	281	-7	24653.13	15130.00
13	Jorge BERENDT	Arg	70	72	71	69	282	-6	20844.36	12792.50
	Thomas BJÖRN	Den	67	71	72	72	282	-6	20844.36	12792.50
	Van PHILLIPS	Eng	71	70	69	72	282	-6	20844.36	12792.50
	Greg OWEN	Eng	68	70	74	70	282	-6	20844.36	12792.50
17	Miguel Angel MARTIN	Sp	69	76	70	68	283	-5	17912.76	10993.34
	Thomas GÖGELE	Ger	69	76	69	69	283	-5	17912.76	10993.34
	Darren CLARKE	N.Ire	71	70	69	73	283	-5	17912.76	10993.34
20	Tony JOHNSTONE	Zim	72	74	68	70	284	-4	15909.25	9763.75
	Peter MITCHELL	Eng	68	74	72	70	284	-4	15909.25	9763.75
	Roger WINCHESTER	Eng	72	75	65	72	284	-4	15909.25	9763.75
	John BICKERTON	Eng	69	75	68	72	284	-4	15909.25	9763.75
24	Jean-Francois REMESY	Fr	69	76	70	70	285	-3	13988.57	8585.00
	José Maria OLAZABAL	Sp	71	74	68	72	285	-3	13988.57	8585.00
	Ian GARBUTT	Eng	66	76	74	69	285	-3	13988.57	8585.00
	David PARK	Wal	71	71	69	74	285	-3	13988.57	8585.00
	Jarmo SANDELIN	Swe	68	79	63	75	285	-3	13988.57	8585.00
29	Justin LEONARD	USA	72	73	68	73	286	-2	12326.56	7565.00
	Tom GILLIS	USA	70	74	69	73	286	-2	12326.56	7565.00
	Gary ORR	Scot	68	75	70	73	286	-2	12326.56	7565.00
32	Roger CHAPMAN	Eng	67	78	71	71	287	-1	10747.65	6596.00
	Eduardo ROMERO	Arg	71	73	70	73	287	-1	10747.65	6596.00
	Steve WEBSTER	Eng	73	74	69	71	287	-1	10747.65	6596.00
	Alex CEJKA	Ger	70	74	72	71	287	-1	10747.65	6596.00
	Bradley DREDGE	Wal	70	77	70	70	287	-1	10747.65	6596.00
37	Mats LANNER	Swe	69	74	75	70	288	0	8725.54	5355.00
	Wayne RILEY	Aus	68	76	68	76	288	0	8725.54	5355.00
	Andrew MCLARDY	SA	74	72	70	72	288	0	8725.54	5355.00
	Thomas LEVET	Fr	74	69	71	74	288	0	8725.54	5355.00
	Soren HANSEN	Den	68	76	71	73	288	0	8725.54	5355.00
	Jyoti RANDHAWA	Ind	70	75	72	71	288	0	8725.54	5355.00
	Carl SUNESON	Sp	68	77	68	75	288	0	8725.54	5355.00
	Phillip PRICE	Wal	73	74	70	71	288	0	8725.54	5355.00
	David LYNN	Eng	70	75	73	70	288	0	8725.54	5355.00
46	Kyi Hla HAN	Myan	75	72	73	69	289	1	6371.03	3910.00
	Mark O'MEARA	USA	73	72	71	73	289	1	6371.03	3910.00
	Brian DAVIS	Eng	76	71	68	74	289	1	6371.03	3910.00
	Colin MONTGOMERIE	Scot	71	75	70	73	289	1	6371.03	3910.00
	Miguel Angel JIMÉNEZ	Sp	69	75	70	75	289	1	6371.03	3910.00
	Nicolas VANHOOTEGEM	Bel	74	72	69	74	289	1	6371.03	3910.00
	Rolf MUNTZ	Hol	69	76	73	71	289	1	6371.03	3910.00
	Peter LONARD	Aus	69	78	74	68	289	1	6371.03	3910.00
54	Lian-Wei ZHANG	PRC	71	73	75	71	290	2	4986.03	3060.00
	Peter BAKER	Eng	69	75	74	72	290	2	4986.03	3060.00
56	Fredrik LINDGREN	Swe	70	76	72	73	291	3	4258.90	2613.75
	Jonathan LOMAS	Eng	70	77	73	71	291	3	4258.90	2613.75
	Ricardo GONZALEZ	Arg	71	75	71	74	291	3	4258.90	2613.75
	David CARTER	Eng	69	77	69	76	291	3	4258.90	2613.75
60	Mark DAVIS	Eng	72	74	75	71	292	4	3739.52	2295.00
	Johan SKOLD	Swe	70	73	72	77	292	4	3739.52	2295.00
	Daren LEE	Eng	74	73	70	75	292	4	3739.52	2295.00
63	Gary EVANS	Eng	69	70	77	77	293	5	3462.52	2125.00
64	Santiago LUNA	Sp	70	74	75	75	294	6	3116.27	1912.50
	David HOWELL	Eng	74	73	71	76	294	6	3116.27	1912.50
	Jim PAYNE	Eng	69	78	71	76	294	6	3116.27	1912.50
	Wei-Tze YEH	Tai	71	73	74	76	294	6	3116.27	1912.50
68	Des SMYTH	Ire	74	73	73	75	295	7	2770.01	1700.00
69	André BOSSERT	Swi	74	72	74	76	296	8	2668.18	1637.50
	Stephen ALLAN	Aus	70	76	79	71	296	8	2668.18	1637.50
71	Gary MURPHY	Ire	68	79	75	75	297	9	2076.50	1274.38
	Christopher HANELL	Swe	70	77	75	75	297	9	2076.50	1274.38
73	Felix CASAS	Phil	71	76	73	78	298	10	2072.00	1271.62
74	Peter DOWNIE	Scot	71	75	81	78	305	17	2069.00	1269.78

Seminal Moment

DOHA GOLF CLUB, QATAR

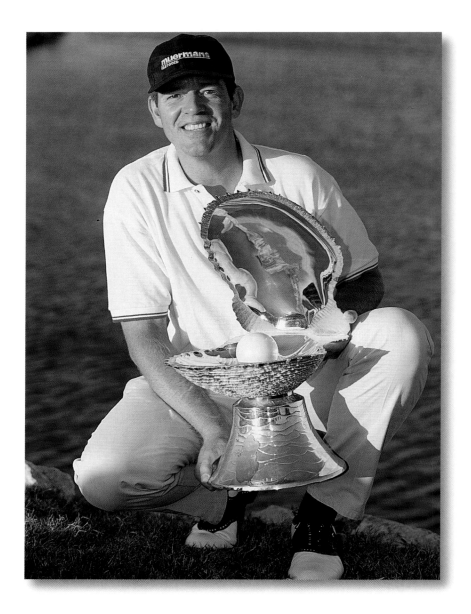

*I*t was two hours and more after he had experienced the greatest moment of his professional life, the instant when the faith and trust he had had in himself had been vindicated after years of trying.

He could have been back in his hotel, planning what he would do on the first day of the rest of a life that had been changed, perhaps for ever.

He could have been in the bar over there in the clubhouse, surrendering himself to the welcoming arms of Bacchus, a guy's best pal when in the mood for a celebration. Say what you like about old Bacchus, he's never boring.

His friends and rivals had all disappeared into the velvet Arabian night, gone to lick their wounds after being battered halfway to insensibility for four solid days by the elements.

The Course

In 1999, 39 players broke par for the tournament. This time around, there were only two, which even in the presence of a constant and melancholy wind, said something about the way the course was set up. Like its cousins, The Emirates and Dubai Creek, down the road in Dubai, Doha is a testimony to the course designer's art. It's tough enough when it's calm. When the wind blows, as it did, it's a wonderful but punishing brute.

Rolf Muntz

For most of them, the only aim was to forget what they had been through, for it had not been pleasant. But for this man, the moment had been special, and he wanted to hold on to it for as long as humanly possible.

He had received the acclamation of the crowd, he had pocketed the biggest check of a career that was suddenly adorned not with tin but with precious metal, he had given his champion's press conference, and still he was rolling the flavour of victory round his mouth like a Master of Wine tasting the Rhone Valley's finest.

There were still plenty of people left at Doha Golf Club as a dusty moon rose — courtesy car drivers, clubhouse staff, a few lingering spectators, the massed ranks of the media, hunched over their computers, spreading the good word about this man's exploits. From time to time the elusive, wraithlike figure of a Qatari wearing the traditional snowy-white dish-dash could be seen flitting from tent to tent, tournament office to clubhouse.

Oh yes, there were people around, all right. But Rolf Muntz was scarcely aware of any of them; he was wrapped up, cocooned in a little world inhabited only by himself and Vanessa, his partner. He had won, you see, and, my, did it feel good.

The third Qatar Masters was a seminal moment in not only Muntz's life but also in the life of golf itself in his native country. In claiming a runaway victory with a total of 272, eight under par, at a stroke Muntz raised the profile of the game in Holland by several notches

— now they could boast another successful export in addition to Edam cheese and tulips from Amsterdam.

In a seven-year career as a professional, Muntz could have laid claim to being Holland's best player in modern times before he struck his first shot in the tiny, oil-rich sheikdom, but still he had not managed what Joop Ruhl, his compatriot, had achieved long ago in 1947 — victory in a ranking European event.

Ruhl had his moment of glory in his country's Open back then, but Muntz had to travel a good deal further to emulate him. It had been a pretty rocky road at times, too, but through it all he had never lost belief in himself, even when he lost his card in 1995.

Now he had the one entry on his CV that would validate him as a professional golfer. And a comprehensive success it was, too, as he won by five strokes from no less a luminary than Ian Woosnam, who himself was the length of a medium-sized straat from the next men in the list, Eduardo Romero and Stephen Leaney.

Woosnam was typically gracious in defeat. "He's beaten me by five and I've beaten the rest by four," he said. "That just goes to show how good he's been this week."

Woosie was dead right. In a four-day battering from the wicked, malicious shamal, the cruel wind that sweeps in from the desert in these parts, Muntz played a different game to the rest. They all took

Van Phillips

Shot of the Week

It didn't actually mean a great deal in the wider context of the tournament, but the moment experienced by Jamie Spence in the second round was one to savour for the player. In 25 years in the game he had never had a hole in one, but he rectified the situation at last on the 13th with a two iron. It brought personal delight to Spence and also at least partly silenced his long-time caddie, Janet Squire. She had had six before her boss got his first.

Ian Woosnam and Miguel Angel Martin find themselves in the deep stuff.

on the challenge — only the tall Dutchman could be said to have beaten it.

Alongside David Lynn, the young Englishman, he was a stroke behind Peter Lonard, the Australian, after 18 holes, 68 to 67. It was the last time he was headed.

He shared the lead after 36 holes with Matthias Grônberg, already a tournament winner in 2000 when he took the Alfred Dunhill Championship title in South Africa. He led on his own after 54, a marvellous five under par 67 on the blowiest day of the tournament putting him six strokes ahead of Leaney.

It was on this day that Muntz won the tournament, no doubt about

it. With 18 holes to go, his biggest battle now would not be with the conditions, the golf course or his closest rivals; it would be with himself.

As it transpired, he won that little skirmish hands down, a clear and handsome winner on points. They could have stopped the contest at halfway to stop the other 78 from unnecessary punishment. Even when he was dropping shots at three consecutive holes from the fifth, he was still in control of himself and the tournament.

He thought so, too. "There was only one contestant, and that was me," he said. "I didn't have to beat anybody else. I just tried to be my own friend. You don't have control over other people, so there wasn't any point in worrying about them — I just tried to play my own game."

Which is exactly what he did, splendidly and with massive authority. In 1990 he became the first Dutchman to take the British Amateur title, and now he had become the first man from the flatlands of Holland to win on the modern European Tour.

He faced an uncertain future when he dropped out of his degree course in law at Leiden University to turn professional in 1992. Right now, the law, which can be as dry, dusty and arid as the sandy wastes in which he had had his finest moment, must have seemed a million miles away. And that, as far as Rolf Frederick Cornelis Muntz was concerned, was exactly where it could stay.

Mel Webb

DOHA GOLF CLUB, QATAR, 9-12 MARCH 2000, PAR 72, 7110 YARDS, 6500 METRES

Pos.	Name		Rd1	Rd2	Rd3	Rd4	Total	Par	Prize Money Euro	£
1	Rolf MUNTZ	Hol	68	73	67	72	280	-8	129964.42	79063.88
2	Ian WOOSNAM	Wal	71	75	71	68	285	-3	86504.32	52624.92
3	Eduardo ROMERO	Arg	75	74	71	69	289	1	43901.98	26707.78
	Stephen LEANEY	Aus	70	74	70	75	289	1	43901.98	26707.78
5	Miguel Angel MARTIN	Sp	73	73	71	73	290	2	30177.75	18358.64
	Brian DAVIS	Eng	75	70	75	70	290	2	30177.75	18358.64
7	Peter FOWLER	Aus	72	72	73	74	291	3	18987.81	11551.24
	Soren KJELDSEN	Den	73	70	73	75	291	3	18987.81	11551.24
	Paul MCGINLEY	Ire	72	70	74	75	291	3	18987.81	11551.24
	José COCERES	Arg	74	73	71	73	291	3	18987.81	11551.24
11	Steve WEBSTER	Eng	72	75	72	73	292	4	13438.32	8175.20
	Ian POULTER	Eng	74	71	73	74	292	4	13438.32	8175.20
	Andrew BUTTERFIELD	Eng	72	77	70	73	292	4	13438.32	8175.20
14	Soren HANSEN	Den	73	75	69	76	293	5	10994.98	6688.80
	Olivier EDMOND	Fr	74	73	74	72	293	5	10994.98	6688.80
	Angel CABRERA	Arg	71	76	74	72	293	5	10994.98	6688.80
	Markus BRIER	Aut	70	76	73	74	293	5	10994.98	6688.80
	David CARTER	Eng	73	74	72	74	293	5	10994.98	6688.80
19	Malcolm MACKENZIE	Eng	75	75	72	72	294	6	8729.06	5310.33
	Wayne RILEY	Aus	73	76	72	73	294	6	8729.06	5310.33
	Barry LANE	Eng	71	79	74	70	294	6	8729.06	5310.33
	Peter BAKER	Eng	75	72	74	73	294	6	8729.06	5310.33
	Carl SUNESON	Sp	74	73	72	75	294	6	8729.06	5310.33
	Per NYMAN	Swe	77	72	71	74	294	6	8729.06	5310.33
	Van PHILLIPS	Eng	72	75	70	77	294	6	8729.06	5310.33
	Patrik SJÖLAND	Swe	74	74	73	73	294	6	8729.06	5310.33
27	Eamonn DARCY	Ire	74	73	75	73	295	7	6823.13	4150.85
	José RIVERO	Sp	75	71	76	73	295	7	6823.13	4150.85
	Gary MURPHY	Ire	75	75	72	73	295	7	6823.13	4150.85
	Richard S JOHNSON	Swe	74	72	78	71	295	7	6823.13	4150.85
	Mathias GRÖNBERG	Swe	71	70	75	79	295	7	6823.13	4150.85
	David LYNN	Eng	68	76	77	74	295	7	6823.13	4150.85
	Greg OWEN	Eng	71	78	72	74	295	7	6823.13	4150.85
	Jarmo SANDELIN	Swe	74	74	75	72	295	7	6823.13	4150.85
35	Roger CHAPMAN	Eng	75	74	73	74	296	8	5536.48	3368.12
	Lian-Wei ZHANG	PRC	73	74	75	74	296	8	5536.48	3368.12
	Craig HAINLINE	USA	73	76	72	75	296	8	5536.48	3368.12
	Matthew BLACKEY	Eng	75	74	74	73	296	8	5536.48	3368.12
	John BICKERTON	Eng	73	74	75	74	296	8	5536.48	3368.12
40	Santiago LUNA	Sp	75	75	72	75	297	9	4678.72	2846.30
	David HOWELL	Eng	78	72	75	72	297	9	4678.72	2846.30
	Sven STRÜVER	Ger	72	76	77	72	297	9	4678.72	2846.30
	Roger WINCHESTER	Eng	75	75	72	75	297	9	4678.72	2846.30
	Alex CEJKA	Ger	72	77	75	73	297	9	4678.72	2846.30
	Phillip PRICE	Wal	72	73	73	79	297	9	4678.72	2846.30
46	Jamie SPENCE	Eng	74	71	78	75	298	10	3587.02	2182.16
	Russell CLAYDON	Eng	71	72	75	80	298	10	3587.02	2182.16
	Gary ORR	Scot	70	74	79	75	298	10	3587.02	2182.16
	Stephen SCAHILL	NZ	73	74	78	73	298	10	3587.02	2182.16
	Niclas FASTH	Swe	73	74	74	77	298	10	3587.02	2182.16
	Ola ELIASSON	Swe	75	75	73	75	298	10	3587.02	2182.16
	John MELLOR	Eng	72	74	78	74	298	10	3587.02	2182.16
	Christopher HANELL	Swe	73	73	78	74	298	10	3587.02	2182.16
54	Thomas LEVET	Fr	72	73	76	78	299	11	2588.89	1574.95
	Robin BYRD	USA	78	71	72	78	299	11	2588.89	1574.95
	Per-Ulrik JOHANSSON	Swe	73	77	70	79	299	11	2588.89	1574.95
	Peter LONARD	Aus	67	78	78	76	299	11	2588.89	1574.95
	David PARK	Wal	75	74	72	78	299	11	2588.89	1574.95
59	Marc FARRY	Fr	74	74	75	77	300	12	2066.44	1257.12
	Philip GOLDING	Eng	72	75	74	79	300	12	2066.44	1257.12
	Gary EVANS	Eng	73	76	76	75	300	12	2066.44	1257.12
	Ricardo GONZALEZ	Arg	74	71	76	79	300	12	2066.44	1257.12
	Steven RICHARDSON	Eng	76	73	75	76	300	12	2066.44	1257.12
	Max ANGLERT	Swe	72	72	77	79	300	12	2066.44	1257.12
65	Philip WALTON	Ire	73	77	78	73	301	13	1676.54	1019.92
	Ross MCFARLANE	Eng	74	75	77	75	301	13	1676.54	1019.92
	José Manuel CARRILES	Sp	74	76	74	77	301	13	1676.54	1019.92
	Thomas GÖGELE	Ger	74	72	76	79	301	13	1676.54	1019.92
69	Tony JOHNSTONE	Zim	76	73	75	78	302	14	1300.12	790.93
	Paul AFFLECK	Wal	75	75	74	78	302	14	1300.12	790.93
	Nicolas VANHOOTEGEM	Bel	73	75	80	74	302	14	1300.12	790.93
	Francisco CEA	Sp	73	76	77	76	302	14	1300.12	790.93
	Raymond RUSSELL	Scot	74	75	74	79	302	14	1300.12	790.93
74	Jim PAYNE	Eng	73	76	73	81	303	15	1161.00	706.29
75	Simon D. HURLEY	Eng	72	78	78	76	304	16	1152.00	700.82
	Stephen FIELD	Eng	75	75	76	78	304	16	1152.00	700.82
	André BOSSERT	Swi	76	74	78	76	304	16	1152.00	700.82
	Bradley DREDGE	Wal	74	76	71	83	304	16	1152.00	700.82
	Johan SKOLD	Swe	73	77	75	79	304	16	1152.00	700.82

Pro-Golf 2001

Pro-Golf, the European Tour Media Guide respected throughout the golfing world as an essential work of reference, has been chronicling the achievements of the European Tour for 30 years and the 2001 edition is packed full of records and revealing statistics.

In an arena full of great champions find out how Thomas Björn, Michael Campbell, Darren Clarke, Ernie Els, and Lee Westwood, winner of no fewer than five European Tour titles, challenged Colin Montgomerie's seven-year reign as Europe's Number One. Pro-Golf tells the full story of the race for the Volvo Order of Merit title.

On the world stage Tiger Woods spent the millennium year re-writing the record books, but European Tour Members pushed him harder than anyone. Darren Clarke rose to the challenge by defeating Woods in the 36-hole final of the

WGC - Andersen Consulting Match Play. Then after the excitement of Augusta, Pebble Beach and St Andrews, Bob May almost tamed the Tiger at Valhalla when he tied for the title after a thrilling duel before losing a sudden-death play-off. The figures and facts behind the winning of the major championships and all the events that make up the European Tour International Schedule can be found in Pro-Golf 2001.

Suberb biographies of the international stars who make the European Tour unique combined with more than 400 pages on the Tour history, tournament results, prize money and facts and figures make the illustrated Pro-Golf 2001, a must for all students of the game.

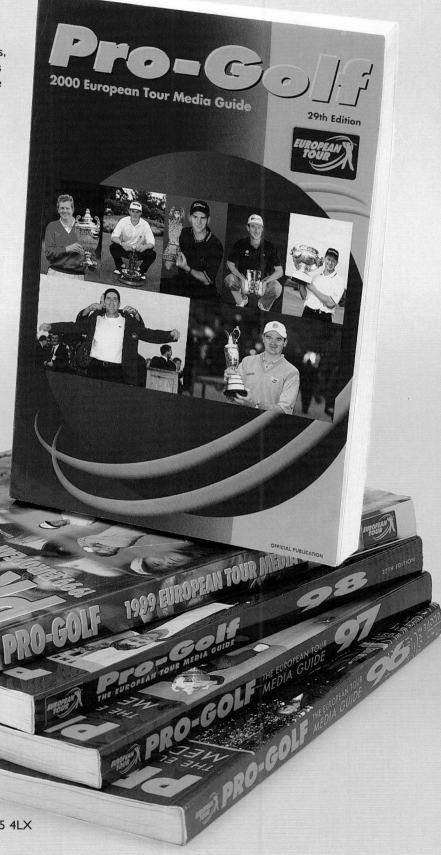

Ordering a copy of Pro-Golf 2001 is simple: send a cheque for £15 UK and Europe (which includes postage and packaging) and £20 Overseas (which includes postage and packaging), made payable to the PGA European Tour to Emily Doughty, Communications Division, European Tour, Wentworth Drive, Virginia Water, Surrey GU25 4LX or call +44 1344 840442 with credit card details.

Island of Dreams

SANTO DA SERRA, MADEIRA

Perhaps it is the spectacular scenery, perhaps the mountainous course, or perhaps mere coincidence, but whatever it is about Santo da Serra, Swedish players seem to feel very much at home in Madeira.

When Niclas Fasth led from start to finish to claim his first European Tour title he became the fourth Swedish winner of the Madeira Island Open in the past eight years, following in the footsteps of his countrymen Mats Lanner, champion in 1994 and 1998, and Jarmo Sandelin, who won in 1996.

To further emphasise the Swedish presence in this event there were no fewer than six Swedes in the top seven on the leaderboard after three rounds. But ultimately it was Fasth who triumphed, rounds of

66, 72, 68 and 73 giving the 27-year-old Swede a nine under par total of 279 and a two-stroke victory over another Swede Richard S Johnson, England's Mark Davis and Scotland's Ross Drummond.

It has been a long road to success for Fasth since he turned professional in 1993. That year he won three times on the Challenge Tour to earn his place on the European Tour and when he lost his card in 1996 by the small matter of 1,120 euro (£800) he bounced straight back by winning the European Tour Qualifying School Finals. But in November, 1999, he was back on Spain's Costa del Sol, finishing second behind Alastair Forsyth to reclaim his Tour card once again.

Niclas Fasth

Twice over the past five years Fasth had come close to making a winning breakthrough, but on both occasions he was denied by two European Tour Number Ones. First, in 1995 Colin Montgomerie won the Volvo German Open by a shot and then two years later Bernhard Langer finished with a string of birdies to win the Chemapol Trophy Czech Open. This time he was not to be denied.

From the outset, Fasth was the man to beat, his opening six under par 66, in which he twice chipped in for birdie, gave him a two shot lead and prompted him to say: "I will win. It might not be this week, but I will win."

That confidence stayed with him throughout the week as he held his place at the top of the leaderboard. A level par 72 in the second round kept him at the head of the field although his lead was down to one but he regained his two stroke cushion with a third round of 68 with England's Jim Payne occupying second.

As the final day unfolded, Payne back after recovering from the thumb injury which put him out of action for much of 1999 made the initial progress, narrowing the gap to one with a wonderful chip and putt for birdie on the third. But his hopes faded when his tee shot on the fourth, one of the most spectacular holes on the European circuit, bounced over the green and down the side of the mountain. It cost him a double bogey and when he made another double on the next hole he was effectively out of the running.

Golf in the clouds

Johnson, a Challenge Tour winner last year, then took up the challenge with an eagle three on the 11th and then a birdie on the next hole but two bogeys over the closing stretch proved costly.

There was also a welcome return to the leaderboard for both Davis and Drummond. Davis, twice a European Tour winner, didn't play at all for ten months last year having been struck down with a knee injury. Indeed, he wasn't even sure if he would ever play again. But after visiting a specialist, Volker Smasal, who works with the

Richard S Johnson

The Course

Perched high in the mountains, Santo da Serra is undoubtedly one of the most spectacular courses on the European Tour. Fine views of mountain tops and the Atlantic Ocean only add to the enjoyment of playing this course. A new wall had been added to the tee on the treacherous 11th, and the 15th green was re-shaped. The new pond on the 16th makes a marvellous feature and when played in glorious sunshine as it was all week, the course is a wonder to behold.

Olympic skiers and skaters in Munich, Davis underwent extensive surgery and physiotherapy to repair the damage. Playing on a medical exemption this year, he emerged from the pack with a final round of 67.

For Drummond it was his first start of the year after putting his clubs away following the European Tour Qualifying School Finals in November. The 43-year-old picked up six birdies on the back nine for a round of 67 to finish in a share of second place and equal his best finish on the European Tour.

Fasth meanwhile made steady progress, opening with seven solid pars before dropping a shot at the short eighth hole when he came up short. But with two birdies from the turn he was clear and, despite two late bogeys, on his way to victory.

"It really does feel good," he said. "It was the first time for me to be in the position of leading all week and it was more difficult than I thought. I was trying to make a good score in the final round but it was tough. It was a case of being patient. I played solid golf all week. I was really happy with everything. Of course it was difficult but I made it in the end."

Roddy Williams

Seve Ballesteros

Shot of the Week

This week it was not one shot of the week but two, both equally important as they provided the springboard for Niclas Fasth to claim his maiden European Tour victory. During the first round, Fasth twice chipped in for birdie. On the fifth he holed from about 20 feet and then he repeated the shot from the back of the 15th green from some 30 feet, both judged to perfection. Those two shots paved the way for an opening 66 and he never looked back.

SANTO DA SERRA, MADEIRA, 16-19 MARCH 2000, PAR 72, 7079 YARDS, 6166 METRES

Pos.	Name		Rd1	Rd2	Rd3	Rd4	Total	Par	Prize Money Euro	£
1	Niclas FASTH	Swe	66	72	68	73	279	-9	91630.00	56040.76
2	Ross DRUMMOND	Scot	72	69	73	67	281	-7	40993.33	25071.45
	Mark DAVIS	Eng	73	69	72	67	281	-7	40993.33	25071.45
	Richard S JOHNSON	Swe	70	75	67	69	281	-7	40993.33	25071.45
5	Raimo SJÖBERG	Swe	71	69	70	72	282	-6	21285.00	13017.87
	John BICKERTON	Eng	70	70	73	69	282	-6	21285.00	13017.87
7	Thomas GÖGELE	Ger	74	69	71	69	283	-5	13392.50	8190.83
	Bradley DREDGE	Wal	74	71	71	67	283	-5	13392.50	8190.83
	David LYNN	Eng	74	72	69	68	283	-5	13392.50	8190.83
	Markus BRIER	Aut	69	70	75	69	283	-5	13392.50	8190.83
11	Andrew BEAL	Eng	70	70	75	69	284	-4	9790.00	5987.55
	Simon HURD	Eng	72	73	70	69	284	-4	9790.00	5987.55
13	Frédéric CUPILLARD	Fr	70	71	73	71	285	-3	8855.00	5415.70
14	Peter LAWRIE	Ire	72	72	70	72	286	-2	7920.00	4843.86
	Francis VALERA	Sp	75	69	73	69	286	-2	7920.00	4843.86
	Jim PAYNE	Eng	71	69	68	78	286	-2	7920.00	4843.86
	Christopher HANELL	Swe	69	73	73	71	286	-2	7920.00	4843.86
18	Jose Manuel LARA	Sp	71	69	77	70	287	-1	6531.67	3994.76
	Henrik STENSON	Swe	68	73	70	76	287	-1	6531.67	3994.76
	Steen TINNING	Den	71	73	70	73	287	-1	6531.67	3994.76
	Stuart CAGE	Eng	70	74	73	70	287	-1	6531.67	3994.76
	Desmond TERBLANCHE	SA	71	74	69	73	287	-1	6531.67	3994.76
	Daren LEE	Eng	72	71	71	73	287	-1	6531.67	3994.76
24	Fredrik HENGE	Swe	71	71	70	76	288	0	5555.00	3397.43
	Alberto BINAGHI	It	71	70	76	71	288	0	5555.00	3397.43
	Jesus Maria ARRUTI	Sp	73	75	72	68	288	0	5555.00	3397.43
	Diego BORREGO	Sp	67	74	75	72	288	0	5555.00	3397.43
	Mikael LUNDBERG	Swe	69	71	72	76	288	0	5555.00	3397.43
29	Justin ROSE	Eng	74	72	71	72	289	1	4248.75	2598.53
	Gary EMERSON	Eng	71	71	75	72	289	1	4248.75	2598.53
	Simon D. HURLEY	Eng	75	71	74	69	289	1	4248.75	2598.53
	Peter MITCHELL	Eng	73	71	73	72	289	1	4248.75	2598.53
	Sam LITTLE	Eng	73	72	72	72	289	1	4248.75	2598.53
	Scott ROWE	USA	73	70	71	75	289	1	4248.75	2598.53
	Jeremy ROBINSON	Eng	72	74	78	65	289	1	4248.75	2598.53
	Fernando ROCA	Sp	71	73	74	71	289	1	4248.75	2598.53
	Jorge BERENDT	Arg	72	71	74	72	289	1	4248.75	2598.53
	Tomas Jesus MUÑOZ	Sp	74	72	72	71	289	1	4248.75	2598.53
	Matthew BLACKEY	Eng	77	67	73	72	289	1	4248.75	2598.53

Pos.	Name		Rd1	Rd2	Rd3	Rd4	Total	Par	Prize Money Euro	£
	Nic HENNING	SA	70	72	74	73	289	1	4248.75	2598.53
41	Robert Jan DERKSEN	Hol	74	70	70	76	290	2	3245.00	1984.64
	Eric CARLBERG	Swe	70	72	78	70	290	2	3245.00	1984.64
	Andrew MCLARDY	SA	76	71	72	71	290	2	3245.00	1984.64
	James HEPWORTH	Eng	72	74	73	71	290	2	3245.00	1984.64
	Peter GUSTAFSSON	Swe	70	72	74	74	290	2	3245.00	1984.64
46	Rudi SAILER	Aut	73	72	75	71	291	3	2640.00	1614.62
	Elliot BOULT	NZ	68	76	77	70	291	3	2640.00	1614.62
	Paul NILBRINK	Swe	76	68	71	76	291	3	2640.00	1614.62
	Jean-François LUCQUIN	Fr	75	70	73	73	291	3	2640.00	1614.62
	Paul MCGINLEY	Ire	70	77	69	75	291	3	2640.00	1614.62
	Henrik NYSTROM	Swe	73	72	75	71	291	3	2640.00	1614.62
52	Peter FOWLER	Aus	76	71	74	71	292	4	2145.00	1311.88
	Marc PENDARIES	Fr	76	67	72	77	292	4	2145.00	1311.88
	Lorne KELLY	Scot	71	74	75	72	292	4	2145.00	1311.88
55	Mats LANNER	Swe	70	75	74	73	293	5	1738.00	1062.96
	Wayne RILEY	Aus	74	74	74	71	293	5	1738.00	1062.96
	Ian POULTER	Eng	74	74	77	68	293	5	1738.00	1062.96
	Stephen DODD	Wal	72	72	72	77	293	5	1738.00	1062.96
	Luis CLAVERIE	Sp	71	76	73	73	293	5	1738.00	1062.96
60	Steven RICHARDSON	Eng	73	73	77	71	294	6	1540.00	941.86
61	Carlos RODILES	Sp	73	71	75	76	295	7	1292.50	790.49
	Richard BLAND	Eng	70	78	76	71	295	7	1292.50	790.49
	Christian PENA	USA	73	72	72	78	295	7	1292.50	790.49
	Victor CASADO	Sp	73	74	73	75	295	7	1292.50	790.49
	Ian HUTCHINGS	SA	73	69	78	75	295	7	1292.50	790.49
	António SOBRINHO	Port	74	73	74	74	295	7	1292.50	790.49
	Mark PILKINGTON	Wal	71	76	75	73	295	7	1292.50	790.49
	Pedro LINHART	Sp	75	73	73	74	295	7	1292.50	790.49
69	Johan RYSTRÖM	Swe	77	70	75	74	296	8	980.00	599.37
	Leon STANFORD	Eng	73	75	73	75	296	8	980.00	599.37
	Nicolas MARIN	Fr	68	74	78	76	296	8	980.00	599.37
72	Garry HOUSTON	Wal	74	73	76	73	297	9	820.50	501.82
	Gianluca BARUFFALDI	It	72	75	76	74	297	9	820.50	501.82
74	Joao UMBELINO (AM)	Port	69	74	81	74	298	10		
	Peter HEDBLOM	Swe	70	77	78	73	298	10	814.50	498.15
	José DIAS	Port	72	76	74	76	298	10	814.50	498.15
76	Kevin CARISSIMI	USA	79	69	76	76	300	12	810.00	495.39
77	Fredrik WIDMARK	Swe	75	71	75	80	301	13	807.00	493.56

Nice Guys do Win

ITANHANGÁ, RIO DE JANEIRO, BRAZIL

*I*f all the world's a stage and, with due acknowledgment to William Shakespeare, golf had been Roger Chapman's proscenium arch for the last 20 years of his life, he'd most often been an anonymous spear-carrier or, sometimes, the Fourth Praetorian Guard, with the occasional appearance as some such as Banquo in the Best Supporting Actor role.

If all the men and women are merely players, then Chapman had been merely a player in more golf tournaments than he would care to count.

If they have their exits and entrances, our hero had had more premature exits than he would care to admit to.

If one man in his time plays many parts, for Chapman it had been, more often than not, a minor and (very) peripheral part.

The whole of Chapman's professional life had been there, in microcosm, in the pages of As You Like It. But in the heat of Rio de Janeiro one Sunday afternoon in late March, he stepped out of character for a few precious, glorious hours and was Romeo and Othello and Macbeth all rolled into one.

Chapman's victory in the Brazil Rio de Janeiro 500 Years Open was witness to Shakespeare's wisdom in a sporting context. Here, truly, was life imitating art. In Hamlet the Great Bard tells a man "to thine own self be true" and, even when his future appeared at its

Padraig Harrington

Roger Chapman

blackest, Chapman was just that. Even when he lost his player's card on the European Tour at the end of 1999 and was sorely tempted to walk away from the game, he couldn't do it.

It was the tragic death of Payne Stewart that moved him to try again. "I looked at myself and thought 'he wanted to play but can't any more; I can and don't want to'." he said. "It took poor Payne's death to make me realise that there were people worse off than me and that I was spoilt."

The consequence was that he took himself off to the Qualifying School, the European Tour's version of thumb racks and Chinese water torture, and won his card back in twelfth place. "Golf is my life," he had said then. "It's all I've ever wanted to do. I will not leave this Tour until I win."

Well, now he had done it, and just about the entire constituency of his peers in Europe rejoiced with him that evening, not excluding Padraig Harrington, whom he had defeated on the second hole of a sudden-death play-off.

"I couldn't have lost to a nicer guy," the characteristically gracious Harrington said. "He's been out there a long time, and he deserves it." See? Even at the moment when Harrington had been deprived of his second European victory, he was happy — genuinely happy — for the man who had beaten him. That's what knowing the personable Chapman does to people.

Shakespeare delivered a further homily in Hamlet that "we know what we are but know not what we may be," and Chapman, with his six second-place finishes in a long career that had been studded with, if not victory, then grace in defeat, had maybe never quite known what he may be.

He must have known that he was a good player who was blessed with a swing to die for, but he also knew that hundreds of competitive appearances - the tournament in Brazil was his 472nd - had yielded him nothing beyond the knowledge that he was making a good life for Cathy, his wife of 15 years, and Christopher and Thomas, his sons.

At the age of 40, he must have thought his day had gone. Sure, he had made some money and, certainly. he had seen the world in the pursuit of his profession. But he still hadn't won and, because he loved golf, his life's work would not be complete if he faded from the scene without handling that trophy, hearing that applause, making that acceptance speech, being suffused in the warm glow that only victory can bring.

He knew that ambition should be made of sterner stuff (let's cut to Julius Caesar for a moment), and he still had ambition. Events would prove, there in the warm, early-evening Brazilian sun, that he was made of sterner stuff, too. If he were mortally struck by lightning the next day or got run over by the inattentive driver of a runaway bus, he could shuffle off this mortal coil a happy man.

Sport is, by its very nature, a trivial thing, but its innate triviality renders it all the more important. Ask any supporter of Manchester United, the most famous football club in the world — it is said that they have infinitely more fans who will never see them play than those who will. To them, their club is life itself. They weep, literally, when their team is beaten, they exult when it wins. The result of one of its matches can make or mar their weekend. It is that important, that meaningless.

Being an intelligent sort of fellow, Chapman would have known all that if he had stopped to think about it. But, for just this one wonderful moment, sport as defined by golf was the most crucial thing in his life, not in the least bit trivial. And, my oh my, did it feel good.

The manner in which he won was not particularly glorious, as it happened. A par four at the second extra hole to Harrington's bogey five was enough. It didn't matter — he had played one fewer stroke than his Irish opponent, and that was all that counted right now.

He had, to invoke the immortal Will again, suited the action to the word, and the word to the action. And it felt absolutely marvellous. He had started the final day five strokes behind Harrington, the overnight leader, and thrust his way into the play-off with a coruscating seven under par 65 to leave him alongside the Dubliner on an 18 under par total of 270.

Chapman's day of days was an eloquent statement in favour of a philosophy that is a core value of the European Tour — opportunity and incentive.

Thomas Levet

Shot of the Week

Without doubt, Roger Chapman's ten foot par putt on the 72nd hole. Chapman had raced his first effort from 35 feet past the hole and knew he must hole out to secure a chance of a play-off. He held his nerve supremely well...and the rest is history.

Sure, the fat cats were away from Europe as they pursued their pursuit of another Masters victory with a warm-up tournament at Arnie Palmer's course at Bay Hill. And certainly, it was the very devil of a long way to go to fulfil a life's ambition.

But, when it happened, Chapman could not have cared less. All he knew was that years and years of unavailing effort had finally been vindicated in sunny Rio. He had undoubtedly had the incentive and had been granted the opportunity. And taken both, and then some.

He had travelled, sometimes footsore, weary and ready to give in, many thousands of miles down this road and finally he had reached his goal. Now all the self-doubt had been smashed into a million fragments, scattered onto the four winds by the South American breeze.

So let us finish, as we began, with a quotation: The reward of a thing well done is to have done it. Shakespeare again?

No — Ralph Waldo Emerson, actually. Which goes to show that back there in the 20th Century — remember it? — the greatest philosophical minds were talking about Roger Chapman, even if they didn't know it. He had done a thing well, and his reward was that he had done it. And nobody could ask more of a man than that.

Mel Webb

Robert Karlsson

The Course

An old-fashioned, tree-lined, traditional course opened in 1933. Shorter than the average on the European Tour but a delight to play, with a premium on the ability to move the ball both ways on the winding fairways.

ITANHANGÁ, RIO DE JANEIRO, BRAZIL, 23-26 MARCH 2000, PAR 72, 6618 YARDS, 6052 METRES

Pos.	Name		Rd1	Rd2	Rd3	Rd4	Total	Par	Euro	£
1	Roger CHAPMAN	Eng	70	64	71	65	270	-18	111707.97	68952.56
2	Padraig HARRINGTON	Ire	67	62	71	70	270	-18	74427.28	45940.78
3	José COCERES	Arg	66	70	69	66	271	-17	41974.31	25908.95
4	Joakim HAEGGMAN	Swe	69	67	69	68	273	-15	30977.85	19121.30
	Jorge BERENDT	Arg	67	67	69	70	273	-15	30977.85	19121.30
6	Santiago LUNA	Sp	70	70	65	70	275	-13	17755.27	10959.57
	Robin BYRD	USA	70	71	66	68	275	-13	17755.27	10959.57
	Mathias GRÖNBERG	Swe	66	75	67	67	275	-13	17755.27	10959.57
	Nicolas VANHOOTEGEM	Bel	71	71	70	63	275	-13	17755.27	10959.57
	Alastair FORSYTH	Scot	65	62	75	73	275	-13	17755.27	10959.57
11	Paolo QUIRICI	Swi	65	69	69	73	276	-12	11935.19	7367.08
	Ignacio GARRIDO	Sp	70	65	69	72	276	-12	11935.19	7367.08
13	Paul EALES	Eng	71	69	67	70	277	-11	10091.27	6228.91
	Greg OWEN	Eng	69	68	67	73	277	-11	10091.27	6228.91
	David PARK	Wal	71	67	68	71	277	-11	10091.27	6228.91
	Raymond RUSSELL	Scot	68	66	70	73	277	-11	10091.27	6228.91
17	Johan RYSTRÖM	Swe	71	68	72	67	278	-10	8515.55	5256.29
	Pedro Rodolfo MARTINEZ	Par	73	68	67	70	278	-10	8515.55	5256.29
	Peter LONARD	Aus	62	74	71	71	278	-10	8515.55	5256.29
	Robert COLES	Eng	69	72	70	67	278	-10	8515.55	5256.29
21	Peter FOWLER	Aus	73	65	70	71	279	-9	7484.64	4619.95
	Angel CABRERA	Arg	68	71	70	70	279	-9	7484.64	4619.95
	Desmond TERBLANCHE	SA	72	67	69	71	279	-9	7484.64	4619.95
	Francisco CEA	Sp	67	69	73	70	279	-9	7484.64	4619.95
25	Malcolm MACKENZIE	Eng	68	75	69	68	280	-8	6571.05	4056.03
	Roger WINCHESTER	Eng	70	70	69	71	280	-8	6571.05	4056.03
	Olivier EDMOND	Fr	71	70	67	72	280	-8	6571.05	4056.03
	Grant HAMERTON	Eng	69	69	74	68	280	-8	6571.05	4056.03
	Jarmo SANDELIN	Swe	72	68	69	71	280	-8	6571.05	4056.03
30	Eduardo ROMERO	Arg	68	70	72	71	281	-7	5475.88	3380.03
	Marc FARRY	Fr	67	73	67	74	281	-7	5475.88	3380.03
	Robert KARLSSON	Swe	67	69	67	78	281	-7	5475.88	3380.03
	David LYNN	Eng	69	72	69	71	281	-7	5475.88	3380.03
	Angel FRANCO	Par	74	67	66	74	281	-7	5475.88	3380.03
	Walter Alberto MIRANDA	Arg	70	70	70	71	281	-7	5475.88	3380.03
36	Miguel Angel MARTIN	Sp	71	70	70	71	282	-6	4693.61	2897.16
	José Manuel CARRILES	Sp	67	72	72	71	282	-6	4693.61	2897.16
	Christian PENA	USA	73	68	71	70	282	-6	4693.61	2897.16
	Henrik NYSTROM	Swe	72	69	70	71	282	-6	4693.61	2897.16
40	Philip WALTON	Ire	69	72	76	66	283	-5	4157.20	2566.06
	Massimo FLORIOLI	It	71	70	74	68	283	-5	4157.20	2566.06
	Stuart CAGE	Eng	71	67	71	74	283	-5	4157.20	2566.06
	Fredrik JACOBSON	Swe	73	67	72	71	283	-5	4157.20	2566.06
44	Steve WEBSTER	Eng	76	67	69	72	284	-4	3352.58	2069.40
	Hennie OTTO	SA	67	70	75	72	284	-4	3352.58	2069.40
	Alberto BINAGHI	It	69	72	74	69	284	-4	3352.58	2069.40
	Per NYMAN	Swe	70	71	74	69	284	-4	3352.58	2069.40
	Diego BORREGO	Sp	69	70	70	75	284	-4	3352.58	2069.40
	Tomas Jesus MUÑOZ	Sp	73	70	71	70	284	-4	3352.58	2069.40
	Gerry NORQUIST	USA	70	68	74	72	284	-4	3352.58	2069.40
	Daniel Alfredo VANCSIK	Arg	68	72	70	74	284	-4	3352.58	2069.40
52	Tom GILLIS	USA	69	73	74	69	285	-3	2749.11	1696.91
53	Kevin CARISSIMI	USA	68	74	74	70	286	-2	2241.44	1383.55
	Philip GOLDING	Eng	65	73	75	73	286	-2	2241.44	1383.55
	Paul AFFLECK	Wal	71	71	72	72	286	-2	2241.44	1383.55
	Iain PYMAN	Eng	70	67	73	76	286	-2	2241.44	1383.55
	Ola ELIASSON	Swe	69	69	72	76	286	-2	2241.44	1383.55
	Max ANGLERT	Swe	76	66	69	75	286	-2	2241.44	1383.55
	Ivo GINER	Sp	67	70	74	75	286	-2	2241.44	1383.55
60	Costantino ROCCA	It	70	73	74	70	287	-1	1676.29	1034.70
	Silvio GRAPPASONNI	It	72	69	73	73	287	-1	1676.29	1034.70
	Steven RICHARDSON	Eng	69	74	70	74	287	-1	1676.29	1034.70
	Andrew RAITT	Eng	72	71	74	70	287	-1	1676.29	1034.70
	Andrew BUTTERFIELD	Eng	72	70	72	73	287	-1	1676.29	1034.70
	Johan SKOLD	Swe	71	72	74	70	287	-1	1676.29	1034.70
	John MELLOR	Eng	72	68	74	73	287	-1	1676.29	1034.70
67	José RIVERO	Sp	69	74	76	69	288	0	1332.65	822.59
	Jean-Francois REMESY	Fr	70	73	74	71	288	0	1332.65	822.59
	Raphaël JACQUELIN	Fr	68	75	76	69	288	0	1332.65	822.59
	Simon D. HURLEY	Eng	71	72	73	72	288	0	1332.65	822.59
71	Gustavo ROJAS	Arg	71	72	74	73	290	2	1006.00	620.96
72	Andrew SHERBORNE	Eng	69	73	76	73	291	3	1000.00	617.26
	Rafael NAVARRO	Bra		72	76	73	291	3	1000.00	617.26
	Didier DE VOOGHT	Bel	70	72	77	72	291	3	1000.00	617.26
75	Derrick COOPER	Eng	72	69	76	79	296	8	994.00	613.55

The Good and The Bad

SAO PAULO GOLF CLUB, SAO PAULO, BRAZIL

When Roger Chapman secured that long-overdue and largely unexpected victory in Rio de Janeiro, much play was made of the Englishman's record of six second place finishes over an 18-year span before he finally achieved that breakthrough.

It went almost completely unnoticed, however, that Padraig Harrington - the man who lost a two-hole play-off for the Brazil Rio de Janeiro 500 Years Open - made Chapman's sequence of seconds pale by comparison.

While Chapman accumulated his seconds over nearly two decades on the European Tour, Harrington had gathered no fewer than nine in under four seasons, and seven within the previous eleven months.

Five of those second places came during 1999, when he performed heroics to qualify for the Ryder Cup without managing to enter the winner's enclosure. In 2000 he had already finished runner-up in the Benson and Hedges Malaysian Open in February 2000 then in the sudden-death play-off against Chapman.

Admittedly Harrington, unlike Chapman, had already savoured the winning feeling in 1996 when he captured the Peugeot Open de España on only the tenth start of his professional career, but coming second can be habit forming and, worse, can often lead to the mind playing strange tricks on sportsmen well versed in the theory that golf is a game played between the ears.

A champagne moment for Padraig Harrington

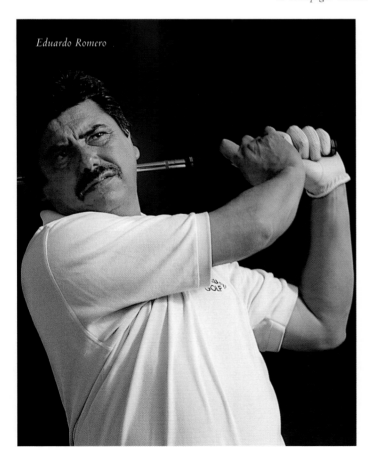

Eduardo Romero

Harrington, though, is true to the spirit and etiquette of golf. He bore another colossal disappointment stoically, just as he had done on eight previous occasions, paid a glowing tribute to Chapman - "I couldn't have lost to a more deserving guy" - packed his suitcase and caught the short flight to the vast, teeming urban sprawl of Sao Paulo.

If there were any residual mental scars, they certainly were not visible by the time the 1999 Ryder Cup rookie teed up at the Sao Paulo Golf Club, a venue which radiated an old-English feel of Berkshire or Surrey.

This time there were no mistakes; no mental or physical errors; no acceptance of second best. Harrington was a man driven by more than simply a basic need to win another tournament. He had endured the agonies of being runner-up, and no-one was going to ruin an otherwise pleasant Sunday afternoon.

With four supremely controlled rounds in the sixties, the urbane Dubliner ended the streak of seconds with a 14 under par total of 270 and a two stroke victory over American Gerry Norquist. This time around, Sunday was a picnic in the park as no-one ever looked like getting close to Harrington.

"This is great because I've had a lot of second places," he conceded. "But I felt very relaxed even after losing in a play-off to Roger. I didn't let things get on top of me. I believe that what will be will be and everything went smoothly."

He had only flown to Brazil at the last minute, receiving invitations after missing the cut at Bay Hill in Florida. With only eleven competitive rounds behind him in 2000 following a prolonged winter break, Harrington decided enough of rest, it was time to play golf.

He added: "I came to Brazil to get competitive again and I achieved that. I travelled a lot in 1999. It was a very long year and I didn't perform towards the end of it. I didn't want to play. It's only since arriving here that I felt I wanted to play again.

"You know, this is a very strange game. I won my first title in only my tenth event in 1996. I led the field from the gun and nothing went wrong. Since then I've had to learn a lot about winning and losing...and I've lost a lot. I have had good and bad days but the main thing is that you're always learning."

Harrington, who had nudged his way into contention subtly and without fuss, fired a final round 68 to prove that he deserved to be on top of the podium again. In a fortnight in Brazil, Harrington won

a total of 202,975 euro (£124,506) from his second and first place finishes.

Norquist, winner of the Benson and Hedges Malaysian Open in 1999, closed with birdie putts from six, 35 and six feet for a 68 and 12 under par total of 272, leaving five players sharing third place a further two strokes behind.

Paul Affleck of Wales had taken the first round lead with a five under par 66 over the superb, traditional lay-out at Sao Paulo Golf Club. Harrington, who opened with a 69, followed it with a 68 to lie five behind halfway leader, rookie Matt Blackey from Hampshire.

After three rounds, Harrington was sharing the top spot on 11 under par after a controlled 65 which left him level with Welshman David Park, who birdied the final two holes on Saturday for a 68 and total of 202.

However on the last day, Harrington seldom looked like putting a foot wrong. A birdie at the first and back-to-back birdies at the 11th and 12th sealed the fate of his rivals.

Gordon Simpson

The Course

A wonderfully traditional tree-lined parkland course which earned rave reviews from the players, who might have been mistaken for thinking they were playing golf in Britain. Not long, but tricky and with enough rough to penalise an errant tee shot.

Greg Owen

Shot of the Week

Fabrice Tarnaud had the honour of becoming the first European Tour Member of the new millennium to record that rarest of birds, an albatross. The Frenchman holed his five wood second shot from 233 yards on the 17th hole of the first round.

SAO PAULO GOLF CLUB, SAO PAULO, BRAZIL, 30 MARCH - 2 APRIL 2000, PAR 71, 6646 YARDS, 6077 METRES

Pos.	Name		Rd1	Rd2	Rd3	Rd4	Total	Par	Prize Money Euro	£
1	Padraig HARRINGTON	Ire	69	68	65	68	270	-14	128548.08	78566.94
2	Gerry NORQUIST	USA	69	71	64	68	272	-12	85561.60	52294.15
3	Eduardo ROMERO	Arg	68	69	69	68	274	-10	33936.69	20741.67
	Steve WEBSTER	Eng	71	66	68	69	274	-10	33936.69	20741.67
	Ian POULTER	Eng	69	67	69	69	274	-10	33936.69	20741.67
	Pedro Rodolfo MARTINEZ	Par	69	68	68	69	274	-10	33936.69	20741.67
	Greg OWEN	Eng	68	70	71	65	274	-10	33936.69	20741.67
8	Miguel Angel MARTIN	Sp	69	68	66	72	275	-9	17328.28	10590.82
	Jean-Francois REMSEY	Fr	69	67	68	71	275	-9	17328.28	10590.82
	Anders HANSEN	Den	71	66	69	69	275	-8	17328.28	10590.82
11	Richard S JOHNSON	Swe	67	72	68	69	276	-8	13728.94	8390.95
	Mathias GRÖNBERG	Swe	73	68	65	70	276	-8	13728.94	8390.95
13	Andrew McLARDY	SA	70	70	68	69	277	-7	11607.89	7094.59
	Robert KARLSSON	Swe	70	69	68	70	277	-7	11607.89	7094.59
	Jorge BERENDT	Arg	71	66	69	71	277	-7	11607.89	7094.59
	Matthew BLACKEY	Eng	70	63	71	73	277	-7	11607.89	7094.59
17	José RIVERO	Sp	71	66	71	70	278	-6	9633.91	5888.12
	Andrew SHERBORNE	Eng	69	68	69	72	278	-6	9633.91	5888.12
	Paul AFFLECK	Wal	66	72	72	68	278	-6	9633.91	5888.12
	Gustavo ROJAS	Arg	70	73	65	70	278	-6	9633.91	5888.12
	David PARK	Wal	67	67	68	76	278	-6	9633.91	5888.12
22	Brian DAVIS	Eng	73	67	70	69	279	-5	8137.10	4973.29
	Knud STORGAARD	Den	70	70	66	73	279	-5	8137.10	4973.29
	Thomas LEVET	Fr	69	71	72	67	279	-5	8137.10	4973.29
	Robin BYRD	USA	72	69	68	70	279	-5	8137.10	4973.29
	Max ANGLERT	Swe	70	72	68	69	279	-5	8137.10	4973.29
	Adilson JOSE da SILVA	Bra	70	73	66	70	279	-5	8137.10	4973.29
28	Scott ROWE	USA	68	73	67	72	280	-4	6748.77	4124.76
	Carl SUNESON	Sp	69	72	68	71	280	-4	6748.77	4124.76
	Per NYMAN	Swe	67	68	72	73	280	-4	6748.77	4124.76
	Didier DE VOOGHT	Bel	73	68	68	71	280	-4	6748.77	4124.76
	Angel CABRERA	Arg	75	68	69	68	280	-4	6748.77	4124.76
	Peter LONARD	Aus	72	65	72	71	280	-4	6748.77	4124.76
34	Peter FOWLER	Aus	69	73	71	68	281	-3	5630.40	3441.23
	Paolo QUIRICI	Swi	71	71	69	70	281	-3	5630.40	3441.23
	Andrew BEAL	Eng	72	70	70	69	281	-3	5630.40	3441.23
	José COCERES	Arg	69	73	67	72	281	-3	5630.40	3441.23
	Jean Marie KULA	Fr	71	66	68	76	281	-3	5630.40	3441.23
39	Roger CHAPMAN	Eng	73	70	71	68	282	-2	4550.60	2781.27
	Mark MOULAND	Wal	71	72	71	68	282	-2	4550.60	2781.27

Pos.	Name		Rd1	Rd2	Rd3	Rd4	Total	Par	Prize Money Euro	£
	Christian PENA	USA	70	68	73	71	282	-2	4550.60	2781.27
	Thomas GÖGELE	Ger	70	72	71	69	282	-2	4550.60	2781.27
	Ian GARBUTT	Eng	72	69	71	70	282	-2	4550.60	2781.27
	David LYNN	Eng	72	70	71	69	282	-2	4550.60	2781.27
	Ola ELIASSON	Swe	72	70	69	71	282	-2	4550.60	2781.27
	Daniel CHOPRA	Swe	72	70	72	68	282	-2	4550.60	2781.27
	Benoit TEILLERIA	Fr	70	72	67	73	282	-2	4550.60	2781.27
48	Simon D. HURLEY	Eng	74	69	70	70	283	-1	3015.04	1842.75
	Roger WINCHESTER	Eng	74	68	70	71	283	-1	3015.04	1842.75
	Massimo FLORIOLI	It	75	68	68	72	283	-1	3015.04	1842.75
	Fernado ROCA	Sp	69	73	69	72	283	-1	3015.04	1842.75
	Diego BORREGO	Sp	70	71	69	73	283	-1	3015.04	1842.75
	Nicolas VANHOOTEGEM	Bel	71	65	74	73	283	-1	3015.04	1842.75
	Desmond TERBLANCHE	SA	68	70	73	72	283	-1	3015.04	1842.75
	Fredrik JACOBSON	Swe	70	69	70	74	283	-1	3015.04	1842.75
	Johan SKOLD	Swe	68	72	75	68	283	-1	3015.04	1842.75
	Carlos LARRAIN	Ven	70	73	69	71	283	-1	3015.04	1842.75
	Acacio Jorge PEDRO	Bra	72	71	68	72	283	-1	3015.04	1842.75
59	Tom GILLIS	USA	72	68	72	72	284	0	1928.21	1178.50
	Joakim HAEGGMAN	Swe	70	71	71	72	284	0	1928.21	1178.50
	Jonathan LOMAS	Eng	68	74	70	72	284	0	1928.21	1178.50
	Ricardo GONZALEZ	Arg	73	70	69	72	284	0	1928.21	1178.50
	Tomas Jesus MUÑOZ	Sp	67	68	75	74	284	0	1928.21	1178.50
	Pascal EDMOND	Fr	72	71	70	71	284	0	1928.21	1178.50
	Andrew BUTTERFIELD	Eng	72	69	70	73	284	0	1928.21	1178.50
	Simon WAKEFIELD	Eng	70	72	70	72	284	0	1928.21	1178.50
	Angel FRANCO	Par	72	71	66	75	284	0	1928.21	1178.50
68	Philip ARCHER	Eng	70	72	74	69	285	1	1522.01	930.23
69	Jarmo SANDELIN	Swe	74	70	72	69	285	1	1522.01	930.23
70	Alberto BINAGHI	It	68	74	73	71	286	2	1311.22	801.40
	Scott WATSON	Eng	71	72	73	70	286	2	1311.22	801.40
72	Rodolfo GONZALEZ	Arg	70	69	74	74	287	3	1152.50	704.39
	Ruberiel FELIZARDO	Bra	67	73	71	76	287	3	1152.50	704.39
74	Justin HOBDAY	SA	75	68	72	73	288	4	1148.00	701.64
75	Soren KJELDSEN	Den	72	68	70	79	289	5	1142.00	697.98
	Ignacio GARRIDO	Sp	70	69	72	78	289	5	1142.00	697.98
	Raymond RUSSELL	Scot	71	71	76	71	289	5	1142.00	697.98
78	Luiz MARTINS	Bra	69	72	79	73	293	9	1136.00	694.31
79	Daniel Alfredo VANCSIK	Arg	73	68	76	80	297	13	1133.00	692.48
80	Paul NILBRINK	Swe	73	70	77	78	298	14	1130.00	690.64

A BRIGHTER IDEA FOR GOLF.

HIT IT HARD, BRILLIANT DISTANCE REACTION. HIT IT SOFT, BRILLIANT FEEL REACTION.

The Wilson Smart-Core™ is golf's first smart ball. It has the brains to react with distance *or* feel, on demand, to optimize every shot. Next to Smart-Core,™ every other ball is just mindless.

www.wilsonsmartcore.com

Crossing the Equator

AUGUSTA NATIONAL, GEORGIA, USA

The clubhouse at Augusta sits like a left-over set from Gone With The Wind. But, standing in its shadow, the view has a distinctly English flavour. Look out across the lawns to the towering Georgia pines that guard the fairways, and study the patrons. This could be Ascot or Henley; blazers are *de rigueur*.

In the last quarter of the 20th century Augusta also became a shrine to European golf. Seve Ballesteros, Bernhard Langer and José Maria Olazábal all won twice; Sandy Lyle and Ian Woosnam triumphed, and Nick Faldo, of course, secured three famous victories.

Bobby Jones, who started The Masters in 1934 as an invitation tournament, did not live to witness this extraordinary European take-over of the course he built. If he had then Jones, one of the finest golfers in the history of the game and a proponent of good sportsmanship, would have celebrated the international coming-of-age of his tournament.

After all, the plantation on which the course was built was first developed on land on which General James Edward Oglethorpe, an English soldier who joined the Guards, made peace with the Cherokees and obtained a charter for the colony of Georgia. Moreover Dr Alister Mackenzie, a Scottish-born physician who on immigrating to America abandoned medicine in favour of designing courses, masterminded the operation with Clifford Roberts, an investment broker, and Jones.

Their love affair with the game turned Augusta into the garden of golf as the Masters became as much a celebration as a sporting contest. This unique appeal has been rewarded by a roll call of champions extending beyond America, with Gary Player of South Africa first setting a trend for "overseas" winners. So, perhaps, it was fitting that the first major championship of the new millennium should be won by a player from a country which more than 100 years ago was a British colony where Indians were taken to work on the plantations.

It might be a fantasy – almost fictional – story from the wet lowlands of Fiji, not to mention the rainforest of Borneo, to the green, green grass of Augusta, but for Vijay Singh winning the coveted Masters Jacket was the culmination of an unforgettable journey that was a triumph for diligence and determination.

Singh's victory in the 1998 US PGA Championship has assured him of a special place in golf's record books. Yet it was at Augusta National, where traditionally among the azalea and the dogwood the Masters annually blooms, that he indelibly carved his place in sporting history while simultaneously sparking cause for great celebration in his homeland.

Fiji is a country made up of 332 islands and about 500 islets in the Pacific Ocean. Sugar is an important export, coconuts provide food, rice grows on the wet lowlands and there is an abundance of breadfruit, mango, soursop, tapioca and yams. There are also now ten golf courses in Fiji and at one of them, the Fiji Golf Club, the

Ernie Els

Members toasted one of their own in the early hours of Monday morning as many thousands of miles away Vijay Singh followed in the footsteps of Gene Sarazen and Byron Nelson, Sam Snead and Ben Hogan, Arnold Palmer and Jack Nicklaus, Tom Watson and Tiger Woods.

Singh was taught to play golf from the age of 13 on Viti Levu, Fiji's largest and most populous island, by his father, Mohan, a refueler at Nadi airport, and grooved his swing at Fiji Golf Club where he played with his two brothers, Krishna and Mira. The islanders, quite rightly, take pride in the global achievements of their sons, and Singh's success at Augusta National took their appreciation of him and the sport to a new level. That would have appealed to Jones since he always believed that golf could unite the world and that there was always a place for the underdog in sport.

Not that Singh had arrived in Augusta for the Masters as an underdog, but the journey that led to him being the Master Golfer was such that it is safe to assume that no player in the history of the game is likely to follow a similar trail.

For the route from Fiji, where as a child he dreamed like all others with a passion for the game of emulating the deeds of the then all-conquering Jack Nicklaus, took him in the early 1980s down a pockmarked track from Kota Kinabalu, on Borneo's north-east coast, across the Croker Range of mountains to the Klube Golf Keningau. Borneo is a large island in South East Asia. The equator crosses Borneo where the prevailing conditions are hot and wet.

He was paid £25 a week to give lessons to the locals and the 100 active members many of whom were Chinese contractors who gambled huge sums on individual matches. To supplement his income Singh sold balls retrieved from the water hazards and gambled beyond his means on the then nine-hole golf course by examining his game against all-comers. In one match against a timber baron he apparently played for $700, with only $10 in his pocket, and, level at the last, fired his drive out of bounds. He said: "The feeling when I stood over the next drive was the worst feeling I have ever had in the game. How would I pay if I lost? Would I lose my job? What would I tell my wife?" There have been many in similar circumstances, such as Lee Trevino as a youth, and Singh's ability to play under pressure was demonstrated during the next ten minutes as he made an eagle with the second ball to win the match.

Such strength of character impressed the members and two of them, Chris Kah Jin, the club captain, and Datuk Rahim Ismail, a local politician, helped to fund Singh's return to more conventional surroundings as he relaunched his career at the 1987 European Tour Qualifying School at La Manga in Spain. He had won the 1984 Malaysian PGA Championship, prior to his hiatus in Borneo, but he finished three shots the wrong side of the 72-hole cut at La Manga and once again found himself compelled to go in another direction. Even so victory in the Nigerian Open and the Swedish PGA

Championship provided the impetus for him to return to the School at the end of 1988 and this time only Jesper Parnevik finished ahead of him as he emerged triumphant along with the likes of Carlos Franco, Miguel Angel Jiménez and Jean Van de Velde.

Singh had led the Safari Tour money list in 1988, winning the small fortune of 35,200 euro (£22,000), and his return to Africa at the start of 1989 signalled the transformation of his career as he followed victory in the Zimbabwe Open with others in the Nigerian and Ivory Coast Opens. Yet the big breakthrough that year came with his first win on the European Tour when at the Is Molas club in Sardinia he captured the Volvo Open Championship and a first prize of 53,328 euro (£33,330) by following an opening 72 with three 68s.

At that time Singh, who used in his early days the swing of Tom Weiskopf on which to model his own, gave credit to Bob Torrance, Sam's father, for technical advice, and Singh had by now become a slave to the practice range as he determined that nothing would now stop him from becoming a respected world class player.

This Singh had achieved by the time he arrived at Augusta National as with 26 wins world-wide , including nine on the European Tour, the World Match Play Championship at Wentworth and the 1998 US PGA Championship, he had built an enviable record and, of course, a bank balance to match. Now he was chasing glory and this was only four days around the corner. Singh felt he was assisted because with rain falling before the tournament, and again on the Saturday, the greens were a tad slower than is the custom at Augusta. Singh said: "If you asked me two years ago I would have said I couldn't win at Augusta the way I was putting. Augusta's greens are so severe that if you're not a good putter, you're not going to win. It's as simple as that. I think an attitude change was a big boost."

On a sunny and warm opening day, Singh's 72 left him four shots behind the initial pacemaker, Dennis Paulson, of the United States, but, more significantly, three shots ahead of Tiger Woods. By dropping two shots at the tenth and three at the short 12th, Woods provided the bookmakers, who had installed him as the hottest favourite in Masters history, as well as his rivals with more than a little relief.

Tom Lehman had climbed onto the leader board with a 69, one ahead of Sergio Garcia and Steve Stricker, but, like Paulson, they faded from the scene as the conditions cooled on Friday. David Duval surged to the front by storming home in 30 for a 65 to set the halfway target with a six under par 138 - one ahead of Ernie Els, who followed a 72 with a 67, Phil Mickelson, who shot 68, and Singh, whose 67 was to be his lowest score of the week.

Shot of the Week

Crunch time at The Masters Tournament traditionally comes on the back nine on the last day. Vijay Singh had kept a one shot lead at the 12th by virtue of a superb bunker shot to three feet, but it was at the 13th that he applied the pressure. There he laced a superb three iron onto the green which left David Duval, one shot behind at the time, wondering whether to take a four or five for his shot from 196 yards. He selected the five iron, and the ball hopped into Rae's Creek. But the feeling remained that Singh had put the pressure on Duval by hitting the right shot at the right time.

The Course

Initially it was suggested that Augusta National, opened in January, 1933, should be a site for the US Open, but Bobby Jones and Clifford Roberts wanted their own tournament and The Masters was born.

Jack Nicklaus tees off at the 18th

Woods had failed to make an impact for the second successive day - he had five bogeys in a 72 - but Jack Nicklaus most certainly did as, despite missing more than a dozen putts of inside 20 feet in the first 36-holes, he shot 74-70 to be only six behind Duval. Nicklaus said: "I don't know whether I should be leading, but I've certainly played better than I've scored. I've still got a lot of guys in front of me, but I've still got a chance."

High winds with violent gusts in excess of 35mph, and a drop in temperature of some 40 degrees from the opening day, contributed to Nicklaus's third round 81, but as that fairytale evaporated so Singh's sped closed to fruition as with a round of 70 he moved to seven under par. This was three shots ahead of Duval, who took 74, and four in front of Loren Roberts (71) and Els (74). All this was achieved by Singh in spite of being compelled to complete his round on Sunday morning after a two hour delay because of the inclement weather.

A bogey at the third hole of the fourth round was not the start Singh was seeking, but on a glorious final afternoon with the sun shining he characteristically recovered with birdies at the sixth, eighth and ninth. Duval, however, had four birdies in an outward 32 to Singh's 34 to be one behind. At that stage Singh was on nine under with Duval at eight, Roberts at six, following an outward 33, and Woods and Els, out in 33 and 35 respectively, at four under. Duval missed

Lee Westwood in Rae's Creek at the 13th

the green at the tenth to drop a shot as Roberts bogeyed the 11th where Els holed from 18 feet for a birdie three. Singh hit his second shot into the water at the 11th and with Els and Roberts both making birdies at the 13th he was being strongly challenged. Indeed Singh had to get up and down from a bunker at the 12th to remain at eight under - one ahead of Duval, two in front of Els, three in front of Roberts and four ahead of Woods.

Singh, however, gave himself a commanding three shot lead ahead of Duval, Els and Roberts when he made a birdie with two good putts at the 13th where Duval found a watery grave with his second shot and took six.

Els also holed from 20 feet at the 15th although moments later both Duval and Singh made birdies at that hole. Singh's three putts at the 16th gave his rivals a glimmer of hope, but he was two shots ahead teeing off at the 18th where he holed from 20 feet for a birdie whereas Duval took five to leave Els in outright second place.

So the fairytale was complete and as wife, Ardina, and their son, Qass Seth, joyfully celebrated, Singh went to the Butler Cabin where José Maria Olazábal, the 1999 champion, helped him into that coveted green jacket.

Mitchell Platts

AUGUSTA NATIONAL, GEORGIA, USA, 6-9 APRIL 2000, PAR 72, 6985 YARDS, 6387 METRES

Pos.	Name		Rd1	Rd2	Rd3	Rd4	Total	Par	Prize Money Euro	£
1	Vijay SINGH	Fiji	72	67	70	69	278	-10	864844.49	520035.17
2	Ernie ELS	SA	72	67	74	68	281	-7	518906.69	312021.10
3	Loren ROBERTS	USA	73	69	71	69	282	-6	278672.12	167566.89
	David DUVAL	USA	73	65	74	70	282	-6	278672.12	167566.89
5	Tiger WOODS	USA	75	72	68	69	284	-4	192187.66	115563.37
6	Tom LEHMAN	USA	69	72	75	69	285	-3	172968.89	104007.03
7	Davis LOVE III	USA	75	72	68	71	286	-2	149746.22	90043.13
	Carlos Daniel FRANCO	Par	79	68	70	69	286	-2	149746.22	90043.13
	Phil MICKELSON	USA	71	68	76	71	286	-2	149746.22	90043.13
10	Hal SUTTON	USA	72	75	71	69	287	-1	129726.68	78005.28
11	Greg NORMAN	Aus	80	68	70	70	288	0	110507.91	66448.94
	Nick PRICE	Zim	74	69	73	72	288	0	110507.91	66448.94
	Fred COUPLES	USA	76	72	70	70	288	0	110507.91	66448.94
14	Chris PERRY	USA	73	75	72	69	289	1	84082.10	50558.97
	Jim FURYK	USA	73	74	71	71	289	1	84082.10	50558.97
	John HUSTON	USA	77	69	72	71	289	1	84082.10	50558.97
	Dennis PAULSON	USA	68	76	73	72	289	1	84082.10	50558.97
18	Jeff SLUMAN	USA	73	69	77	71	290	2	72070.37	43336.26
19	Padraig HARRINGTON	Ire	76	69	75	71	291	3	56214.89	33802.28
	Steve STRICKER	USA	70	73	75	73	291	3	56214.89	33802.28
	Jean VAN DE VELDE	Fr	76	70	75	70	291	3	56214.89	33802.28
	Colin MONTGOMERIE	Scot	76	69	77	69	291	3	56214.89	33802.28
	Bob ESTES	USA	72	71	77	71	291	3	56214.89	33802.28
	Glen DAY	USA	79	67	74	71	291	3	56214.89	33802.28
25	Larry MIZE	USA	78	67	73	74	292	4	39238.31	23594.19
	Craig PARRY	Aus	75	71	72	74	292	4	39238.31	23594.19
	Steve JONES	USA	71	70	76	75	292	4	39238.31	23594.19
28	Nick FALDO	Eng	72	72	74	75	293	5	29949.24	18008.62
	Bernhard LANGER	Ger	71	71	75	76	293	5	29949.24	18008.62

Pos.	Name		Rd1	Rd2	Rd3	Rd4	Total	Par	Prize Money Euro	£
	Justin LEONARD	USA	72	71	77	73	293	5	29949.24	18008.62
	Stewart CINK	USA	75	72	72	74	293	5	29949.24	18008.62
	Mike WEIR	Can	75	70	70	78	293	5	29949.24	18008.62
	Dudley HART	USA	75	71	72	75	293	5	29949.24	18008.62
	Paul AZINGER	USA	72	72	77	72	293	5	29949.24	18008.62
	Masashi OZAKI	Jpn	72	72	74	75	293	5	29949.24	18008.62
	Thomas BJÖRN	Den	71	77	73	72	293	5	29949.24	18008.62
37	Fred FUNK	USA	75	68	78	73	294	6	22582.05	13578.70
	Jay HAAS	USA	75	71	75	73	294	6	22582.05	13578.70
	Notah BEGAY III	USA	74	74	73	73	294	6	22582.05	13578.70
40	Ian WOOSNAM	Wal	74	70	76	75	295	7	18257.83	10978.52
	Sergio GARCIA	Sp	70	72	75	78	295	7	18257.83	10978.52
	Jesper PARNEVIK	Swe	77	71	70	77	295	7	18257.83	10978.52
	Darren CLARKE	N.Ire	72	71	78	74	295	7	18257.83	10978.52
	Mark BROOKS	USA	72	76	73	74	295	7	18257.83	10978.52
	Retief GOOSEN	SA	73	69	79	74	295	7	18257.83	10978.52
46	Shigeki MARUYAMA	Jpn	76	71	74	75	296	8	14414.07	8667.25
	Scott GUMP	USA	75	70	78	73	296	8	14414.07	8667.25
48	Brandt JOBE	USA	73	74	76	74	297	9	13164.85	7916.09
49	Miguel Angel JIMÉNEZ	Sp	76	71	79	72	298	10	12139.86	7299.76
	Steve PATE	USA	78	69	77	74	298	10	12139.86	7299.76
	David TOMS	USA	74	72	73	79	298	10	12139.86	7299.76
52	Steve ELKINGTON	Aus	74	74	78	73	299	11	11435.17	6876.02
	Rocco MEDIATE	USA	71	74	75	79	299	11	11435.17	6876.02
54	Jack NICKLAUS	USA	74	70	81	78	303	15	11146.89	6702.68
	David GOSSETT (AM)	USA	75	71	79	78	303	15		
56	Skip KENDALL	USA	76	72	77	83	308	20	11050.78	6644.89
57	Tommy AARON	USA	72	74	86	81	313	25	10954.69	6587.11

OFFICIAL SPONSOR

OFFICIAL SPONSOR

OFFICIAL GOLF CAR AND UTILITY VEHICLE

OFFICIAL SUPPLIER

We build relationships that drive the game.

OFFICIAL SUPPLIER

OFFICIAL GOLF CAR AND UTILITY VEHICLE

OFFICIAL SUPPLIER

play to win™

1-800-ClubCar • www.clubcar.com
(using AT&T Direct Dial Access #)

 P.O. Box 2 • Chorley New Road • Horwich Bolton BL6 6JN UK

The Spirit of Enterprise

*W*hen the 21st century dawned, the first Eurobet Seve Ballesteros Trophy wasn't even on the schedule, but by the time Seve was handed his own creation on the evening of Sunday 16th April, we all knew something most worthwhile had been added to European golf.

Ever since the Americans had invented the Presidents Cup for biennial competition in the years between the Ryder Cup, there was a feeling they had once again given themselves an edge in that great contest. Always anxious to trump any American ace, and mindful now that the Continent really could be competitive against Great Britain & Ireland, Seve put his name to a trophy to be played for between the old adversaries.

The chosen venue was the Old Course at Sunningdale, an inspired choice for a new event given the reputation and standing of

England's premier inland courses. The only pity was the weather was not to match. Torrential rain had soaked the course in the days leading up to the match and it is doubtful the thermometer ever rose more than a few points above freezing.

The first series of foursomes went the way of Great Britain & Ireland by three matches to one, seeming to give the lie to the apparent evenness of the teams on paper. To be fair, it should have been two all, but Thomas Björn and Robert Karlsson squandered a lead of two up with four to play, losing on the last green, when the Dane missed from inside two feet for a half.

Colin Montgomerie showed throughout what a good job he will make of the Ryder Cup captaincy when the time comes and won his first game playing top with Ian Woosnam. To select Woosnam and then choose to play with him, was a gesture that somehow captured the spirit of the entire week.

Certainly Montgomerie's pairings throughout showed logic. Lee Westwood and Darren Clarke, after swamping their foursomes opposition, were split up to take senior partner roles with two new boys, David Howell and John Bickerton; Montgomerie himself reuniting with Paul Lawrie in a reprise of their successful Ryder Cup partnership. Unfortunately logic doesn't always work against Seve. That afternoon the Continentals hit back, led by the unlikely figure of Björn. Forgiven for his morning lapse, he almost won his

José Maria Olazábal and Miguel Angel Jiménez

Darren Clarke

David Howell, Colin Montgomerie, Sergio Garcia and Jean Van de Velde on the 7th green

fourball with Miguel Angel Jiménez single-handed. Round in 65 with his own ball, they beat Clarke and Bickerton on the last green.

The stars of the afternoon though were Sergio Garcia and Jarmo Sandelin, who were heading for a better ball of 61 when they took care of Montgomerie and Lawrie by 3 and 2. In the end the morning score was reversed and the teams level going into day two.

Further heavy rain overnight meant only one series of matches could be completed on Saturday. Even in good conditions the scoring that dank, chilly afternoon would have been exceptional. Out of form and low on confidence, José Maria Olazábal had drawn a blank on Friday, but his skipper kept faith and sent him out top in the company of Jiménez against Montgomerie and Woosnam.

If one shot can revitalise a player, then Olazábal's one iron to three feet at the second was that shot. It launched the Spaniards on an outward nine of 28, a five hole lead and an eventual victory by 6 and 5. Elsewhere honours were even, and it was only fair that no side should gain any advantage in such vile conditions.

The loss of a round on Saturday, meant two on Sunday, with greensomes in the morning being followed by ten singles in the afternoon. It was hereabouts Montgomerie discovered the

Sergio Garcia

Captains shake hands

impossibility of being both captain and player. Having just completed a fine recovery in his match with Howell, turning two down after ten into a 2 and 1 victory over Garcia and Jean Van de Velde, and in the process enabling GB&I to share yet another series of matches, he then had to dash into the press tent to sort out the afternoon pairings with his opposite number.

That done, and with scarcely time to grab a sandwich, he was back on the first tee in a clash of the Captains. Seve may be but a shadow of the man who won all those major championships in the 1980s, but he instinctively knew circumstances had given him a great chance against Europe's best player. It was an opportunity he didn't squander.

Keeping the ball in play any way he could, he fashioned three birdies in the first four holes to go two up. A haywire drive at the fifth and a Montgomerie birdie at seven meant all square by the turn, but crucial mistakes at ten and 11 put GB&I's captain two down once more, and that was that. A win for Seve 2 and 1. Most impressively, a four at the last would have had him round in 67.

Obviously with the overall match so close, that win was both a bonus

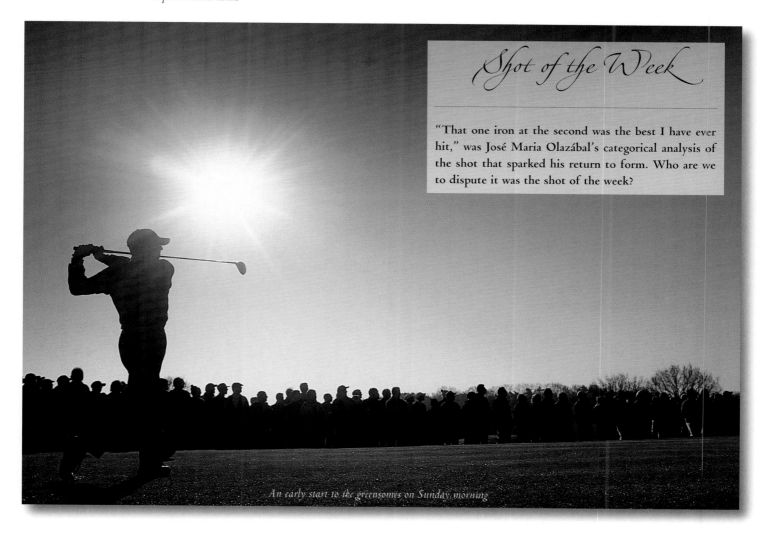

Shot of the Week

"That one iron at the second was the best I have ever hit," was José Maria Olazábal's categorical analysis of the shot that sparked his return to form. Who are we to dispute it was the shot of the week?

An early start to the greensomes on Sunday morning

The Course

The Old Course at Sunningdale has scarcely changed since Willie Park Jnr laid it out through rolling heather and gorse just on 100 years ago. Certainly it has been lengthened, but bunkers, dykes and ditches are much as they have always been and only pine and silver birch have grown up around what would have seemed an inland links when first created. Small greens are synonymous with a course of such age, and sharp, intricate slopes do much to protect the course's reputation against technology's relentless advance.

to his side and a tremendous lift. Immediately behind Sergio Garcia had been down all the way to Darren Clarke, but finished with three birdies in the last five holes, including threes at both the 17th and 18th to snatch a half. Those two results, both delivering more than they promised, were to be the vital difference that afternoon.

The balance thereafter always seemed to be with Continental Europe and in due course they ran out the winners by a single point. Of special note was Bernhard Langer's victory over Ian Woosnam. Out in 29, he was two up and further birdies at 11th and 14th were too much for the gallant Welshman, who was himself heading for a 65 when beaten 4 and 3. Best of all though, the winning point was delivered by José Maria Olazábal, with whom Seve has shared so many historic moments in the Ryder Cup.

It was a fitting climax to a memorable week. Had there been any doubts as to the worth of such a contest, they were dispelled by the closeness of the competition, the spirit in which it was played and the desire of all to do the very best for their team. Unquestionably too, the Old Course at Sunningdale played its part in what has to be the first of many outings for The Eurobet Seve Ballesteros Trophy.

Bruce Critchley

SUNNINGDALE GOLF CLUB, BERKSHIRE, ENGLAND
14-16 APRIL 2000, PAR 70, 6601 YARDS, 6035 METRES

GB & IRELAND		CONTINENTAL EUROPE	
Captain: Colin Montgomerie		**Captain: Seve Ballesteros**	
Friday April 14			
Foursomes: Morning			
C Montgomerie & I Woosnam (2&1)	1	J M Olazábal & J A Jiménez	0
D Clarke & L Westwood (4&3)	1	A Cejka & B Langer	0
P Harrington & P Price (1 hole)	1	T Björn & R Karlsson	0
P Lawrie & G Orr	0	S Garcia & J Van de Velde (3&2)	1
	3		1
Fourballs: Afternoon			
L Westwood & D Howell (2&1)	1	J M Olazábal & S Ballesteos	0
D Clarke & J Bickerton	0	T Björn & M A Jiménez (1 hole)	1
I Woosnam & P Harrington	0	A Cejka & B Langer (2&1)	1
P Lawrie & C Montgomerie	0	J Sandelin & S Garcia (3&2)	1
	4		4
Saturday April 15			
Fourballs: Afternoon			
I Woosnam & C Montgomerie	0	M A Jiménez & J M Olazábal (6&5)	1
P Lawrie & G Orr (1 hole)	1	J Sandelin & R Karlsson	0
J Bickerton & P Price	0	T Björn & S Garcia (1 hole)	1
D Clarke & L Westwood (3&1)	1	A Cejka & J Van de Velde	0
	6		6
Sunday April 16			
Greensomes: Morning			
P Lawrie & G Orr (halved)	½	M A Jiménez & J M Olazábal (halved)	½
C Montgomerie & D Howell (2&1)	1	S Garcia & J Van de Velde	0
D Clarke & L Westwood	0	B Langer & T Björn (4&3)	1
P Harrington & P Price (halved)	½	A Cejka & R Karlsson (halved)	½
	8		8
Singles			
C Montgomerie	0	S Ballesteros (2&1)	1
D Clarke (halved)	½	S Garcia (halved)	½
J Bickerton	0	J Sandelin (2&1)	1
L Westwood (1 hole)	1	T Björn	0
P Price (2&1)	1	A Cejka	0
I Woosnam	0	B Langer (4&3)	1
D Howell	0	R Karlsson (2&1)	1
G Orr	0	J M Olazábal (2&1)	1
P Lawrie (5&4)	1	J Van de Velde	0
P Harrington (1 hole)	1	M A Jiménez	0
Total	**12½**	**Total**	**13½**

London Print and Design PLC

*Creative Design,
Electronic Artwork, Printing,
Binding & Distribution*

In conjunction with our designers
TC Communications, London Print and
Design produce and publish high quality
programmes, posters and drawsheets, in
addition to publications such as
The European Tour Yearbook.

London Print & Design Plc
020 7242 6051
printmanagement@londonprint.com

TC Communications Plc
01344 622280
timl@tc-comms.co.uk

Top Gunner

GOLF D'AMELKIS, MARRAKECH, MOROCCO

Jamie Spence has always derived enjoyment from an evening spent wining and dining in far-flung corners of the globe in the entertaining company of good friends Sam Torrance, Mark James and Gordon Brand Jnr. It is one of life's little pleasures after a hard working day on the European Tour.

As he sat at the dinner table, though, Spence occasionally reflected on why his friends had accumulated almost 50 European Tour titles between them, while his grand total amounted to the derisory digit of one.

It was not that he lacked the ability or the courage to be a winner - as evidenced by his maiden victory in 1992 when he overturned a ten-shot deficit in the final round of the Canon European Masters,

shooting a round of 60 before beating Anders Forsbrand in a play-off.

It is a well known fact (or should that be an old wives tale?) that the second win is always easier than the first, so why could he not finish off the job? What were Sam, Mark and Gordon doing that he wasn't?

"I suppose it irritated me a bit and I once mentioned it to Jesse (Mark James) that they seemed to possess that indefinable something which made them winners," revealed Spence. "He said that there was no big secret to it; just that I should always try to play my own game and not be put off by any setbacks and to make the most of my chances."

Thomas Levet

In essence, be true to yourself and what will be will be.

Those sage words from a wise old owl filtered their way into Spence's psyche during the final round of the Moroccan Open Méditel at the picturesque Golf D'Amelkis Club in Marrakech. After several close attempts which rattled the crossbar, and the golfing equivalent of an own goal when he was disqualified when leading a tournament in 1993, this passionate Arsenal FC supporter finally located the back of the net.

At 36, and in the midst of his 12th unbroken season on Tour, the man from Tunbridge Wells in Kent was a winner once more. Breaking bread with his close friends would be an even sweeter experience in future!

It was a relieved and emotional Spence who hugged his caddie, Janet Squire, after getting up and down at the 72nd hole for the birdie four which clinched that long-awaited second Tour title with a 22 under par total of 266. He had shot four sub-70 rounds and reserved the best for last, becoming the fifth player that week to shoot the course record of 64.

He admitted: "It's been a long wait, that's for sure. It feels like I've won the British Open, to be honest. I've had my chances in the past but maybe backed off. My policy was to attack and go for birdies and I kept doing that right to the final hole. I had chances in the past

Jamie Spence

but maybe I played a bit conservatively when I needed to play positively. I think I've learned that from the better players."

Spence added: "I feel I should probably have won the Moroccan Open in 1992 but didn't and have hardly been back since. But I heard the course and the weather were good and I had hardly played at home for five weeks so decided to come out here. Maybe it owed me one!"

It was a popular win for a player who had been inspired by the epic Tom Watson-Jack Nicklaus duel in the Open Championship as an impressionable 14-year-old. Two years later he left school to work for a bank in the City of London but quit to focus on playing full-time amateur golf. Jamie worked as a part-time barman and labourer to indulge his passion for the game.

In 1993 he was disqualified from the Roma Masters after holding the 54 hole lead. He signed for an incorrect score after incurring a two-shot penalty for playing from the wrong place. By the time the error was spotted, Spence was back in his hotel, and disqualification was inevitable.

"That was painful" he acknowledged. "It was a Ryder Cup year and winning would have put me in good shape to qualify. Sadly, it set me back and I suffered from shingles during the season and that was that. Hopefully there is still time for me yet."

Ian Poulter

Shot of the Week

Although he had a hole in one on the first day, Spence nominated his 55 yards lob wedge to the 16th in the last round. He flipped the ball over a mound and spun it back to three feet for the par four which he felt closed out his rivals. A difficult shot under pressure, brilliantly executed.

The Course

American-designed parkland course affording superb views of the Atlas Mountains. Water hazards figure prominently and ensured an interesting finish with the par five 15th and 18th both rewarding those who got up in two. The huge greens putted beautifully and led to low scoring and favourable comments.

Ignacio Garrido

Spence began the final day three behind 54-hole leader Ignacio Garrido of Spain and quickly turned that deficit into a single shot advantage thanks to a pair of birdies to open his round and another pair to close the front nine. Three more birdies in a row from the 13th opened up a gap between Spence and the field and he drilled a four iron through the 18th and chipped back to four feet for his eighth birdie of the day and a wonderfully controlled 64.

As he gathered momentum, his nearest rivals went into reverse. Garrido, who had looked solid after rounds of 68, 64 and 67, threw in two birdies and four bogeys over the first 12 holes to let his chance evaporate. He ended with a 74 and a share of sixth place. It was a similar story for Pedro Martinez of Paraguay, whose opening scores of 64 and 66 earned him pole position through 18 and 36 holes. He began the day alongside Spence on 202, 14 under par, but was unable to make any progress and he joined Adam Scott, then an amateur, on 273 after a round of 72. Three players, England's Ian Poulter and Frenchmen Seb Delagrange and Thomas Levet finished tied for second on 270, 18 under par, four behind the winner.

Gordon Simpson

GOLF D'AMELKIS, MARRAKECH, MOROCCO, 20-23 APRIL 2000, PAR 72, 7281 YARDS, 6657 METRES

Pos.	Name		Rd1	Rd2	Rd3	Rd4	Total	Par	Prize Money Euro	£
1	Jamie SPENCE	Eng	66	68	68	64	266	-22	110509.11	66640.00
2	Ian POULTER	Eng	69	64	68	69	270	-18	49439.45	29813.33
	Thomas LEVET	Fr	66	74	64	66	270	-18	49439.45	29813.33
	Sebastien DELAGRANGE	Fr	66	69	65	70	270	-18	49439.45	29813.33
5	Desmond TERBLANCHE	SA	68	68	65	70	271	-17	28124.77	16960.00
6	Pedro Rodolfo MARTINEZ	Par	64	66	71	72	273	-15	23216.20	14000.00
	Adam SCOTT (AM)	Aus	66	66	69	72	273	-15		
8	Malcolm MACKENZIE	Eng	68	67	68	71	274	-14	16151.84	9740.00
	Elliot BOULT	NZ	67	70	69	68	274	-14	16151.84	9740.00
	Ignacio GARRIDO	Sp	68	64	67	75	274	-14	16151.84	9740.00
	Bradley DREDGE	Wal	67	68	68	71	274	-14	16151.84	9740.00
12	Mårten OLANDER	Swe	68	69	70	68	275	-13	11807.10	7120.00
	Shaun WEBSTER	Eng	69	65	70	71	275	-13	11807.10	7120.00
14	Santiago LUNA	Sp	68	67	69	72	276	-12	9203.57	5550.00
	Mark DAVIS	Eng	69	70	71	66	276	-12	9203.57	5550.00
	Ulrik GUSTAFSSON	Swe	69	66	73	68	276	-12	9203.57	5550.00
	Robin BYRD	USA	71	68	69	68	276	-12	9203.57	5550.00
	Scott ROWE	USA	68	68	70	70	276	-12	9203.57	5550.00
	Roger WINCHESTER	Eng	69	71	65	71	276	-12	9203.57	5550.00
	Patrik SJÖLAND	Swe	71	65	70	70	276	-12	9203.57	5550.00
	Mikael LUNDBERG	Swe	66	72	69	69	276	-12	9203.57	5550.00
22	Roger CHAPMAN	Eng	69	67	71	70	277	-11	6902.21	4162.22
	Jose Manuel LARA	Sp	69	67	68	73	277	-11	6902.21	4162.22
	Silvio GRAPPASONNI	It	70	70	67	70	277	-11	6902.21	4162.22
	Soren KJELDSEN	Den	68	66	70	73	277	-11	6902.21	4162.22
	Tom GILLIS	USA	71	68	66	72	277	-11	6902.21	4162.22
	Joakim HAEGGMAN	Swe	70	68	69	70	277	-11	6902.21	4162.22
	Stephen DODD	Wal	70	66	72	69	277	-11	6902.21	4162.22
	Ola ELIASSON	Swe	71	66	70	70	277	-11	6902.21	4162.22
	Nic HENNING	SA	70	67	68	72	277	-11	6902.21	4162.22
31	Klas ERIKSSON	Swe	68	72	70	68	278	-10	5181.27	3124.45
	Mattias ELIASSON	Swe	68	68	69	73	278	-10	5181.27	3124.45
	Paul SHERMAN	Eng	70	66	71	71	278	-10	5181.27	3124.45
	Peter MITCHELL	Eng	68	69	72	69	278	-10	5181.27	3124.45
	Andrew RAITT	Eng	71	69	69	69	278	-10	5181.27	3124.45
	Fredrik JACOBSON	Swe	65	71	70	72	278	-10	5181.27	3124.45
	Fredrik ANDERSSON	Swe	70	68	70	70	278	-10	5181.27	3124.45
	David HIGGINS	Ire	68	70	69	71	278	-10	5181.27	3124.45
	Peter GUSTAFSSON	Swe	70	68	67	73	278	-10	5181.27	3124.45
40	Ross DRUMMOND	Scot	66	68	73	72	279	-9	3913.59	2360.00
	Des SMYTH	Ire	68	70	71	70	279	-9	3913.59	2360.00
	Robert Jan DERKSEN	Hol	69	67	72	71	279	-9	3913.59	2360.00
	Fredrik HENGE	Swe	73	67	73	66	279	-9	3913.59	2360.00
	Thomas GÖGELE	Ger	70	69	71	69	279	-9	3913.59	2360.00
	Andrew BUTTERFIELD	Eng	72	67	69	71	279	-9	3913.59	2360.00
	Mark PILKINGTON	Wal	67	66	73	73	279	-9	3913.59	2360.00
	Jean Marie KULA	Fr	73	67	67	72	279	-9	3913.59	2360.00
	Christopher HANELL	Swe	68	72	69	70	279	-9	3913.59	2360.00
49	Raphaël JACQUELIN	Fr	67	72	70	71	280	-8	2984.94	1800.00
	Robert COLES	Eng	71	66	71	72	280	-8	2984.94	1800.00
	Andrew COLTART	Scot	67	70	71	72	280	-8	2984.94	1800.00
	John BICKERTON	Eng	70	67	67	76	280	-8	2984.94	1800.00
	Benoit TEILLERIA	Fr	70	70	70	70	280	-8	2984.94	1800.00
54	Wayne RILEY	Aus	73	67	70	71	281	-7	2520.62	1520.00
	Van PHILLIPS	Eng	66	69	75	71	281	-7	2520.62	1520.00
56	Kevin CARISSIMI	USA	69	71	70	72	282	-6	2096.09	1264.00
	Knud STORGAARD	Den	70	69	68	75	282	-6	2096.09	1264.00
	Scott WATSON	Eng	70	70	68	74	282	-6	2096.09	1264.00
	Simon HURD	Eng	71	69	70	72	282	-6	2096.09	1264.00
	Rodolfo GONZALEZ	Arg	68	72	71	71	282	-6	2096.09	1264.00
61	Frédéric CUPILLARD	Fr	70	70	69	74	283	-5	1824.13	1100.00
	Daniel CHOPRA	Swe	72	68	75	68	283	-5	1824.13	1100.00
63	Paul WAY	Eng	69	71	71	73	284	-4	1591.97	960.00
	Simon D. HURLEY	Eng	73	66	72	73	284	-4	1591.97	960.00
	Massimo FLORIOLI	It	70	67	71	76	284	-4	1591.97	960.00
	Fernando ROCA	Sp	69	68	72	75	284	-4	1591.97	960.00
	Christophe POTTIER	Fr	70	68	71	75	284	-4	1591.97	960.00
68	Fredrik LINDGREN	Swe	69	70	73	73	285	-3	1318.35	795.00
	Tomas Jesus MUÑOZ	Sp	70	69	73	73	285	-3	1318.35	795.00
	Brian NELSON	USA	66	72	70	77	285	-3	1318.35	795.00
	Iain PYMAN	Eng	68	69	76	72	285	-3	1318.35	795.00
72	Gary MURPHY	Ire	69	71	73	73	286	-2	993.50	599.11
	Steven RICHARDSON	Eng	70	70	72	74	286	-2	993.50	599.11
74	Alberto BINAGHI	It	70	70	74	73	287	-1	987.50	595.49
	Neil CHEETHAM	Eng	70	67	75	75	287	-1	987.50	595.49
76	Tony CAROLAN	Aus	69	69	74	77	289	1	983.00	592.78
77	Bjorn PETTERSSON	Swe	68	72	74	76	290	2	980.00	590.97
78	Ivo GINER	Sp	67	72	74	80	293	5	977.00	589.16

Independent Spirit

PGA GOLF DE CATALUNYA, GIRONA, SPAIN

eware the sick golfer. Oh no, not that old one again, comes the anguished cry. And to be sure, it does cause a flush of embarrassment to rise, unbidden and unwelcome, from the base of the neck and climb rapidly to the top of the head just by the mere act of setting the old maxim down on paper again. It's just that, this time, no other form of words will fit the case quite as perfectly.

The subject under discussion is the Peugeot Open de España and more particularly the golfers who figured in the upper reaches of it. A total of 156 players descended upon the PGA Golf de Catalunya course in April and, curious though it might appear, it seemed that the only ones who prospered throughout the four days of the tournament were the crocks. At times the leaderboard looked like a cast-list from "Casualty".

The first man on the treatment table was Dean Robertson, who not long before had been sick and tired of being sick and tired. Then there was Gary Evans, who over the years had suffered more than most by the slings and arrows – and especially the slings – of outrageous fortune.

All through the piece Colin Montgomerie, who, although fit and well physically, was afflicted by a nasty case of *putticushorribilis* and just felt generally queasy about the whole situation.

And finally, we had Brian Davis, who could offer a whole compendium of maladies which, apparently, had its root in a particularly unpleasant bout of chickenpox in South Africa a couple of years before and eventually led to his being confined to an intensive care unit in Dubai, body all aching and racked with pain. Great line for a song, that . . . but no, it would never sell.

Well, if the medical misfortune that had befallen Davis in the Veldt had been the precursor to the performance he produced in the heartland of the independent spirit of Catalunya, it could very rapidly become the paediatric disease of choice. You can see the slogan right off . . . "Catch chickenpox; it's so healthy". The brothers Saatchi, gurus of advertising spin, would love it.

The records will show for posterity that Davis won the venerable Spanish Open, one of the oldest championships on the European

Brian Davis

The Course

PGA Golf de Catalunya is the newest of the European Tour's own courses and is possibly the pick of the entire portfolio. Designed by Neil Coles and Angel Gallardo, it winds its sinuous way through groves of pine and cork trees and presents a constant challenge – the players loved it. Peter Baker's course-record 64 on the closing day was a remarkable round, for it does not yield birdies without a stern battle.

Tour International Schedule – it dates from 1912 – with a total of 274, 14 under par. What the bald statistics will not display is the manner of his victory, achieved as it was against a backdrop of ill-health and a putting touch the observation of which had sometimes been painfully close to intrusion on private grief.

In his darkest days Davis, 25 at the time of his victory, had even come to believe that his tournament career might be over, and it was only with the help of two coaches, one American and one English, that his rehabilitation was achieved.

Davis is a great lover of all things American, to the extent that one of his career ambitions is to have playing privileges on both sides of the Atlantic. He had almost managed it the previous autumn when he won the first stage of the US Tour Qualifying School by eight strokes but missed out by a couple at the second stage.

He had worked hard during the winter with Tony Ziegler, his coach in Orlando, and when back in England took the advice of Tony Bryan, the head professional at the East Herts club that sponsors him, on an ailing putting stroke. The combined talents of Messrs Ziegler and Bryan worked a treat as their client had the tournament of his life.

Robertson did not quite scale the lofty heights that Davis managed, but to the slim Scot it was enough just to be out there playing. He had succumbed to a mystery stomach virus while playing for Scotland in the World Cup of Golf in Kuala Lumpur the previous November that left him feeling nauseous and exhausted for weeks on end.

He had virtually no sleep for the first three months of the year and, like Davis, at one time could see no way back. But at last he had made it, and celebrated with a 65 that equalled the course record on the first day. To him the greater pleasure was in being able to play a full round and feel fine afterwards. Davis was neither in the piece nor out of it with a 71.

The lead after the second round was held by Juan Quiros, making a rare tournament appearance, but the round of the day was played by Gary Evans, once one of the great white hopes of European golf who was once terribly afflicted by a wrist injury that made him uncompetitive for years rather than weeks or months. After a 67 he slid down the leaderboard with a third-round 77 but fought back pluckily with his second 67 of the tournament on the final day to finish in a tie for seventh.

All this time Montgomerie was going through all sorts of travails. He had a 67 in the first round, but then his putting problems hit him and he was not able to recover the touch in his last three rounds.

In full flow: Peter Baker

It was a shot only one man in the field could have played. Severiano Ballesteros sprayed his opening drive of the tournament way out to the right and seemed to have no shot. For others a double-bogey six would have beckoned at the very least; so Seve eagled it. With a seven iron from 155 yards he hit a huge curling fade that missed everything on its way, bounced twice on the green and obediently rolled into the hole for a two. A stroke of genius; he missed the cut, but he made a unique contribution to the tournament with this one shot alone.

Phillips

Sergio García

After being five under par for his first 18 holes, he was only four under for the next 54. Montgomerie, it is fair to say, was not happy; it is a measure of the man that he could finish tied for fifth and still feel dissatisfied.

Leaders came and went as the tournament established its own rhythm, but through it all Davis was plotting a safe course. He had a 68 in round two then took a one-stroke lead into the final day with a glittering 66 in the third round.

His main challenger on a tense closing afternoon was Eduardo Romero, who pushed Davis every inch of the way. Although the gentle giant from Argentina faltered at the 72nd hole with a bogey that dropped him into share of third place alongside Peter Baker, who set a course record with his 64, his was the most concerted challenge to Davis.

Davis knew it, too; knew that if he scored better that Romero, he would probably win the tournament. And he did, too, 69 to 71, to win by three strokes from Markus Brier, the Austrian in his rookie season.

Davis said that the first thing he would do with the largest pay-cheque of his career was to try to persuade his parents, Linda and Bob, to take early retirement from their florist's business. The way he blossomed in Catalunya, he deserved a bouquet of his own.

Mel Webb

PGA GOLF DE CATALUNYA, GIRONA, SPAIN, 28 APRIL - 1 MAY 2000, PAR 72, 7205 YARDS, 6588 METRES

Pos.	Name		Rd1	Rd2	Rd3	Rd4	Total	Par	Prize Money Euro	£
1	Brian DAVIS	Eng	71	68	66	69	274	-14	166600.00	98988.72
2	Markus BRIER	Aut	69	70	67	71	277	-11	111000.00	65952.87
3	Eduardo ROMERO	Arg	70	72	65	71	278	-10	56300.00	33451.77
	Peter BAKER	Eng	70	73	71	64	278	-10	56300.00	33451.77
5	Colin MONTGOMERIE	Scot	67	71	70	71	279	-9	42400.00	25192.81
6	Gary ORR	Scot	68	73	68	71	280	-8	35000.00	20795.95
7	Carlos RODILES	Sp	72	69	67	73	281	-7	25800.00	15329.59
	Gary EVANS	Eng	70	67	77	67	281	-7	25800.00	15329.59
	Niclas FASTH	Swe	70	73	70	68	281	-7	25800.00	15329.59
10	Paolo QUIRICI	Swi	66	78	71	67	282	-6	19200.00	11408.06
	Van PHILLIPS	Eng	73	70	70	69	282	-6	19200.00	11408.06
12	Miguel Angel MARTIN	Sp	73	74	68	68	283	-5	15480.00	9197.75
	Gary MURPHY	Ire	72	72	70	69	283	-5	15480.00	9197.75
	Sergio GARCIA	Sp	70	74	66	73	283	-5	15480.00	9197.75
	Iain PYMAN	Eng	71	69	72	71	283	-5	15480.00	9197.75
	Dean ROBERTSON	Scot	65	76	73	69	283	-5	15480.00	9197.75
17	Juan QUIROS	Sp	66	70	77	71	284	-4	12700.00	7545.96
	Phillip PRICE	Wal	70	73	69	72	284	-4	12700.00	7545.96
	Greg OWEN	Eng	70	72	73	69	284	-4	12700.00	7545.96
	Andrew COLTART	Scot	70	69	73	72	284	-4	12700.00	7545.96
21	Sven STRÜVER	Ger	68	74	69	74	285	-3	10858.33	6451.69
	Anders HANSEN	Den	71	73	70	71	285	-3	10858.33	6451.69
	Scott ROWE	USA	70	71	70	74	285	-3	10858.33	6451.69
	Thomas GÖGELE	Ger	72	70	67	76	285	-3	10858.33	6451.69
	Massimo FLORIOLI	It	73	74	69	69	285	-3	10858.33	6451.69
	Angel CABRERA	Arg	73	72	70	70	285	-3	10858.33	6451.69
27	Roger CHAPMAN	Eng	74	71	70	71	286	-2	9050.00	5377.24
	Steen TINNING	Den	71	72	74	69	286	-2	9050.00	5377.24
	Olivier EDMOND	Fr	72	73	72	69	286	-2	9050.00	5377.24
	Carl SUNESON	Sp	71	70	70	75	286	-2	9050.00	5377.24
	Emanuele CANONICA	It	73	67	77	69	286	-2	9050.00	5377.24
	Didier DE VOOGHT	Bel	72	70	72	72	286	-2	9050.00	5377.24
33	Tony JOHNSTONE	Zim	73	70	74	70	287	-1	7010.00	4165.13
	Ian WOOSNAM	Wal	73	69	75	70	287	-1	7010.00	4165.13
	José Maria OLAZABAL	Sp	69	76	71	71	287	-1	7010.00	4165.13
	John SENDEN	Aus	71	69	71	76	287	-1	7010.00	4165.13
	Nick O'HERN	Aus	66	77	74	70	287	-1	7010.00	4165.13
	José COCERES	Arg	73	70	73	71	287	-1	7010.00	4165.13
	Stephen SCAHILL	NZ	69	69	73	76	287	-1	7010.00	4165.13
	Francisco CEA	Sp	69	76	70	72	287	-1	7010.00	4165.13
	John BICKERTON	Eng	70	76	70	71	287	-1	7010.00	4165.13
	David CARTER	Eng	72	72	72	71	287	-1	7010.00	4165.13
43	Malcolm MACKENZIE	Eng	72	73	70	73	288	0	5500.00	3267.94
	Soren HANSEN	Den	70	74	67	77	288	0	5500.00	3267.94
	Diego BORREGO	Sp	74	72	71	71	288	0	5500.00	3267.94
	Thomas BJÖRN	Den	66	76	73	71	288	0	5500.00	3267.94
	Ola ELIASSON	Swe	71	76	68	73	288	0	5500.00	3267.94
48	David HOWELL	Eng	70	75	73	71	289	1	4600.00	2733.18
	Richard S JOHNSON	Swe	71	76	67	75	289	1	4600.00	2733.18
	Jarrod MOSELEY	Aus	74	71	71	73	289	1	4600.00	2733.18
	Per-Ulrik JOHANSSON	Swe	69	78	72	70	289	1	4600.00	2733.18
52	Elliot BOULT	NZ	71	75	68	76	290	2	4000.00	2376.68
	Patrik SJÖLAND	Swe	72	75	73	70	290	2	4000.00	2376.68
54	Steve WEBSTER	Eng	74	71	75	71	291	3	3250.00	1931.05
	Juan Carlos AGUERO	Sp	72	72	73	74	291	3	3250.00	1931.05
	Hennie OTTO	SA	72	73	78	70	291	3	3250.00	1931.05
	Thomas LEVET	Fr	72	68	76	75	291	3	3250.00	1931.05
	Domingo HOSPITAL	Sp	72	73	74	72	291	3	3250.00	1931.05
	Jonathan LOMAS	Eng	71	71	73	77	291	3	3250.00	1931.05
60	Gordon BRAND JNR.	Scot	71	76	71	74	292	4	2550.00	1515.13
	Richard GREEN	Aus	73	72	71	76	292	4	2550.00	1515.13
	Ian HUTCHINGS	SA	72	74	73	73	292	4	2550.00	1515.13
	Tomas Jesus MUÑOZ	Sp	72	72	74	74	292	4	2550.00	1515.13
	Robert COLES	Eng	71	76	71	74	292	4	2550.00	1515.13
	David LYNN	Eng	73	70	74	75	292	4	2550.00	1515.13
	Richard FINCH (AM)	Eng	73	74	73	72	292	4		
67	Paul AFFLECK	Wal	73	77	70	73	293	5	2030.00	1206.17
	Fernando ROCA	Sp	72	73	72	76	293	5	2030.00	1206.17
	Jarmo SANDELIN	Swe	68	77	73	75	293	5	2030.00	1206.17
	Stephen GALLACHER	Scot	73	74	76	72	293	5	2030.00	1206.17
	Alastair FORSYTH	Scot	78	69	71	75	293	5	2030.00	1206.17
72	Mats LANNER	Swe	74	72	75	73	294	6	1495.50	888.58
	Santiago LUNA	Sp	75	68	78	73	294	6	1495.50	888.58
	Barry LANE	Eng	70	74	72	78	294	6	1495.50	888.58
	Jesus Maria ARRUTI	Sp	73	71	76	74	294	6	1495.50	888.58
76	David GILFORD	Eng	73	72	76	74	295	7	1488.00	884.12
	Eduardo DE LA RIVA (AM)	Sp	71	73	76	76	296	8		
78	Benoit TEILLERIA	Fr	72	73	74	78	297	9	1485.00	882.34

MARQUÉS DE RISCAL
150 Years of Modern Wine Making

All You Need is Love

LE GOLF NATIONAL, PARIS, FRANCE

'Tres bien ensemble'. Colin Montgomerie back on song - with lyrics by Lennon and McCartney.

The reigning European number one took his first title of the season with a little help from his friends.

And on the way to climbing up to fourth on the Volvo Order of Merit and launching his 2000 season in earnest by winning the Novotel Perrier Open de France at Le Golf National, Montgomerie proved, all you need is love.

A new putter, several hours practice, and then on Friday, the arrival of wife Eimear, provided Montgomerie with the stimulus and the relaxation to overcome a determined Jonathan Lomas in an exhilarating eagle-eagle finale.

In the end the 200,000 euro (£116,500) first prize became a battle between two men, one a player bent on adding to his only title four years beforehand, the other a player bent on capturing his 23rd trophy on the European Tour. On paper there could be only one result. But Montgomerie had proved that paper results counted for nothing three weeks before in The Eurobet Seve Ballesteros Trophy.

When he struck the imperious three-wood approach to just nine inches on the 14th for his first eagle, to move three strokes ahead of the dogged Lomas, however, it looked no-contest. All Montgomerie's troubles seemed so far away.

An overhit approach at the first island finishing hole, the 15th, though, which took his ball into the lake, and a stunning birdie putt of 20 feet by Lomas on the 17th, reduced the advantage to only a stroke. Would it still prove to be a hard day's night for Montgomerie?

Lomas increased the tension by finding the island in two. But now the confidence born of a week when everything had at last come together, settled Montgomerie. His rapier six-iron might just as well

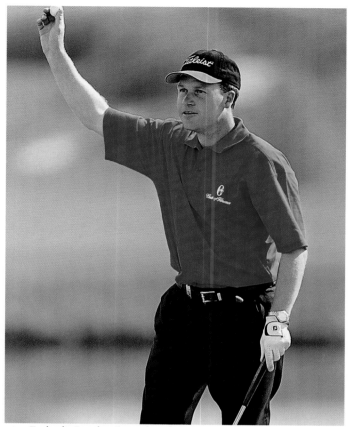

England's Jonathan Lomas kept the pressure on right to the 72nd hole

The Course

A return to Le Golf National after a brief sojourn to Bordeaux and there were no significant changes to the par-72, 7,098 yards course. Opened in 1990, American-style holes alternate with those typically found at the coast in a panorama of large, critical dunes. The smallest error can prove costly.

Shot of the Week

Three shots by Colin Montgomerie would have qualified, his five-wood - only the second time he had used it - to just four feet on the 17th after a lightning stoppage on Saturday, earned him his final round lead. On the last day his three-wood to nine inches was supreme, but you had to plump for his six-iron at the 72nd to two feet, which finally ended Jonathan Lomas's challenge.

have struck his 32-year-old opponent to the heart than to within two feet of the flag on the 18th green. Eagle. Hello? Goodbye!

When the week began, however, victory seemed far away for Montgomerie as he duelled with a wayward putting stroke and an unusually lax swing which inhibited his scoring to a 71 in the first round. That left the Scot five strokes in arrears of the front-runner, Italy's Alberto Binaghi, who led the field by one. 'Not good enough by a long chalk,' said the fastidious Montgomerie. It was the old Achilles Heel, the putting, which was holding him back, seeping lack of confidence into his all-round game, frustrating him to boiling point.

At that juncture Montgomerie decided on one palliative and had another provided him by friends Peter Mitchell and Peter Baker. Baker was practising with a 'White Hot' putter on Thursday afternoon. Montgomerie liked the look of it and dashed off to the Callaway caravan to secure one before the workshop closed for the day. Mitchell then looked at his stroke: 'Do you want to know a secret Monty?' To prove he had imparted good advice, Mitchell took the Scot on in a nine-hole competition on the practice green. Montgomerie won, something he had not done for a long while. Help had arrived at last.

If the putting revival was a boost then the arrival of his wife, who had booked a ticket to ride on Eurostar when she heard hubby was

Miguel Angel Martin

feeling down, turned the previously tetchy Montgomerie into a cuddly teddy bear. A candlelit dinner and a putter he felt he could trust turned Montgomerie into a new man.

After a 68 in a second round affected first by fog and then by a thunderstorm, he hovered dangerously, four behind the joint leaders Anders Hansen, Fernando Roca and Jarmo Sandelin. He was just three adrift of the second placed men, Lomas and New Zealander Michael Campbell. Campbell was looking for his third European Tour title of the season, a formidable opponent for the European number one.

On Saturday Montgomerie's putter really did live up to its name. His 65 to earn a one-shot lead took him second on the putting statistics, a point which was to provide an extra fillip the next day.

When this time the putts would not drop early in the final round, his confidence would not be shaken, as it had been six days before in Girona. Rivals slipped away with the exception of Lomas.

Montgomerie's finish was truly champion. He was back in the USSR - the Usual Sweet Swing Routine.

Norman Dabell

Rodger Davis

LE GOLF NATIONAL, PARIS, FRANCE, 4-7 MAY 2000, PAR 72, 7098 YARDS, 6498 METRES

Pos.	Name		Rd1	Rd2	Rd3	Rd4	Total	Par	Prize Money Euro	£
1	Colin MONTGOMERIE	Scot	71	68	65	68	272	-16	199920.00	116778.43
2	Jonathan LOMAS	Eng	72	64	69	69	274	-14	133200.00	77805.56
3	Rodger DAVIS	Aus	69	68	70	70	277	-11	75120.00	43879.53
4	John SENDEN	Aus	73	67	70	68	278	-10	50960.00	29767.05
	Roger WESSELS	SA	69	70	72	67	278	-10	50960.00	29767.05
	Fredrik JACOBSON	Swe	71	70	69	68	278	-10	50960.00	29767.05
7	David GILFORD	Eng	73	69	68	69	279	-9	24660.00	14404.54
	Carlos RODILES	Sp	70	70	68	71	279	-9	24660.00	14404.54
	Jean VAN DE VELDE	Fr	68	74	68	69	279	-9	24660.00	14404.54
	Soren HANSEN	Den	68	74	68	69	279	-9	24660.00	14404.54
	Peter O'MALLEY	Aus	68	75	68	68	279	-9	24660.00	14404.54
	Robert COLES	Eng	71	68	71	66	279	-9	24660.00	14404.54
	Andrew COLTART	Scot	69	68	70	72	279	-9	24660.00	14404.54
	Michael CAMPBELL	NZ	70	66	69	74	279	-9	24660.00	14404.54
15	Santiago LUNA	Sp	72	70	67	71	280	-8	16224.00	9476.86
	Anders HANSEN	Den	70	65	74	71	280	-8	16224.00	9476.86
	Nick O'HERN	Aus	69	70	71	70	280	-8	16224.00	9476.86
	Nicolas VANHOOTEGEM	Bel	70	74	70	66	280	-8	16224.00	9476.86
	José COCERES	Arg	70	71	71	68	280	-8	16224.00	9476.86
20	Miguel Angel MARTIN	Sp	69	70	71	71	281	-7	14190.00	8288.75
	Robin BYRD	USA	69	71	71	70	281	-7	14190.00	8288.75
22	Des SMYTH	Ire	70	73	72	67	282	-6	12120.00	7079.60
	Stephen LEANEY	Aus	71	72	68	71	282	-6	12120.00	7079.60
	Scott ROWE	USA	70	72	68	72	282	-6	12120.00	7079.60
	Alex CEJKA	Ger	70	70	69	73	282	-6	12120.00	7079.60
	Fernando ROCA	Sp	67	68	72	75	282	-6	12120.00	7079.60
	Ricardo GONZALEZ	Arg	74	70	69	69	282	-6	12120.00	7079.60
	Van PHILLIPS	Eng	76	69	69	68	282	-6	12120.00	7079.60
	Nicolas JOAKIMIDES	Fr	73	69	71	69	282	-6	12120.00	7079.60
	David PARK	Wal	71	69	69	73	282	-6	12120.00	7079.60
31	Soren KJELDSEN	Den	70	69	72	72	283	-5	9624.00	5621.63
	Richard GREEN	Aus	73	71	67	72	283	-5	9624.00	5621.63
	Alberto BINAGHI	It	66	73	71	73	283	-5	9624.00	5621.63
	Joakim HAEGGMAN	Swe	69	68	73	73	283	-5	9624.00	5621.63
	Robert KARLSSON	Swe	71	72	68	72	283	-5	9624.00	5621.63
36	Gary MURPHY	Ire	76	69	68	71	284	-4	8280.00	4836.56
	Jamie SPENCE	Eng	73	69	73	69	284	-4	8280.00	4836.56
	Steen TINNING	Den	69	70	74	71	284	-4	8280.00	4836.56
	Ignacio GARRIDO	Sp	72	73	72	67	284	-4	8280.00	4836.56
	Retief GOOSEN	SA	73	70	73	68	284	-4	8280.00	4836.56
41	Eduardo ROMERO	Arg	73	67	73	72	285	-3	7320.00	4275.80
	Anthony WALL	Eng	71	72	73	69	285	-3	7320.00	4275.80
	Greg OWEN	Eng	70	72	70	73	285	-3	7320.00	4275.80
44	Olivier EDMOND	Fr	70	74	70	72	286	-2	6600.00	3855.23
	Grant HAMERTON	Eng	71	72	73	70	286	-2	6600.00	3855.23
	Alastair FORSYTH	Scot	73	71	72	70	286	-2	6600.00	3855.23
47	José RIVERO	Sp	70	75	75	67	287	-1	5880.00	3434.66
	Jean-Francois REMESY	Fr	70	70	74	73	287	-1	5880.00	3434.66
	Mathias GRÖNBERG	Swe	71	72	75	69	287	-1	5880.00	3434.66
50	Sven STRÜVER	Ger	73	67	71	77	288	0	4800.00	2803.80
	Thomas LEVET	Fr	75	70	71	72	288	0	4800.00	2803.80
	Roger WINCHESTER	Eng	69	71	75	73	288	0	4800.00	2803.80
	Gustavo ROJAS	Arg	70	73	71	74	288	0	4800.00	2803.80
	Bradley DREDGE	Wal	71	71	73	73	288	0	4800.00	2803.80
	Stephen GALLACHER	Scot	72	70	71	75	288	0	4800.00	2803.80
56	Seve BALLESTEROS	Sp	72	71	72	74	289	1	3760.00	2196.31
	Peter LONARD	Aus	70	70	76	73	289	1	3760.00	2196.31
	Benoit TEILLERIA	Fr	72	72	72	73	289	1	3760.00	2196.31
59	Malcolm MACKENZIE	Eng	73	68	72	77	290	2	3120.00	1822.47
	Brian DAVIS	Eng	71	73	71	75	290	2	3120.00	1822.47
	Raphaël JACQUELIN	Fr	75	69	75	71	290	2	3120.00	1822.47
	Peter BAKER	Eng	74	69	76	71	290	2	3120.00	1822.47
	Fabrice TARNAUD	Fr	74	71	74	71	290	2	3120.00	1822.47
	David LYNN	Eng	73	72	72	73	290	2	3120.00	1822.47
	Ola ELIASSON	Swe	72	70	75	73	290	2	3120.00	1822.47
66	Craig HAINLINE	USA	72	71	72	76	291	3	2580.00	1507.04
	Stephen ALLAN	Aus	68	77	70	76	291	3	2580.00	1507.04
68	Per-Ulrik JOHANSSON	Swe	72	73	77	70	292	4	2340.00	1366.85
	Paul MCGINLEY	Ire	70	74	74	74	292	4	2340.00	1366.85
	Sebastien DELAGRANGE	Fr	73	70	73	76	292	4	2340.00	1366.85
71	Lionel ALEXANDRE	Fr	71	74	76	72	293	5	1800.00	1051.43
	Bruno LECUONA (AM)	Fr	70	73	76	74	293	5		
73	Ian POULTER	Eng	77	68	71	78	294	6	1795.50	1048.80
	Russell CLAYDON	Eng	72	71	76	75	294	6	1795.50	1048.80
75	Philip GOLDING	Eng	73	70	75	77	295	7	1791.00	1046.17
76	Geoff OGILVY	Aus	74	70	75	77	296	8	1788.00	1044.42
77	Michael JONZON	Swe	71	74	72	81	298	10	1785.00	1042.66
78	Marcus CAIN	Aus	74	70	80	83	307	19	1782.00	1040.91

Fit for Golf?

These days it is no longer sufficient to rely on talent and the desire to win. The right training and the right skills are important factors in performance. However, a balanced diet is also very much part of the package. Nestlé Nutrition will provide golf professionals and enthusiasts with information and up-to-date advice on sports nutrition, innovative foods and beverage products, giving them the winning edge.

Please come and ask for your free copy of the "Fit for golf" booklet at the upcoming Tour Event.

Nestlé
NUTRITION

OFFICIAL PARTNER OF THE PGA EUROPEAN TOUR

Man of Dignity

THE DE VERE BELFRY, SUTTON COLDFIELD, ENGLAND

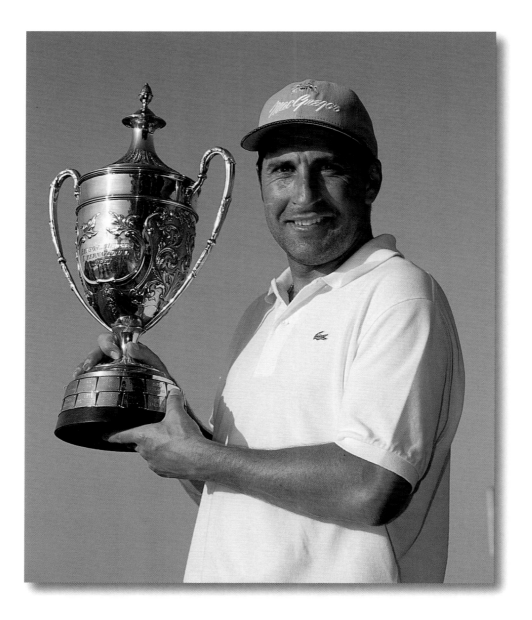

*I*n the wake of Padraig Harrington's disqualification from the Benson and Hedges International Open, there was always the danger that the eventual winner might be seen to have won the title by default.

Mercifully, that did not begin to apply, for José Maria Olazábal captured the title in style, following one glorious 66 with another over the weekend to defeat Phillip Price by three shots.

Olazábal's aggregate was as many as 13 under par, while the win was his first since he collected his green jacket at Augusta National in 1999. In his own quiet way, the Spaniard was elated.

Like Price, he had bedded down on Saturday night in second place at seven under par, five shots behind Harrington with scores of 71, 69 and 64. But, not much more than an hour before the leaders were due to set out on their fourth round, there was the news which

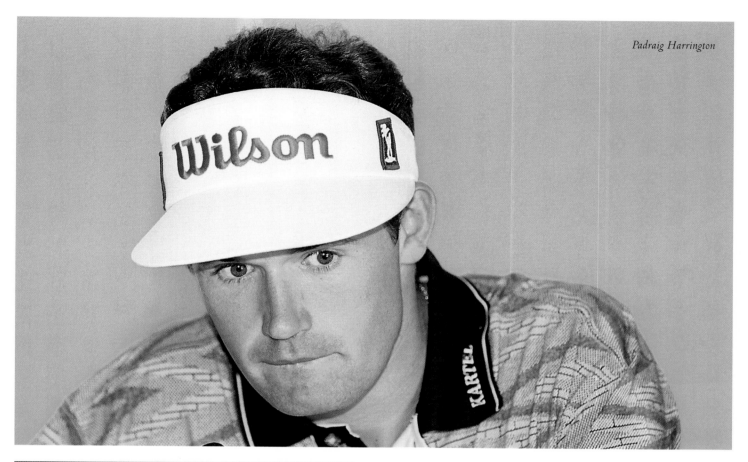

Padraig Harrington

José Maria Olazábal

left everyone at The De Vere Belfry in a state of shock.

European Tour officials had discovered, that he had failed to sign for his opening 71. This sad lapse had occurred in the scorer's caravan after Jamie Spence, who was marking for Harrington, affixed his signature to the card before passing it on to Harrington via Michael Campbell, the third member of their party. Campbell thought the card was his and did as he always does in signing it first before checking the figures. When he realised the figures were not his, he passed it to Harrington.

The 28-year-old Ryder Cup player proceeded to go through the numbers with all the thoroughness you would expect of a player who had qualified as an accountant before turning professional. However, when he reached the point where he would normally have penned his name, he must have assumed that he had signed already.

"I can only think that I thought Jamie Spence's signature was mine," he said. "Yes, it was on the marker's line rather than the player's, but in terms of shape and length it looked much the same."

Andy McFee, the Tour's Senior Referee, had the unenviable task of bringing the matter to Harrington's attention. He showed him the card and Harrington noticed at once that his name was missing. He knew the implications and, to his endless credit, he was not complaining.

Adam Scott

"It's unfortunate, but the rules are the rules - we live by them and they are there to protect everybody," he noted, ruefully. "If," he continued, "you were to do away with this rule, at what stage would you do away with another? It's not like we don't know... I've been signing cards since I was 12."

The relevant ruling - Rule 6-6b - is as follows: "The competitor shall ensure that the marker has signed the card, countersign the card himself and return it to the Committee as soon as possible. Penalty for breach of Rule 6-6b: Disqualification."

So well did Harrington handle his demise that it was no surprise when, a few weeks later, he was highly considered for the Asprey and Garrard Golfer of the Month award for June.

Olazábal, than whom there is no more sensitive soul on Tour, wasted no time in prefixing his winner's press conference with a few words about Harrington. Then he told how his initial shock at the news had given way to the realisation that he would have to change his game plan. "I had planned to be aggressive but, with no Padraig out in front, I decided I had to play consistently and see what happened," he said.

Shot of the Week

When spectators swarmed deep into the copse to the right of the 428 yards eighth, the assumption was that they were about to watch a Seve spectacular. Instead, the trouble-shot artist was none other than Colin Montgomerie, who was in the throes of putting together a second-round 69 on his way to a share of fifth place.

To begin with, the Scot planned on hacking the ball out sideways. Then, as people were cleared out of the way and only trees remained, he saw a route to the green.

With silver birch branches dangling about his head and a look of furious concentration on his face, he knocked a seven iron to 10 feet. The spectators could not believe what they were seeing - and were clearly a little miffed when their "I was there" story was diluted as Montgomerie missed his birdie putt.

The Course

The 5,600,000 euro (£3.5 million) spent on The Brabazon Course since the 1993 Ryder Cup could not be said to have evaporated. One player after another spoke of how the course had improved both scenically - in terms of the maturing trees and waterways - and as an out-and-out test of golf.

The 473 yards 18th, which has always engendered more than its share of drama, is nowadays every bit the demanding hole its architects intended. Olazábal said he would not have felt happy with anything less than a two shot cushion as he teed up there on the last day, a judgement which was in keeping with the findings of the AXA statistic people. They rated it the most difficult hole in terms of all three of their categories of tee-shot, second and green.

Jean Van de Velde

As it turned out, the consistent approach yielded two birdies in the first three holes. But, with the valiant Price matching one of those and making another at the sixth, the two were still level at the turn. At this point, both had the feeling they were embarking on a match-play situation, with each throwing birdies at the other until Olazábal holed from 12 feet for an eagle at the 17th to go two ahead.

Olazábal's iron play had been at its considerable best all through, while John Jacobs, his mentor, must have been rejoicing at the way in which his charge was at last teeing the ball up a little higher and turning rather than sliding through his drives.
Away from the golf, the week will go down as one in which the key figures behaved with a dignity which spoke volumes for the game.

Who, for example, will ever forget that moment when Harrington, amid his disappointment, stepped on to the practice putting green to send Olazábal and Price on their way with a good-luck pat on the back?

Lewine Mair

José Maria Olazábal putts on the 18th

THE DE VERE BELFRY, SUTTON COLDFIELD, ENGLAND, 11-14 MAY 2000, PAR 72, 7118 YARDS, 6509 METRES

Pos.	Name		Rd1	Rd2	Rd3	Rd4	Total	Par	Prize Money Euro	£
1	José Maria OLAZÁBAL	Sp	75	68	66	66	275	-13	284482.81	166599.99
2	Phillip PRICE	Wal	69	72	68	69	278	-10	189541.38	111000.00
3	José COCERES	Arg	74	74	68	67	283	-5	96136.76	56300.00
	Andrew COLTART	Scot	75	71	71	66	283	-5	96136.76	56300.00
5	Anthony WALL	Eng	75	69	73	70	287	-1	61131.36	35800.00
	Colin MONTGOMERIE	Scot	76	69	73	69	287	-1	61131.36	35800.00
	Stephen GALLACHER	Scot	76	71	69	71	287	-1	61131.36	35800.00
	Adam SCOTT (AM)	Aus	71	75	67	74	287	-1		
9	Jean-Francois REMESY	Fr	73	76	70	69	288	0	35176.15	20600.00
	Miguel Angel JIMÉNEZ	Sp	76	72	71	69	288	0	35176.15	20600.00
	Jonathan LOMAS	Eng	71	71	73	73	288	0	35176.15	20600.00
	Peter O'MALLEY	Aus	73	75	69	71	288	0	35176.15	20600.00
	Angel CABRERA	Arg	72	72	77	67	288	0	35176.15	20600.00
14	Anders HANSEN	Den	76	73	72	68	289	1	25699.08	15050.00
	John SENDEN	Aus	73	73	69	74	289	1	25699.08	15050.00
	Jean VAN DE VELDE	Fr	70	75	70	74	289	1	25699.08	15050.00
	Geoff OGILVY	Aus	73	75	68	73	289	1	25699.08	15050.00
18	Bernhard LANGER	Ger	76	70	73	71	290	2	21686.27	12700.00
	Richard GREEN	Aus	78	69	72	71	290	2	21686.27	12700.00
	Massimo FLORIOLI	It	76	75	68	71	290	2	21686.27	12700.00
	Paul MCGINLEY	Ire	73	71	72	74	290	2	21686.27	12700.00
22	Tom GILLIS	USA	77	74	70	70	291	3	18541.47	10858.33
	Ian POULTER	Eng	73	74	72	72	291	3	18541.47	10858.33
	Peter MITCHELL	Eng	76	74	67	74	291	3	18541.47	10858.33
	Paolo QUIRICI	Swi	73	73	72	73	291	3	18541.47	10858.33
	Darren CLARKE	N.Ire	78	72	72	69	291	3	18541.47	10858.33
	Niclas FASTH	Swe	75	75	70	71	291	3	18541.47	10858.33
28	Costantino ROCCA	It	74	70	74	74	292	4	15453.60	9050.00
	Brian DAVIS	Eng	76	73	71	72	292	4	15453.60	9050.00
	Nick O'HERN	Aus	75	74	71	72	292	4	15453.60	9050.00
	Soren HANSEN	Den	75	76	70	71	292	4	15453.60	9050.00
	Robert KARLSSON	Swe	76	70	70	76	292	4	15453.60	9050.00
	David CARTER	Eng	79	70	68	75	292	4	15453.60	9050.00
34	Eduardo ROMERO	Arg	75	73	74	71	293	5	13020.30	7625.00
	Maarten LAFEBER	Hol	77	72	68	76	293	5	13020.30	7625.00
	Carlos RODILES	Sp	74	77	72	70	293	5	13020.30	7625.00
	Ian GARBUTT	Eng	76	71	72	74	293	5	13020.30	7625.00

Pos.	Name		Rd1	Rd2	Rd3	Rd4	Total	Par	Prize Money Euro	£
38	Gordon BRAND JNR.	Scot	71	80	70	73	294	6	11270.03	6600.00
	Raphaël JACQUELIN	Fr	77	73	75	69	294	6	11270.03	6600.00
	Sven STRÜVER	Ger	76	71	70	77	294	6	11270.03	6600.00
	Knud STORGAARD	Den	81	69	71	73	294	6	11270.03	6600.00
	Desmond TERBLANCHE	SA	76	74	73	71	294	6	11270.03	6600.00
	David LYNN	Eng	77	72	73	72	294	6	11270.03	6600.00
44	Ian WOOSNAM	Wal	77	73	68	77	295	7	9391.69	5500.00
	Carl SUNESON	Sp	73	78	73	71	295	7	9391.69	5500.00
	Ricardo GONZALEZ	Arg	78	72	71	74	295	7	9391.69	5500.00
	Greg OWEN	Eng	76	69	75	75	295	7	9391.69	5500.00
	Dean ROBERTSON	Scot	72	78	76	69	295	7	9391.69	5500.00
49	Santiago LUNA	Sp	78	72	73	73	296	8	8025.63	4700.00
	Steen TINNING	Den	75	74	75	72	296	8	8025.63	4700.00
	David PARK	Wal	75	72	73	76	296	8	8025.63	4700.00
52	Peter LONARD	Aus	77	72	75	73	297	9	7171.84	4200.00
	Michael CAMPBELL	NZ	78	73	72	74	297	9	7171.84	4200.00
54	Robin BYRD	USA	71	76	73	78	298	10	5976.53	3500.00
	Paul AFFLECK	Wal	76	73	75	74	298	10	5976.53	3500.00
	Bradley DREDGE	Wal	77	73	76	72	298	10	5976.53	3500.00
	Matthew BLACKEY	Eng	75	75	72	76	298	10	5976.53	3500.00
	Lee WESTWOOD	Eng	77	74	76	71	298	10	5976.53	3500.00
59	David GILFORD	Eng	75	75	70	79	299	11	5037.36	2950.00
	Ola ELIASSON	Swe	74	77	75	73	299	11	5037.36	2950.00
61	Miguel Angel MARTIN	Sp	75	76	69	80	300	12	4695.85	2750.00
	Domingo HOSPITAL	Sp	76	69	78	77	300	12	4695.85	2750.00
63	Soren KJELDSEN	Den	79	71	71	80	301	13	4354.33	2550.00
	Jorge BERENDT	Arg	74	76	78	73	301	13	4354.33	2550.00
65	Andrew SHERBORNE	Eng	75	73	76	78	302	14	4098.19	2400.00
66	Francisco CEA	Sp	76	75	75	77	303	15	3756.68	2200.00
	Jim PAYNE	Eng	75	74	77	77	303	15	3756.68	2200.00
	John BICKERTON	Eng	73	76	73	81	303	15	3756.68	2200.00
69	Peter SENIOR	Aus	76	75	76	77	304	16	3329.79	1950.01
	Sam TORRANCE	Scot	77	72	79	76	304	16	3329.79	1950.01
	Elliot BOULT	NZ	76	75	73	80	304	16	3329.79	1950.01
72	Massimo SCARPA	It	77	72	75	81	305	17	2561.00	1499.78
73	Barry LANE	Eng	77	74	83	78	312	24	2558.00	1498.03

All Change in Hamburg

GUT KADEN, HAMBURG, GERMANY

All of the ingredients were in place. With eight of the world's top-20 players in the field alongside, for the first time since Brookline 1999, all 12 members of the European Ryder Cup squad, we should have known that this would be a special week on the European Tour.

So it proved. Only eight days after telling the world that he "can't see where the next good round is coming from," Lee Westwood played "one of the best rounds of my career" to win the Deutsche Bank-SAP Open TPC of Europe.

Indeed, rarely can the fickleness of golf have been better demonstrated. After a disappointing third round of 76 at The De Vere Belfry during the Benson and Hedges International Open, Westwood appeared in despair. His comments - "I've not been able

to motivate myself. I'm losing interest. It's making me miserable. I don't know what to do. I'm probably not thinking about golf as much as I used to," - were those of a man in search of both himself and his game.

But golf, as someone once said, is a funny game. Sometimes, all it needs is a spark, a new challenge, or maybe a return to a favourite venue and a struggling golfer can be transformed into a world-beater.

Make that world's number one beater. With 18 holes to play, Westwood's steady rounds of 71-69-69 over the picturesque Gut Kaden course (where he had shot an 11 under par 61 en route to victory in this same event two years before) left him two shots behind the man at the top of the Official World Golf Ranking, Tiger Woods.

Darren Clarke and Tiger Woods paired again for the first time since the final of the WGC - Andersen Consulting Match Play

In such situations, Woods is invariably a winner. Fourteen times the American had previously led or shared the lead going into the final round of an event; 13 times he had emerged victorious.

But not on this day. Although he was right in contention until a pushed seven iron approach into water at the 439 yards 11th, the American fell short in his bid to retain the title he had won at St. Leon Rot, Heidelberg, in 1999. His closing 70, while respectable, was never going to be enough in the face of the excellence shown by Westwood and others. By the end, he was tied for third with Jean Van de Velde and Ian Woosnam.

Earlier, the final round started with a rush from, it seemed, almost everyone in contention. Putts were going in from everywhere as the likes of Jesper Parnevik, Colin Montgomerie, Miguel Angel Jiménez, Paul Lawrie and the aforementioned Woosnam and Van de Velde made their bids for the richest prize in European golf outside of the four majors and the three World Golf Championship events with a 450,000 euro (£269,300) first prize at stake from a prize fund of 2,700,000 euro (£1,635,000).

By the turn, the leaderboard resembled a who's-who of world golf, all of whom had at least a chance of victory.

Until, that is, Westwood moved into overdrive. Birdies at Woods's nemesis, the 11th, and the 12th suddenly moved the 27-year-old Englishman three shots clear and looking the likely champion. There was, however, one more challenge to repel.

Ian Woosnam

Shot of the Week

Two hundred and eighty yards from the green after a "big" drive at the 559 yards 17th on the final day, Lee Westwood smacked a three-wood into the heart of the green. "I hit it perfectly," he said. "When I saw where it finished, I knew I had won."

Emanuele Canonica

Indeed, had it not been for the fact that the Italian was playing in the same group, and given all that was going on around him, it could have been easy for Westwood to miss the steady play from Emanuele Canonica.

And that would have been a mistake. Europe's longest hitter, Canonica played the round of his life en route to the highest finish of his career. Under the severest pressure, the Torino native never looked like "going away" and, when he holed for a birdie at the 166-yards 16th, momentarily got to within one shot of his playing companion. Only when Westwood followed him in for a matching two did Canonica mentally concede defeat.

Westwood wasn't finished either. Yet another birdie - his eighth of the day - came at the long 17th and suddenly his lead was back to three. He could enjoy the leisurely stroll and comfortable par he made at the last. His 64 was the lowest round of the day and the week. Afterwards, he was, as you'd expect, a very happy young man.

"I proved today I cannot be intimidated," he said. "I felt in total control even when the pressure was on me. I did exactly what I knew I had to do. I proved that I can come out of a slump, not panic, and win. All my negative thoughts have gone." What a difference a week can make.

John Huggan

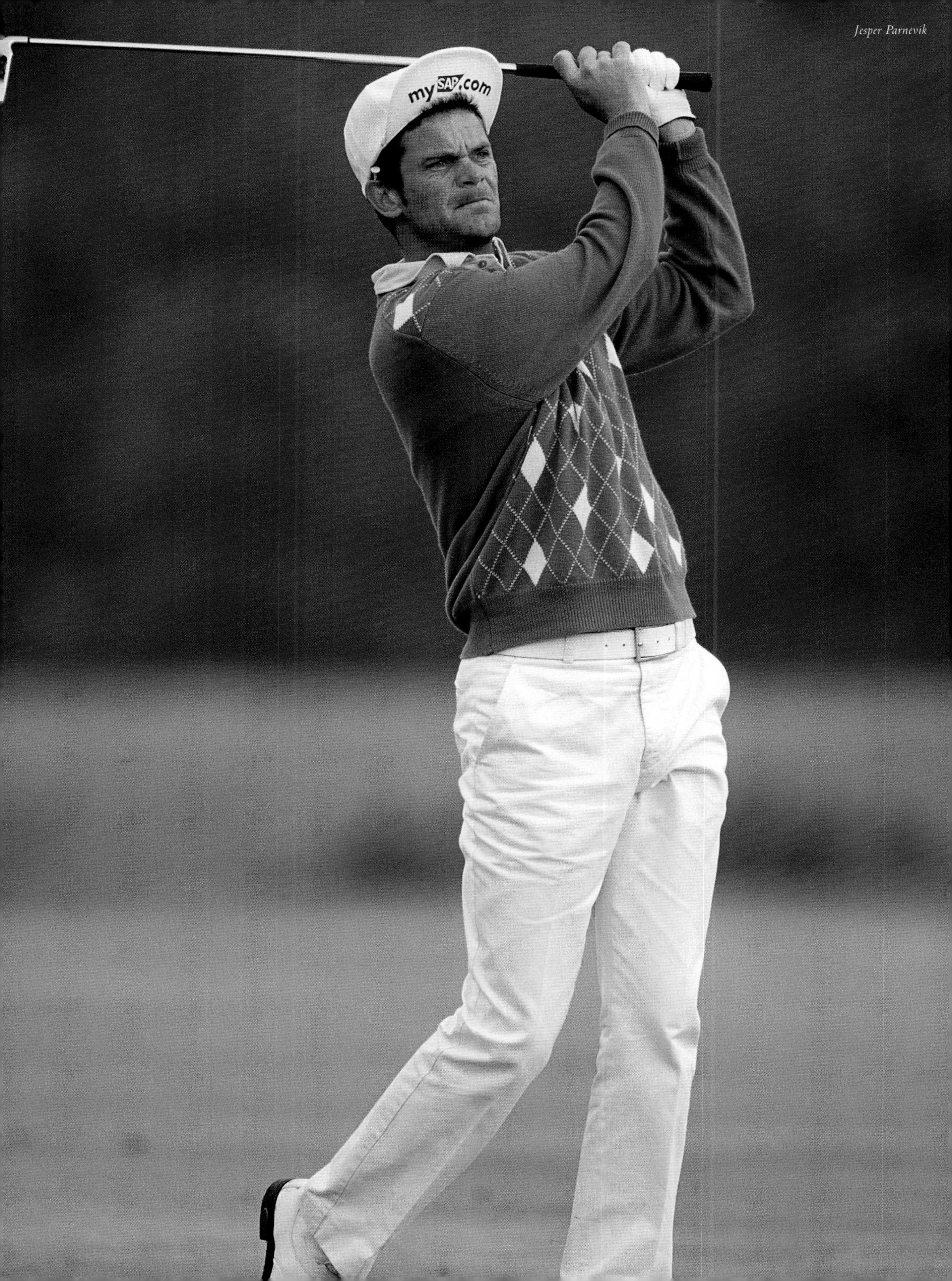
mySAP.com

The Course

Gut Kaden is a course of two halves, the inward half very much newer than the front nine holes. Not that you'd notice, however. With the narrowing of the fairways and the addition of some thick rough, the course played much harder than in previous years. No longer could the players unthinkingly hit driver from every tee; this year strategic planning was a much bigger part of the challenge presented.

GUT KADEN, HAMBURG, GERMANY, 18-21 MAY 2000, PAR 72, 7085 YARDS, 6487 METRES

Pos.	Name		Rd1	Rd2	Rd3	Rd4	Total	Par	Prize Money Euro	£
1	Lee WESTWOOD	Eng	71	69	69	64	273	-15	450000.00	269311.10
2	Emanuele CANONICA	It	69	69	71	67	276	-12	300000.00	179540.73
3	Ian WOOSNAM	Wal	71	71	69	66	277	-11	139500.00	83486.44
	Tiger WOODS	USA	70	70	67	70	277	-11	139500.00	83486.44
	Jean VAN DE VELDE	Fr	69	71	70	67	277	-11	139500.00	83486.44
6	Colin MONTGOMERIE	Scot	73	70	68	67	278	-10	81000.00	48476.00
	Miguel Angel JIMÉNEZ	Sp	67	69	73	69	278	-10	81000.00	48476.00
	Geoff OGILVY	Aus	72	71	66	69	278	-10	81000.00	48476.00
9	David HOWELL	Eng	71	69	72	67	279	-9	52650.00	31509.40
	Soren KJELDSEN	Den	77	67	66	69	279	-9	52650.00	31509.40
	Paul MCGINLEY	Ire	73	65	72	69	279	-9	52650.00	31509.40
	Gary ORR	Scot	73	66	72	68	279	-9	52650.00	31509.40
13	Brian DAVIS	Eng	72	68	72	68	280	-8	42390.00	25369.11
	Retief GOOSEN	SA	68	71	71	70	280	-8	42390.00	25369.11
15	Darren CLARKE	N.Ire	72	69	68	72	281	-7	38880.00	23268.48
	Paul LAWRIE	Scot	68	73	70	70	281	-7	38880.00	23268.48
17	Miguel Angel MARTIN	Sp	69	71	71	71	282	-6	33187.50	19861.69
	Padraig HARRINGTON	Ire	73	70	69	70	282	-6	33187.50	19861.69
	Nick PRICE	Zim	72	71	70	69	282	-6	33187.50	19861.69
	Ian POULTER	Eng	71	70	72	69	282	-6	33187.50	19861.69
	Peter BAKER	Eng	71	69	71	71	282	-6	33187.50	19861.69
	Peter MITCHELL	Eng	71	72	67	72	282	-6	33187.50	19861.69
23	Jesper PARNEVIK	Swe	70	73	68	72	283	-5	28890.00	17289.77
	Steve WEBSTER	Eng	72	67	73	71	283	-5	28890.00	17289.77
	Angel CABRERA	Arg	75	69	67	72	283	-5	28890.00	17289.77
26	Mark JAMES	Eng	74	70	70	70	284	-4	25650.00	15350.73
	Raphaël JACQUELIN	Fr	71	72	68	73	284	-4	25650.00	15350.73
	Joakim HAEGGMAN	Swe	69	71	73	71	284	-4	25650.00	15350.73
	Benoit TEILLERIA	Fr	70	75	70	69	284	-4	25650.00	15350.73
	Michael CAMPBELL	NZ	74	66	71	73	284	-4	25650.00	15350.73
31	Sergio GARCIA	Sp	70	72	71	72	285	-3	22005.00	13169.31
	Domingo HOSPITAL	Sp	69	74	69	73	285	-3	22005.00	13169.31
	Paolo QUIRICI	Swi	70	73	71	71	285	-3	22005.00	13169.31
	Peter O'MALLEY	Aus	72	72	70	71	285	-3	22005.00	13169.31
35	Roger CHAPMAN	Eng	68	74	72	72	286	-2	17820.00	10664.72
	Ronan RAFFERTY	N.Ire	72	71	69	74	286	-2	17820.00	10664.72
	José Maria OLAZABAL	Sp	75	65	74	72	286	-2	17820.00	10664.72
	Greg TURNER	NZ	73	72	70	71	286	-2	17820.00	10664.72
	Stephen LEANEY	Aus	70	70	74	72	286	-2	17820.00	10664.72

Pos.	Name		Rd1	Rd2	Rd3	Rd4	Total	Par	Prize Money Euro	£
	Mathias GRÖNBERG	Swe	71	74	70	71	286	-2	17820.00	10664.72
	Thomas BJÖRN	Den	75	70	73	68	286	-2	17820.00	10664.72
	David LYNN	Eng	74	68	74	70	286	-2	17820.00	10664.72
	John BICKERTON	Eng	72	73	70	71	286	-2	17820.00	10664.72
	David CARTER	Eng	72	73	71	70	286	-2	17820.00	10664.72
45	Gary MURPHY	Ire	74	69	73	71	287	-1	13230.00	7917.75
	Sven STRÜVER	Ger	72	71	74	70	287	-1	13230.00	7917.75
	Philip GOLDING	Eng	72	73	69	73	287	-1	13230.00	7917.75
	Richard S JOHNSON	Swe	72	69	73	73	287	-1	13230.00	7917.75
	Phillip PRICE	Wal	72	69	71	75	287	-1	13230.00	7917.75
	Markus BRIER	Aut	72	73	69	73	287	-1	13230.00	7917.75
	Bob MAY	USA	71	68	74	74	287	-1	13230.00	7917.75
52	Eamonn DARCY	Ire	71	72	74	71	288	0	9281.25	5554.54
	Mark MCNULTY	Zim	70	74	70	74	288	0	9281.25	5554.54
	Jamie SPENCE	Eng	73	72	71	72	288	0	9281.25	5554.54
	Paul EALES	Eng	75	68	74	71	288	0	9281.25	5554.54
	Alex CEJKA	Ger	73	69	78	68	288	0	9281.25	5554.54
	Nicolas VANHOOTEGEM	Bel	70	74	73	71	288	0	9281.25	5554.54
	Van PHILLIPS	Eng	73	70	71	74	288	0	9281.25	5554.54
	Johan SKOLD	Swe	72	73	73	70	288	0	9281.25	5554.54
60	Rodger DAVIS	Aus	72	71	73	73	289	1	7020.00	4201.25
	Nick O'HERN	Aus	72	70	75	72	289	1	7020.00	4201.25
	Jeremy ROBINSON	Eng	74	71	78	66	289	1	7020.00	4201.25
	Jorge BERENDT	Arg	72	73	72	72	289	1	7020.00	4201.25
	Stephen ALLAN	Aus	69	74	73	73	289	1	7020.00	4201.25
65	Ignacio GARRIDO	Sp	72	73	72	73	290	2	6075.00	3635.70
	Jarmo SANDELIN	Swe	74	71	70	75	290	2	6075.00	3635.70
67	Marc FARRY	Fr	71	73	72	75	291	3	5445.00	3258.66
	Craig HAINLINE	USA	73	72	71	75	291	3	5445.00	3258.66
	Lucas PARSONS	Aus	71	72	67	81	291	3	5445.00	3258.66
70	Costantino ROCCA	It	71	73	74	74	292	4	4590.00	2746.97
	Ricardo GONZALEZ	Arg	72	73	73	74	292	4	4590.00	2746.97
72	Knud STORGAARD	Den	71	72	75	75	293	5	4044.00	2420.21
	Michael JONZON	Swe	72	73	74	74	293	5	4044.00	2420.21
	Dean ROBERTSON	Scot	71	72	74	76	293	5	4044.00	2420.21
75	Tony JOHNSTONE	Zim	71	74	72	78	295	7	4036.50	2415.72
	Carl SUNESON	Sp	74	70	76	75	295	7	4036.50	2415.72
77	Anders HANSEN	Den	75	70	77	74	296	8	4032.00	2413.03
78	Stuart MCGREGOR	Scot	72	73	77	81	303	15	4029.00	2411.23

Welcome TPC fans!

Deutsche Bank - SAP Open

Lee Westwood, winner 2000

May 17 – 20, 2001

Golf Club St. Leon-Rot
near Heidelberg

For further information please contact the
Deutsche Bank - SAP Tournament office
Ticket-Hotline: +49 (0) 4193 9000-0
http://www.deutschebank-sap-open.de

Deutsche Bank

SAP

Flagship Day

At times, the routine consistency of Colin Montgomerie's supremacy masks the enormity of his achievement and makes the winning outcome seem not only predictable but nothing less than was expected of him.

And yet the familiar pose of Montgomerie triumphantly holding another trophy is invariably preceded by a less certain narrative during which the hero himself has to overcome a combination of crises, challenges and other pressures before he prevails.

So it was with the Volvo PGA Championship over the West Course at Wentworth Club where a monumental task awaited him. He had already made one successful defence of the title and thus faced the possibility of becoming the first golfer in history to win the championship three years in succession quite apart from emulating Nick Faldo's feat of winning a hat-trick of European Tour titles as the Englishman did in the Irish Open between 1991 and 1993.

Shot of the Week

A comfortable four-stroke lead had disappeared and Colin Montgomerie was aware that his fellow countryman, Andrew Coltart was gaining in confidence. As he walked towards his ball on the eighth fairway after a colossal tee shot he decided to give himself a serious talking-to: "I realised that a loose approach shot would give the initiative to Andrew. I knew this was a crucial hole." He drilled a seven iron unerringly towards the flagstick and the ball finished close enough for a birdie to restore his lead. He said: "That really was the pivotal moment."

Thus the objective was clear enough but the outcome was open to inevitable vagaries because although Montgomerie was cruising back into form with victory a few weeks earlier in the Novotel Perrier Open de France, he was now facing the combined threats from a legion of rivals all of whom were at their best and determined to make their own bid for the most prestigious title in the European professional game.

Darren Clarke had usurped Montgomerie's position at the top of the Volvo Order of Merit after his inspiring match play victory over Tiger Woods at the start of the year. Lee Westwood had suddenly regained his touch and improved sight through laser surgery to win a Tour event a week before his Wentworth assault. José Maria Olazábal, twice US Masters champion, had also produced a compelling triumph two weeks before the Championship. New Zealander Michael Campbell, who dominated the early season in the Far East and Australia, was an obvious contender while Open champion Paul Lawrie as well as Sergio Garcia and Andrew Coltart, a resurgent Ian Woosnam and ever-present Bernhard Langer all added to the challenge Montgomerie faced (although Lawrie was forced to retire with a recurring groin injury in the second round).

Mel Pyatt and HRH The Duke of York

Darren Clarke

Sergio Garcia and caddie
Glenn Murray

And then there was the rain. Not just the irritation of personal saturation and slippery grips but the kind of massive playing disruption that Montgomerie and the rest of the assembled company faced as Wentworth endured monsoon-like conditions that halted play for hours and left rounds incomplete overnight as course superintendent Chris Kennedy and his 40-strong staff worked tirelessly - and through the night - to clear away water from flooded greens, fairways and bunkers.

Consider the Montgomerie schedule for the second day's play after he had been obliged to stop when he was two under par after eight holes of his delayed opening round as darkness fell. He returned to the course for a 7.30am re-start which meant getting out of bed at his Oxshott home at 5.00am and driving to Wentworth in time for his customary warm-up routine.

Even so, his concentration remained sharply focused as if entirely oblivious to the interrupted routine and blustery conditions and he finished with a 67 to find himself two strokes behind the pace-setting target set by Australia's Nick O'Hern. With just a forty-minute break during which he consumed a hearty English breakfast, Montgomerie was back on the course and this time put together a stunning

Rupert Lendrum, Director of Moët Hennessy UK Ltd, presents Colin Montgomerie
with a jeroboam of Moët & Chandon.

display of four birdies in the first five holes for an eventual 65 which had the dual effect of giving him a two-stroke lead over Australian left-hander Richard Green as well as warning the entire cast that Europe's top money winner for the last seven years was in hungry mood again.

Of course afterwards the completed leaderboard bore no hint of the fragmented manner in which the scores were produced and how Europe's finest golfers stuck to their task without complaint in such dire conditions. Clarke put together a brace of 68s, Coltart scored 67-69 while Westwood (71-70) remained within reasonable touch, Robert Karlsson (67-69) kept pace and Garcia (68-71) was still close enough to pose a threat.

As halfway leader and therefore last man out, Montgomerie faced more problems on the third day because a further delay of more than three hours due to rain compelled him to tee off in early evening and he had negotiated only 13 holes when darkness fell so that he and others had to stop play. Weather experts had calculated that in just 12 hours the average rainfall for the entire month of May had descended upon Wentworth Club.

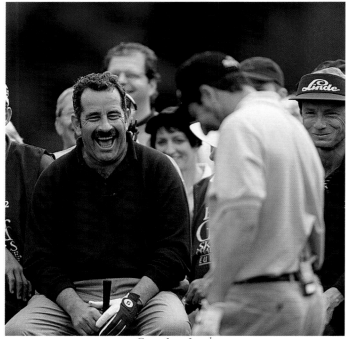

Game for a Laugh

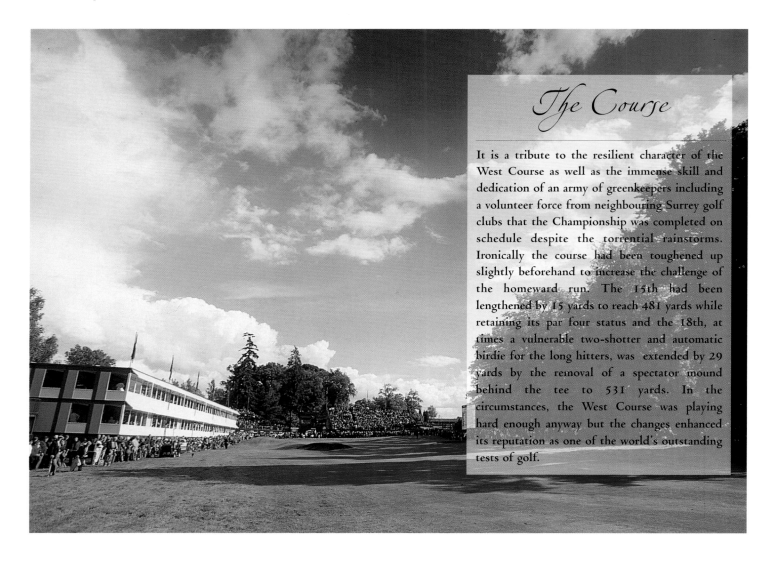

The Course

It is a tribute to the resilient character of the West Course as well as the immense skill and dedication of an army of greenkeepers including a volunteer force from neighbouring Surrey golf clubs that the Championship was completed on schedule despite the torrential rainstorms. Ironically the course had been toughened up slightly beforehand to increase the challenge of the homeward run. The 15th had been lengthened by 15 yards to reach 481 yards while retaining its par four status and the 18th, at times a vulnerable two-shotter and automatic birdie for the long hitters, was extended by 29 yards by the removal of a spectator mound behind the tee to 531 yards. In the circumstances, the West Course was playing hard enough anyway but the changes enhanced its reputation as one of the world's outstanding tests of golf.

Asprey & Garrard

LONDON

A team led by Bernhard Langer won the NSPCC Pro-Am held in the presence of HRH The Duke of York on the eve of the Volvo PGA Championship. The European Tour raised £169,000 for the NSPCC from the event which was presented by Invensys Plc. HRH The Duke of York, who is chairman of the NSPCC's Full Stop Campaign, is pictured with Sergio Garcia in the team with Allen Yurko, Chief Executive of Invensys Plc, and Jan Engström, President and CEO Volvo Bus Corporation, Sweden

Colin Montgomerie won the European edition of the EMC Golf Skills Challenge, sanctioned by The European Tour, and he received his cheque from Ronald Slate, EMC's Vice President of Global Communications

Victor Chandler On Course at Wentworth Club

It meant that Montgomerie and the rest of the leading contenders faced another early start and long-playing ordeal on the final day as the third round was completed and the drama of the fourth round unfolded with all the main characters facing their individual moments of opportunity but unable to take proper advantage.

Clarke put together a blistering final 66 that included one eagle and six birdies but felt he had wasted his chance of drawing even closer to the leader by failing to birdie either of the two closing long holes in the third round. Westwood, four behind at the start of the final round due largely to the brilliance of a homeward 30 in the third round in which he had five birdies in six holes, could not recapture such accuracy in the final round and took 68 for a share of second place with Clarke and Coltart.

Seve Ballesteros, on behalf of the Members of The European Tour, congratulated and thanked Evan Kaloussis (second from left), Senior Vice President of Nestlé, for the Nestlé Nutrition Physiotherapy Unit. They are joined by Guy Delacave, Director of Physiotherapy, and George O'Grady, Managing Director of PGA European Tour Productions

The annual European Tour Dinner took place at Wentworth Club during the Volvo PGA Championship, and later in the year, John Jacobs, the Father of the European Tour, and Neil Coles were inducted into the World Golf Hall of Fame

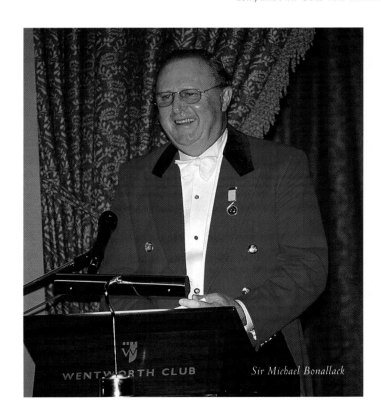

Sir Michael Bonallack

Ken Schofield CBE

Huge galleries gathered at Wentworth Club

Andrew Coltart

The lean Scot made a spirited challenge and put Montgomerie under acute pressure by drawing level with a birdie on the seventh hole after his fellow-countryman endured an uncharacteristic miss. But even though Montgomerie's lead had slipped away there was to be no further collapse because he restored his advantage at the next hole with a spectacular approach to set up a birdie then eased away with three birdies in succession from the 11th hole to put the title beyond reach and his own supremacy beyond doubt with a closing 69 and a 17 under par 271 total.

What gave him most satisfaction was the quality of players assembled for the Championship and he reflected: "It was a great honour for me to win. This is our flagship event. Everybody on the European Tour was playing here and playing well. The future is very, very bright in Europe. The standard is very good and I have to play at my very best to stay up there." One fact underlined that point. A record 81 players made the halfway cut in such tough conditions. Montgomerie got it right. Again.

Michael McDonnell

Colin Montgomerie's approach to the final hole

WENTWORTH CLUB, SURREY, ENGLAND, 26-29 MAY 2000, PAR 72, 7047 YARDS, 6445 METRES

Pos.	Name		Rd1	Rd2	Rd3	Rd4	Total	Par	Prize Money Euro	£
1	Colin MONTGOMERIE	Scot	67	65	70	69	271	-17	415130.00	250000.00
2	Darren CLARKE	N.Ire	68	68	72	66	274	-14	185734.70	111853.34
	Andrew COLTART	Scot	67	69	69	69	274	-14	185734.70	111853.34
	Lee WESTWOOD	Eng	71	70	65	68	274	-14	185734.70	111853.34
5	Sergio GARCIA	Sp	68	71	68	70	277	-11	96393.19	58050.00
	Richard GREEN	Aus	67	67	73	70	277	-11	96393.19	58050.00
7	Ian WOOSNAM	Wal	72	71	68	68	279	-9	60650.49	36525.00
	Olivier EDMOND	Fr	68	74	69	68	279	-9	60650.49	36525.00
	Peter O'MALLEY	Aus	68	73	69	69	279	-9	60650.49	36525.00
	Retief GOOSEN	SA	74	70	68	67	279	-9	60650.49	36525.00
11	Nick O'HERN	Aus	65	74	71	70	280	-8	44335.88	26700.00
	Michael CAMPBELL	NZ	73	68	71	68	280	-8	44335.88	26700.00
13	Roger CHAPMAN	Eng	71	72	70	68	281	-7	37486.24	22575.00
	Raphaël JACQUELIN	Fr	70	75	71	65	281	-7	37486.24	22575.00
	Robert KARLSSON	Swe	67	69	74	71	281	-7	37486.24	22575.00
	Bob MAY	USA	68	75	68	70	281	-7	37486.24	22575.00
17	Bernhard LANGER	Ger	69	71	71	71	282	-6	32214.09	19400.00
	Padraig HARRINGTON	Ire	72	74	69	67	282	-6	32214.09	19400.00
	Gary EMERSON	Eng	69	69	73	71	282	-6	32214.09	19400.00
20	Anders HANSEN	Den	70	73	69	71	283	-5	27813.71	16750.00
	Miguel Angel JIMÉNEZ	Sp	69	75	70	69	283	-5	27813.71	16750.00
	Roger WINCHESTER	Eng	71	75	68	69	283	-5	27813.71	16750.00
	Thomas GÖGELE	Ger	71	73	74	65	283	-5	27813.71	16750.00
	Paul MCGINLEY	Ire	70	70	72	71	283	-5	27813.71	16750.00
	Phillip PRICE	Wal	72	67	69	75	283	-5	27813.71	16750.00
26	Des SMYTH	Ire	77	69	70	68	284	-4	24036.03	14475.00
	Peter MITCHELL	Eng	71	73	71	69	284	-4	24036.03	14475.00
	Ricardo GONZALEZ	Arg	73	68	70	73	284	-4	24036.03	14475.00
	Gary ORR	Scot	72	71	72	69	284	-4	24036.03	14475.00
30	Wayne RILEY	Aus	72	70	70	73	285	-3	21047.09	12675.00
	Stuart LITTLE	Eng	68	75	74	68	285	-3	21047.09	12675.00
	Dean ROBERTSON	Scot	73	71	73	68	285	-3	21047.09	12675.00
	John BICKERTON	Eng	69	74	73	69	285	-3	21047.09	12675.00
34	Jean-Francois REMESY	Fr	74	70	73	69	286	-2	18431.77	11100.00
	Mark MCNULTY	Zim	71	71	72	72	286	-2	18431.77	11100.00
	Alex CEJKA	Ger	71	71	72	72	286	-2	18431.77	11100.00
	Iain PYMAN	Eng	72	71	70	73	286	-2	18431.77	11100.00
38	Barry LANE	Eng	73	71	73	70	287	-1	16190.07	9750.00
	Soren KJELDSEN	Den	68	73	76	70	287	-1	16190.07	9750.00
	Jean VAN DE VELDE	Fr	68	75	73	71	287	-1	16190.07	9750.00
	David CARTER	Eng	76	70	73	68	287	-1	16190.07	9750.00
	Alastair FORSYTH	Scot	72	71	74	70	287	-1	16190.07	9750.00
43	Tony JOHNSTONE	Zim	72	73	74	69	288	0	12952.06	7800.00
	Mats LANNER	Swe	73	70	75	70	288	0	12952.06	7800.00
	Sam TORRANCE	Scot	69	72	73	74	288	0	12952.06	7800.00
	Lian-Wei ZHANG	PRC	75	71	70	72	288	0	12952.06	7800.00
	Stephen LEANEY	Aus	71	71	74	72	288	0	12952.06	7800.00
	Jamie SPENCE	Eng	75	70	73	70	288	0	12952.06	7800.00
	Olle KARLSSON	Swe	72	74	74	68	288	0	12952.06	7800.00
	Gustavo ROJAS	Arg	68	75	71	74	288	0	12952.06	7800.00
51	Miguel Angel MARTIN	Sp	72	73	73	71	289	1	9714.04	5850.00
	José RIVERO	Sp	70	72	76	71	289	1	9714.04	5850.00
	Carl SUNESON	Sp	71	72	74	72	289	1	9714.04	5850.00
	Angel CABRERA	Arg	71	73	73	72	289	1	9714.04	5850.00
	Benoit TEILLERIA	Fr	72	73	73	71	289	1	9714.04	5850.00
56	Santiago LUNA	Sp	72	71	75	72	290	2	7389.31	4450.00
	Eduardo ROMERO	Arg	72	73	71	74	290	2	7389.31	4450.00
	José Maria OLAZABAL	Sp	71	75	70	74	290	2	7389.31	4450.00
	Andrew MCLARDY	SA	74	71	74	71	290	2	7389.31	4450.00
	Geoff OGILVY	Aus	68	76	72	74	290	2	7389.31	4450.00
	Christopher HANELL	Swe	73	72	72	73	290	2	7389.31	4450.00
62	Costantino ROCCA	It	69	77	73	72	291	3	5728.79	3450.00
	David HOWELL	Eng	69	76	70	76	291	3	5728.79	3450.00
	Peter BAKER	Eng	70	76	70	75	291	3	5728.79	3450.00
	Emanuele CANONICA	It	72	73	73	73	291	3	5728.79	3450.00
	Massimo SCARPA	It	72	71	78	70	291	3	5728.79	3450.00
	Ignacio GARRIDO	Sp	73	73	74	71	291	3	5728.79	3450.00
	Thomas BJÖRN	Den	70	75	75	71	291	3	5728.79	3450.00
69	Van PHILLIPS	Eng	72	71	76	73	292	4	4641.15	2795.00
	Jarmo SANDELIN	Swe	72	70	78	72	292	4	4641.15	2795.00
71	Mark JAMES	Eng	73	73	73	74	293	5	3731.50	2247.19
	Maarten LAFEBER	Hol	69	71	75	78	293	5	3731.50	2247.19
	André BOSSERT	Swi	70	76	74	73	293	5	3731.50	2247.19
	Des TERBLANCHE	SA	73	73	75	72	293	5	3731.50	2247.19
75	Steve WEBSTER	Eng	71	72	74	77	294	6	3724.00	2242.67
76	Paul WAY	Eng	72	72	77	74	295	7	3721.00	2240.86
77	Peter SENIOR	Aus	70	75	77	74	296	8	3715.00	2237.25
	John SENDEN	Aus	72	74	78	72	296	8	3715.00	2237.25
	John MELLOR	Eng	72	72	77	75	296	8	3715.00	2237.25
80	Paul R SIMPSON	Eng	70	74	78	77	299	11	3709.00	2233.64
81	Seve BALLESTEROS	Sp	70	74	79	80	303	15	3706.00	2231.83

OPERATIONAL EXCELLENCE

VOLVO

Seriously Stylish

MARRIOTT FOREST OF ARDEN HOTEL, WARWICKSHIRE, ENGLAND

Right, let us begin with a question: Which is better, a round of 63 or one of 65?

Well, whichever way logic dictates the answer should be, the correct reply in this instance is, of course, the 65 that Darren Clarke recorded in a final round that took him to a quite sensational victory at The Compass Group English Open.

The 63, meanwhile, was the first round compiled by Kiwi Michael Campbell, a bouquet of birdies, and one eagle, that took him so far ahead of the rest of a glittering field at Marriott's increasingly splendid Forest of Arden lay-out that even the Colin Montgomerie's of this golfing world were reaching for binoculars.

Indeed, Campbell's six shot lead after the opening 18 holes was a record for the European Tour. It was also, at least to those of us who

have spent most of our lives examining the detail of pro golf, a sure sign that things could only get worse.

And, of course, they did. Not disastrously but Campbell, a rejuvenated player these days, could not quite reignite the brilliant flame that propelled him through this first day.

But then it is always difficult to know what to do when this most curious of games decides to embrace, rather than kick, you. Should he continue to attack? Should he now play safe and leave the others to play catch-up? Should he enjoy a three hour lunch in Compass's seriously stylish entertaining unit by the 18th green?

The third choice would have been mine. Campbell, to his credit however, kept trying to push forward after what he described as "the best round of my professional career."

Golf, on the other hand, decided to be contrary. After caressing Campbell on day one, the grand, old game suddenly turned all negative on him, putts that had dropped previously just sliding by the hole as Michael threw back his head in anguish.

It was not disaster but his second, third and fourth rounds of 69, 72 and 72 failed to propel him over the distant horizon he had been heading for on Thursday.

By Saturday evening Campbell was still in the lead but by now it was by two shots over Lee Westwood with Colin Montgomerie five shots back. Mark James, meanwhile, had taken time off from writing books to filling in scorecards. This he did to some effect with a third round 65 that owed much to a putting tip from a spectator who suggested his left wrist was turning to jelly on the stroke.

"I just tried to firm up my grip by putting all my weight forward and hitting down on the ball and it worked. I found a part of the putter head that I'd forgotten existed. Apparently it's called the sweet spot", said James with his usual mixture of revelation and laconic comment.

It all prompted Campbell to identify Westwood and Montgomerie as his main rivals for the final round. Fair enough, except that Clarke had other ideas. When the big Ulsterman is hot, he can melt any course as he had proved earlier in the year in the USA when he crushed Tiger Woods in his powerful paws. For Clarke, as with all the really successful players, golf is about trying to win, not securing

Mark James

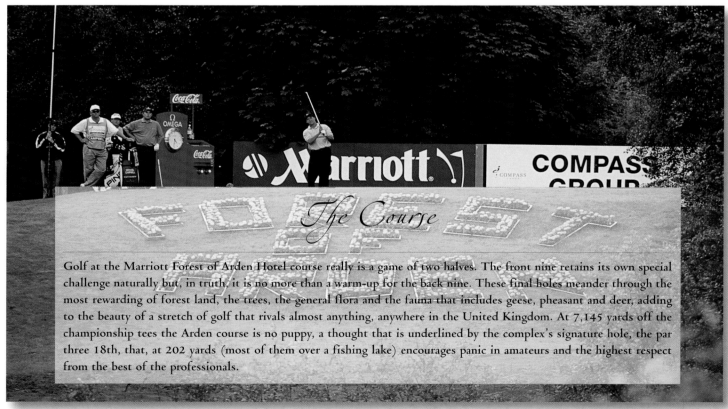

The Course

Golf at the Marriott Forest of Arden Hotel course really is a game of two halves. The front nine retains its own special challenge naturally but, in truth, it is no more than a warm-up for the back nine. These final holes meander through the most rewarding of forest land, the trees, the general flora and the fauna that includes geese, pheasant and deer, adding to the beauty of a stretch of golf that rivals almost anything, anywhere in the United Kingdom. At 7,145 yards off the championship tees the Arden course is no puppy, a thought that is underlined by the complex's signature hole, the par three 18th, that, at 202 yards (most of them over a fishing lake) encourages panic in amateurs and the highest respect from the best of the professionals.

a high enough place for a reassuringly large cheque. His mission statement for the last 18 holes was simple...Go For It Big Style.

And this he proceeded to do. While Westwood and Montgomerie struggled and James fought off another attack of the jellies, Clarke bombarded the flag. By the time he stood on the 13th tee his six shot deficit had been halved. It was then that he decided he needed to finish with five birdies until the thought struck him that he actually had six holes left.

In fact he made four in a row, narrowly failing to convert the fifth and by the time he walked off the last green he was in the lead by a shot. Over this closing stretch the big man signalled his advance by igniting his favourite stogies. As his ball peppered the pin it was the first recorded case of 'close and several cigars into the bargain'.

As he waited to see if he had won Campbell missed a crucial 30ft eagle putt on the 17th by the width of a putter head and then watched in horror at the last as his birdie effort to tie turned obstinately away from the hole at the last possible nano-second.

Clarke, eyes narrowed like a pair of slit-trenches, watched, then grunted and finally relit his cigar while Campbell had to settle for a share of second spot alongside James and the dawning realisation that sometimes a 65 can be lower than a 63. If you see what I mean.

Bill Elliott

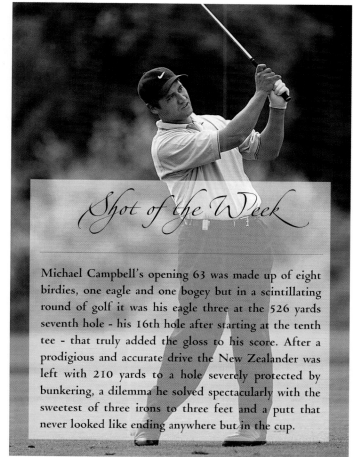

Shot of the Week

Michael Campbell's opening 63 was made up of eight birdies, one eagle and one bogey but in a scintillating round of golf it was his eagle three at the 526 yards seventh hole - his 16th hole after starting at the tenth tee - that truly added the gloss to his score. After a prodigious and accurate drive the New Zealander was left with 210 yards to a hole severely protected by bunkering, a dilemma he solved spectacularly with the sweetest of three irons to three feet and a putt that never looked like ending anywhere but in the cup.

Darren Clarke and Lee Westwood share a joke

Michael Campbell under close scrutiny from one of the locals

MARRIOTT FOREST OF ARDEN HOTEL, WARWICKSHIRE, ENGLAND 1-4 JUNE 2000, PAR 72, 7167 YARDS, 6553 METRES

Pos.	Name		Rd1	Rd2	Rd3	Rd4	Total	Par	Prize Money Euro	£
1	Darren CLARKE	N.Ire	70	72	68	65	275	-13	208330.00	130390.43
2	Mark JAMES	Eng	73	69	65	69	276	-12	108565.00	67949.10
	Michael CAMPBELL	NZ	63	69	72	72	276	-12	108565.00	67949.10
4	Ricardo GONZALEZ	Arg	71	69	69	69	278	-10	57750.00	36144.80
	Lee WESTWOOD	Eng	69	70	67	72	278	-10	57750.00	36144.80
6	Brian DAVIS	Eng	74	67	70	68	279	-9	40625.00	25426.54
	Gary ORR	Scot	69	72	71	67	279	-9	40625.00	25426.54
8	Colin MONTGOMERIE	Scot	71	68	69	72	280	-8	31250.00	19558.88
9	David LYNN	Eng	70	73	68	70	281	-7	28000.00	17524.75
10	Peter O'MALLEY	Aus	72	65	71	74	282	-6	24000.00	15021.22
	Ian GARBUTT	Eng	72	69	74	67	282	-6	24000.00	15021.22
12	Marc FARRY	Fr	75	69	71	68	283	-5	19350.00	12110.86
	Greg TURNER	NZ	73	71	67	72	283	-5	19350.00	12110.86
	Maarten LAFEBER	Hol	76	67	68	72	283	-5	19350.00	12110.86
	Nick O'HERN	Aus	73	69	70	71	283	-5	19350.00	12110.86
	Mathias GRÖNBERG	Swe	73	67	71	72	283	-5	19350.00	12110.86
17	Tony JOHNSTONE	Zim	72	70	73	69	284	-4	15354.17	9609.93
	Wayne RILEY	Aus	73	72	71	68	284	-4	15354.17	9609.93
	Mark MCNULTY	Zim	69	75	70	70	284	-4	15354.17	9609.93
	Anthony WALL	Eng	72	74	69	69	284	-4	15354.17	9609.93
	Gary EVANS	Eng	70	73	70	71	284	-4	15354.17	9609.93
	Thomas BJÖRN	Den	73	71	68	72	284	-4	15354.17	9609.93
23	David HOWELL	Eng	72	69	74	70	285	-3	13375.00	8371.20
	Steve WEBSTER	Eng	70	69	71	75	285	-3	13375.00	8371.20
	John BICKERTON	Eng	73	73	69	70	285	-3	13375.00	8371.20
26	Tom GILLIS	USA	74	72	70	70	286	-2	11687.50	7315.02
	Soren HANSEN	Den	74	71	69	72	286	-2	11687.50	7315.02
	Roger WINCHESTER	Eng	75	70	73	68	286	-2	11687.50	7315.02
	Gustavo ROJAS	Arg	73	72	68	73	286	-2	11687.50	7315.02
	David CARTER	Eng	73	70	70	73	286	-2	11687.50	7315.02
	Christopher HANELL	Swe	76	68	69	73	286	-2	11687.50	7315.02
32	Gordon BRAND JNR.	Scot	74	70	70	73	287	-1	9843.75	6161.05
	Miguel Angel MARTIN	Sp	73	72	71	71	287	-1	9843.75	6161.05
	Gary MURPHY	Ire	73	73	71	70	287	-1	9843.75	6161.05
	José Manuel CARRILES	Sp	72	69	72	74	287	-1	9843.75	6161.05
36	Peter MITCHELL	Eng	69	74	75	70	288	0	8625.00	5398.25
	Olivier EDMOND	Fr	73	72	72	71	288	0	8625.00	5398.25
	Nicolas VANHOOTEGEM	Bel	73	69	71	75	288	0	8625.00	5398.25
	Nick LUDWELL	Eng	72	71	73	72	288	0	8625.00	5398.25
	Benoit TEILLERIA	Fr	69	74	74	71	288	0	8625.00	5398.25
41	Mark DAVIS	Eng	76	70	72	71	289	1	7250.00	4537.66
	Peter BAKER	Eng	75	70	68	76	289	1	7250.00	4537.66
	Fredrik LINDGREN	Swe	74	71	70	74	289	1	7250.00	4537.66
	Fredrik JACOBSON	Swe	74	72	71	72	289	1	7250.00	4537.66
	Iain PYMAN	Eng	74	69	73	73	289	1	7250.00	4537.66
	Retief GOOSEN	SA	74	71	71	73	289	1	7250.00	4537.66
47	Roger CHAPMAN	Eng	74	72	70	74	290	2	5625.00	3520.60
	Santiago LUNA	Sp	74	72	71	73	290	2	5625.00	3520.60
	Mattias ELIASSON	Swe	75	71	73	71	290	2	5625.00	3520.60
	Stephen LEANEY	Aus	73	70	72	75	290	2	5625.00	3520.60
	Hennie OTTO	SA	71	71	74	74	290	2	5625.00	3520.60
	Stephen FIELD	Eng	71	75	70	74	290	2	5625.00	3520.60
	Joakim HAEGGMAN	Swe	72	74	72	72	290	2	5625.00	3520.60
54	Costantino ROCCA	It	72	74	69	76	291	3	4150.00	2597.42
	Sam TORRANCE	Scot	70	75	74	72	291	3	4150.00	2597.42
	Per NYMAN	Swe	73	70	74	74	291	3	4150.00	2597.42
	John MELLOR	Eng	75	69	73	74	291	3	4150.00	2597.42
	Brett RUMFORD	Aus	70	73	80	68	291	3	4150.00	2597.42
59	Andrew OLDCORN	Scot	72	74	72	74	292	4	3437.50	2151.48
	Jeremy ROBINSON	Eng	75	71	74	72	292	4	3437.50	2151.48
	Ian HUTCHINGS	SA	74	69	75	74	292	4	3437.50	2151.48
	Raymond RUSSELL	Scot	71	74	75	72	292	4	3437.50	2151.48
63	Sandy LYLE	Scot	74	71	75	73	293	5	3062.50	1916.77
	Daren LEE	Eng	72	74	73	74	293	5	3062.50	1916.77
65	Craig HAINLINE	USA	74	71	77	72	294	6	2569.17	1608.00
	Paolo QUIRICI	Swi	75	71	77	71	294	6	2569.17	1608.00
	Massimo FLORIOLI	It	71	75	76	72	294	6	2569.17	1608.00
	Diego BORREGO	Sp	73	73	74	74	294	6	2569.17	1608.00
	David PARK	Wal	74	71	76	73	294	6	2569.17	1608.00
	Stephen GALLACHER	Scot	75	69	73	77	294	6	2569.17	1608.00
71	Greig HUTCHEON	Scot	73	71	73	78	295	7	1870.50	1170.72
	Chris HALL	Eng	70	75	76	74	295	7	1870.50	1170.72
	Francisco CEA	Sp	74	72	74	75	295	7	1870.50	1170.72
	Ivo GINER	Sp	72	72	76	75	295	7	1870.50	1170.72
75	Peter FOWLER	Aus	72	72	76	79	299	11	1863.00	1166.02
76	Johan SKOLD	Swe	73	71	76	80	300	12	1860.00	1164.14

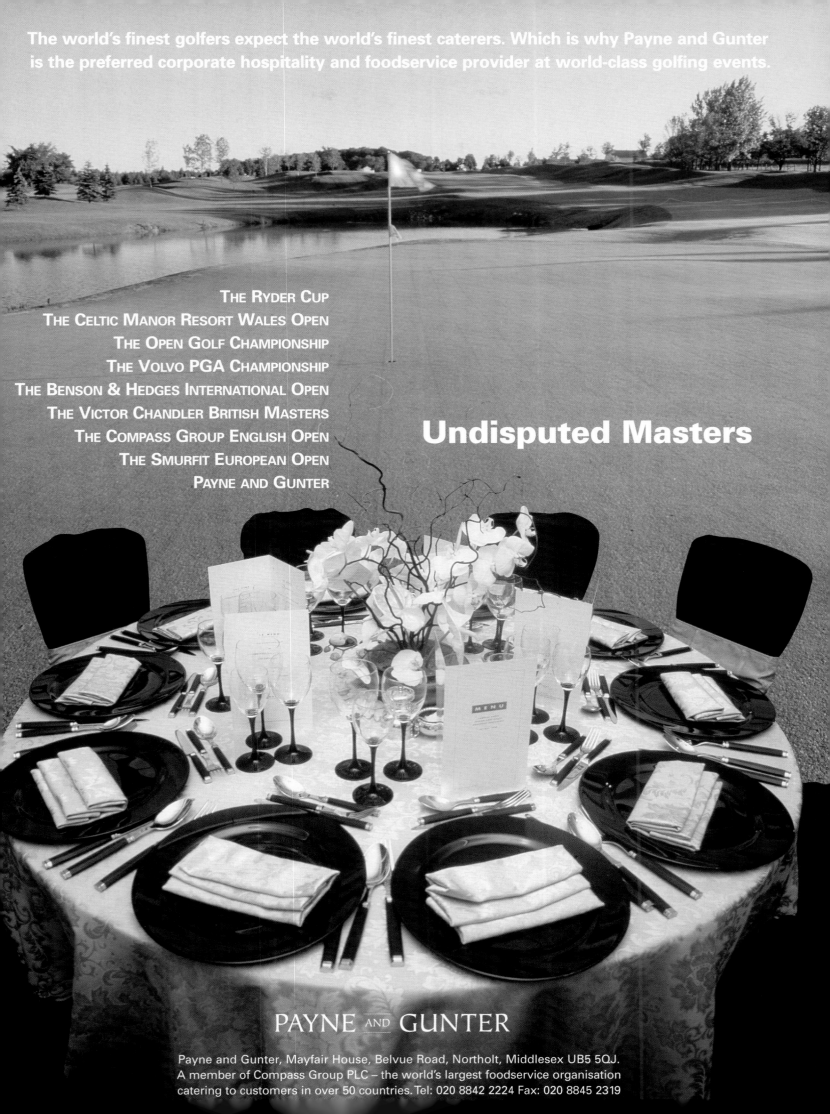

Crossing the Rubicon

CELTIC MANOR RESORT, NEWPORT, WALES

When Steen Tinning crossed the Severn Bridge from England into Wales in his hire car, he had no idea he would have to pay a toll charge of £4.20. When he made the return drive four days later he was even more surprised to be in possession of a cheque for 200,000 euro (£125,000).

The 37-year-old Danish journeyman, after setting sail from Copenhagen for the European Tour 14 long years ago, landed his maiden victory, appropriately enough, at Newport, the haven for the inaugural Celtic Manor Resort Wales Open.

It was Tinning's first visit to the Principality but it won't be his last. More often than not he had pitched up at a tournament without anywhere to stay but when he arrived at the Celtic Manor Resort he was delighted to find he was in five star splendour.

Nor did he know what to expect of Wentwood Hills, the third and most extravagant course built in Celtic Manor's rolling hillsides. "When I first saw it I thought I should have brought my skis," Tinnings said, "but I grew to love it."

Steen Tinning

Despite the misgivings of several players, who thought they were in Beverly Hills rather than the Usk Valley, Wentwood Hills, almost 7,400 yards off the back tees, did not behave like a precocious newcomer.

Robert Coles, a young Londoner, set the target on day one with a stunning 64. Also on the leaderboard were Mark James, Ian, Woosnam and Garbutt, and a Dane – Anders Hansen. Woosnam, naturally, was the local favourite.

At a resort which he had helped to promote an indoor academy and a bar both bear his name - the little Welshman was at home. "It's nice to have the crowd behind you," he said. "It's lovely to hear the Welsh accent coming out. They were willing my putts to go in."

Fredrik Jacobson

Wentwood Hills, which only opened in 1999, was designed by the Trent Jones dynasty of America (Robert Trent Jones Snr was born in Aberystwyth) for Dr Terry Matthews to the highest specification. Matthews, an electronics billionaire who was born at a nursing home on the site, did not only want a championship layout but a course that would bring the Ryder Cup to Wales.

On the eve of the first Wales Open, Celtic Manor's bid to host the Cup in 2009 was officially launched. At a Gala Dinner in one of the hotel's enormous conference rooms, Max Boyce, the Welsh comedian, was able to say: "I was there." So was the regimental goat of the Royal Welsh Fusiliers.

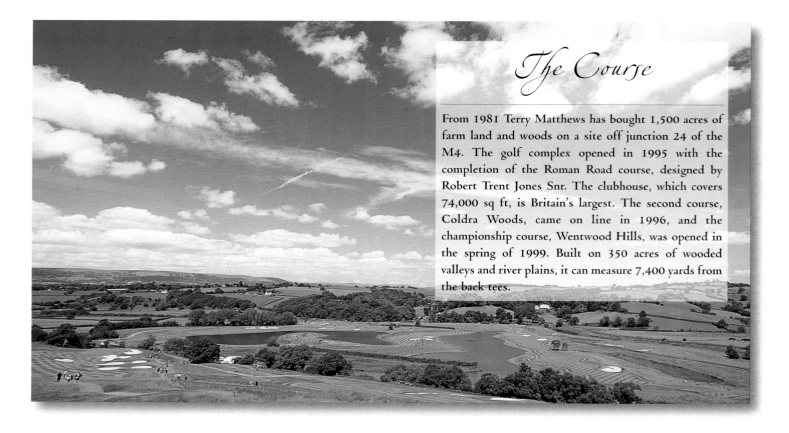

The Course

From 1981 Terry Matthews has bought 1,500 acres of farm land and woods on a site off junction 24 of the M4. The golf complex opened in 1995 with the completion of the Roman Road course, designed by Robert Trent Jones Snr. The clubhouse, which covers 74,000 sq ft, is Britain's largest. The second course, Coldra Woods, came on line in 1996, and the championship course, Wentwood Hills, was opened in the spring of 1999. Built on 350 acres of wooded valleys and river plains, it can measure 7,400 yards from the back tees.

David Howell

And go in they did. As Coles crashed with a 79, Woosnam followed a 68 with a 69 to move to seven under par, level with Mark McNulty and a stroke ahead of Tinning. The cut was made at two over par.

At the age of 42, Woosnam had not won anything since 1997 but he was where the public wanted him to be, on top of the leaderboard. The third round was played in perfect conditions and the Welshman carried on the good work, particularly over the front nine. He went to the turn in just 30 strokes but, significantly perhaps, came home with nine pars. The inward half is the more severe test, particularly its closing holes which are uphill. Woosnam's 66 was matched by Tinning who remained a stroke off the lead.

The two were paired for the final assault on Sunday when a crowd of 15,000 took to the Hills. The question: Would Woosnam have the stamina to hold on? Tinning had said he would not feel at all uncomfortable playing with a Welshman in front of a Welsh crowd and so it proved.

As Woosnam failed to reproduce the form of the first three rounds, coming in with a 73 that included five bogeys, the baton was taken up by David Howell, who hit the front at 14 under par. However, Howell's 68 included a fatal bogey five on the penultimate hole where he missed a three foot putt.

Tinning impressively negotiated the back nine, recovering from a bogey on the short 12th with three birdies to come home in 34 for a 69. At 15 under for the championship, he finished a stroke in front of Howell and three in front of Woosnam and Fredrik Jacboson.

"This is fantastic for me," Tinning said. "The only thing better than this was the birth of my two kids." His previous highest finish had been joint fourth in the Madeira Island Open in 1995 but his career had been seriously interrupted by amateur drivers. He nearly lost his right arm in a car crash in Germany in 1990 and in1999 had the thumb on his right hand smashed by a ball driven by an amateur on a company day. Restored to physical well being, Tinning had been working on the mental side of the game with Arne Nielsson, a Danish world champion canoeist. For one thing, it meant he wasn't up the Usk without a paddle. "If your game is good but you are not mentally strong you are never going to win," Tinning said. "Of course I was shaking over the last putt but playing with Woosie was a pleasure and the crowd couldn't have been fairer."

For Tinning, who received a handsome silver trophy complete with dragon from Dr Matthews, the victory represented an irrevocable step, the crossing not so much of the rivers Severn and Usk as the Rubicon. That was the waterway crossed by Julius Caesar, precipitating the war which brought him to power, and as Celtic Manor occupies the site of what was once a Roman fortress there is only one salute: et tu Steen.

Tim Glover

Bunkered! Ian Woosnam escapes

Shot of the Week

The 14th hole at Celtic Manor is an uphill par three of 184 yards and it had a crucial bearing on the destiny of The Celtic Manor Resort Wales Open in the final round. Five birdies in 13 holes lifted David Howell to 15 under par and the outright lead. However, at the 14th he missed the green and took bogey. Tinning, who had dropped a shot at the 12th, then hit the greatest five iron of his career, to within a foot at the 14th for a tap in two.

Shot with a View: Mark James

CELTIC MANOR RESORT, NEWPORT, WALES, 8-11 JUNE 2000, PAR 72, 7324 YARDS, 6698 METRES

Pos.	Name		Rd1	Rd2	Rd3	Rd4	Total	Par	Prize Money Euro	£
1	Steen TINNING	Den	70	68	66	69	273	-15	199838.75	125000.00
2	David HOWELL	Eng	72	67	67	68	274	-14	133220.50	83330.00
3	Ian WOOSNAM	Wal	68	69	66	73	276	-12	67505.53	42225.00
	Fredrik JACOBSON	Swe	71	68	70	67	276	-12	67505.53	42225.00
5	Mark MCNULTY	Zim	70	67	72	69	278	-10	42925.37	26850.00
	Nick O'HERN	Aus	71	68	69	70	278	-10	42925.37	26850.00
	Phillip PRICE	Wal	71	70	72	65	278	-10	42925.37	26850.00
8	Gordon BRAND JNR.	Scot	72	70	68	69	279	-9	25719.25	16087.50
	Mark JAMES	Eng	67	72	69	71	279	-9	25719.25	16087.50
	Ian GARBUTT	Eng	68	71	67	73	279	-9	25719.25	16087.50
	Robert COLES	Eng	64	79	67	69	279	-9	25719.25	16087.50
12	David LYNN	Eng	71	73	69	68	281	-7	19963.89	12487.50
	Henrik NYSTROM	Swe	71	71	64	75	281	-7	19963.89	12487.50
14	John SENDEN	Aus	69	75	70	68	282	-6	17625.78	11025.00
	Andrew COLTART	Scot	72	74	65	71	282	-6	17625.78	11025.00
	Brett RUMFORD	Aus	70	71	71	70	282	-6	17625.78	11025.00
17	Andrew OLDCORN	Scot	70	74	68	71	283	-5	15227.71	9525.00
	Maarten LAFEBER	Hol	73	69	71	70	283	-5	15227.71	9525.00
	Richard GREEN	Aus	74	71	69	69	283	-5	15227.71	9525.00
	Jamie SPENCE	Eng	71	70	70	72	283	-5	15227.71	9525.00
21	Robert Jan DERKSEN	Hol	72	70	68	74	284	-4	13009.51	8137.50
	Soren KJELDSEN	Den	72	71	72	69	284	-4	13009.51	8137.50
	Jeremy ROBINSON	Eng	73	71	70	70	284	-4	13009.51	8137.50
	Carl SUNESON	Sp	70	71	67	76	284	-4	13009.51	8137.50
	Roger WESSELS	SA	70	76	69	69	284	-4	13009.51	8137.50
	David PARK	Wal	69	71	73	71	284	-4	13009.51	8137.50
27	Roger CHAPMAN	Eng	69	73	73	70	285	-3	11570.67	7237.50
	Stephen ALLAN	Aus	74	69	72	70	285	-3	11570.67	7237.50
29	Barry LANE	Eng	69	73	67	77	286	-2	9532.31	5962.50
	Marc FARRY	Fr	73	72	72	69	286	-2	9532.31	5962.50
	Anders HANSEN	Den	68	73	70	75	286	-2	9532.31	5962.50
	Thomas LEVET	Fr	69	73	71	73	286	-2	9532.31	5962.50
	Peter BAKER	Eng	70	76	68	72	286	-2	9532.31	5962.50
	Fredrik LINDGREN	Swe	74	72	67	73	286	-2	9532.31	5962.50
	Gary EVANS	Eng	72	74	71	69	286	-2	9532.31	5962.50
	Pierre FULKE	Swe	71	75	69	71	286	-2	9532.31	5962.50
	Gary ORR	Scot	71	74	71	70	286	-2	9532.31	5962.50
	David CARTER	Eng	76	68	71	71	286	-2	9532.31	5962.50
39	Mark MOULAND	Wal	74	71	73	69	287	-1	7314.10	4575.00
	Marcus CAIN	Aus	73	71	70	73	287	-1	7314.10	4575.00
	Jarrod MOSELEY	Aus	72	72	70	73	287	-1	7314.10	4575.00
	Roger WINCHESTER	Eng	70	71	74	72	287	-1	7314.10	4575.00
	Paul AFFLECK	Wal	74	70	71	72	287	-1	7314.10	4575.00
	Iain PYMAN	Eng	67	75	74	71	287	-1	7314.10	4575.00
	Alastair FORSYTH	Scot	73	72	69	73	287	-1	7314.10	4575.00
46	Stephen LEANEY	Aus	72	74	65	77	288	0	5395.65	3375.00
	Domingo HOSPITAL	Sp	73	72	69	74	288	0	5395.65	3375.00
	Thomas GÖGELE	Ger	73	71	74	70	288	0	5395.65	3375.00
	Per NYMAN	Swe	72	69	75	72	288	0	5395.65	3375.00
	Nicolas VANHOOTEGEM	Bel	70	71	76	71	288	0	5395.65	3375.00
	Van PHILLIPS	Eng	74	69	75	70	288	0	5395.65	3375.00
	Dean ROBERTSON	Scot	71	75	67	75	288	0	5395.65	3375.00
	Daren LEE	Eng	74	70	72	72	288	0	5395.65	3375.00
	Ivo GINER	Sp	67	77	70	74	288	0	5395.65	3375.00
55	Anthony WALL	Eng	70	72	76	71	289	1	3866.88	2418.75
	Paul EALES	Eng	72	71	71	75	289	1	3866.88	2418.75
	Joakim HAEGGMAN	Swe	71	71	74	73	289	1	3866.88	2418.75
	Simon DYSON	Eng	72	72	70	75	289	1	3866.88	2418.75
59	Sam TORRANCE	Scot	73	71	71	75	290	2	3297.34	2062.50
	Philip GOLDING	Eng	70	76	74	70	290	2	3297.34	2062.50
	Steven RICHARDSON	Eng	73	69	74	74	290	2	3297.34	2062.50
	Wei-Tze YEH	Taiwan	72	73	72	73	290	2	3297.34	2062.50
63	Ross DRUMMOND	Scot	70	74	70	77	291	3	2817.73	1762.50
	Ross MCFARLANE	Eng	70	68	78	75	291	3	2817.73	1762.50
	Elliot BOULT	NZ	71	75	75	70	291	3	2817.73	1762.50
	Max ANGLERT	Swe	72	68	78	73	291	3	2817.73	1762.50
67	Peter O'MALLEY	Aus	75	71	76	70	292	4	2458.02	1537.50
	Mark PLUMMER	Eng	72	74	72	74	292	4	2458.02	1537.50
69	Andrew BEAL	Eng	74	69	74	76	293	5	2089.46	1306.97
	Paul MCGINLEY	Ire	77	67	68	81	293	5	2089.46	1306.97
	Simon WAKEFIELD	Eng	70	75	74	74	293	5	2089.46	1306.97
72	Soren HANSEN	Den	72	73	75	74	294	6	1794.00	1122.15
	Raymond RUSSELL	Scot	70	69	80	75	294	6	1794.00	1122.15
	Lucas PARSONS	Aus	72	74	73	75	294	6	1794.00	1122.15
75	Philip WALTON	Ire	72	70	80	73	295	7	1786.00	1117.15
	Mark LITTON	Wal	70	76	73	76	295	7	1786.00	1117.15
	Richard DINSDALE	Wal	73	70	73	79	295	7	1786.00	1117.15
78	Michael JONZON	Swe	74	70	79	74	297	9	1780.00	1113.40

We'd like to introduce you to the biggest hitter on the European Tour...

...National Car Rental! With more than 250,000 vehicles at nearly 3000 locations worldwide, we're confident we can get you the right car in the right place for the right price - wherever you are.

As the official car rental company of the PGA European Tour, we know a thing or two about getting from tee to green. And even more about driving. If you or your company rent cars, you won't find a more versatile or dependable partner than National. We offer the widest choice of quality self drive cars at preferential rates. Whether it's business or pleasure, we'll design the right package for you. So don't under-club your next trip, drive National and get there with ease. Call us now on: **+44 (0) 1273 223308** or visit our website at: **www.nationalcar-europe.com**

As Good as it Gets

PEBBLE BEACH GOLF LINKS, CALIFORNIA, USA

By any yardstick, European golfers had a good week at Pebble Beach. There was only one huge problem. Tiger Woods had the kind of week that made the 100th US Open, already an historic occasion, truly special. If it is possible, Woods produced an even greater performance than his first major victory at the Masters Tournament in 1997.

Then Woods won by 12 strokes but here, in more testing conditions, the reigning US PGA champion won by 15 strokes from Ernie Els and Miguel Angel Jiménez. Woods smashed an 138-year-old record for major championships. Old Tom Morris won the third Open Championship in 1862 by 13 shots when a small group of Scots played three 12-hole rounds at Prestwick in one day.

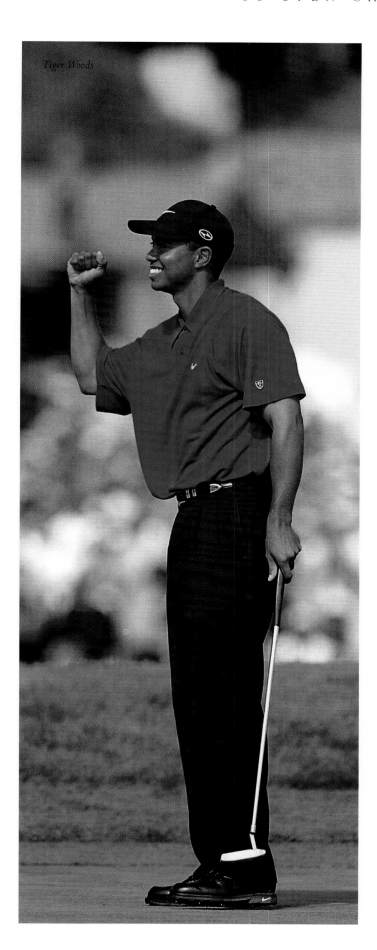

Tiger Woods

It was Woods's third win in a different major, leaving only a victory in the Open Championship to join Gene Sarazen, Ben Hogan, Gary Player and Jack Nicklaus as winners of all four. "That's what I had in mind coming into this week," Woods said. "If there were any two tournaments to seal the Grand Slam, Pebble Beach and St Andrews are the ones. It doesn't get any better than that.

"The other two majors were great wins but, for an American, it is an incredible feeling being our national champion. You think about this as a kid and to do it on Father's Day. I can't wait to give the trophy to my dad to hold.

"All week I had a sense of calm that I haven't had for a while, since Augusta. Whatever happened I was able to keep focused and concentrate on every shot. Today I was determined not to make a bogey."

Starting the final day with a ten-stroke lead, a new record for the US Open, Woods, the first wire-to-wire winner for 30 years, did not need to go low as he had with an opening 65. But as then he did not drop a stroke in his 67. After parring the entire front nine, Woods finally birdied the tenth and added another at the 12th, making him only the second player, after Gil Morgan at Pebble Beach eight years ago, to reach ten under par in the US Open.

The 24-year-old became the first to finish in double digits after further birdies at the 13th and 14th. He missed only three greens in

Joint runner-up: Miguel Angel Jiménez

José Maria Olazábal

regulation, saving par each time and nearly holing a bunker shot at the 17th. He finished 12 under par, while his aggregate of 272 equalled the record held by Nicklaus and Lee Janzen.

Woods might have improved on that figure further but for the US Golf Association's decision to reduce the second hole from a par five to a tough par four of 484 yards. There was also the little matter of the triple bogey at the fourth on Saturday. On a day when the windy conditions sent the average score up to 77, Woods still managed a level par 71. The only player to score better was Els with a 68.

The South African played alongside Woods on the final day. "It was kind of embarrassing to be 15 shots back," said Els, the double US Open champion. "You knew he meant business today. He was awesome. It was a dominating performance. Whatever I say will be an understatement. Who knows where he will go from here? It has always been my goal to win all four major championships but with Tiger I've got my work cut out for the next ten years."

This was a sublime performance by the game's best player in peak form. With Pebble Beach proving an exacting test in the wind, precise ball-striking alone would not have been enough. Imagination in shot-making was essential and no one has more variety of shots than Woods.

His putting was reminiscent of his 12-stroke Masters win. When he needed to hole a putt, it disappeared. "What has surprised me is I've been able to do it in a US Open," Woods said.

Joint runner up: Ernie Els

"At a US Open it is so hard to go low. At Augusta then there was no rough and you could bomb the ball as far as you wanted and knew it would be on the fairway. This week it is not that way. You need to grind away and hit the fairway at all costs. I've hit some weird clubs off the tees, but I've kept it in play.

"And I've been able to make the big putts this week. There comes a point in a round where you have to make that big par putt to keep the momentum going and I've done that. It's the weirdest feeling but to hole a par putt in a major championship from eight or ten feet is an even better feeling than making a birdie."

Els said: "It seems we have really got a dominant figure in golf, in any sport, with Tiger. He's probably the most recognisable sportsman on the planet right now. It's good for golf but it would be even better if someone could step up and play with him. I've had my run-ins with Tiger but not enough. I'd like some more battles with him."

Els was unable to win the race for second place on his own, Jiménez catching him with a closing 71. The 36-year-old gave Spain their best ever US Open result after opening with a 66. "I feel great," said Jiménez. "After two rounds, Tiger was playing a different tournament and I was playing against everyone else. On this course you had to concentrate and keep your intensity on all the time. It says something about the quality of players around the world."

Jack Nicklaus

Tiger Woods, well supported in all sorts of guises

Lee Westwood

It was an atypical US Open leaderboard with five European Tour players in the top seven. Padraig Harrington and Lee Westwood had superb weeks to tie for fifth, as did Nick Faldo. His seventh place was his first top-ten in a major championship for four years and it booked his place in the US Open for next year. "My other goal was to finish less than 20 behind Tiger!" Faldo said.

Westwood claimed his own piece of history by becoming the first player to eagle the par-five 18th in the second round, holing an 80-foot putt from off the front of the green. "I never thought I'd see 12 under in a US Open," Westwood said.

"They do their best for people not to shoot 12 under here. They thought level par would win this week and it has won the other tournament. But it was nice to see the leaderboard crammed with Europeans. It shows we can play a bit. It was not so much the conditions, we just played better than most of the Americans - apart from the one who turned it into a parade."

Andy Farrell

Padraig Harrington

Shot of the Week

At the sixth hole on Friday evening, Woods drove into the thick rough on the right of the fairway. He had over 200 yards to the green and was hitting uphill over a tree. Demonstrating his immense strength, Woods hit a seven iron onto the green and two-putted for birdie. He even allowed himself a smile after the shot. Other players were still talking about it days later. "Most of us would have to punch the ball out 30 yards," said Darren Clarke.

Tiger Woods left everyone else chasing shadows

PEBBLE BEACH GOLF LINKS, CALIFORNIA, USA, 15-18 JUNE 2000, PAR 71, 6846 YARDS, 6261 METRES

Pos.	Name		Rd1	Rd2	Rd3	Rd4	Total	Par	Prize Money Euro	£
1	Tiger WOODS	USA	65	69	71	67	272	-12	839806.35	530539.16
2	Miguel Angel JIMÉNEZ	Sp	66	74	76	71	287	3	409563.07	258737.32
	Ernie ELS	SA	74	73	68	72	287	3	409563.07	258737.32
4	John HUSTON	USA	67	75	76	70	288	4	223366.45	141109.49
5	Padraig HARRINGTON	Ire	73	71	72	73	289	5	170612.96	107783.01
	Lee WESTWOOD	Eng	71	71	76	71	289	5	170612.96	107783.01
7	Nick FALDO	Eng	69	74	76	71	290	6	144029.95	90989.46
8	Loren ROBERTS	USA	68	78	73	72	291	7	118377.00	74783.47
	David DUVAL	USA	75	71	74	71	291	7	118377.00	74783.47
	Stewart CINK	USA	77	72	72	70	291	7	118377.00	74783.47
	Vijay SINGH	Fiji	70	73	80	68	291	7	118377.00	74783.47
12	José Maria OLAZÁBAL	Sp	70	71	76	75	292	8	90513.28	57180.85
	Paul AZINGER	USA	71	73	79	69	292	8	90513.28	57180.85
	Retief GOOSEN	SA	77	72	72	71	292	8	90513.28	57180.85
	Michael CAMPBELL	NZ	71	77	71	73	292	8	90513.28	57180.85
16	Justin LEONARD	USA	73	73	75	72	293	9	68458.92	43248.23
	Mike WEIR	Can	76	72	76	69	293	9	68458.92	43248.23
	Fred COUPLES	USA	70	75	75	73	293	9	68458.92	43248.23
	Scott HOCH	USA	73	76	75	69	293	9	68458.92	43248.23
	Phil MICKELSON	USA	71	73	73	76	293	9	68458.92	43248.23
	David TOMS	USA	73	76	72	72	293	9	68458.92	43248.23
22	Notah BEGAY III	USA	74	75	72	73	294	10	55747.39	35217.85
23	Hal SUTTON	USA	69	73	83	70	295	11	47802.82	30198.95
	Bob MAY	USA	72	76	75	72	295	11	47802.82	30198.95
	Tom LEHMAN	USA	71	73	78	73	295	11	47802.82	30198.95
	Mike BRISKY	USA	71	73	79	72	295	11	47802.82	30198.95
27	Tom WATSON	USA	71	74	78	73	296	12	35761.05	22591.68
	Nick PRICE	Zim	77	70	78	71	296	12	35761.05	22591.68
	Steve STRICKER	USA	75	74	75	72	296	12	35761.05	22591.68
	Steve JONES	USA	75	75	74	72	296	12	35761.05	22591.68
	Hale IRWIN	USA	68	78	81	69	296	12	35761.05	22591.68
32	Tom KITE	USA	72	77	77	71	297	13	29652.51	18732.67
	Chris PERRY	USA	75	72	78	72	297	13	29652.51	18732.67
	Richard ZOKOL	Can	74	74	80	69	297	13	29652.51	18732.67
	Rocco MEDIATE	USA	69	76	75	77	297	13	29652.51	18732.67
	Lee PORTER	USA	74	70	83	70	297	13	29652.51	18732.67
37	Woody AUSTIN	USA	77	70	78	73	298	14	23153.45	14626.96
	Jerry KELLY	USA	73	73	81	71	298	14	23153.45	14626.96
	Larry MIZE	USA	73	72	76	77	298	14	23153.45	14626.96
	Craig PARRY	Aus	73	74	76	75	298	14	23153.45	14626.96
	Bobby CLAMPETT	USA	68	77	76	77	298	14	23153.45	14626.96
	Angel CABRERA	Arg	69	76	79	74	298	14	23153.45	14626.96
	Lee JANZEN	USA	71	73	79	75	298	14	23153.45	14626.96
	Ted TRYBA	USA	71	73	79	75	298	14	23153.45	14626.96
	Charles WARREN	USA	75	74	75	74	298	14	23153.45	14626.96
46	Rick HARTMANN	USA	73	75	75	76	299	15	16681.71	10538.50
	Sergio GARCIA	Sp	75	71	81	72	299	15	16681.71	10538.50
	Colin MONTGOMERIE	Scot	73	74	79	73	299	15	16681.71	10538.50
	Scott VERPLANK	USA	72	74	78	75	299	15	16681.71	10538.50
	Thomas BJÖRN	Den	70	70	82	77	299	15	16681.71	10538.50
51	Warren SCHUTTE	SA	74	75	74	77	300	16	14253.62	9004.58
	Mark O'MEARA	USA	74	74	78	74	300	16	14253.62	9004.58
53	Darren CLARKE	N.Ire	71	75	83	72	301	17	13381.27	8453.48
	Keith CLEARWATER	USA	74	74	80	73	301	17	13381.27	8453.48
	Jeff COSTON	USA	70	77	80	74	301	17	13381.27	8453.48
56	Kirk TRIPLETT	USA	70	71	84	77	302	18	12757.70	8059.55
57	Dave EICHELBERGER	USA	78	69	77	79	303	19	12345.16	7798.93
	Jimmy GREEN	USA	74	75	77	77	303	19	12345.16	7798.93
59	Jeffrey WILSON (Am)	USA	74	72	82	76	304	20		
60	Jim FURYK	USA	72	74	84	75	305	21	11993.48	7576.76
61	Brandel CHAMBLEE	USA	70	77	82	77	306	22	11698.50	7390.41
	Carlos Daniel FRANCO	Par	74	75	75	82	306	22	11698.50	7390.41
63	Robert DAMRON	USA	72	73	84	84	313	29	11402.48	7203.40

Let the Good Times Roll

DE VERE SLALEY HALL, NORTHUMBERLAND, ENGLAND

Compaq Managing Director Joe McNally stepped in when Lee Westwood claimed he hadn't had time to buy wife Laurae a birthday present - he handed over her 27-year-old husband's 170,276 euro (£108,330) cheque after the Englishman had completed a three-stroke win in the Compaq European Grand Prix at De Vere Slaley Hall.

Compaq will return next year to back the tournament and, hopefully, so will Westwood to defend his title, and perhaps then he will have the US Open trophy to give Laurae as a birthday present.

Westwood's dash back from Pebble Beach was probably a good enough excuse not to have had time to buy the birthday present, but Laurae surely forgave him after a performance of consummate quality to win at De Vere Slaley Hall.

A closing round of 70, two under par, held off Sweden's Fredrik Jacobson, who made a determined late bid to come from three shots back and snatch victory. Jacobson did get it down to one with three holes left but crucially bogeyed the 16th and Westwood birdied to re-establish his three-shot cushion and that's how it finished.

Westwood had moved into the lead at the halfway stage of the tournament when it seemed the week would belong to Ryder Cup captain Sam Torrance, who scored a hole in one at the 14th on his way to a six under par 66 and the first round lead.

The 46-year-old Scot arrived at Slaley having won a pro-am at Sunningdale with a sparkling 64 and he continued that form when he covered the back nine in 30 following that seven iron ace and equalled the Tour record of 20 putts, he needed just eight on the back nine.

Darren Clarke and Westwood were both feeling the effects of jet lag following the US Open and professed they were finding it hard to adjust back to British time. But their respective scores of 69 and 68 indicated their golf was in fine shape even if they were not.

Torrance's hopes - and those of many others - were blown away on day two with winds gusting up to 40 miles an hour and only Westwood, Jacobson and Belgian Nicolas Vanhootegem mastered the conditions to break par.

Westwood was simply superb with a second successive 68 to lead by three from Jacobson and it was, in the opinion of many, one of the best rounds of golf seen on the European Tour so far during 2000.

Fredrik Jacobson

Emanuele Canonica

Shot of the Week

Sam Torrance's seven iron ace at the 179 yards 14th in
the first round would normally qualify for shot of the
week and it was a remarkable first day three ball
because Peter Mitchell had holed a four iron from 220
yards at the 562 yards par five 11th for an albatross two
and Australian Lucas Parsons came within a whisker of
making an ace at the 17th and winning the car that was
on offer there. But the shot of the week was
undoubtedly Lee Westwood's chip in from 80 yards for
a stunning eagle three at the 12th on day two in gusting
40 mph winds as he cruised to a stunning back nine of
31, five under par, after being one over at the turn.

Body Language: Stephen Allan shows the way

Westwood put together a stunning back nine of 31, five under par, after being one over at the turn with a three-putt at the third. It was shot-making at its very best and he birdied the tenth from 30 feet, belted a six iron on to the par five 11th to set up another birdie and then chipped in from 80 yards for a stunning eagle three at the 12th.

He nearly chipped in again at the 16th after his drive had clipped a tree and he missed the green with his second before lipping out for birdie at the 17th. The round ended in real style with a 15 foot downhill putt for birdie at the 18th.

There was no change at the top of the leaderboard or the margin of Westwood's lead on day three, but the 27-year-old had to grind out a two under par 70 after struggling with a painful back problem.

Jacobson also posted a 70 with a brave birdie on the 18th to be one ahead of Andrew Oldcorn, who shot the best round of the day, a 66, one off the course record. Meanwhile Clarke moved back into contention with a 68 to be six shots back - the same gap he made up at the Marriott Forest of Arden Hotel to win The Compass Group English Open.

Westwood pulled a muscle in his back when he hit his tee shot on the fourth and he needed treatment from physiotherapist Rob Hillman and also took some painkillers. He missed a short putt on the second to drop a shot but immediately got it back with a birdie at the next and did exactly the same when he bogeyed the eighth by picking up a birdie at Slaley's signature hole, the ninth.

Despite, or perhaps because of, the treatment for his back problems, Westwood birdied both the 11th and the 16th to stay in front of Jacobson, who ended a disappointing day with some cheer when he birdied from 20 feet on the 18th.

Oldcorn's best of the day 66 was a welcome return to form after he had missed ten weeks on Tour with a virus he picked up on the way back from Australia. Clarke's 68 was frustrating for the big Ulsterman, who reckoned he had needed a 65 to put pressure on the leaders. His coach, Butch Harmon, left a message on his phone that he had seen Clarke on The Golf Channel and that he was moving his head when he putted.

It seemed it would be a procession when Westwood birdied the first in the final round but he could not find the spark to ignite his game and Jacobson mounted a real charge when he birdied 11, 12 and 15. But the Swede ruined his chance when he pushed his tee shot into the bunker at 16 and didn't come out well enough to make the green. Westwood immediately wedged to five feet and made birdie to Jacobson's bogey and the gap was back to three.

"I expected it to be difficult," said Westwood, ``and I was actually a bit relieved when no-one really came at me on the front nine. Freddie came at me a little bit and then birdied 15 to get it down to one but then I birdied 16 and he bogeyed and it was back to three so I suppose I made the most of his mistake."

Both players bogeyed the last after indifferent shots with Westwood nearly making par, his 35 footer hanging over the hole so much that he felt he had to tap it in instead of following the tradition of making it the last shot of the tournament.

"Somebody started celebrating early and opened a can of Newcy Brown on the last tee and it put me off a bit, but it wasn't a problem," he said. "When the putt finished it was overhanging the hole quite a bit and I didn't want to mark it in case it fell into the hole when I replaced it or addressed the ball. I didn't want it all to get a bit silly and Freddie's putt wasn't going to affect the result anyway and he was okay about it.

"When you're in front it's easy to lose your composure and you see people do that when they're in that position and the key is not to panic and not to deviate from your game plan.

"I knew I was playing well coming back from Pebble Beach. My short game was sharp, my putting was pretty good and my game tee to green was pretty good as well. The key was not letting the jetlag get to me on the first day and play myself out of the tournament and just keep plugging away."

Only a month before Slaley, Westwood had been in the depths of despair with his game and then everything clicked at Gut Kaden in the Deutsche Bank – SAP Open TPC of Europe where he shot a closing 64 to overhaul Tiger Woods and win the tournament.

"Winning in Germany after going through a bad patch did me good," he added. "It makes you appreciate the good times more when you have been through a bad patch."

Alan Hedley

The Course

There were some changes made to the David Thomas-designed Hunting course (there is now a second course, the Priestman) at De Vere Slaley Hall. Lee Westwood described the course as being in the best condition he had seen it – and that was before he won! New greens had been built at the third and seventh to reduce slopes, but Slaley's difficulty still lies in it's undulating greens and good mix of tree-lined, moorland and parkland holes with the front nine undoubtedly the tougher test.

Lee Westwood, en route to victory

DE VERE SLALEY HALL, NORTHUMBERLAND, ENGLAND, 22-25 JUNE 2000, PAR 72, 7088 YARDS, 6480 METRES

Pos.	Name		Rd1	Rd2	Rd3	Rd4	Total	Par	Euro	£
1	Lee WESTWOOD	Eng	68	68	70	70	276	-12	170276.35	108330.00
2	Fredrik JACOBSON	Swe	69	70	70	70	279	-9	113517.56	72220.00
3	Emanuele CANONICA	It	69	73	71	68	281	-7	57521.12	36595.00
	Darren CLARKE	N.Ire	69	75	68	69	281	-7	57521.12	36595.00
5	Andrew OLDCORN	Scot	71	73	66	72	282	-6	43319.63	27560.00
6	Jamie SPENCE	Eng	69	74	72	69	284	-4	33204.91	21125.00
	Stephen ALLAN	Aus	71	73	71	69	284	-4	33204.91	21125.00
8	Nicolas VANHOOTEGEM	Bel	70	71	72	72	285	-3	25542.24	16250.00
9	Greg TURNER	NZ	71	76	70	69	286	-2	21659.82	13780.00
	Elliot BOULT	NZ	69	76	71	70	286	-2	21659.82	13780.00
11	Peter FOWLER	Aus	70	80	69	68	287	-1	18799.08	11960.00
12	Gary EMERSON	Eng	71	74	70	73	288	0	17011.13	10822.50
	Massimo SCARPA	It	70	75	73	70	288	0	17011.13	10822.50
14	Sam TORRANCE	Scot	66	79	71	73	289	1	14712.33	9360.00
	Ian POULTER	Eng	69	78	70	72	289	1	14712.33	9360.00
	Olle KARLSSON	Swe	70	79	70	70	289	1	14712.33	9360.00
	Henrik NYSTROM	Swe	72	76	67	74	289	1	14712.33	9360.00
18	Richard GREEN	Aus	73	78	70	69	290	2	12490.16	7946.25
	Simon D. HURLEY	Eng	70	75	72	73	290	2	12490.16	7946.25
	Francisco CEA	Sp	67	77	74	72	290	2	12490.16	7946.25
	Andrew COLTART	Scot	68	81	72	69	290	2	12490.16	7946.25
22	Gordon BRAND JNR.	Scot	70	75	77	69	291	3	10472.32	6662.50
	Carl SUNESON	Sp	75	73	71	72	291	3	10472.32	6662.50
	Steven RICHARDSON	Eng	75	74	69	73	291	3	10472.32	6662.50
	Iain PYMAN	Eng	73	79	66	73	291	3	10472.32	6662.50
	Dean ROBERTSON	Scot	72	75	72	72	291	3	10472.32	6662.50
	Daren LEE	Eng	73	75	71	72	291	3	10472.32	6662.50
	David CARTER	Eng	72	75	71	73	291	3	10472.32	6662.50
	Graeme STORM	Eng	72	76	72	71	291	3	10472.32	6662.50
30	Nick O'HERN	Aus	73	79	72	68	292	4	8939.79	5687.50
	Alberto BINAGHI	It	70	75	75	72	292	4	8939.79	5687.50
32	Brian DAVIS	Eng	76	76	73	68	293	5	8045.81	5118.75
	Peter MITCHELL	Eng	71	79	73	70	293	5	8045.81	5118.75
	Diego BORREGO	Sp	72	74	75	72	293	5	8045.81	5118.75
	Paul LAWRIE	Scot	77	75	69	72	293	5	8045.81	5118.75
36	Mark MOULAND	Wal	74	77	70	73	294	6	6640.98	4225.00
	Anders HANSEN	Den	70	78	73	73	294	6	6640.98	4225.00
	Kenneth FERRIE	Eng	74	77	72	71	294	6	6640.98	4225.00
	Peter BAKER	Eng	73	76	73	72	294	6	6640.98	4225.00
	Domingo HOSPITAL	Sp	74	76	75	69	294	6	6640.98	4225.00
	Paul EALES	Eng	75	76	71	72	294	6	6640.98	4225.00
	Scott ROWE	USA	75	75	72	72	294	6	6640.98	4225.00
	Neil CHEETHAM	Eng	72	78	71	73	294	6	6640.98	4225.00
	David LYNN	Eng	77	75	68	74	294	6	6640.98	4225.00
45	Santiago LUNA	Sp	73	78	73	71	295	7	5006.28	3185.00
	Jean-Francois REMESY	Fr	75	75	72	73	295	7	5006.28	3185.00
	Greig HUTCHEON	Scot	76	74	71	74	295	7	5006.28	3185.00
	Shaun P WEBSTER	Eng	70	80	70	75	295	7	5006.28	3185.00
	Jonathan LOMAS	Eng	73	79	75	68	295	7	5006.28	3185.00
	Bradley DREDGE	Wal	71	79	70	75	295	7	5006.28	3185.00
	Jim PAYNE	Eng	73	76	76	70	295	7	5006.28	3185.00
52	Derrick COOPER	Eng	73	79	72	72	296	8	3439.69	2188.33
	Tom GILLIS	USA	74	77	75	70	296	8	3439.69	2188.33
	Euan LITTLE	Scot	77	74	72	73	296	8	3439.69	2188.33
	Michael ARCHER	Eng	71	81	73	71	296	8	3439.69	2188.33
	Jeremy ROBINSON	Eng	74	75	73	74	296	8	3439.69	2188.33
	Stephen FIELD	Eng	71	79	72	74	296	8	3439.69	2188.33
	Gary EVANS	Eng	73	77	73	73	296	8	3439.69	2188.33
	Tomas Jesus MUÑOZ	Sp	73	76	73	74	296	8	3439.69	2188.33
	Raymond RUSSELL	Scot	70	81	68	77	296	8	3439.69	2188.33
61	John BICKERTON	Eng	71	79	72	75	297	9	2707.48	1722.50
	Adam SCOTT	Aus	72	79	69	77	297	9	2707.48	1722.50
63	Marcus CAIN	Aus	75	76	76	71	298	10	2452.05	1560.00
	Robert WRAGG	Eng	75	77	77	69	298	10	2452.05	1560.00
	Wei-Tze YEH	Taiwan	73	76	76	73	298	10	2452.05	1560.00
66	Robin BYRD	USA	78	73	76	72	299	11	2145.55	1365.00
	Sebastien DELÁGRANGE	Fr	71	74	77	77	299	11	2145.55	1365.00
	Daniel CHOPRA	Swe	73	78	74	74	299	11	2145.55	1365.00
69	José Manuel CARRILES	Sp	72	80	74	74	300	12	1941.21	1235.00
70	Ian HUTCHINGS	SA	73	74	74	81	302	14	1870.48	1190.00
71	Stephen SCAHILL	NZ	73	79	78	73	303	15	1532.00	974.66
72	Nick LUDWELL	Eng	75	77	78	75	305	17	1529.00	972.75
73	Tony CAROLAN	Aus	76	76	74	80	306	18	1526.00	970.84

Patrik's Day

BALLYBUNION GOLF CLUB, CO KERRY, IRELAND

*I*t is the nature of seaside links to test the character of a man as well as his golf in what is essentially a battle against the elements and an examination of skills. Indeed when Patrik Sjöland first beheld the towering landscape of Ballybunion on the west coast of Ireland he declared: "This is an awesome course."

Moreover he wondered whether low scoring was actually possible on this stretch of majestic coastline that has become a shrine to so many golfers - Tom Watson (the millennium club captain) in particular - and was the setting for the Murphy's Irish Open. And

yet by the end of a momentus week, the genial Swede had held both Ballybunion and the massed ranks of the European Tour's finest campaigners at arm's length to become champion.

It had been a comprehensive display of scoring ability as well as downright determination as he edged past more high profile contenders with a performance none of them could quite match. From the outset, the two points of discussion centred on whether Sergio Garcia would become the youngest professional ever to successfully defend a Tour title or if one of the local favourites,

Shot of the Week

In the closing moments it became obvious that the title could be won or lost by a simple error and Patrik Sjöland looked to have made it on the short 16th when his tee shot finished tight against the wall of a greenside bunker. He could only play the ball from a kneeling position with one foot in the bunker. He said: "It was a key moment because Jacobson would have had more confidence going to the 17th if I missed." Sjöland coolly coaxed his recovery clear of the bunker wall and although the the ball ran 18 feet away from the hole he dispatched the saving putt briskly. It was a grevious blow for Jacobson, whose moment had passed as Sjöland marched to glory.

Darren Clarke, Padraig Harrington and Paul McGinley and could end the 18-year absence of an Irish name on the trophy.

In truth Garcia justified the first part of the debate when he opened with a 64 to share both course record and lead with 29-year-old Sjöland, whose first Tour win came with the Italian Open in 1998 and who had celebrated the birth of his first son, Hugo, seven weeks earlier. But perhaps the most popular performer on that first day was Sweden's Fredrik Lindgren, who holed in one at the third hole and in so doing earned every ticket holder a free pint of the sponsor's product.

There was understandable patriotic enthusiasm, too, for the efforts of Des Smyth, making a welcome return to the competitive ranks, who scored 65 while McGinley had 67 along with Philip Walton and Harrington, who took on the course as the wind strengthened in the afternoon.

When Sjöland put a second round 65 alongside his opening effort to take the halfway lead there was a growing awareness that some famous names might be caught napping unless they kept pace even though fellow countryman Jacobson closed within three strokes after lowering the course record with a 63.

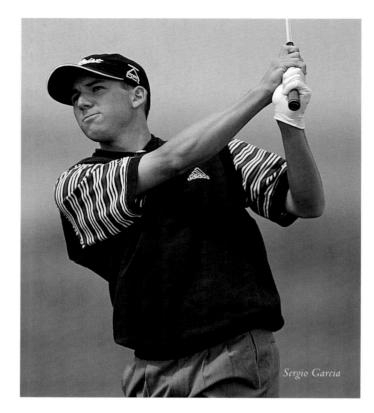

Sergio Garcia

Fredrik Jacobson, runner-up for the second successive week

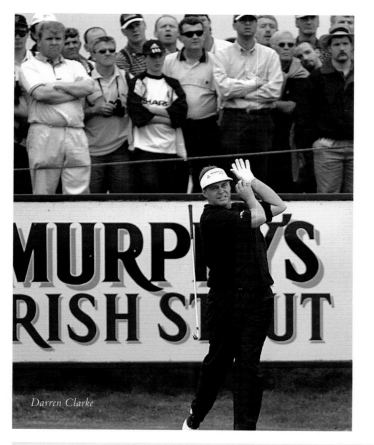

Darren Clarke

By the third day both had made way for a new challenger who occupied centre stage as Dutch professional Rolf Muntz took clear advantage of Ballybunion's relatively benign mood to produce a 68 and capture a marginal lead. Even so, amid all the excitement and virtually unnoticed, Sjöland demonstrated the precise qualities so essential for successful links golf with a performance that assuredly maintained his prospects of victory.

He dropped four strokes in four holes from the 12th hole and looked to be fading fast until he revived with three successive closing birdies to find himself tied with Garcia, two strokes behind Muntz, as they headed for the final round. Earlier José Maria Olazábal had salvaged some personal pride with two consecutive birdies -one from a bush on the 17th - to finish with 66, but was already lagging too far behind to pose a serious threat.

McGinley maintained the Irish challenge with a 66 and Smyth was still within range but there was a general awareness that Garcia might still be the man to beat on the final day particularly if he launched one of his customary charges. Indeed Sjöland admitted as much when he said: "I expected Garcia to be the man to catch, but it didn't happen."

Instead the Spaniard never found his stride and suffered a savage setback on the fourth hole when his approach rolled off the green

Padraig Harrington

The Course

Ironically, the demands of modern tournament golf - grandstands, television platforms, tented villages etc - meant that Ballybunion reverted to its original sequence of holes for the championship with the long fifth serving as the closing hole (as it was before 1971). But the change also meant that the gruelling encounter with the cliff-top holes came much earlier in the round and put several contenders on the defensive.

Jarmo Sandelin

and he hit two pitch shots that failed to climb the hill and landed back at his feet as he took a triple-bogey seven and eventual 77. Muntz was having a wretched day, too, as he toiled to a 76 so that the title clearly rested between Sjöland and his playing partner, Jacobson, who was a stroke ahead as they played the short 16th.

Sjöland found a bunker with his tee shot and looked in danger of slipping even further behind as his rival nestled on the green. Even so, Patrik salvaged a remarkable par, holing from 18 feet, to keep the pressure on his fellow countryman. In truth Jacobson lost his customary focus on the 17th tee and carved his drive against a boundary fence for an eventual bogey six while Sjöland eased past him with a chip and putt birdie four.

Jacobson then took six down the last hole while Sjöland made a sensible par to become champion. In the meantime McGinley gave his Irish fans a hint of things to come when he holed a 17 yards chip shot for an eagle three on the 17th to finish with a 71 and share third place with Muntz. But the day belonged to Sjöland, who had produced a 14 under par 270 winning total to prove beyond question that yet another generation of campaigners had adjusted to the traditional demands of seaside golf— and mastered them, too.

Michael McDonnell

Fredrik Jacobson and Patrik Sjöland

BALLYBUNION GOLF CLUB, CO KERRY, IRELAND, 29 JUNE - 2 JULY 2000, PAR 71, 6651 YARDS, 6082 METRES

Pos.	Name		Rd1	Rd2	Rd3	Rd4	Total	Par	Prize Money Euro	£
1	Patrik SJÖLAND	Swe	64	65	71	70	270	-14	267319.31	166660.00
2	Fredrik JACOBSON	Swe	69	63	69	71	272	-12	178218.22	111110.00
3	Paul MCGINLEY	Ire	67	70	66	71	274	-10	90304.08	56300.00
	Rolf MUNTZ	Hol	66	64	68	76	274	-10	90304.08	56300.00
5	Peter LONARD	Aus	69	68	72	66	275	-9	68008.75	42400.00
6	Eduardo ROMERO	Arg	68	66	70	72	276	-8	45071.84	28100.00
	Des SMYTH	Ire	65	70	70	71	276	-8	45071.84	28100.00
	Nick O'HERN	Aus	69	68	70	69	276	-8	45071.84	28100.00
	Bradley DREDGE	Wal	70	68	73	65	276	-8	45071.84	28100.00
10	Bernhard LANGER	Ger	73	66	70	68	277	-7	24797.53	15460.00
	Philip WALTON	Ire	67	67	71	72	277	-7	24797.53	15460.00
	Sergio GARCIA	Sp	64	70	66	77	277	-7	24797.53	15460.00
	Mark DAVIS	Eng	73	66	69	69	277	-7	24797.53	15460.00
	José Maria OLAZABAL	Sp	73	67	66	71	277	-7	24797.53	15460.00
	Angel CABRERA	Arg	69	69	72	67	277	-7	24797.53	15460.00
	Roger WESSELS	SA	68	68	71	70	277	-7	24797.53	15460.00
	Jarmo SANDELIN	Swe	71	71	66	69	277	-7	24797.53	15460.00
	David CARTER	Eng	67	70	72	68	277	-7	24797.53	15460.00
	Adam SCOTT	Aus	73	68	67	69	277	-7	24797.53	15460.00
20	Thomas LEVET	Fr	69	68	72	69	278	-6	19247.76	12000.00
21	Peter MITCHELL	Eng	69	70	69	71	279	-5	18365.57	11450.00
	Retief GOOSEN	SA	69	68	74	68	279	-5	18365.57	11450.00
23	Rodger DAVIS	Aus	72	67	73	68	280	-4	16681.39	10400.00
	Andrew MCLARDY	SA	73	66	71	70	280	-4	16681.39	10400.00
	Robert KARLSSON	Swe	71	70	68	71	280	-4	16681.39	10400.00
	Stephen GALLACHER	Scot	70	66	74	70	280	-4	16681.39	10400.00
	Alastair FORSYTH	Scot	72	66	70	72	280	-4	16681.39	10400.00
28	Padraig HARRINGTON	Ire	67	71	72	71	281	-3	14516.02	9050.00
	Steen TINNING	Den	69	71	70	71	281	-3	14516.02	9050.00
	Jeremy ROBINSON	Eng	70	70	69	72	281	-3	14516.02	9050.00
	Ricardo GONZALEZ	Arg	74	68	70	69	281	-3	14516.02	9050.00
32	Roger CHAPMAN	Eng	73	66	72	71	282	-2	11929.60	7437.50
	Marc FARRY	Fr	72	67	70	73	282	-2	11929.60	7437.50
	Sven STRÜVER	Ger	71	71	73	67	282	-2	11929.60	7437.50
	Stephen LEANEY	Aus	71	68	71	72	282	-2	11929.60	7437.50
	Hennie OTTO	SA	70	69	74	69	282	-2	11929.60	7437.50
	Darren CLARKE	N.Ire	72	70	68	72	282	-2	11929.60	7437.50
	José COCERES	Arg	70	67	77	68	282	-2	11929.60	7437.50
	Simon DYSON	Eng	67	69	68	78	282	-2	11929.60	7437.50
40	Anders FORSBRAND	Swe	70	68	72	73	283	-1	9784.28	6100.00
	Gary EMERSON	Eng	71	69	67	76	283	-1	9784.28	6100.00
	Andrew BUTTERFIELD	Eng	71	68	71	73	283	-1	9784.28	6100.00

Pos.	Name		Rd1	Rd2	Rd3	Rd4	Total	Par	Prize Money Euro	£
	Raymond RUSSELL	Scot	67	69	72	75	283	-1	9784.28	6100.00
	Christopher HANELL	Swe	69	73	68	73	283	-1	9784.28	6100.00
45	Andrew OLDCORN	Scot	69	71	71	73	284	0	7699.10	4800.00
	Jarrod MOSELEY	Aus	67	75	71	71	284	0	7699.10	4800.00
	André BOSSERT	Swi	69	69	74	72	284	0	7699.10	4800.00
	Thomas BJÖRN	Den	68	69	70	77	284	0	7699.10	4800.00
	Greg OWEN	Eng	70	68	74	72	284	0	7699.10	4800.00
	Stephen ALLAN	Aus	73	68	73	70	284	0	7699.10	4800.00
	Dean ROBERTSON	Scot	71	68	73	72	284	0	7699.10	4800.00
	Paddy GRIBBEN	Ire	69	67	70	78	284	0	7699.10	4800.00
53	Tony JOHNSTONE	Zim	73	69	73	70	285	1	5480.27	3416.67
	Malcolm MACKENZIE	Eng	73	69	73	70	285	1	5480.27	3416.67
	Steve WEBSTER	Eng	73	66	74	72	285	1	5480.27	3416.67
	Thomas GÖGELE	Ger	72	68	70	75	285	1	5480.27	3416.67
	Ian GARBUTT	Eng	65	71	73	76	285	1	5480.27	3416.67
	Van PHILLIPS	Eng	72	70	71	72	285	1	5480.27	3416.67
59	Stephen HAMILL	N.Ire	72	65	74	75	286	2	4410.95	2750.00
	Massimo SCARPA	It	73	63	75	75	286	2	4410.95	2750.00
	David LYNN	Eng	70	70	78	68	286	2	4410.95	2750.00
	Niclas FASTH	Swe	72	67	71	76	286	2	4410.95	2750.00
63	Ian WOOSNAM	Wal	71	68	73	75	287	3	3689.15	2300.00
	Domingo HOSPITAL	Sp	76	66	72	73	287	3	3689.15	2300.00
	Richard S JOHNSON	Swe	73	68	72	74	287	3	3689.15	2300.00
	Benoit TEILLERIA	Fr	72	67	74	74	287	3	3689.15	2300.00
	Lucas PARSONS	Aus	65	73	76	73	287	3	3689.15	2300.00
68	Soren HANSEN	Den	71	67	73	77	288	4	3127.76	1950.00
	Johan SKOLD	Swe	65	74	79	70	288	4	3127.76	1950.00
70	Barry LANE	Eng	70	72	74	73	289	5	2581.43	1609.39
	Richard COUGHLAN	Ire	71	70	75	73	289	5	2581.43	1609.39
	Gustavo ROJAS	Arg	74	67	68	80	289	5	2581.43	1609.39
73	Peter O'MALLEY	Aus	69	70	72	79	290	6	2397.00	1494.41
	Emanuele CANONICA	It	71	71	75	73	290	6	2397.00	1494.41
	Grant HAMERTON	Eng	70	72	74	74	290	6	2397.00	1494.41
76	Joakim HAEGGMAN	Swe	73	69	74	75	291	7	2391.00	1490.67
77	Mats LANNER	Swe	70	71	75	76	292	8	2386.50	1487.86
	Peter FOWLER	Aus	71	71	75	75	292	8	2386.50	1487.86
	Mark MURPHY (AM)	Ire	70	70	79	73	292	8		
80	Greg TURNER	NZ	65	77	73	78	293	9	2382.00	1485.06
81	Damian MCGRANE	Ire	73	69	74	78	294	10	2377.50	1482.25
	Sean QUINLIVAN	Ire	72	70	69	83	294	10	2377.50	1482.25
83	Maarten LAFEBER	Hol	71	70	75	79	295	11	2373.00	1479.44

Smiles Better

THE K CLUB, DUBLIN, IRELAND

Darren Clarke, Lee Westwood and Colin Montgomerie were well established as the modern day Great Triumvirate of European golf when they arrived at the elegant K Club in the County Kildare, the heart of Ireland's pasture land. Each had won twice and were placed in the above order as the top Europeans on the Volvo Order of Merit.

In the two months before they arrived in Ireland they had dominated the Tour to the extent that when all three competed for the same title, only once, did they fail to produce the champion. There were five victories, two seconds, a third and four other top tens while, in cash, they amassed a combined total of more than 2,112,000 euro (£1,320,000).

Angel Cabrera

It seemed, therefore, on a mere matter of form that one of them would win again. The prize was the Smurfit European Open Championship, a crown to be defended by Westwood but never won by either of the other two. Clarke's victory in the WGC - Andersen Consulting Match Play had kept him at the top of the Volvo Order of Merit, but Westwood was the man in form.

The Arnold Palmer course had never been better prepared for the challenge of Europe's elite. The first eight holes on each nine were reversed with the ninth and 18th remaining the same, an alteration that made for a stronger finish. The addition of many more maturing trees and penal rough increased the premium on the tee shot, but the landing areas were generous and fair and the greens in better condition than previous years. Furthermore the club's resident Tour professional, Paul McGinley, had designed a new, intimidating tee at the 17th that encroached on the borders of the free flowing River Liffey. The course, in fact, was presented in excellent condition.

All this with a view to the Ryder Cup in 2005 and as Clarke said: "It is great that we play one of our top tournaments on a future Ryder Cup course and that we will play it every year until the match comes around."

The Course

The course was designed by Arnold Palmer and will host the 2005 Ryder Cup. Alterations and extensions stretched the championship yardage to 7,227 through lush parkland in County Kildare just 35 minutes from Dublin Airport. The tree planting campaign which has been ongoing for four years will reach 1,700 by the end of the programme. A 19 million euro (£12 million) investment will embody a second 18 hole Championship course, clubhouse and conference centre planned for completion towards the end of 2003. The five star on site Hotel has 36 rooms with a further 33 under construction.

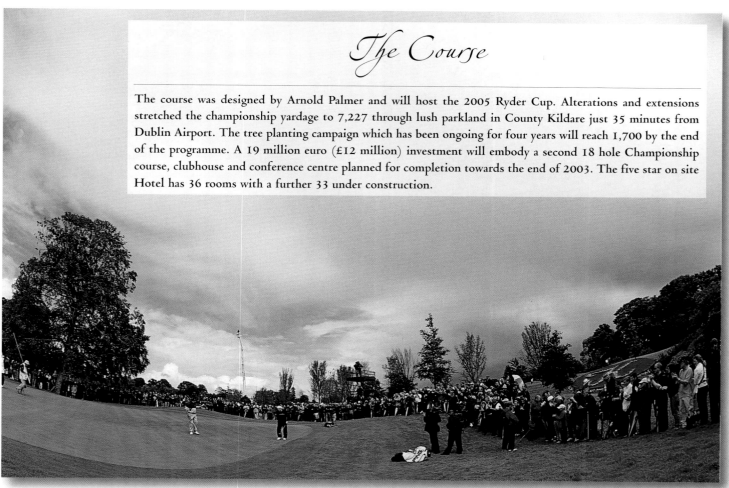

The set up of the course made it unlikely that any one player would run away from the field and such was the case. On his arrival Montgomerie expressed his desire to add the Smurfit European Open to his impressive list of titles. He soon set the standard for the others to follow, although his beginning was benign. Eight pars was pedestrian to his normal pace, but he touched the accelerator around the turn to produce an eagle and four birdies in consecutive holes from the ninth. He eased towards the finish and set a mark at five under that was to be equalled by Argentina's Angel Cabrera and Massimo Scarpa from Italy. The Scot did not sustain the challenge, nor did Scarpa, but Cabrera was there to the very end.

Tom Gillis, an American with a European Tour card, scored 66 on day two, but Cabrera remained in the joint lead with Gary Emerson, Gary Evans and Westwood at the half way stage. Cabrera took over on his own going into the last day, but by then others had gathered near the top of the leaderboard. Significantly, Jarmo Sandelin and Westwood were just a shot behind while Clarke and McGinley raised the home hopes by joining Per-Ulrik Johansson and Ignacio Garrido a further shot away.

Mathias Grönberg

Per-Ulrik Johansson and caddie Mick Donaghy

That third day produced a weather cocktail that was wet, windy and cold and the fourth was not a lot better, but Westwood proved that he is a man for all seasons. His final 66 was an awesome production. Four birdies in the first six holes and great saves at the seventh and eighth put him out in 31 and two ahead of the field. He went three ahead at the tenth but it was indicative of the strength of the Tour that there was little room for complacency. Indeed he won by only a single shot from Cabrera with the top six all within four shots.

So Westwood's renaissance, following the most depressive slump of his career, was almost complete. Celebrating his third win in six starts, the 27-year-old from Worksop, said: "I hit so many great shots out there today that it would take too long to list them. Yet, I was surprised how close it was in the end. Full credit to Angel and Per-Ulrik for the way they hung on."

The finishing charge was reminiscent of his 65 of the previous year but he said "Today's 66 was better than the 65 because the course is so much tougher now and so were the conditions. Yet, I really felt comfortable and in control all day." In fact, he felt so good that he risked the river with a second shot of 220 yards at the par five 16th, a signature hole of the Palmer design. "I just thought I would put some pressure on the tournament," he said with a smile.

Colm Smith

Shot of the Week

Too many to mention, was Westwood's summary of great shots in his final round of 66. A couple do stand out, like his 220 yards second across the River Liffey at the 16th and his second to the final green for a closing birdie. But his best par of the tournament came at the seventh. He hit his drive behind a tree, chopped out onto the fairway and produced a precision wedge of 99 yards for what he considered a vital four.

Weathering the storm: Lee Westwood

THE K CLUB, DUBLIN, IRELAND, 6-9 JULY 2000, PAR 72, 7227 YARDS, 6607 METRES

Pos.	Name		Rd1	Rd2	Rd3	Rd4	Total	Par	Prize Money Euro	£
1	Lee WESTWOOD	Eng	71	68	71	66	276	-12	396280.00	250000.00
2	Angel CABRERA	Arg	67	72	70	68	277	-11	264176.10	166660.00
3	Per-Ulrik JOHANSSON	Swe	70	71	70	67	278	-10	148842.77	93900.00
4	Mathias GRÖNBERG	Swe	73	69	70	67	279	-9	118884.00	75000.00
5	Ignacio GARRIDO	Sp	70	70	71	69	280	-8	92016.22	58050.00
	Jarmo SANDELIN	Swe	70	71	69	70	280	-8	92016.22	58050.00
7	Darren CLARKE	N.Ire	72	67	72	71	282	-6	71330.40	45000.00
8	Colin MONTGOMERIE	Scot	67	73	73	72	285	-3	51001.24	32175.00
	Gary EVANS	Eng	69	70	76	70	285	-3	51001.24	32175.00
	Thomas BJÖRN	Den	70	74	69	72	285	-3	51001.24	32175.00
	Paul LAWRIE	Scot	74	73	68	70	285	-3	51001.24	32175.00
12	David LYNN	Eng	75	70	69	72	286	-2	40896.10	25800.00
13	Mark DAVIS	Eng	72	71	70	74	287	-1	32990.31	20812.50
	Steve WEBSTER	Eng	74	73	71	69	287	-1	32990.31	20812.50
	Paul MCGINLEY	Ire	69	72	70	76	287	-1	32990.31	20812.50
	Phillip PRICE	Wal	70	69	73	75	287	-1	32990.31	20812.50
	José COCERES	Arg	75	67	70	75	287	-1	32990.31	20812.50
	Roger WESSELS	SA	75	71	69	72	287	-1	32990.31	20812.50
	Dean ROBERTSON	Scot	75	67	73	72	287	-1	32990.31	20812.50
	Christopher HANELL	Swe	69	72	76	70	287	-1	32990.31	20812.50
21	David GILFORD	Eng	70	71	72	75	288	0	26511.13	16725.00
	Peter O'MALLEY	Aus	70	72	76	70	288	0	26511.13	16725.00
	Greg OWEN	Eng	69	77	73	69	288	0	26511.13	16725.00
	Stephen ALLAN	Aus	72	68	75	73	288	0	26511.13	16725.00
25	Eduardo ROMERO	Arg	72	72	73	72	289	1	24014.57	15150.00
	Soren KJELDSEN	Den	71	75	71	72	289	1	24014.57	15150.00
	Jamie SPENCE	Eng	72	75	71	71	289	1	24014.57	15150.00
28	Andrew OLDCORN	Scot	70	73	72	75	290	2	20804.70	13125.00
	Marc FARRY	Fr	73	70	77	70	290	2	20804.70	13125.00
	Sven STRÜVER	Ger	71	73	70	76	290	2	20804.70	13125.00
	Steen TINNING	Den	72	72	72	74	290	2	20804.70	13125.00
	Massimo SCARPA	It	67	77	75	71	290	2	20804.70	13125.00
	Retief GOOSEN	SA	74	73	69	74	290	2	20804.70	13125.00
34	Andrew MCLARDY	SA	74	72	72	73	291	3	17357.06	10950.00
	Gary ORR	Scot	72	74	71	74	291	3	17357.06	10950.00
	David CARTER	Eng	69	77	74	71	291	3	17357.06	10950.00

Pos.	Name		Rd1	Rd2	Rd3	Rd4	Total	Par	Prize Money Euro	£
	Lucas PARSONS	Aus	70	74	72	75	291	3	17357.06	10950.00
	Michael CAMPBELL	NZ	77	69	73	72	291	3	17357.06	10950.00
39	Roger CHAPMAN	Eng	73	73	76	70	292	4	14503.85	9150.00
	Sam TORRANCE	Scot	71	73	76	72	292	4	14503.85	9150.00
	Padraig HARRINGTON	Ire	73	71	71	77	292	4	14503.85	9150.00
	Tom GILLIS	USA	75	66	78	73	292	4	14503.85	9150.00
	Niclas FASTH	Swe	72	74	72	74	292	4	14503.85	9150.00
	Matthew BLACKEY	Eng	74	71	74	73	292	4	14503.85	9150.00
	Stephen GALLACHER	Scot	72	73	74	73	292	4	14503.85	9150.00
46	Sandy LYLE	Scot	71	73	78	71	293	5	11412.86	7200.00
	Jean-Francois REMESY	Fr	69	75	75	74	293	5	11412.86	7200.00
	Stephen LEANEY	Aus	72	74	77	70	293	5	11412.86	7200.00
	Justin ROSE	Eng	76	70	72	75	293	5	11412.86	7200.00
	Pierre FULKE	Swe	68	72	77	76	293	5	11412.86	7200.00
	Ricardo GONZALEZ	Arg	69	71	73	80	293	5	11412.86	7200.00
52	José Maria OLAZABAL	Sp	74	72	74	74	294	6	9272.95	5850.00
	Thomas LEVET	Fr	73	73	72	76	294	6	9272.95	5850.00
	Diego BORREGO	Sp	70	74	74	76	294	6	9272.95	5850.00
55	Bernhard LANGER	Ger	72	73	78	72	295	7	7513.47	4740.00
	Barry LANE	Eng	73	73	72	77	295	7	7513.47	4740.00
	Nick O'HERN	Aus	71	71	75	78	295	7	7513.47	4740.00
	Emanuele CANONICA	It	75	72	74	74	295	7	7513.47	4740.00
	Nicolas VANHOOTEGEM	Bel	70	75	73	77	295	7	7513.47	4740.00
60	Des SMYTH	Ire	72	75	76	73	296	8	6538.62	4125.00
	Brian DAVIS	Eng	70	76	77	73	296	8	6538.62	4125.00
62	Philip WALTON	Ire	69	73	78	77	297	9	6063.09	3825.00
	Maarten LAFEBER	Hol	72	75	76	74	297	9	6063.09	3825.00
64	Malcolm MACKENZIE	Eng	75	71	77	75	298	10	5349.78	3375.00
	Paul EALES	Eng	77	68	75	78	298	10	5349.78	3375.00
	Jarrod MOSELEY	Aus	73	73	77	75	298	10	5349.78	3375.00
	Robert KARLSSON	Swe	72	71	79	76	298	10	5349.78	3375.00
68	Ola ELIASSON	Swe	72	73	75	79	299	11	4755.36	3000.00
69	Gary EMERSON	Eng	70	69	85	76	300	12	4430.41	2795.00
	Per NYMAN	Swe	75	72	78	75	300	12	4430.41	2795.00
71	Jean VAN DE VELDE	Fr	71	75	79	77	302	14	3567.00	2250.30
72	Johan SKOLD	Swe	74	72	78	81	305	17	3564.00	2248.41

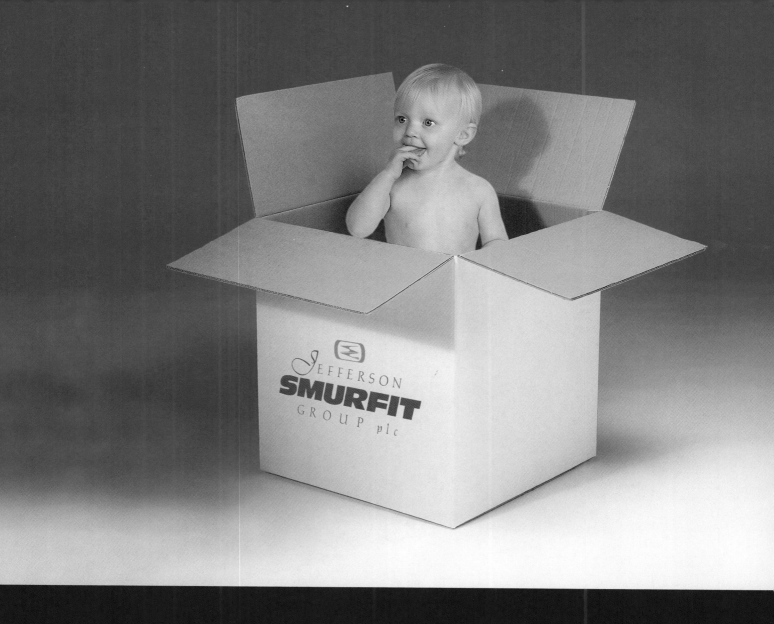

future

The development of global export markets has created sophisticated demands for packaging which will protect, present and promote a diverse range of products. Jefferson Smurfit Group has over sixty years' experience in meeting these demands innovatively and cost-effectively.

Together with its associates, Jefferson Smurfit Group is the world's largest paper-based packaging organisation and largest recycler of paper, with operations throughout Europe, Scandinavia and North and South America.

Smurfit has total control of the packaging manufacturing process, starting with sourcing and sorting waste paper for its own mills and producing virgin pulp from its own sustainable forests, through to the manufacture of paper and board and the production of a wide range of packaging for diverse markets.

From corrugated board to sturdy cases and complex cartons, Smurfit is skilled in answering the world's packaging needs, and with specialist Research and Design centres in Europe and the USA supporting its operations and customers globally, Smurfit is uniquely placed to develop paper and packaging solutions which meet today's needs and those of generations to come.

Developing packaging solutions for future generations

Jefferson Smurfit Group plc, World Headquarters, Beech Hill, Clonskeagh, Dublin 4, Ireland, Phone: 00 353 1 2027000, Web Site: www.smurfit.ie

Ace of Clubs

LOCH LOMOND, GLASGOW, SCOTLAND

After playing tennis with Jim Courier at Skibo Castle and relaxing with his family at their Wentworth home near London, Ernie Els came into the Standard Life Loch Lomond feeling so laid back he was almost horizontal.

The South African felt he needed a break after the US Open and three weeks away from the game meant he came into the tournament feeling relaxed but rusty. Although he was too polite to view an event on a course as illustrious as Loch Lomond as just a warm-up, Els conceded that his presence on the bonnie banks was about blowing away the cobwebs in time for the Open Championship at St Andrews.

"I've got some rust on my game," he admitted. "After three weeks off, I don't know if I can look for a win."

With the benefit of hindsight, of course, this mood of self-deprecation should have alerted astute punters to wager the mortgage on Els at Loch Lomond. After all, 17 months had elapsed since the South African's last official Tour win at the Nissan Open in Los Angeles.

Although he'd finished second in both the US Open at Pebble Beach and the Masters Tournament at Augusta National, there were some who wondered if the Big Easy was more uptight about winning than

Runner-up: America's Tom Lehman

during the early years of his career. At Loch Lomond, though, Els was clearly at ease with himself from the start.

On Wednesday, he began with a solid rather than spectacular 69. Tom Weiskopf's fabulous lay-out was at its most benign and another South African, Retief Goosen, took centre stage thanks to an opening 65.

Notah Begay III, the Native American who was fresh from back-to-back victories on the US PGA Tour, also matched this figure. Having once signed for 59 on the Buy.Com Tour in the States, Begay was no stranger to shooting low numbers.

Aberdeen's Paul Lawrie had played with Begay on the other side of the Atlantic and was mighty impressed by his driving which was straight as an arrow and putting, either right or left handed, that was measured and true.

Begay was quick to remind everyone, though, that there's usually about as much chance of a first round leader winning a golf tournament as there is of snow falling in the desert.

No sign of the bonnie banks here for José Maria Olazábal

The Course

Even by Loch Lomond's high standards, this was a vintage week for Tom Weiskopf's lay-out. Phil Mickelson hailed the fast greens as the truest he'd ever putted on; Ernie Els waxed lyrical about the tightly cut fairways and Tom Lehman described the course as second only to Pebble Beach in terms of beauty.

His words were to prove prophetic as a 72 in the second round dropped Begay out of a share of the lead and opened the way for a revived Nick Faldo, the impressive Australian teenager Adam Scott, and left-hander Richard Green to join Els at the head of the pack.

Once again, the former US Open champion looked to be playing well within himself. His form was smooth and steady in compiling a 67 with the only moment of high drama coming when he holed a bunker shot at the par five third for eagle.

While Tiger roars, Ernie purrs through tournaments. In the third round, he was at it again with another 69 as the Championship moved towards a gripping climax. Going into the final round, Begay and former winner Tom Lehman were on the same eight under par mark as Els while defending champion Colin Montgomerie was also in hot pursuit.

Els and Montgomerie went down the stretch together during the US Open at Congressional when Els came out on top. The climax of the 2000 staging of the Standard Life Loch Lomond was to be a similarly rewarding day for the South African as any remaining patches of rust were scraped off his game.

For all his relaxed approach, Els is a fiery competitor who relishes head to head challenges with his peers. Although he started the final

Notah Begay III

round with three birdies over the opening four holes and threatened to blow everyone else away, a couple of bogeys at the seventh and eighth acted like a bucket of cold water on any aspirations of a runaway victory.

"I lost a lot of momentum around there," Els recalled later, "and that brought a lot of guys back into the picture, especially Colin. He's won a lot more tournaments than I've done and, overall, he's probably the better player."

Certainly, when Montgomerie added a birdie to an eagle midway through the back nine and joined Els in a share of the lead, it looked as if the home crowd were going to get their wish and see a Scot successfully defend a title on home soil.

Els, though, forged ahead thanks to a sweet birdie putt on the 17th while Montgomerie dropped a shot at the last and Lehman followed suit with a hooked tee shot off the 18th tee into the loch.

It meant that a 68 - his fourth consecutive sub-70 round - for the 11 under total of 273 was good enough to collect Els's first title on the European Tour since the Alfred Dunhill South African PGA in 1999. The Big Easy was back.

Mike Aitken

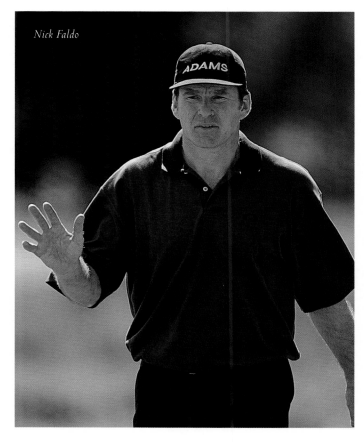

Nick Faldo

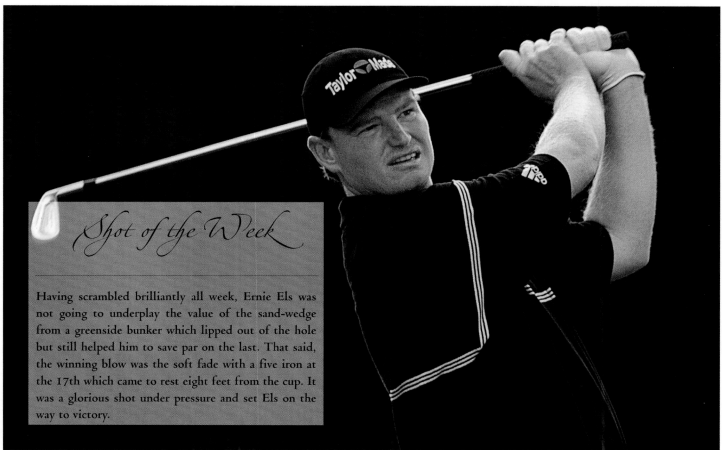

Shot of the Week

Having scrambled brilliantly all week, Ernie Els was not going to underplay the value of the sand-wedge from a greenside bunker which lipped out of the hole but still helped him to save par on the last. That said, the winning blow was the soft fade with a five iron at the 17th which came to rest eight feet from the cup. It was a glorious shot under pressure and set Els on the way to victory.

Retief Goosen

LOCH LOMOND, GLASGOW, SCOTLAND, 12-15 JULY 2000, PAR 71, 7050 YARDS, 6446 METRES

Pos.	Name		Rd1	Rd2	Rd3	Rd4	Total	Par	Prize Money Euro	£
1	Ernie ELS	SA	69	67	69	68	273	-11	292721.18	183330.00
2	Tom LEHMAN	USA	66	71	68	69	274	-10	195147.45	122220.00
3	Colin MONTGOMERIE	Scot	70	68	68	69	275	-9	109948.07	68860.00
4	Stephen ALLAN	Aus	66	72	72	67	277	-7	74586.71	46713.33
	Retief GOOSEN	SA	65	72	69	71	277	-7	74586.71	46713.33
	Notah BEGAY III	USA	65	72	68	72	277	-7	74586.71	46713.33
7	Jarmo SANDELIN	Swe	67	69	73	69	278	-6	48299.88	30250.00
	Phil MICKELSON	USA	68	72	73	65	278	-6	48299.88	30250.00
9	Nick FALDO	Eng	67	69	70	73	279	-5	35595.54	22293.33
	José Maria OLAZABAL	Sp	70	71	72	66	279	-5	35595.54	22293.33
	Michael CAMPBELL	NZ	70	67	70	72	279	-5	35595.54	22293.33
12	Adam SCOTT	Aus	66	70	71	73	280	-4	30209.37	18920.00
13	Gary ORR	Scot	69	73	71	68	281	-3	27574.84	17270.00
	Raymond RUSSELL	Scot	69	71	69	72	281	-3	27574.84	17270.00
15	Per-Ulrik JOHANSSON	Swe	67	73	71	71	282	-2	24764.66	15510.00
	Bob MAY	USA	69	71	72	70	282	-2	24764.66	15510.00
	Duffy WALDORF	USA	71	69	74	68	282	-2	24764.66	15510.00
	David GOSSETT (AM)	USA	70	71	72	69	282	-2		
19	Phillip PRICE	Wal	67	72	70	74	283	-1	21837.40	13676.67
	Thomas BJÖRN	Den	74	69	73	67	283	-1	21837.40	13676.67
	Paul LAWRIE	Scot	67	72	74	70	283	-1	21837.40	13676.67
22	Stephen LEANEY	Aus	67	77	69	71	284	0	19583.40	12265.00
	Richard GREEN	Aus	69	67	72	76	284	0	19583.40	12265.00
	Matt KUCHAR (AM)	USA	69	73	73	69	284	0		
	Jarrod MOSELEY	Aus	69	71	72	72	284	0	19583.40	12265.00
	José COCERES	Arg	70	74	71	69	284	0	19583.40	12265.00
27	Jim CARTER	USA	70	72	74	69	285	1	18002.68	11275.00
	Iain PYMAN	Eng	71	72	69	73	285	1	18002.68	11275.00
29	Angel CABRERA	Arg	72	72	73	69	286	2	16685.41	10450.00
	Niclas FASTH	Swe	69	74	72	71	286	2	16685.41	10450.00
	David CARTER	Eng	73	70	71	72	286	2	16685.41	10450.00
32	José RIVERO	Sp	75	69	71	72	287	3	14343.60	8983.33
	Eduardo ROMERO	Arg	72	71	72	72	287	3	14343.60	8983.33
	Barry LANE	Eng	71	72	73	71	287	3	14343.60	8983.33
	Nick O'HERN	Aus	69	73	73	72	287	3	14343.60	8983.33
	Andrew COLTART	Scot	71	71	73	72	287	3	14343.60	8983.33
	Dean ROBERTSON	Scot	72	67	76	72	287	3	14343.60	8983.33
38	Ian WOOSNAM	Wal	70	73	73	72	288	4	12470.15	7810.00
	Maarten LAFEBER	Hol	69	72	76	71	288	4	12470.15	7810.00
	Jonathan LOMAS	Eng	72	71	72	73	288	4	12470.15	7810.00
41	David HOWELL	Eng	69	74	76	70	289	5	10713.79	6710.00
	Thomas LEVET	Fr	69	72	77	71	289	5	10713.79	6710.00
	Geoff OGILVY	Aus	68	74	74	73	289	5	10713.79	6710.00
	Paolo QUIRICI	Swi	68	74	74	73	289	5	10713.79	6710.00
	Olivier EDMOND	Fr	72	70	74	73	289	5	10713.79	6710.00
	David PARK	Wal	70	74	73	72	289	5	10713.79	6710.00
	Christopher HANELL	Swe	69	68	75	77	289	5	10713.79	6710.00
48	David DUVAL	USA	70	73	76	71	290	6	8957.43	5610.00
	Anders HANSEN	Den	72	72	76	70	290	6	8957.43	5610.00
	Alastair FORSYTH	Scot	69	69	80	72	290	6	8957.43	5610.00
51	Malcolm MACKENZIE	Eng	74	71	72	74	291	7	7727.98	4840.00
	Paul EALES	Eng	71	74	76	70	291	7	7727.98	4840.00
	Ignacio GARRIDO	Sp	69	74	74	74	291	7	7727.98	4840.00
	Roger WESSELS	SA	73	70	74	74	291	7	7727.98	4840.00
55	Thomas GÖGELE	Ger	72	71	78	71	292	8	6498.53	4070.00
	Alex CEJKA	Ger	73	70	74	75	292	8	6498.53	4070.00
	Jorge BERENDT	Arg	71	73	76	72	292	8	6498.53	4070.00
58	Marc FARRY	Fr	72	71	76	74	293	9	5620.34	3519.99
	Richard S JOHNSON	Swe	74	71	77	71	293	9	5620.34	3519.99
60	David GILFORD	Eng	73	71	74	76	294	10	5093.44	3190.00
	John SENDEN	Aus	68	75	76	75	294	10	5093.44	3190.00
	Robert COLES	Eng	69	75	74	76	294	10	5093.44	3190.00
3	Russell CLAYDON	Eng	68	74	74	79	295	11	4654.35	2915.00
	Stephen GALLACHER	Scot	70	73	77	75	295	11	4654.35	2915.00
65	Anthony WALL	Eng	72	73	76	75	296	12	4127.45	2585.00
	Craig HAINLINE	USA	72	73	77	74	296	12	4127.45	2585.00
	Gary NICKLAUS	USA	73	72	76	75	296	12	4127.45	2585.00
	Benoit TEILLERIA	Fr	68	75	77	76	296	12	4127.45	2585.00
69	Andrew MCLARDY	SA	73	72	76	76	297	13	3512.72	2200.00
	Mathias GRÖNBERG	Swe	70	75	80	72	297	13	3512.72	2200.00
	Patrik SJÖLAND	Swe	72	73	76	76	297	13	3512.72	2200.00
72	Ricardo GONZALEZ	Arg	75	70	76	77	298	14	2922.18	1830.15
	Peter LONARD	Aus	72	71	76	79	298	14	2922.18	1830.15
74	Hennie OTTO	SA	71	73	85	78	307	23	2632.00	1648.41

The Undisputed Standard Bearer

ST ANDREWS, FIFE, SCOTLAND

*W*hen the immortal Bobby Jones beheld Jack Nicklaus at his peak, he defined the difference between their personal talents thus: "He plays a game with which I am not familiar." It was a sentiment that the assembly of great golf stars could rightfully echo as Tiger Woods left St Andrews as the undisputed standard bearer of the Royal and Ancient game for a new century.

What happened over the Old Course in the 129th Open Championship went beyond a sublime demonstration of superior skill as the gifted American left his rivals so far behind they might as well have been playing in their own event. The truth of it was that Woods took the game to a new level and bestowed upon it an exciting awareness of what lies beyond and how limitless human achievement really can be.

It will be remembered as the week that changed the face of golf and there was a certain historical neatness that this milestone should be reached at the Home of Golf where the game itself began in centuries past. Moreover, Woods confirmed with the manner of his performance that he possessed a technique and strategy that spanned both modern and traditional demands. Most important of all, he had brought athleticism to the game and in so doing unlocked the door to even greater and more measurable improvement.

Tiger Woods

And all this at the age of 24 as he became the youngest golfer ever to win the Grand Slam of four major titles - the other victors being Gene Sarazen, Ben Hogan, Gary Player and Jack Nicklaus - within four years of turning professional. Even before his triumph in which he clipped a stroke off the previous record winning total at St Andrews set by Nick Faldo in 1990, Tiger's presence had been felt by his opponents when he took the US Open by a massive 15 stroke margin at Pebble Beach.

Such is his dominance that when another champion arrived on the first tee at St Andrews to start his challenge for the title his first question to his caddie was: "Any idea how Tiger's doing?" The man had them all transfixed because he had set standards by which they must all judge themselves and towards which they must aspire.

And if the reflective view of this Championship suggests an inevitability about Tiger's triumph, the daily narrative held a different emphasis with various twists and turns as others flitted across the stage and dared to hope for - and even promise - better things. Indeed if any reminder was needed that the game will always be bigger that its participants then it was to be found in the array of 21 pasts champions - the oldest being 88-year-old Sam Snead - who turned up to pay homage in their own not-too-serious four hole contest over the Old Course.

Thomas Björn

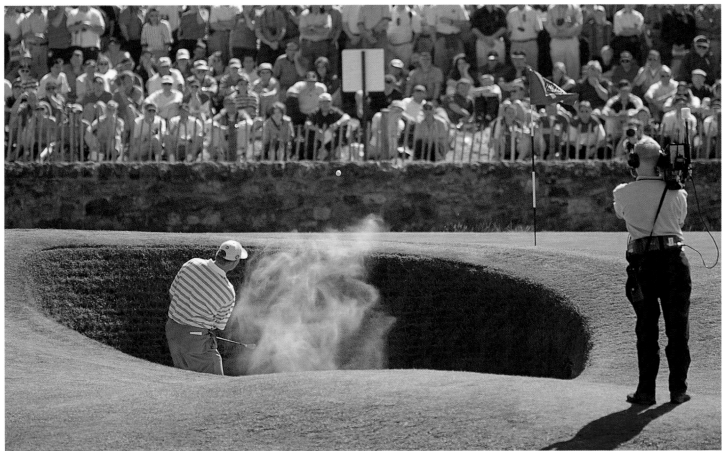

Ernie Els escapes from the Road Hole Bunker

When it comes to sports results, you could say we really know the score.

In sports – just like business – results are everything. And not just to the millions worldwide who depend on our systems to deliver real-time scores and analysis of premier sporting events on the Web and on TV – but to the networks and press that cover them. Like the golf tournaments within the PGA European, Southern African, Asian and Australasian Tours, The Open Championship, U.S. Open, U.S. Women's Open, U.S. Seniors Open, Australian Open, Rugby World Cup and many more. We ensure the results keep pouring in thanks to the powerful teaming of Unisys software, Windows NT servers and our dedicated people. It's the same combination our customers around the world rely on to solve their real-time business problems and get them results. Which is why we take sports very seriously – it's what keeps us ahead of the game. www.unisys.com.

UNISYS

We eat, sleep and drink this stuff.

The Course

The perceived tradition is that the Old Course evolved naturally amid the sandhills on this stretch of Scottish coastline yet the reality is that it still needs adjustments from time to time to match the improving skills of those who play it. The challenge and threat of the Road Hole with its menacing bunker remains timeless but some other bunkers needed to be brought back into play for this Championship by extending several tees. The fourth, tenth ,15th and 16th tees were pushed back for this purpose while the sixth tee was re-positioned to increase the accuracy of play between bunkers. The overall aim was to seek out a rightful winner and nobody can argue about the credentials of the Millennium winner.

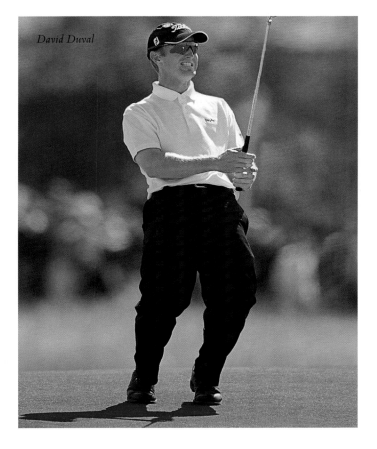

David Duval

In truth the Old Course itself was in benign mood for all four days of the Championship with no serious sign of wind to blow the contestants into what the essayist Bernard Darwin once called "those hungry lurking enemies" - the bunkers - although there were enough horror stories of campaigners who still managed to find some of those 112 disaster spots. And yet it was a decisive feature of Tiger's winning performance that he managed to stay clear of such problems throughout all four days.

More to the point, the quality of his approach play was so precise and under such control on landing that he could boldly attack the flagstick positions and thereby eliminate the vagaries of those massive rolling greens that thwarted the efforts of his rivals. That said, Tiger was edged marginally out of the spotlight on the first day when his flawless 67 was bettered by a 66 from Ernie Els, whose opening effort contained eight birdies.

Others, too, settled comfortably to the pace with Sergio Garcia tucked nicely four strokes off the lead with a 68 - 21 strokes better than his first round effort at Carnoustie a year earlier he reminded the media - and Padraig Harrington among others on a similar score. And while Lee Westwood's 70, Colin Montgomerie's 71 and Darren Clarke's 70 reminded each of them there was ground to make up, a mood of confidence existed among the contenders.

Tiger Woods

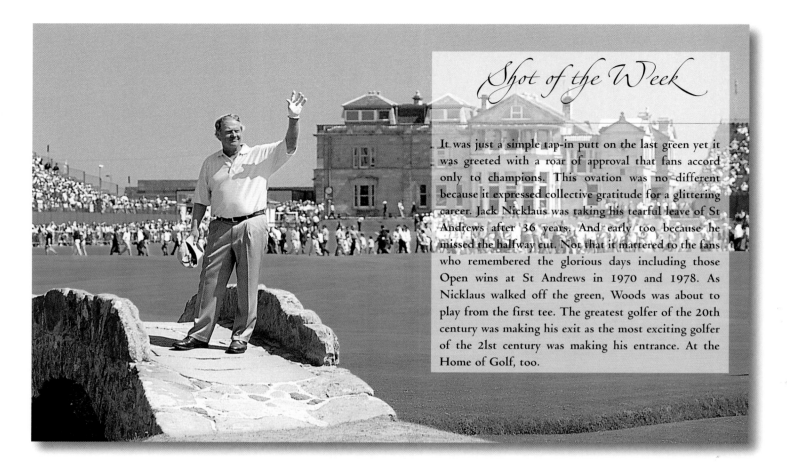

Shot of the Week

It was just a simple tap-in putt on the last green yet it was greeted with a roar of approval that fans accord only to champions. This ovation was no different because it expressed collective gratitude for a glittering career. Jack Nicklaus was taking his tearful leave of St Andrews after 36 years. And early too because he missed the halfway cut. Not that it mattered to the fans who remembered the glorious days including those Open wins at St Andrews in 1970 and 1978. As Nicklaus walked off the green, Woods was about to play from the first tee. The greatest golfer of the 20th century was making his exit as the most exciting golfer of the 21st century was making his entrance. At the Home of Golf, too.

Darren Clarke

Yet by the end of the second day, signs of a familiar pattern began to take shape as Tiger added a 66 - lowest score of the day - to his name and fellow American David Toms, making his Open debut, became his nearest challenger with a 67 to be three strokes adrift. Garcia kept pace four strokes behind although the margin began to widen on Europe's other main hopes. Sadly nine former champions including 1999 winner Paul Lawrie and the legendary Jack Nicklaus, failed to beat the halfway cut of 144.

Then, quite suddenly, the drama looked about to depart from the script as Els threatened to throw the denouement into doubt as he picked up five birdies in the first seven holes of the third round to move within two strokes of Tiger. At that point he faced the dilemma that the Old Course invariably presents. Attack and risk calamity? Or play safe and allow chances to pass? Els went for the former strategy and paid the price particularly on the driveable 12th hole when his tee shot found a bunker and cost him a double bogey six and much of his momentum. Even Garcia could not keep pace, especially when Tiger opened a six stroke lead after a 67.

On the final day, David Duval, Tiger's playing partner, stepped forward to pick up the challenge with a blistering start which closed the margin between them to three strokes after seven holes, but his threat was thwarted by his own punishing errors particularly the four attempts to escape from the Road Bunker on the 17th hole.

And yet the truth of it was that even before that Duval horror had occurred there was no other threat to Tiger's Championship march.

His last round 69 gave him a 19 under par 269 total to the delight of record crowds each of whom can claim they witnessed the dawn of golf's new era including one man who held up his infant son above the multitude on the 18th hole and said in biblical tones: "You have seen Tiger!" Others could take their leave of St Andrews with a different sense of achievement. Ernie Els slipped into second place for his third major championship of the year. Thomas Björn confirmed the growing opinion that he is player of considerable substance on the big occasion by sharing second place. And Darren Clarke maintained his presence with seventh place along with Pierre Fulke among others.

Of course, that still leaves the pressing problem that simply will not go away and was best defined by Jesper Parnevik on behalf of all his fellow professionals when he said: "We've got to find a way to beat Tiger." It will be the ultimate tribute to this charismatic American; that his exploits raised the standard of the game which was changed beyond recognition because he played it.

Michael McDonnell

Pierre Fulke

Fred Couples plays off the road at the 17th hole

A Star is Born

ST ANDREWS, FIFE, SCOTLAND, 20-23 JULY 2000, PAR 72, 7115 YARDS, 6506 METRES

Pos.	Name		Rd1	Rd2	Rd3	Rd4	Total	Par	Prize Money Euro	£
1	Tiger WOODS	USA	67	66	67	69	269	-19	799550.00	500000.00
2	Ernie ELS	SA	66	72	70	69	277	-11	391779.50	245000.00
	Thomas BJÖRN	Den	69	69	68	71	277	-11	391779.50	245000.00
4	Tom LEHMAN	USA	68	70	70	70	278	-10	207883.00	130000.00
	David TOMS	USA	69	67	71	71	278	-10	207883.00	130000.00
6	Fred COUPLES	USA	70	68	72	69	279	-9	159910.00	100000.00
7	Loren ROBERTS	USA	69	68	70	73	280	-8	105940.38	66250.00
	Paul AZINGER	USA	69	72	72	67	280	-8	105940.38	66250.00
	Pierre FULKE	Swe	69	72	70	69	280	-8	105940.38	66250.00
	Darren CLARKE	N.Ire	70	69	68	73	280	-8	105940.38	66250.00
11	Bernhard LANGER	Ger	74	70	66	71	281	-7	59344.38	37111.11
	Mark MCNULTY	Zim	69	72	70	70	281	-7	59344.38	37111.11
	David DUVAL	USA	70	70	66	75	281	-7	59344.38	37111.11
	Stuart APPLEBY	Aus	73	70	68	70	281	-7	59344.38	37111.11
	Davis LOVE III	USA	74	66	74	67	281	-7	59344.38	37111.11
	Vijay SINGH	Fiji	70	70	73	68	281	-7	59344.38	37111.11
	Phil MICKELSON	USA	72	66	71	72	281	-7	59344.38	37111.11
	Bob MAY	USA	72	72	66	71	281	-7	59344.38	37111.11
	Dennis PAULSON	USA	68	71	69	73	281	-7	59344.38	37111.11
20	Steve FLESCH	USA	67	70	71	74	282	-6	40777.05	25500.00
	Padraig HARRINGTON	Ire	68	72	70	72	282	-6	40777.05	25500.00
	Steve PATE	USA	73	70	71	68	282	-6	40777.05	25500.00
	Bob ESTES	USA	72	69	70	71	282	-6	40777.05	25500.00
	Paul MCGINLEY	Ire	69	72	71	70	282	-6	40777.05	25500.00
	Notah BEGAY III	USA	69	73	69	71	282	-6	40777.05	25500.00
26	Mark O'MEARA	USA	70	73	69	71	283	-5	31982.00	20000.00
	Colin MONTGOMERIE	Scot	71	70	72	70	283	-5	31982.00	20000.00
	Miguel Angel JIMÉNEZ	Sp	68	73	71	71	283	-5	31982.00	20000.00
	Mark CALCAVECCHIA	USA	73	70	71	69	283	-5	31982.00	20000.00
	Dean ROBERTSON	Scot	73	70	68	72	283	-5	31982.00	20000.00
31	José Maria OLAZÁBAL	Sp	72	70	71	71	284	-4	26784.93	16750.00
	Jean VAN DE VELDE	Fr	71	68	72	73	284	-4	26784.93	16750.00
	Steve JONES	USA	70	70	72	72	284	-4	26784.93	16750.00
	Jarmo SANDELIN	Swe	70	70	75	69	284	-4	26784.93	16750.00
35	Eduardo ROMERO	Arg	71	68	72	74	285	-3	24786.05	15500.00
36	Sergio GARCIA	Sp	68	69	73	76	286	-2	22387.40	14000.00
	Jesper PARNEVIK	Swe	73	69	72	72	286	-2	22387.40	14000.00

Pos.	Name		Rd1	Rd2	Rd3	Rd4	Total	Par	Prize Money Euro	£
	Craig PARRY	Aus	72	72	71	71	286	-2	22387.40	14000.00
	José COCERES	Arg	74	66	69	77	286	-2	22387.40	14000.00
	Robert ALLENBY	Aus	72	71	72	71	286	-2	22387.40	14000.00
41	Nick FALDO	Eng	72	71	75	71	287	-1	16543.42	10345.46
	Justin LEONARD	USA	70	74	72	71	287	-1	16543.42	10345.46
	Stewart CINK	USA	69	73	76	69	287	-1	16543.42	10345.46
	Jim FURYK	USA	69	71	75	72	287	-1	16543.42	10345.46
	Nick O'HERN	Aus	69	74	70	74	287	-1	16543.42	10345.46
	Jarrod MOSELEY	Aus	70	71	70	76	287	-1	16543.42	10345.46
	Gary ORR	Scot	72	71	72	72	287	-1	16543.42	10345.46
	Jeff MAGGERT	USA	72	71	69	75	287	-1	16543.42	10345.46
	Retief GOOSEN	SA	72	72	71	72	287	-1	16543.42	10345.46
	Lucas PARSONS	Aus	70	72	71	74	287	-1	16543.42	10345.46
	Tsuyoshi YONEYAMA	Jpn	74	69	70	74	287	-1	16543.42	10345.46
52	Mike WEIR	Can	75	68	70	75	288	0	13432.44	8400.00
	Ian GARBUTT	Eng	68	75	70	75	288	0	13432.44	8400.00
	Rocco MEDIATE	USA	74	69	76	69	288	0	13432.44	8400.00
55	David FROST	SA	73	71	71	74	289	1	12472.98	7800.00
	Tom WATSON	USA	73	71	72	73	289	1	12472.98	7800.00
	Shigeki MARUYAMA	Jpn	68	76	69	76	289	1	12472.98	7800.00
	Greg OWEN	Eng	70	74	72	73	289	1	12472.98	7800.00
	Andrew COLTART	Scot	70	72	73	74	289	1	12472.98	7800.00
60	Christy O'CONNOR JNR	Ire	69	75	72	74	290	2	11873.32	7425.00
	Jeff SLUMAN	USA	72	68	75	75	290	2	11873.32	7425.00
	Steve ELKINGTON	Aus	73	69	74	74	290	2	11873.32	7425.00
	Kirk TRIPLETT	USA	73	71	74	72	290	2	11873.32	7425.00
64	Desvonde BOTES	SA	71	70	76	74	291	3	11553.50	7225.00
	Ian POULTER	Eng	74	69	73	75	291	3	11553.50	7225.00
	Per-Ulrik JOHANSSON	Swe	72	69	76	74	291	3	11553.50	7225.00
	Lee WESTWOOD	Eng	70	70	76	75	291	3	11553.50	7225.00
68	Gordon BRAND JNR.	Scot	69	72	80	71	292	4	11313.64	7075.00
	Ian WOOSNAM	Wal	72	72	73	75	292	4	11313.64	7075.00
70	Tom KITE	USA	72	72	76	74	294	6	11193.70	7000.00
	Kazuhiko HOSOKAWA	Jpn	75	69	77	73	294	6	11193.70	7000.00
72	Peter SENIOR	Aus	71	71	74	79	295	7	11193.70	7000.00
	Lionel ALEXANDRE	Fr	75	68	76	76	295	7	11193.70	7000.00

ROLEX

CRAFTSMANSHIP FOR THE EAGLE-EYED.

ROLEX.

OFFICIAL TIMEKEEPER TO THE

PGA EUROPEAN TOUR.

In Love With the Links

NOORDWIJKSE GOLF CLUB, NOORDWIJK, THE NETHERLANDS

Winning the TNT Dutch Open might not match up to taking the Open title at the Home of Golf but Tiger Woods himself would surely have been delighted with Stephen Leaney's victory in Noordwijk.

Western Australian Leaney dropped but one stroke to par in four days and, like the Tiger at St Andrews the week before, never once in 72 holes tangled with a bunker on the testing North Sea links.

It was a remorseless, even ruthless display of precision golf to set up a second TNT Dutch title triumph in three years for the man who first raised eyebrows on this side of the world with his eight strokes victory in the 1998 Moroccan Open on another majestic links layout in Royal Agadir.

In Noordwijk, he had to settle for a "modest" four strokes victory margin over the redoubtable Bernhard Langer, the second of whose own Dutch Open wins came over the same course in 1992.

Lee Westwood, who had collected three victories and more than 1,280,000 euro (£800,000) on his previous seven outings, had to settle for joint third place a stroke further back with Swede Mathias Grönberg and Argentinian Angel Cabrera.

Leaney, looking more like David Duval than Tiger Woods in his wrap-around "shades", shot 66, 70, 65, 68 for an impressive 19 under par 269 total.

In seven previous Opens over the steeply undulating Frank Pennink - designed layout only one man had bettered that - double US Open Champion Payne Stewart, whose 267 aggregate in 1991 swept him nine strokes clear of the field. Langer and José Maria Olazábal won in Noordwijk with scores of 277 and Colin Montgomerie shot 281 to take the 1993 title.

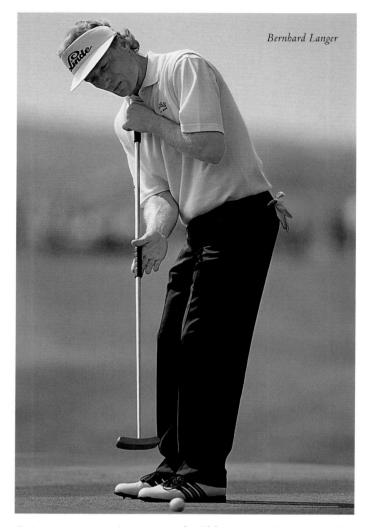

Bernhard Langer

Mathias Grönberg

Quiet man Leaney, who was out of golf for 18 months in 1993 after surgery to remove a blood clot - it entailed extracting two ribs through his right shoulder - admitted: "My goal all week was to go out and not make a bogey. I like a course where you have to use your brain.

"There have probably been guys who have made more birdies but I averaged five a round. I love links golf. Keeping it in play with three-woods and long irons and staying patient rather than getting too aggressive is the key."

Leaney made so few mistakes his rivals never got closer than within two strokes of him on the final afternoon. The only shot he dropped was by missing a two footer in round three.

He explained: "I felt if I shot four under it would be hard for the guys to catch me. I enjoy front running. Eight of my nine tournament victories - all three in Europe - have come when I've lead going into the final round. I feel comfortable in that situation.

"I was two ahead in Hilversum in 1998 and went head to head with Westwood on that occasion too, and held him off along with Darren

Clarke and Nick Price. It proved I was really on my game mentally. I had a total belief in my golf swing and wasn't intimidated.

"After winning the ANZ Players' Championship as well as the Dutch and Moroccan Opens in 1998 I set unreasonable goals. I'd got starts in three majors the following year and didn't work as hard mentally.

"I got a bit lost and put a lot of pressure on myself and it hurt me. I got frustrated at going 18 months without a victory but my new coach Denis Pugh turned things around with a lesson at the Murphy's Irish Open."

The 31-year-old former Eisenhower Trophy amateur, who helped Australia reach the final of the 1999 Alfred Dunhill Cup with victories over Jarmo Sandelin, Katsuyoshi Tomori and Gary Orr, was swift to capitalise.

Langer, chasing his first win for three years, and Westwood still had Leaney in their sights after six holes on day four but a birdie three at the seventh, where the Australian hit a four iron to 25 feet, was a dagger blow. It proved the first of four birdies on eight holes which would lock and bar the door.

Angel Cabrera

Shot of the Week

It was a case of many happy returns to Holland for Justin Rose, who launched his pro career in the 1998 Championship. One of the keys to his career best showing was a spectacular 74 yards pitch he holed for an eagle two at the 15th in round two to revive memories of his 55 yards chip-in at the last to tie fourth in the Open at Royal Birkdale two years earlier to win the amateur silver medal.

The Course

The course that Frank Pennink built, with the help of sketches by club secretary Paul de Jong, opened in 1972 after the seaside resort's previous nine holes layout was built on. It dramatically undulates between high sand dunes and is distinctive by having trees on the fifth, sixth and seventh, the latter being a much debated dogleg left requiring a longish iron off the tee.

Lee Westwood

Langer, who switched back to a steel shafted driver he used to finish second in the 1999 Volvo Masters - "graphite goes a touch further but when its too light I swing too fast and get out of control" - proved he still has much to offer the game as he approached his 43rd birthday.

Westwood, who missed nine putts inside five feet the first three days was philosophical: "Some weeks you get them, some weeks you don't - no worries." He would win again a week later in Stockholm.

Best round of the week was the 63 of Scot Gordon Brand Jnr, who was home in 29, and Justin Rose celebrated his 20th birthday with his best performance of a professional career that began in the TNT Dutch Open two years before with four rounds of par or better for a seven under 281.

But it was Leaney "the meaney", with just one bogey all week, who ended wearing the biggest smile.

Gordon Richardson

Stephen Leaney

NOORDWIJKSE GOLF CLUB, NOORDWIJK, THE NETHERLANDS, 27-30 JULY 2000, PAR 72, 6879 YARDS, 6291 METRES

Pos.	Name		Rd1	Rd2	Rd3	Rd4	Total	Par	Prize Money Euro	£
1	Stephen LEANEY	Aus	66	70	65	68	269	-19	225000.00	138602.27
2	Bernhard LANGER	Ger	69	68	68	68	273	-15	150000.00	92401.52
3	Mathias GRÖNBERG	Swe	68	68	69	69	274	-14	69750.00	42966.70
	Angel CABRERA	Arg	68	69	69	68	274	-14	69750.00	42966.70
	Lee WESTWOOD	Eng	67	72	66	69	274	-14	69750.00	42966.70
6	Roger WESSELS	SA	73	69	68	65	275	-13	47250.00	29106.48
7	Santiago LUNA	Sp	68	69	71	68	276	-12	32872.50	20249.79
	José RIVERO	Sp	70	68	69	69	276	-12	32872.50	20249.79
	Greg OWEN	Eng	68	73	69	66	276	-12	32872.50	20249.79
	Stephen ALLAN	Aus	68	67	69	72	276	-12	32872.50	20249.79
11	Mark MOULAND	Wal	67	70	72	68	277	-11	23265.00	14331.48
	Eduardo ROMERO	Arg	69	67	72	69	277	-11	23265.00	14331.48
	Paolo QUIRICI	Swi	70	73	68	66	277	-11	23265.00	14331.48
14	Gordon BRAND JNR.	Scot	72	71	72	63	278	-10	19845.00	12224.72
	Jarrod MOSELEY	Aus	70	67	72	69	278	-10	19845.00	12224.72
	Peter O'MALLEY	Aus	70	69	71	68	278	-10	19845.00	12224.72
17	Soren KJELDSEN	Den	69	73	65	72	279	-9	15870.00	9776.08
	Euan LITTLE	Scot	69	72	72	66	279	-9	15870.00	9776.08
	Roger WINCHESTER	Eng	67	71	71	70	279	-9	15870.00	9776.08
	Joakim HAEGGMAN	Swe	72	68	72	67	279	-9	15870.00	9776.08
	Miles TUNNICLIFF	Eng	70	67	70	72	279	-9	15870.00	9776.08
	Darren CLARKE	N.Ire	72	69	67	71	279	-9	15870.00	9776.08
	Fredrik JACOBSON	Swe	73	66	70	70	279	-9	15870.00	9776.08
	John BICKERTON	Eng	69	70	71	69	279	-9	15870.00	9776.08
26	Sven STRÜVER	Ger	71	69	71	69	280	-8	13432.50	8274.56
	Russell CLAYDON	Eng	71	72	69	68	280	-8	13432.50	8274.56
28	Padraig HARRINGTON	Ire	69	70	73	69	281	-7	12015.00	7401.36
	Justin ROSE	Eng	68	72	69	72	281	-7	12015.00	7401.36
	Ian POULTER	Eng	73	70	69	69	281	-7	12015.00	7401.36
	Richard S JOHNSON	Swe	66	70	74	71	281	-7	12015.00	7401.36
	Daren LEE	Eng	72	71	68	70	281	-7	12015.00	7401.36
33	Andrew MCLARDY	SA	70	70	73	69	282	-6	9736.88	5998.02
	Soren HANSEN	Den	70	71	72	69	282	-6	9736.88	5998.02
	Massimo FLORIOLI	It	71	68	71	72	282	-6	9736.88	5998.02
	Carl SUNESON	Sp	74	70	70	68	282	-6	9736.88	5998.02
	Ricardo GONZALEZ	Arg	68	70	71	73	282	-6	9736.88	5998.02
	John HUSTON	USA	74	67	70	71	282	-6	9736.88	5998.02
	Van PHILLIPS	Eng	71	71	70	70	282	-6	9736.88	5998.02
	Simon DYSON	Eng	71	68	72	71	282	-6	9736.88	5998.02
41	Ian HUTCHINGS	SA	70	69	72	72	283	-5	8235.00	5072.84

Pos.	Name		Rd1	Rd2	Rd3	Rd4	Total	Par	Prize Money Euro	£
	Ian GARBUTT	Eng	70	72	71	70	283	-5	8235.00	5072.84
	Jorge BERENDT	Arg	71	71	72	69	283	-5	8235.00	5072.84
44	Gary EMERSON	Eng	70	73	72	69	284	-4	7290.00	4490.71
	Gary EVANS	Eng	75	68	70	71	284	-4	7290.00	4490.71
	Grant HAMERTON	Eng	68	76	68	72	284	-4	7290.00	4490.71
	Alastair FORSYTH	Scot	71	71	75	67	284	-4	7290.00	4490.71
48	Eamonn DARCY	Ire	71	73	69	72	285	-3	6345.00	3908.58
	Olle KARLSSON	Swe	69	73	73	70	285	-3	6345.00	3908.58
	Steven RICHARDSON	Eng	68	71	69	77	285	-3	6345.00	3908.58
51	Anders FORSBRAND	Swe	72	69	72	73	286	-2	5265.00	3243.29
	Greg TURNER	NZ	69	73	74	70	286	-2	5265.00	3243.29
	Hayo BENSDORP	Hol	69	73	72	72	286	-2	5265.00	3243.29
	Olivier EDMOND	Fr	73	71	70	72	286	-2	5265.00	3243.29
	Stephen FIELD	Eng	73	71	71	71	286	-2	5265.00	3243.29
56	Anders HANSEN	Den	67	74	75	71	287	-1	4320.00	2661.16
	David PARK	Wal	69	71	74	73	287	-1	4320.00	2661.16
58	Malcolm MACKENZIE	Eng	70	69	72	77	288	0	3645.00	2245.36
	Andrew OLDCORN	Scot	70	73	72	73	288	0	3645.00	2245.36
	David HOWELL	Eng	71	73	71	73	288	0	3645.00	2245.36
	Jean-Francois REMESY	Fr	70	73	73	72	288	0	3645.00	2245.36
	Jeremy ROBINSON	Eng	73	71	71	73	288	0	3645.00	2245.36
	Fabrice TARNAUD	Fr	75	69	74	70	288	0	3645.00	2245.36
	Iain PYMAN	Eng	72	72	75	69	288	0	3645.00	2245.36
65	Paul AFFLECK	Wal	71	70	72	76	289	1	2970.00	1829.55
	Max ANGLERT	Swe	74	70	72	73	289	1	2970.00	1829.55
	Henrik NYSTROM	Swe	73	71	75	70	289	1	2970.00	1829.55
68	José Manuel CARRILES	Sp	69	75	73	73	290	2	2437.50	1501.52
	Simon WAKEFIELD	Eng	73	71	71	75	290	2	2437.50	1501.52
	Ivo GINER	Sp	70	74	75	71	290	2	2437.50	1501.52
	Brendan JONES	Aus	70	74	73	73	290	2	2437.50	1501.52
72	Andrew SHERBORNE	Eng	72	72	73	74	291	3	2019.00	1243.72
	Knud STORGAARD	Den	69	74	71	77	291	3	2019.00	1243.72
	Andrew RAITT	Eng	74	69	73	75	291	3	2019.00	1243.72
75	Brian DAVIS	Eng	74	68	78	72	292	4	2013.00	1240.03
76	Ralph MILLER	Hol	67	72	80	74	293	5	2008.50	1237.26
	Raymond RUSSELL	Scot	70	71	79	73	293	5	2008.50	1237.26
78	Greig HUTCHEON	Scot	71	72	75	76	294	6	2004.00	1234.48
79	Tomas Jesus MUÑOZ	Sp	71	71	77	76	295	7	1999.50	1231.71
	Ola ELIASSON	Swe	69	75	74	77	295	7	1999.50	1231.71
81	Kevin CARISSIMI	USA	69	74	78	78	299	11	1995.00	1228.94

Heaven on Earth

KUNGSÄNGEN, STOCKHOLM, SWEDEN

The sun shouted its warmth from a pellucid sky as thousand upon thousand pine trees sprayed forth nature's aerosol with their sweet, resinous perfume. All was right with the world in a quietly beautiful corner of Sweden on a warm, somnolent Sunday in the early days of August. It could not have been closer to heaven on earth; oh, and incidentally, the golf was pretty darned good, too.

Of course it was. Anything less would have been an insult to the setting and the occasion. The countless thousands who thronged the fairways of Kungsängen, 20 miles or so north-west of the unutterably beautiful Swedish capital of Stockholm, deserved a treat. And they got one as they witnessed a virtuoso performance by a young man at the peak of his considerable powers.

The record books will show that Lee Westwood won the Volvo Scandinavian Masters by three strokes with a total of 270, 14 under par. Yet although the bald statistics tell some of the story, they do not reveal everything of a victory that was just about as comprehensive as it was possible to be. Westwood was magnificent as he claimed his fourth triumph of the European Tour season, the only flaw in such a statement being that the word "magnificent" is a puny, seven-stone weakling of a word to describe the total authority that he brought to the business of winning one of Europe's more coveted titles. If there is anything better than merely utterly magnificent, Westwood was it, and then some.

At that precise moment, as the sturdy scion of Worksop holed the final putt before the vast, enthusiastic and knowledgeable gallery that, as ever, made its contribution to the enduring success of one of the finest tournaments on the calendar, there may have been only one better player in the whole, wide world, and we all know who that might have been, don't we?

To be the second-best as compared with the fabled Woods is not such a bad accolade, actually. In this tournament, Westwood displayed form that put him firmly and justly on a similar plane to young Mr Woods. And he did it all without breaking more than a bead of sweat.

There can be few players in the game who are better able to win prestigious, big-money tournaments with more equability and grace under the pressure of primacy than Westwood. If the casual spectator were to happen upon him by chance as he left the green at a par-five hole in mid-round, there would be no way of knowing by his demeanour whether he had just inscribed an eagle three or a triple-bogey eight on his card. It is, more than any technical ability to play the game supremely well, his over-riding strength.

In a tournament played out on a course that is a living tribute to its designer, Anders Forsbrand, one of the founding fathers of the modern Swedish game, Westwood exceeded the superlatives. His scores grew progressively higher with each round – 63, 67, 69, 71 – but rarely was his domination of the event called into question. Further, it was the first time in his career that he had led from first to last: it was almost as if it were his by right.

His victory continued a nine-tournament sequence that had started with his stunning triumph over Woods et al in the Deutsche Bank - SAP Open TPC of Europe in May. In between had come two more victories and ties for second, third, fourth and fifth, the only blip in an otherwise sweetly smooth parabola of success being a share of 64th place in the Open Championship at St Andrews.

Michael Campbell

The Course

Kungsängen had been blighted by torrential rainfall in the run-up to the event, but was still as well presented as any course on the European rota. Its major strength lay in the testing first five holes of the back nine, but the other 13 were scarcely any simpler. A course to be reckoned with.

Raymond Russell

There is even a reason for that aberration. Westwood has an uneasy relationship with the Old Course, one that he admits with characteristic candour is probably as much to do with him as anything else. He is not alone in that – Bobby Jones, no less, hated the place at first before learning to love it. In time, Westwood will surely grow to like and respect the Home of Golf. Most do.

But that is in the future. This was very much of the present, and it was a privilege to be there to watch it, and him.

He had one of the rounds of the week on the first day, a 63 that could not possibly have been worse. He led by two strokes from Katsuyoshi Tomori, the smiling Japanese, with Diego Borrego and local hero Olle Karlsson a stroke further back and Ian Hutchings, David Gilford and Maarten Lafeber one more adrift on four under par.

He had an eagle and seven birdies, including four in the last five holes, and none of the birdie putts had to be made from 12 feet. He was set fair for a good week; it would get even better.

After the second round, a 67 had maintained his two-shot advantage over Barry Lane, the former Ryder Cup player, who produced a coruscating 63 of his own, the result, he said, of enjoying his golf again armed as he was with a new, philosophical approach to the game.

A mere 24 hours later, Westwood had increased his advantage to six strokes following a 69. With Lane subsiding to a 76, it was left to the inexperienced Lafeber, who had a one-over-par 72, to provide him with his only challenge of note.

The next day, Lafeber was to equal Westwood's closing 71; it was not enough by a long chalk. In comparison with what had gone before, Westwood was muted in the last round, but it was more than enough. He started with a birdie, had a couple of bogeys immediately after the turn and then turned the screw with a birdie at the penultimate hole.

Meanwhile, others were pursuing their own, private targets — Raymond Russell's third place secured his playing rights for 2001, Borrego advanced his lowly earnings for the year by 73,920 euro (£45,500) with his tie for fourth and Michael Campbell strengthened his position in fifth place in the Volvo Order of Merit.

However, they would have been the first to admit that, on this day, they were but sideshows to the main event. Westwood had his maiden European Tour victory in this tournament in 1996. Now he was on top of the world. On the whole, he rather liked the feeling; it was no more than he deserved.

Mel Webb

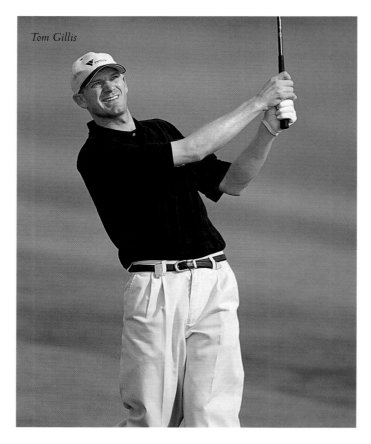

Tom Gillis

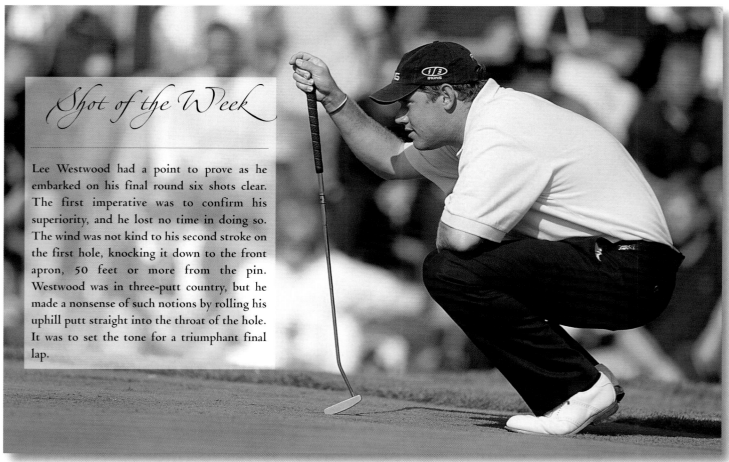

Shot of the Week

Lee Westwood had a point to prove as he embarked on his final round six shots clear. The first imperative was to confirm his superiority, and he lost no time in doing so. The wind was not kind to his second stroke on the first hole, knocking it down to the front apron, 50 feet or more from the pin. Westwood was in three-putt country, but he made a nonsense of such notions by rolling his uphill putt straight into the throat of the hole. It was to set the tone for a triumphant final lap.

Lee Westwood in wonderland

KUNGSÄNGEN, STOCKHOLM, SWEDEN, 3-6 AUGUST 2000, PAR 71, 6761 YARDS, 6182 METRES

Pos.	Name		Rd1	Rd2	Rd3	Rd4	Total	Par	Prize Money Euro	£
1	Lee WESTWOOD	Eng	63	67	69	71	270	-14	266660.00	164095.43
2	Michael CAMPBELL	NZ	69	71	66	67	273	-11	177770.00	109394.90
3	Raymond RUSSELL	Scot	69	69	69	67	274	-10	100160.00	61635.79
4	Jamie SPENCE	Eng	70	69	70	66	275	-9	73920.00	45488.39
	Diego BORREGO	Sp	66	70	71	68	275	-9	73920.00	45488.39
6	Katsuyoshi TOMORI	Jpn	65	73	68	70	276	-8	44960.00	27667.18
	Maarten LAFEBER	Hol	67	66	72	71	276	-8	44960.00	27667.18
	Tom GILLIS	USA	70	69	67	70	276	-8	44960.00	27667.18
	Steen TINNING	Den	71	68	67	70	276	-8	44960.00	27667.18
10	John SENDEN	Aus	70	64	74	69	277	-7	32000.00	19691.94
11	Barry LANE	Eng	69	63	76	70	278	-6	25546.67	15720.74
	Jesper PARNEVIK	Swe	71	69	69	69	278	-6	25546.67	15720.74
	Greg TURNER	NZ	71	70	71	66	278	-6	25546.67	15720.74
	Henrik STENSON	Swe	69	71	70	68	278	-6	25546.67	15720.74
	Ricardo GONZALEZ	Arg	71	68	70	69	278	-6	25546.67	15720.74
	Christopher HANELL	Swe	68	73	68	69	278	-6	25546.67	15720.74
17	Ian WOOSNAM	Wal	72	71	68	68	279	-5	19653.33	12094.13
	Steve WEBSTER	Eng	72	64	73	70	279	-5	19653.33	12094.13
	Colin MONTGOMERIE	Scot	68	71	70	70	279	-5	19653.33	12094.13
	Per-Ulrik JOHANSSON	Swe	69	72	67	71	279	-5	19653.33	12094.13
	Pierre FULKE	Swe	75	67	67	70	279	-5	19653.33	12094.13
	Fabrice TARNAUD	Fr	72	65	69	73	279	-5	19653.33	12094.13
23	David GILFORD	Eng	67	74	69	70	280	-4	16400.00	10092.12
	Andrew MCLARDY	SA	70	69	68	73	280	-4	16400.00	10092.12
	Paolo QUIRICI	Swi	73	68	73	66	280	-4	16400.00	10092.12
	Darren CLARKE	N.Ire	69	66	74	71	280	-4	16400.00	10092.12
	Thomas BJÖRN	Den	71	72	68	69	280	-4	16400.00	10092.12
	Andrew COLTART	Scot	70	73	67	70	280	-4	16400.00	10092.12
29	Daren LEE	Eng	71	68	70	72	281	-3	14480.00	8910.60
	Stephen GALLACHER	Scot	71	70	72	68	281	-3	14480.00	8910.60
31	Gordon BRAND JNR.	Scot	68	70	75	69	282	-2	12832.00	7896.47
	Thomas LEVET	Fr	69	71	68	74	282	-2	12832.00	7896.47
	Olle KARLSSON	Swe	66	69	76	71	282	-2	12832.00	7896.47
	Mathias GRÖNBERG	Swe	71	70	69	72	282	-2	12832.00	7896.47
	Patrik SJÖLAND	Swe	72	70	71	69	282	-2	12832.00	7896.47
36	Sven STRÜVER	Ger	69	71	70	73	283	-1	11520.00	7089.10
	Alastair FORSYTH	Scot	72	70	69	72	283	-1	11520.00	7089.10
38	Knud STORGAARD	Den	73	67	72	72	284	0	10080.00	6202.96
	Justin ROSE	Eng	69	72	71	72	284	0	10080.00	6202.96
	Fredrik LINDGREN	Swe	68	68	74	74	284	0	10080.00	6202.96
	Per NYMAN	Swe	71	69	72	72	284	0	10080.00	6202.96
	Ian HUTCHINGS	SA	67	70	74	73	284	0	10080.00	6202.96
	Gary ORR	Scot	73	69	71	71	284	0	10080.00	6202.96
	David LYNN	Eng	69	71	71	73	284	0	10080.00	6202.96
45	Anders HANSEN	Den	72	70	71	72	285	1	8160.00	5021.45
	Jarrod MOSELEY	Aus	73	66	74	72	285	1	8160.00	5021.45
	Thomas GÖGELE	Ger	71	71	71	72	285	1	8160.00	5021.45
	John BICKERTON	Eng	70	72	70	73	285	1	8160.00	5021.45
	Simon DYSON	Eng	71	68	75	71	285	1	8160.00	5021.45
50	Tony JOHNSTONE	Zim	72	68	75	71	286	2	7040.00	4332.23
	Andrew BUTTERFIELD	Eng	71	71	71	73	286	2	7040.00	4332.23
52	Des SMYTH	Ire	73	70	69	75	287	3	5760.00	3544.55
	Ian POULTER	Eng	69	74	70	74	287	3	5760.00	3544.55
	Philip GOLDING	Eng	73	70	74	70	287	3	5760.00	3544.55
	Joakim HAEGGMAN	Swe	71	72	73	71	287	3	5760.00	3544.55
	Raimo SJÖBERG	Swe	74	69	73	71	287	3	5760.00	3544.55
	Gerry NORQUIST	USA	71	71	74	71	287	3	5760.00	3544.55
58	Klas ERIKSSON	Swe	71	71	72	74	288	4	4560.00	2806.10
	Ross MCFARLANE	Eng	72	71	73	72	288	4	4560.00	2806.10
	Massimo FLORIOLI	It	73	69	73	73	288	4	4560.00	2806.10
	Max ANGLERT	Swe	71	72	72	73	288	4	4560.00	2806.10
62	Roger CHAPMAN	Eng	72	70	74	73	289	5	4080.00	2510.72
	David CARTER	Eng	73	69	71	76	289	5	4080.00	2510.72
64	Gary MURPHY	Ire	72	68	75	75	290	6	3600.00	2215.34
	Stephen FIELD	Eng	70	73	73	74	290	6	3600.00	2215.34
	Phillip PRICE	Wal	72	69	70	79	290	6	3600.00	2215.34
	Grant HAMERTON	Eng	73	70	75	72	290	6	3600.00	2215.34
68	Paul EALES	Eng	71	71	73	76	291	7	3120.00	1919.96
	Lucas PARSONS	Aus	72	71	74	74	291	7	3120.00	1919.96
70	Dennis EDLUND	Swe	70	73	75	74	292	8	2575.67	1585.00
	Massimo SCARPA	It	72	71	73	76	292	8	2575.67	1585.00
	Markus BRIER	Aut	71	72	75	74	292	8	2575.67	1585.00
	Linus PETTERSON (AM)	Swe	69	74	75	76	294	10		
74	Simon D. HURLEY	Eng	71	69	81	74	295	11	2392.50	1472.28
	Jeremy ROBINSON	Eng	71	72	74	78	295	11	2392.50	1472.28
76	Steven RICHARDSON	Eng	70	73	76	77	296	12	2388.00	1469.51

One for the Book

WOBURN GOLF AND COUNTRY CLUB, MILTON KEYNES, ENGLAND

*E*ither way Victor Chandler, on-course Official Bookmakers to the European Tour, were on a winner. "If Montgomerie wins, we get the publicity," explained affable Victor. "If anybody else wins, we get the money."

That was before Colin Montgomerie, hot favourite for the second year running, had failed to deliver the Victor Chandler British Masters - for the second year running.

It was more than an action replay on glorious Woburn's Duke's Course where record crowds of almost 42,000 watched under cloudless skies as birdies galore, eagles and even two holes-in-one in the same match made it four golden days to remember.

In the first year of Chandler sponsorship, it had been gutsy little American Bob May, a 50-1 outsider, who had stopped Montgomerie's gallop. This time it was fellow Scot Gary Orr, at 40-1, who did the bookies a big favour, the only bet of note being one of £300 each-way at 8-1 struck during the winner's record-breaking second round of 62.

The previous year Montgomerie had led by three going into the final day and had been a prohibitive 1-8 favourite, only to fluff his lines. This time, starting two adrift on the Sunday, he stated his intentions straight away with a double-birdie start that equalised the contest, only for unexpected errors to start creeping in, not least missed putts of 18 inches and three feet.

It was Orr's second victory of the year, following a spring success in Portugal after eight years of honest toil awaiting the big breakthrough. Like Montgomerie, he moved away from Scotland years ago to live in stockbroker-belt Surrey, the big difference being that Europe's No 1 has a few more million in the bank!

The 220,500 euro (£133,330) winner's cheque was a far cry from Orr's only other Woburn success. That came in the 1987 Prince of Wales's Trophy and the prizes were a golf bag and a driver. "Winning 130 grand is more fun but it is not as important to me as beating Montgomerie head-to-head," said Orr, whose wife Sarah produced their first-born, Jamie, only three months earlier.

"It's easy to say after the event, but I am not a materialistic person and, of course we do it to earn a living, but it's the winning and the competing that really matter to me."

Per-Ulrik Johansson

Gary Orr

It was quite a week for the Burhill Club in Walton-on-Thames, to which Orr is attached. Only seven days earlier, another club member, Walker Cup star Paul Casey, had won the English Amateur Championship.

How quickly fortunes change. Only two weeks earlier, Orr had been compelled by recurring back pain to withdraw from the TNT Dutch Open after playing just two shots. Here he was packing his bags for a Stateside debut in the year's final major Championship at Valhalla as the Victor Chandler British Masters champion, joining an elite roll of honour which includes most of the greats of European golf.

Not only a champion but also the record-holder for 18 holes, his ten under par 62 in round two beating the 63 set by another Masters winner, Peter Baker, seven years earlier, though Orr failed by one to equal Baker's record low of 266 for 72 holes.

After Montgomerie had romped into the lead on day one with a 64, everyone assumed the tournament was over. Victor Chandler did, anyway. Montgomerie went odds-on, but Orr and Zimbabwe veteran Mark McNulty had other ideas. Orr swept into the halfway lead with his record, with McNulty a shot behind after his second straight 65, a big surprise to him as he was in the middle of swing changes under instruction from David Leadbetter, who said he had been developing bad habits in his old age.

Having taken up the running after six holes of the second round, Orr was never headed again and only briefly equalled. Three birdies and a chip-in eagle on his front nine - the back nine on the card - were followed by five more birdies as he came back in 29 shots, saving the best till last.

Blocked out off the tee, Orr fashioned a three-iron chip-and-run shot from only 130 yards that actually rolled over the hole before settling down a tap-in distance away. "I could easily have made a bogey and been left with a sour taste," admitted modest Orr. "But it was just my day. Everything came off, but that was THE shot of the round and I didn't even see it finish. My caddie told me it was good, but all I was trying to do was squirt it under the branches of the tree."

Having finished off the job on the weekend, holding fast-finishing Swede Per-Ulrik Johansson by two, with Montgomerie third and McNulty hanging on for fourth despite a few hiccups with his new swing, Orr was asked whether it was now a case of "Watch out, Tiger" to which came the dry but realistic reply "Watch out for what?"

Montgomerie, still winless at Woburn, was in less humorous form. "Didn't drive well, didn't hit iron shots well, didn't chip well, never made a putt over six feet, one over par for the last 16 holes. Poor, poor, poor. Every shot I hit after the second hole gave Gary confidence."

Shot of the Week

It has to be the one that broke the record, Gary Orr's 130 yards chip-and-run recovery, cut with a three iron from behind a tree at his final hole on day two to set up the crucial birdie when a bogey looked far more likely. The ball rolled over the hole and finished two feet away. Orr knocked it in for a 62 and was on his way to the second and most important victory of his career.

Gary Orr

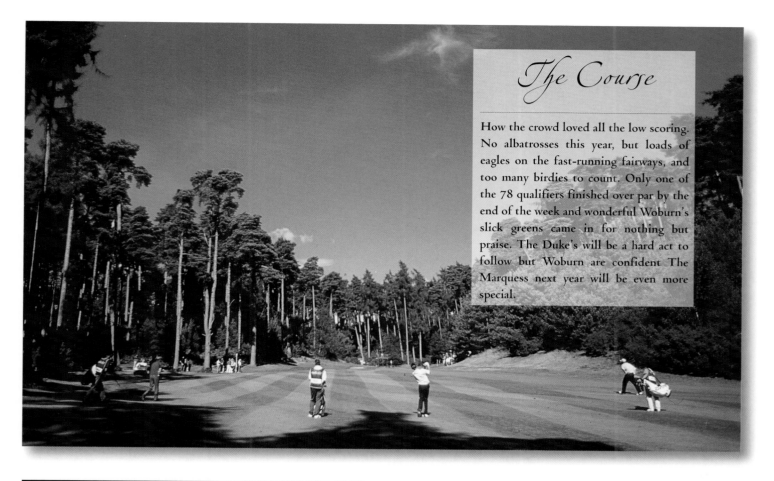

The Course

How the crowd loved all the low scoring. No albatrosses this year, but loads of eagles on the fast-running fairways, and too many birdies to count. Only one of the 78 qualifiers finished over par by the end of the week and wonderful Woburn's slick greens came in for nothing but praise. The Duke's will be a hard act to follow but Woburn are confident The Marquess next year will be even more special.

Colin Montgomerie

Much of the final-day excitement came early when Alastair Forsyth, with a wedge at the 134 yards second, and Roger Chapman, at the 173 yards eighth with a six iron, playing together, aced different holes on the front nine.

Nobody could remember it happening before and nobody, not even Chandler's man, could work out the odds about such a startling turn of events, though figures from 5000-1 to 35,000-1 were bandied about.

It was a fun week all the way off course as well, with the state-of-the-art Victor Chandler betting unit doing roaring trade, spectators being tempted by the four free £1 betting vouchers contained in every programme. From Pro-Am (won by Thomas Björn's men) to winning putt it was a triumph for organiser Amanda Hughes and her gallant team, who will have to do it all over again next year, still at Woburn but on the much-heralded new Marquess Course.

Incidentally, with May and Orr winning the first two runnings of the Victor Chandler, if your name isn't Han, Lee or Cea, there may not be much point in entering. At Woburn, it seems, golf is a three-letter word!

Jeremy Chapman

The picturesque par 3 2nd hole

WOBURN GOLF AND COUNTRY CLUB, MILTON KEYNES, ENGLAND, 10-13 AUGUST 2000, PAR 72, 6979 YARDS, 6382 METRES

Pos.	Name		Rd1	Rd2	Rd3	Rd4	Total	Par	Prize Money Euro	£	Pos.	Name		Rd1	Rd2	Rd3	Rd4	Total	Par	Prize Money Euro	£
1	Gary ORR	Scot	67	62	68	70	267	-21	220703.82	133330.00		Paul AFFLECK	Wal	72	67	70	72	281	-7	8872.52	5360.00
2	Per-Ulrik JOHANSSON	Swe	68	65	69	67	269	-19	147124.84	88880.00		Massimo SCARPA	It	70	71	70	70	281	-7	8872.52	5360.00
3	Colin MONTGOMERIE	Scot	64	69	66	71	270	-18	82898.43	50080.00		Van PHILLIPS	Eng	68	71	71	71	281	-7	8872.52	5360.00
4	Mark MCNULTY	Zim	65	65	71	70	271	-17	66212.80	40000.00	43	Sven STRÜVER	Ger	71	70	70	71	282	-6	7018.56	4240.00
5	Paul LAWRIE	Scot	68	70	64	70	272	-16	47408.36	28640.00		Thomas LEVET	Fr	74	68	69	71	282	-6	7018.56	4240.00
	Andrew COLTART	Scot	70	65	68	69	272	-16	47408.36	28640.00		Stephen FIELD	Eng	69	70	71	72	282	-6	7018.56	4240.00
	Bob MAY	USA	69	68	67	68	272	-16	47408.36	28640.00		Russell CLAYDON	Eng	69	69	75	69	282	-6	7018.56	4240.00
8	Jarmo SANDELIN	Swe	69	72	67	65	273	-15	31384.87	18960.00		Simon WAKEFIELD	Eng	73	69	70	70	282	-6	7018.56	4240.00
	Patrik SJÖLAND	Swe	68	68	68	69	273	-15	31384.87	18960.00		Max ANGLERT	Swe	70	66	73	73	282	-6	7018.56	4240.00
10	Raymond RUSSELL	Scot	67	71	69	67	274	-14	26485.12	16000.00		Christopher HANELL	Swe	69	72	71	70	282	-6	7018.56	4240.00
11	Ian WOOSNAM	Wal	71	69	67	68	275	-13	21638.34	13072.00	50	Sam TORRANCE	Scot	68	69	76	70	283	-5	5429.45	3280.00
	Richard S JOHNSON	Swe	68	70	71	66	275	-13	21638.34	13072.00		Paul EALES	Eng	71	71	69	72	283	-5	5429.45	3280.00
	Jarrod MOSELEY	Aus	70	66	66	73	275	-13	21638.34	13072.00		Nicolas VANHOOTEGEM	Bel	71	70	70	72	283	-5	5429.45	3280.00
	Pierre FULKE	Swe	69	72	68	66	275	-13	21638.34	13072.00		Thomas BJÖRN	Den	69	71	70	73	283	-5	5429.45	3280.00
	Stephen ALLAN	Aus	70	69	70	66	275	-13	21638.34	13072.00		Lucas PARSONS	Aus	76	66	71	70	283	-5	5429.45	3280.00
16	Paolo QUIRICI	Swi	69	67	72	68	276	-12	18274.74	11040.00	55	Mats LANNER	Swe	72	70	73	69	284	-4	4029.52	2434.28
	Ian GARBUTT	Eng	69	65	68	74	276	-12	18274.74	11040.00		Andrew SHERBORNE	Eng	70	72	65	77	284	-4	4029.52	2434.28
18	Mathias GRÖNBERG	Swe	67	70	74	66	277	-11	16751.84	10120.00		David GILFORD	Eng	70	72	70	72	284	-4	4029.52	2434.28
	Johan SKOLD	Swe	70	71	72	64	277	-11	16751.84	10120.00		Andrew MCLARDY	SA	69	71	70	74	284	-4	4029.52	2434.28
20	Peter O'MALLEY	Aus	70	68	68	72	278	-10	15405.51	9306.67		Peter MITCHELL	Eng	70	68	74	72	284	-4	4029.52	2434.28
	Greg OWEN	Eng	69	67	69	73	278	-10	15405.51	9306.67		David PARK	Wal	71	71	75	67	284	-4	4029.52	2434.28
	Niclas FASTH	Swe	71	69	69	69	278	-10	15405.51	9306.67		John BICKERTON	Eng	68	73	73	70	284	-4	4029.52	2434.28
23	Roger CHAPMAN	Eng	71	71	72	65	279	-9	13573.63	8200.00	62	Anders FORSBRAND	Swe	73	69	73	70	285	-3	3045.79	1840.00
	Marc FARRY	Fr	71	67	71	70	279	-9	13573.63	8200.00		Jean-Francois REMESY	Fr	69	72	71	73	285	-3	3045.79	1840.00
	Steve WEBSTER	Eng	72	69	70	68	279	-9	13573.63	8200.00		Tom GILLIS	USA	69	69	75	72	285	-3	3045.79	1840.00
	Steen TINNING	Den	69	70	70	70	279	-9	13573.63	8200.00		Richard COUGHLAN	Ire	75	66	73	71	285	-3	3045.79	1840.00
	Diego BORREGO	Sp	70	71	69	69	279	-9	13573.63	8200.00		Jorge BERENDT	Arg	70	72	73	70	285	-3	3045.79	1840.00
	Alastair FORSYTH	Scot	74	68	72	65	279	-9	13573.63	8200.00		Fabrice TARNAUD	Fr	70	72	70	73	285	-3	3045.79	1840.00
29	Des SMYTH	Ire	71	70	70	69	280	-8	11010.24	6651.43		David CARTER	Eng	71	69	75	70	285	-3	3045.79	1840.00
	Katsuyoshi TOMORI	Jpn	71	70	68	71	280	-8	11010.24	6651.43	69	Kyi Hla HAN	Myan	72	68	75	71	286	-2	2230.10	1347.23
	Barry LANE	Eng	71	69	71	69	280	-8	11010.24	6651.43		Soren KJELDSEN	Den	70	69	75	72	286	-2	2230.10	1347.23
	Anders HANSEN	Den	69	73	69	69	280	-8	11010.24	6651.43		Hennie OTTO	SA	70	72	71	73	286	-2	2230.10	1347.23
	Thomas GÖGELE	Ger	68	70	71	71	280	-8	11010.24	6651.43		Tomas Jesus MUÑOZ	Sp	68	73	67	78	286	-2	2230.10	1347.23
	Per NYMAN	Swe	69	70	73	68	280	-8	11010.24	6651.43	73	Stephen LEANEY	Aus	73	68	73	73	287	-1	1976.50	1194.03
	Gustavo ROJAS	Arg	71	68	73	68	280	-8	11010.24	6651.43		Gary EMERSON	Eng	70	71	74	72	287	-1	1976.50	1194.03
36	Mark MOULAND	Wal	70	72	66	73	281	-7	8872.52	5360.00		Fredrik JACOBSON	Swe	72	70	75	70	287	-1	1976.50	1194.03
	Philip WALTON	Ire	70	69	72	70	281	-7	8872.52	5360.00		Ivo GINER	Sp	68	72	74	73	287	-1	1976.50	1194.03
	Maarten LAFEBER	Hol	71	69	73	68	281	-7	8872.52	5360.00	77	Peter BAKER	Eng	72	67	73	76	288	0	1969.00	1189.50
	Nick O'HERN	Aus	68	73	72	68	281	-7	8872.52	5360.00	78	Ignacio GARRIDO	Sp	71	67	74	78	290	2	1966.00	1187.69

Victor Chandler On Course – the driving force behind sports betting

*Y*ou can make your golf knowledge pay. Pitch your opinion against ours and you could be a winner. Victor Chandler On Course is the name to have on your side for the widest selection of betting options. We play all the players from Love to Lawrie and Woods to Westwood!

As Official Bookmaker to The European Tour and to the Ryder Cup, we look forward to seeing you again throughout 2001. The Victor Chandler Betting Unit will be at Woburn Golf and Country Club for the Victor Chandler British Masters 31st May - 3rd June 2001 and at The Belfry for the Ryder Cup 28th - 30th September 2001. We'll be offering Tax-free betting on all sports at these events and at many other European Tour events throughout the year.

FOR ANY ENQUIRIES OR TO OPEN
AN ACCOUNT PLEASE CALL:

08000 978797

or visit our website at:
www.victorchandler.co.uk

Official Bookmaker to
The European Tour

Official Bookmaker to
The Ryder Cup.

History Makers

VALHALLA GOLF CLUB, LOUISVILLE, KENTUCKY, USA

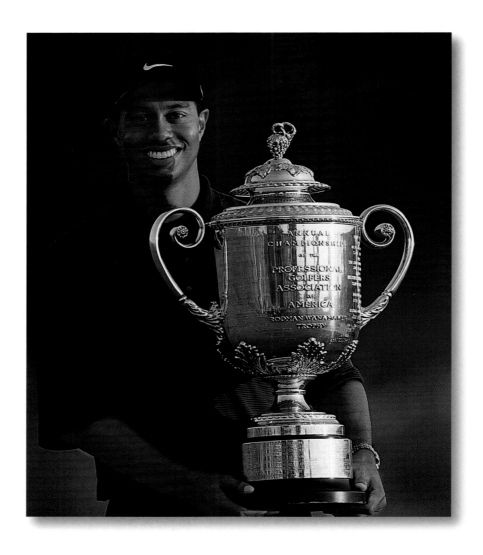

One inspired headline writer in a local Louisville newspaper described the classic duel that provided such a thrilling climax to the US PGA Championship as: "The history man versus the mystery man."

You could see what he meant. Tiger Woods has been making history at the same rate as he has been making birdies almost since he first swung a club in earnest.

Bob May was a mystery even among a large number of American professionals unaware of his formidable reputation as a teenager in Southern California and scarcely any the wiser by his arrival at the beginning of the year on the US Tour.

But May was no mystery among European professionals who had tasted his cold steel in many a tournament on this side of the Atlantic.

Colin Montgomerie had lost his own particular duel with May when, surprisingly, though not entirely so, the American won the 1999 Victor Chandler British Masters at Woburn Golf and Country Club.

Indeed, but for that victory May would not have been at Valhalla and would not have played his prominent role in probably the most dramatic final few hours of a major championship since Tom Watson and Jack Nicklaus closed in on the winning line at Turnberry in the 1977 Open Championship.

There is another sense in which the European Tour contributed hugely to the event aside from the high placings of Members like Thomas Björn (third), José Maria Olazábal (fourth) and Darren Clarke (ninth).

Although May was born and brought up in Southern California - and has been a resident of Las Vegas for a number of years - it was his five campaigns on the European Tour that matured a talent sufficiently to stretch Woods almost to breaking point.

You could tell that May was grateful for the opportunities afforded to him in Europe in the way he unhesitatingly returned to England to defend his Victor Chandler British Masters title in the week preceding the US PGA Championship.

He had played four rounds at Denver the week prior to that. Denver to Valhalla via Woburn was probably the most unlikely and exhausting schedule undertaken by anyone in the field.

Bob May

Thomas Björn

The Course

Valhalla Golf Club is of more than usual interest to Europeans than the average venue for a US PGA Championship. The Jack Nicklaus-designed course in Louisville, Kentucky, will play host to the 2007 Ryder Cup. At 7,167 yards, the par 72 track is neither long nor short, neither memorable nor forgettable, neither particularly scenic nor particularly ugly. Valhalla is reckoned to be a well above average design tee to green. But the putting surfaces boast humps and bumps, ridges and depressions, tiers and ramps; José María Olazábal, who carded a record 63, loved it. But the designer himself confessed he would like to see some of the undulations softened. Expect alterations prior to the Ryder Cup.

Greg Chalmers

To score 31, as May did, on the inward half as a contender in a major championship and not win must have been hard to swallow, though probably more palatable given the identity of the victor and the special circumstances of an extraordinary summer.

Woods reminded me of James Bond strapped to the table with Dr No's laser heading unerringly towards his private parts. You always knew that he would escape, but you did not know precisely how and when.

You always knew that Woods was going to win but you did not know exactly how and when. He prevailed in a play-off though only after the most fantastic putt to tie on the 72nd green. Downhill, very fast, slightly left to right and the best part of seven feet, it required technique and nerve. Woods possesses any amount of both.

If the final afternoon was exciting, the first three days produced no shortage of memorable moments. There was the first competitive meeting of Woods and Jack Nicklaus and the way both produced birdies at the final hole of their two days together, the old master wedging stone dead and the young pretender holing a long putt. Anything you can do.......

Saturday provided one of the great rounds in the history of major championship golf. Olazábal's 63 was the 19th such score in major history and with a comparatively disappointing par, par finish agonisingly close to what would have been the first 62.

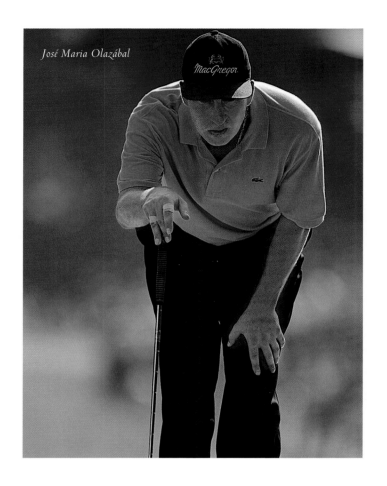

José Maria Olazábal

This proved to be a remarkable turnaround in fortunes for the Spaniard. He had missed the cut in his previous tournament with a second round 81 and opened up at Valhalla with a poor 76 in which he looked a tortured soul.

But there are few who work harder and none more capable of brave fightbacks. He went from 32nd to joint sixth and declared: "It's been a long time since I enjoyed myself this much on a golf course." The reason was apparent for someone with notorious driving problems. He missed only one fairway out of 14!

Björn came of age during the summer of 2000. His second place at St Andrews and third in the US PGA Championship confirmed much of his own self belief and, by his own reckoning, contributed to general signs of a golden new era for European golf.

"We have gone through a period where we had five or six players at the top of the world rankings over a period of 15 years," the Dane said. "Now there are a lot of new faces and younger players who have played majors for three or four years. They are getting used to it. That is the reason why Europeans have done well in the majors. We have not won any, but we are getting up there and we're contending."

No mystery about that. Just a new line of history makers.

Alan Fraser

Shot of the Week

It could have been Jack Nicklaus's wedge at the 36th or that putt of Tiger Woods on the 72nd. But Bob May's second to the 15th during the final round was so audacious and so perfectly executed that Woods himself was struck with admiration. Let Woods describe the seven iron over the water to six feet from the flag. "I doubt if any of the spectators really understood the shot Bob hit. To step up there and hit the ball about eight yards right of the hole and draw it back over the water was an impressive shot. I saw it start out and I said ''Wow, that's a little right. All of a sudden it was drawing back. 'That was impressive,' I told my caddie. To be that committed." May happened to miss the short putt in a key moment. But that error did not affect the greatness of the approach.

Jack Nicklaus salutes the huge galleries on the 18th hole

VALHALLA GOLF CLUB, LOUISVILLE, KENTUCKY, USA, 17-20 AUGUST 2000, PAR 72, 7167 YARDS, 6514 METRES

Pos.	Name		Rd1	Rd2	Rd3	Rd4	Total	Par	Prize Money Euro	£
1	Tiger WOODS	USA	66	67	70	67	270	-18	994912.91	598404.26
2	Bob MAY	USA	72	66	66	66	270	-18	596947.73	359042.55
3	Thomas BJÖRN	Den	72	68	67	68	275	-13	375855.98	226063.83
4	Greg CHALMERS	Aus	71	69	66	70	276	-12	219617.81	132092.20
	José Maria OLAZABAL	Sp	76	68	63	69	276	-12	219617.81	132092.20
	Stuart APPLEBY	Aus	70	69	68	69	276	-12	219617.81	132092.20
7	Franklin LANGHAM	USA	72	71	65	69	277	-11	173557.03	104388.30
8	Notah BEGAY III	USA	72	66	70	70	278	-10	160291.52	96409.57
9	Tom WATSON	USA	76	70	65	68	279	-9	124364.12	74800.54
	Fred FUNK	USA	69	68	74	68	279	-9	124364.12	74800.54
	Davis LOVE III	USA	68	69	72	70	279	-9	124364.12	74800.54
	Darren CLARKE	N.Ire	68	72	72	67	279	-9	124364.12	74800.54
	Scott DUNLAP	USA	66	68	70	75	279	-9	124364.12	74800.54
	Phil MICKELSON	USA	70	70	69	70	279	-9	124364.12	74800.54
15	Stewart CINK	USA	72	71	70	67	280	-8	85673.05	51529.25
	Lee WESTWOOD	Eng	72	72	69	67	280	-8	85673.05	51529.25
	Chris DIMARCO	USA	73	70	69	68	280	-8	85673.05	51529.25
	Michael CLARK II	USA	73	70	67	70	280	-8	85673.05	51529.25
19	Tom KITE	USA	70	72	69	70	281	-7	62126.79	37367.03
	JP HAYES	USA	69	68	68	76	281	-7	62126.79	37367.03
	Angel CABRERA	Arg	72	71	71	67	281	-7	62126.79	37367.03
	Robert ALLENBY	Aus	73	71	68	69	281	-7	62126.79	37367.03
	Lee JANZEN	USA	76	70	70	65	281	-7	62126.79	37367.03
24	Paul AZINGER	USA	72	71	66	73	282	-6	45323.81	27260.64
	Steve JONES	USA	72	71	70	69	282	-6	45323.81	27260.64
	Jarmo SANDELIN	Swe	74	72	68	68	282	-6	45323.81	27260.64
27	Brad FAXON	USA	71	74	70	68	283	-5	37769.84	22717.20
	Skip KENDALL	USA	72	72	69	70	283	-5	37769.84	22717.20
	Tom PERNICE	USA	74	69	70	70	283	-5	37769.84	22717.20
30	Mike WEIR	Can	76	69	68	71	284	-4	31920.12	19198.80
	Jean VAN DE VELDE	Fr	70	74	69	71	284	-4	31920.12	19198.80
	Stephen AMES	T&T	69	71	71	73	284	-4	31920.12	19198.80
	Kenny PERRY	USA	78	68	70	68	284	-4	31920.12	19198.80
34	Sergio GARCIA	Sp	74	69	73	69	285	-3	26531.01	15957.45
	Chris PERRY	USA	72	74	70	69	285	-3	26531.01	15957.45
	Mark CALCAVECCHIA	USA	73	74	71	67	285	-3	26531.01	15957.45
	Ernie ELS	SA	74	68	72	71	285	-3	26531.01	15957.45
	Blaine MCCALLISTER	USA	73	71	70	71	285	-3	26531.01	15957.45
39	Toshimitsu IZAWA	USA	73	73	71	69	286	-2	22661.91	13630.32
	Colin MONTGOMERIE	Scot	74	72	70	70	286	-2	22661.91	13630.32
41	Jeff SLUMAN	USA	73	69	72	73	287	-1	18792.80	11303.19
	Justin LEONARD	USA	73	73	71	70	287	-1	18792.80	11303.19
	Paul STANKOWSKI	USA	75	72	68	72	287	-1	18792.80	11303.19
	Steve PATE	USA	75	70	74	68	287	-1	18792.80	11303.19
	David TOMS	USA	72	68	72	75	287	-1	18792.80	11303.19
46	Bernhard LANGER	Ger	75	69	73	71	288	0	13984.05	8410.90
	Mark O'MEARA	USA	71	72	70	75	288	0	13984.05	8410.90
	Shigeki MARUYAMA	Jpn	77	69	71	71	288	0	13984.05	8410.90
	Duffy WALDORF	USA	75	70	71	72	288	0	13984.05	8410.90
	Brian HENNINGER	USA	70	74	71	73	288	0	13984.05	8410.90
51	Nick FALDO	Eng	79	68	69	73	289	1	12120.57	7290.09
	Jesper PARNEVIK	Swe	72	74	70	73	289	1	12120.57	7290.09
	Steve LOWERY	USA	73	74	73	69	289	1	12120.57	7290.09
	Brian WATTS	USA	72	74	73	70	289	1	12120.57	7290.09
	Glen DAY	USA	76	71	71	71	289	1	12120.57	7290.09
	Andrew COLTART	Scot	74	71	73	71	289	1	12120.57	7290.09
	Jonathan KAYE	USA	69	74	71	75	289	1	12120.57	7290.09
58	Padraig HARRINGTON	Ire	75	72	69	74	290	2	11330.95	6815.16
	Loren ROBERTS	USA	74	72	71	73	290	2	11330.95	6815.16
	Curtis STRANGE	USA	72	76	70	72	290	2	11330.95	6815.16
	Carlos Daniel FRANCO	Par	72	74	74	70	290	2	11330.95	6815.16
	Dennis PAULSON	USA	72	75	70	73	290	2	11330.95	6815.16
	Joe OGILVIE	USA	73	74	71	72	290	2	11330.95	6815.16
64	Wayne GRADY	Aus	71	74	68	78	291	3	10722.95	6449.47
	Craig STADLER	USA	74	69	71	77	291	3	10722.95	6449.47
	Bill GLASSON	USA	73	74	71	73	291	3	10722.95	6449.47
	Miguel Angel JIMÉNEZ	Sp	70	77	74	70	291	3	10722.95	6449.47
	Jay HAAS	USA	73	74	68	76	291	3	10722.95	6449.47
69	Greg KRAFT	USA	71	73	75	73	292	4	10418.95	6266.62
	Kirk TRIPLETT	USA	76	71	73	72	292	4	10418.95	6266.62
71	John HUSTON	USA	75	72	74	72	293	5	10336.05	6216.76
72	Jim FURYK	USA	74	71	74	75	294	6	10253.14	6166.89
	Paul LAWRIE	Scot	75	71	73	75	294	6	10253.14	6166.89
74	Robert DAMRON	USA	72	74	81	70	297	9	10114.95	6083.78
	Billy MAYFAIR	USA	74	73	76	74	297	9	10114.95	6083.78
	Scott HOCH	USA	73	70	75	79	297	9	10114.95	6083.78
77	Masashi OZAKI	Jpn	74	71	76	78	299	11	9976.76	6000.66
	Rory SABBATINI	USA	74	71	76	78	299	11	9976.76	6000.66
79	Hidemichi TANAKA	Jpn	72	73	77	79	301	13	9893.86	5950.80
80	Frank DOBBS	USA	75	72	88	78	313	25	9838.58	5917.55

Chianti e Pasta é ancora il menu di oggi

SLIEVE RUSSELL HOTEL GOLF AND COUNTRY CLUB, CO CAVAN, IRELAND

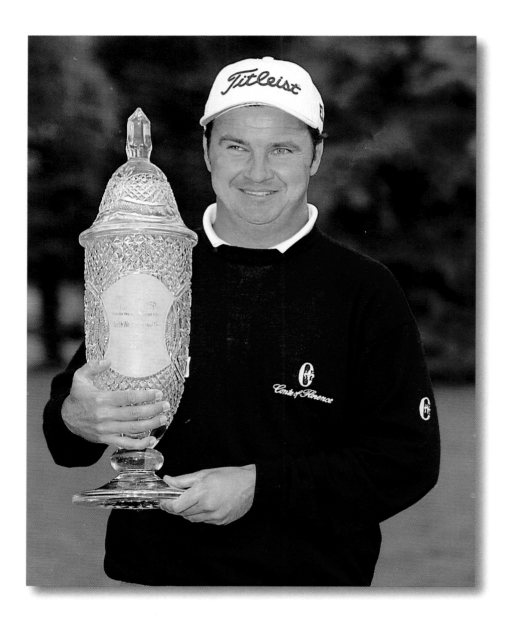

The Italian connection proved a winner again at Slieve Russell where Massimo Scarpa succeeded his esteemed compatriot Costantino Rocca as the champion of the Buzzgolf.com North West of Ireland Open. After a nerve-wracking final day that was initially disrupted by early morning fog, and later by a thunder and lightning storm as the leaders tackled the closing two holes, the 30 year-old Scarpa held off the challenge of the Swede, Mikael Lundberg, to get home by a shot.

The Buzzgolf.com sponsorship once again inspired the contenders in this "double badge" event to demonstrate just how good they are, a point graphically made on Friday evening when the cut came at even par on a 7, 053 yards course in weather that varied from the delightful to the not so pleasant.

There have been times when Italian golfers found it more than a little difficult to make their presence felt at the highest level. Cast your minds back to the 1960s through the 1980s and, yes to be sure, there were Ugo Grappasonni (and much later his son, Silvio), Roberto Bernardino, Baldovino Dassu, Massimo Mannelli, Renato Campagnoli, Alberto Croce, all good, solid performers. But it wasn't until Rocca came like an exciting bolt from the blue out of the Challenge Tour and on to Ryder Cup glory that we at last stood up and took serious notice of Italian golfers.

More recently, Emanuele Canonica made light of the fact that at five feet two inches he is one of the shortest men on Tour by winning the AXA Performance Data Driving Distance category in 1998 and 1999. And now there is Massimo Scarpa, a former semi-professional footballer with his first tournament victory safely tucked away and looking forward to a lot more of the same. Pride in the fact that he had succeeded Rocca as champion was the first sentiment that entered Massimo's head when he finally clinched the first prize cheque of 58,330 euro (£35,000) and perhaps even more importantly, a twelve month exemption on the European Tour.

"Proud to be there with Costantino's name, that's how I feel right now," enthused Scarpa, who putts right handed but chips left handed. "My first Tour win as well and I hope it is not my last. I got used to winning on the Challenge Tour, four times in 1998, but this feels different. Mikael played really well. The eagle on 13 was

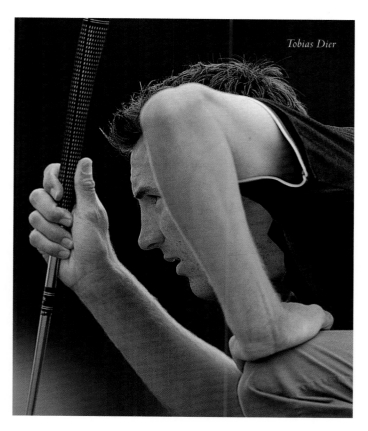

Tobias Dier

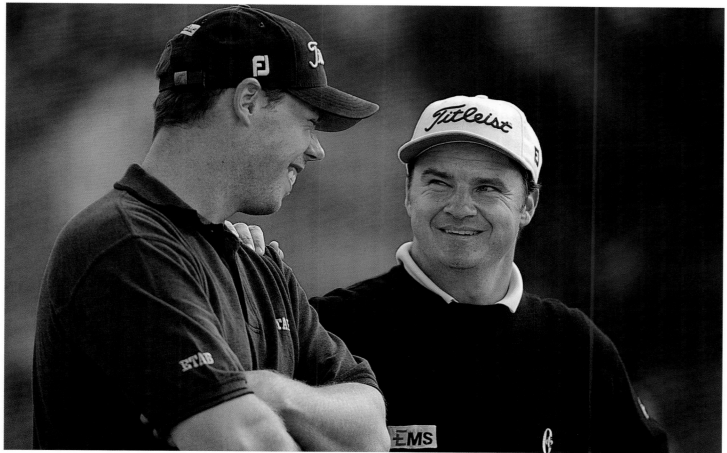

Friendly rivals Mikael Lundberg and Massimo Scarpa

The Course

Slieve Russell Hotel Golf & Country Club is one of the many outstanding golfing venues that have sprung up all over Ireland in the past decade. The course and complex in a remote part of Co Cavan, just inside the southern side of the border from Northern Ireland, are a tribute to the vision of the owner, Sean Quinn. The 7,053 yards, par 72 lay-out was designed by one of Ireland's most noted architects, Patrick Merrigan. It boasts 50 acres of lakes and ponds complementing typical Cavan drumlins and valleys. Tobias Dier of Germany and Henrik Stenson from Sweden set a new record of 65 during the Buzzgolf.com North West of Ireland Open.

Andrew Beal with caddie Roy Robinson

the decisive moment because I didn't putt very well all day. That was the first putt I holed."

Ireland has been good to the Italian this year. In the Murphy's Irish Open in Ballybunion, he came to the ninth, his 18th, needing a par three at a hole measuring just 130 yards to equal the European Tour record for nine holes. He took a bogey but still signed for a course record 63. It was an indication of what he could do and a portent of even greater things to come.

Scarpa arrived in Co Cavan off four sub-par rounds in the previous week's Victor Chandler British Masters at Woburn Golf and Country Club and he duly stretched that to eight with scores of 67, 70, 68 and 70 for a 13 under par total of 275. He was pushed all the way by Lundberg, who recovered bravely from a double bogey six at the third and at the end was only one off the pace. On reflection, Scarpa was absolutely correct in picking out his eagle at the 13th on the final day as the key moment in the tournament. Lundberg, on the other hand, saw his attempt for a three at the same hole roll round the cup and stay out.

The rest, as they say, is history. Chianti and pasta were the order of the day for the second successive year in the west of Ireland!

Charlie Mulqueen

Shot of the Week

Massimo Scarpa was waging a fierce battle with Mikael Lundberg and a number of others when he arrived at Slieve Russell's signature hole, the 529 yards 13th played around the edge of Lough Rud. The hole is fraught with danger for both drive and second shot with the water in play for the man brave to try for the green in two. Scarpa took his courage in both hands and put a little daylight between himself and his rivals when he hit two mighty shots to 20 feet and holed the putt for an eagle. It put him a shot in front and he was never caught again.

SLIEVE RUSSELL HOTEL GOLF AND COUNTRY CLUB, CO CAVAN, IRELAND
17-20 AUGUST 2000, PAR 72, 7053 YARDS, 6449 METRES

Pos.	Name		Rd1	Rd2	Rd3	Rd4	Total	Par	Prize Money Euro	£
1	Massimo SCARPA	It	67	70	68	70	275	-13	58330.00	35083.39
2	Mikael LUNDBERG	Swe	70	69	67	70	276	-12	38880.00	23384.92
3	Andrew BEAL	Eng	67	69	71	70	277	-11	21910.00	13178.08
4	Garry HOUSTON	Wal	67	69	73	69	278	-10	14863.33	8939.76
	Carlos RODILES	Sp	70	71	70	67	278	-10	14863.33	8939.76
	Tobias DIER	Ger	71	71	65	71	278	-10	14863.33	8939.76
7	Ross DRUMMOND	Scot	72	66	69	72	279	-9	8522.50	5125.98
	Gary MURPHY	Ire	70	66	70	73	279	-9	8522.50	5125.98
	Gary EMERSON	Eng	67	75	70	67	279	-9	8522.50	5125.98
	Luis CLAVERIE	Sp	66	72	70	71	279	-9	8522.50	5125.98
11	Henrik STENSON	Swe	72	71	65	72	280	-8	6031.67	3627.83
	Olle KARLSSON	Swe	72	66	68	74	280	-8	6031.67	3627.83
	Robert COLES	Eng	72	70	71	67	280	-8	6031.67	3627.83
14	Katsuyoshi TOMORI	Jpn	71	70	68	72	281	-7	5355.00	3220.84
15	Malcolm MACKENZIE	Eng	71	71	69	71	282	-6	4830.00	2905.07
	Mark MOULAND	Wal	69	72	73	68	282	-6	4830.00	2905.07
	Philip ARCHER	Eng	70	73	67	72	282	-6	4830.00	2905.07
	Trevor IMMELMAN	SA	75	69	71	67	282	-6	4830.00	2905.07
19	Jose Manuel LARA	Sp	66	75	70	72	283	-5	3970.00	2387.81
	Paul SHERMAN	Eng	70	71	71	71	283	-5	3970.00	2387.81
	Justin ROSE	Eng	74	70	70	69	283	-5	3970.00	2387.81
	Stephen FIELD	Eng	71	72	69	71	283	-5	3970.00	2387.81
	Des TERBLANCHE	SA	69	68	72	74	283	-5	3970.00	2387.81
	Mark PILKINGTON	Wal	73	69	67	74	283	-5	3970.00	2387.81
	Joakim RASK	Swe	73	68	71	71	283	-5	3970.00	2387.81
26	Marc PENDARIES	Fr	72	71	73	68	284	-4	3377.50	2031.44
	Dennis EDLUND	Swe	72	70	70	72	284	-4	3377.50	2031.44
	Henrik NYSTROM	Swe	70	73	68	73	284	-4	3377.50	2031.44
	Graeme STORM	Eng	67	73	70	74	284	-4	3377.50	2031.44
30	Kalle VAINOLA	Fin	71	69	71	74	285	-3	2619.17	1575.34
	Mattias ELIASSON	Swe	69	74	73	69	285	-3	2619.17	1575.34
	Grant DODD	Aus	69	74	71	71	285	-3	2619.17	1575.34
	Euan LITTLE	Scot	70	72	70	73	285	-3	2619.17	1575.34
	Fredrik HENGE	Swe	72	71	69	73	285	-3	2619.17	1575.34
	Jesus Maria ARRUTI	Sp	74	68	73	70	285	-3	2619.17	1575.34
	Stephen DODD	Wal	71	73	70	71	285	-3	2619.17	1575.34
	Adam MEDNICK	Swe	73	68	72	72	285	-3	2619.17	1575.34
	Brian NELSON	USA	70	71	69	75	285	-3	2619.17	1575.34
	Steven RICHARDSON	Eng	71	70	72	72	285	-3	2619.17	1575.34
	Simon WAKEFIELD	Eng	71	73	71	70	285	-3	2619.17	1575.34
	Ivo GINER	Sp	74	69	68	74	285	-3	2619.17	1575.34
42	Des SMYTH	Ire	67	73	73	73	286	-2	1855.00	1115.72
	Daniel WESTERMARK	Swe	70	71	70	75	286	-2	1855.00	1115.72
	Graham RANKIN	Scot	71	73	75	67	286	-2	1855.00	1115.72
	Morten BACKHAUSEN	Den	73	70	75	68	286	-2	1855.00	1115.72
	Mikael PILTZ	Fin	72	69	71	74	286	-2	1855.00	1115.72
	Fredrik ANDERSSON	Swe	70	70	75	71	286	-2	1855.00	1115.72
	Sebastien DELAGRANGE	Fr	71	73	75	67	286	-2	1855.00	1115.72
	Erol SIMSEK	Ger	69	71	74	72	286	-2	1855.00	1115.72
	Marco BERNARDINI	It	77	67	70	72	286	-2	1855.00	1115.72
51	Robert Jan DERKSEN	Hol	74	69	69	75	287	-1	1330.00	799.95
	Martin ERLANDSSON	Swe	75	69	69	74	287	-1	1330.00	799.95
	Neil CHEETHAM	Eng	75	67	71	74	287	-1	1330.00	799.95
	Francesco GUERMANI	It	72	69	70	76	287	-1	1330.00	799.95
	Daren LEE	Eng	72	72	72	71	287	-1	1330.00	799.95
	Bjorn PETTERSSON	Swe	74	67	74	72	287	-1	1330.00	799.95
57	Patrik GOTTFRIDSON	Swe	74	70	75	69	288	0	1015.00	610.49
	Nils RORBAEK	Den	68	72	74	74	288	0	1015.00	610.49
	Richard BLAND	Eng	71	73	71	73	288	0	1015.00	610.49
	Johan RYSTRÖM	Swe	70	73	72	73	288	0	1015.00	610.49
	Charles CHALLEN	Eng	69	71	72	76	288	0	1015.00	610.49
62	Andrew SHERBORNE	Eng	72	70	73	74	289	1	857.50	515.76
	Andrew RAITT	Eng	70	70	74	75	289	1	857.50	515.76
	Daniel CHOPRA	Swe	74	67	72	76	289	1	857.50	515.76
	Fredrik WIDMARK	Swe	71	72	72	74	289	1	857.50	515.76
66	Christophe POTTIER	Fr	69	72	75	74	290	2	717.50	431.55
	Raimo SJÖBERG	Swe	72	72	74	72	290	2	717.50	431.55
	Gary CLARK	Eng	71	73	72	74	290	2	717.50	431.55
	Max ANGLERT	Swe	71	71	75	73	290	2	717.50	431.55
70	Costantino ROCCA	It	71	71	74	75	291	3	650.00	390.95
71	Mårten OLANDER	Swe	72	72	77	71	292	4	558.50	335.92
	Dominique NOUAILHAC	Fr	74	70	77	71	292	4	558.50	335.92
73	Tim SPENCE	Eng	70	73	79	71	293	5	554.00	333.21
74	Per G NYMAN	Swe	72	71	71	80	294	6	549.50	330.50
	James HEPWORTH	Eng	73	69	69	83	294	6	549.50	330.50
76	Renaud GUILLARD	Fr	73	71	74	78	296	8	545.00	327.80
77	David MILLS	Eng	74	68	76	79	297	9	542.00	325.99

Triumphant March

FIRESTONE COUNTRY CLUB, AKRON, OHIO, USA

When Tiger Woods arrived at Akron he had more to celebrate than his remarkable victory over a determined Bob May in the US PGA Championship the previous Sunday evening. For despite all that Woods had achieved in his 100th tournament as a professional, winning his fifth major championship and equalling Ben Hogan's record of three in one year, May had done to him what professionals of greater name and stature had been unable to do. May, apparently fearless and not at all intimidated by Woods's reputation, had hunted Woods to the 72nd hole and then nearly beaten him in a three-hole play-off. How would Woods react? Would May's irreverence be taken up by others in the 37-strong field who would push Woods to the limit.

If the answer was not clear after the first round when Woods went round in 64, six under par, and opened a one stroke lead over Jim Furyk and two over Darren Clarke, Carlos Franco, Justin Leonard, Phil Mickelson, Phillip Price, and Lee Westwood, then it was crystal clear after the second, a 61. There are times when Woods confounds everyone. This was one of them. There was no sign of tiredness after the previous week. His 61 was simply sensational, equalling José Maria Olazábal's course record set in 1990.

When Woods was eight under par for the day after 12 holes, the shimmering prospect of a 59, 11 under par, loomed. "I never knew how many under par I was," Woods said later. "I was just concentrating on building a big lead." He did that all right. Woods scarcely put a foot wrong. He was accurate and enormously long from the tee. His iron play was impeccable and his putting, which is perhaps one of the biggest differences between him and his fellow professionals, was excellent. When a player is on song in all these departments he is going to be hard to catch. When that player is Tiger Woods, no one can live with him.

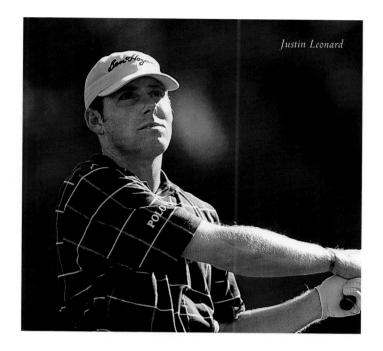

Justin Leonard

Phillip Price

Shot of the Week

Tiger Woods stood in the fairway of the 72nd hole, 168 yards from the flag, in near darkness. It was so dark Woods could hardly see the ball but it did not matter. Such is his control when his game is on song that even with the equivalent of his eyes shut he could hit the ball with pinpoint precision. Using an eight iron, Woods hit his ball to within three feet of the hole. That gave him another birdie and took him to 21 under par. It was the shot of the week, a shot played almost blind.

After the first round Clarke spoke of how he had telephoned Woods after Woods had won the Open Championship. "I left a message on his voicemail saying: "Well done and that the more he won, the better he made me look," Clarke, who had beaten the US Open, Open and US PGA champion in the final of the WGC-Andersen Consulting Match Play in February, said. Woods certainly continued to make Clarke look good as he widened his lead, toying with the field over the difficult South Course. His lead was two strokes after the first round, seven after 36 holes, nine after 54. Woods was making Clarke look better and better the longer the tournament went on.

The only thing that interrupted Woods's triumphant march was the weather, a three-hour delay for rain on the Sunday being an irritant. Hal Sutton, who had so famously outspoken and then outplayed Woods at The Players' Championship in March, fell away from his role as one of the three closest challengers, nine behind. So did Mickelson, whose golf flickered like a guttering candle. Price, in only his second foray had competed in only two major tournaments other than the Open Championship, but he was in contention after rounds of 66, 69 and 66. Boosted by the presence of Alan Fine, his sports psychologist, as well as Sandra, his wife, Price birdied the 12th hole to get to within five strokes of Woods.

Hal Sutton

Phil Mickelson

There is a view that Price is held back because he does not realise how good he is. He is a very good golfer with a much improved swing thanks to recent changes by Dennis Sheehy and a good caddie in Pete Futcher, but perhaps on the thundery Sunday afternoon when he was playing for a prize ten times bigger than the biggest purse he had ever won, Price's diffidence was shown up. Realising that to beat the fast-approaching darkness, Price and the leaders increased their speed. No one wanted to have to return the next morning. Perhaps this was why Price dropped three strokes in his last four holes, thus falling from outright second place into a tie with Justin Leonard and going from winning $500,000 to $437,500.

Three other Europeans joined Price in the top ten. A last 36 holes of 133, seven under par, propelled Colin Montgomerie into joint eighth while Olazábal and the revitalised Thomas Björn, after a second in the US PGA Championship the previous week, shared tenth place.

Nonetheless, this was Woods's tournament from start to finish.

John Hopkins

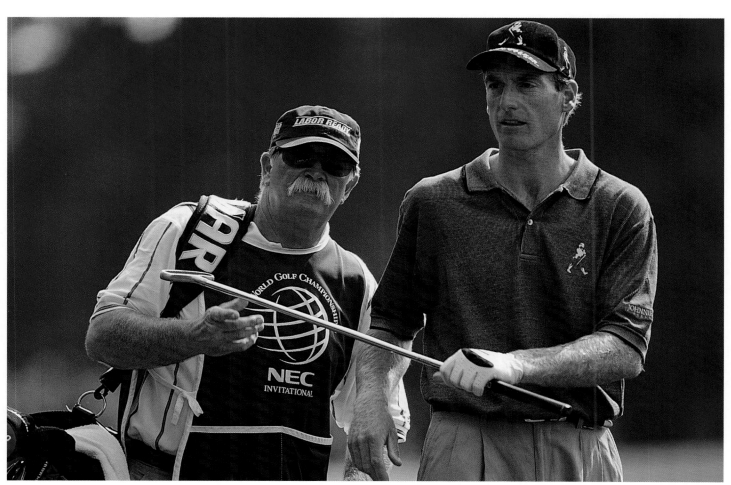

Jim Furyk with caddie Fluff

The Course

The Firestone Country Club opened in 1929 and its courses have hosted 62 golf tournaments since then. The South Course was redesigned in 1960 by Robert Trent Jones, who added 50 bunkers and rebuilt or altered every green, making the course a par 70, stretching it to 7,180 yards and turning it into one of the most feared and respected courses in the US. It is reminiscent of Winged Foot and Oak Hill in the way that trees frame almost every hole and the greens are often above the fairways.

Tiger Woods

FIRESTONE COUNTRY CLUB, AKRON, OHIO, USA, 24-27 AUGUST 2000, PAR 70, 7139 YARDS, 6527 METRES

Pos.	Name		Rd1	Rd2	Rd3	Rd4	Total	Par	Prize Money Euro	£
1	Tiger WOODS	USA	64	61	67	67	259	-21	1102779.46	671366.23
2	Justin LEONARD	USA	66	67	71	66	270	-10	482466.02	293722.73
	Phillip PRICE	Wal	66	69	66	69	270	-10	482466.02	293722.73
4	Jim FURYK	USA	65	69	69	68	271	-9	268342.64	163365.56
	Hal SUTTON	USA	68	68	65	70	271	-9	268342.64	163365.56
	Phil MICKELSON	USA	66	66	69	70	271	-9	268342.64	163365.56
7	Stewart CINK	USA	72	69	68	63	272	-8	187472.51	114132.26
8	Colin MONTGOMERIE	Scot	71	69	66	67	273	-7	162659.97	99026.52
	Paul AZINGER	USA	68	70	70	65	273	-7	162659.97	99026.52
10	José Maria OLAZABAL	Sp	67	73	69	65	274	-6	137847.43	83920.78
	Thomas BJÖRN	Den	69	69	70	66	274	-6	137847.43	83920.78
12	Ernie ELS	SA	67	71	69	68	275	-5	121857.13	74185.97
	Robert ALLENBY	Aus	69	69	70	67	275	-5	121857.13	74185.97
14	Loren ROBERTS	USA	67	69	66	75	277	-3	113586.28	69150.72
15	Shigeki MARUYAMA	Jpn	71	70	68	69	278	-2	105315.43	64115.47
	Michael CAMPBELL	NZ	71	69	70	68	278	-2	105315.43	64115.47
17	Darren CLARKE	N.Ire	66	71	71	71	279	-1	91530.70	55723.40
	Andrew COLTART	Scot	69	69	69	72	279	-1	91530.70	55723.40
	Notah BEGAY III	USA	74	66	69	70	279	-1	91530.70	55723.40
20	Nick PRICE	Zim	70	69	74	67	280	0	75356.23	45876.47
	Stuart APPLEBY	Aus	67	70	70	73	280	0	75356.23	45876.47
	Lee WESTWOOD	Eng	66	69	73	72	280	0	75356.23	45876.47
23	Paul MCGINLEY	Ire	71	72	71	67	281	1	66166.76	40281.97
24	Mike WEIR	Can	68	76	68	71	283	3	57711.76	35134.61
	Jeff MAGGERT	USA	72	69	73	69	283	3	57711.76	35134.61
	Retief GOOSEN	SA	69	74	73	67	283	3	57711.76	35134.61
27	Padraig HARRINGTON	Ire	76	65	71	72	284	4	48522.29	29540.11
	Mark O'MEARA	USA	71	71	70	72	284	4	48522.29	29540.11
	Carlos Daniel FRANCO	Par	66	77	72	69	284	4	48522.29	29540.11
	Gary ORR	Scot	70	68	72	74	284	4	48522.29	29540.11
31	Greg NORMAN	Aus	68	71	76	70	285	5	41905.62	25511.92
	Tom LEHMAN	USA	71	74	70	70	285	5	41905.62	25511.92
33	Ian WOOSNAM	Wal	73	72	72	69	286	6	38321.59	23329.98
	Kirk TRIPLETT	USA	75	67	72	72	286	6	38321.59	23329.98
35	Davis LOVE III	USA	75	72	70	70	287	7	35840.33	21819.40
36	Miguel Angel JIMÉNEZ	Sp	69	74	72	73	288	8	34186.16	20812.35
37	Steve PATE	USA	75	73	69	75	292	12	32531.99	19805.30

Premier Banking

Premier Banking is a genuinely personal service created especially for your convenience, not ours.

In today's volatile financial markets, it's more and more difficult for busy individuals to keep up to date with the latest developments, or to maximise the exciting and challenging opportunities on offer. That's why we provide this bespoke service to clients looking for help and expert advice to ensure their funds work most efficiently and effectively for them.

At Premier Banking, our Account Managers are committed to building close, enduring partnerships with their clients and helping them to make the right financial decisions.

This close relationship is at the heart of the Premier Banking service. Our Managers develop a detailed knowledge of your banking needs, priorities and objectives and offer you a fast track to the financial expertise available within the Barclays Group. And they ensure that our clients are always among the first to hear about new Barclays services and products.

Direct personal contact, fast decision-making, tailored solutions all characterise our Premier Banking service. It's available to you both in the UK, and overseas through International Premier Banking.

If you want to discover more, call us on 024 7653 4672.

Premier Banking Central Office, PO Box 122, 2 The Oaks
Westwood Business Park, Coventry CV4 8YZ

Happy Returns

GLENEAGLES HOTEL, AUCHTERARDER, SCOTLAND

*I*f anyone had suggested to Sweden's Pierre Fulke early last season that he would have won again on the European Tour International Schedule by the end of August, he would have felt he was more likely to find a playable course in the north of his country in mid-December.

Such were his injury problems going into the new millennium that his main concern was whether or not he would be able to play golf again.

From November 1999 to May 2000, he was an absentee from the Tour, scarcely able to make contact with a ball because of the persistent pain in his right wrist. He had consulted the best hand surgeon in Sweden, but after hitting only 300 balls in six days in Dubai in March he came home early, a frustrated and very worried golfer.

Now he had to look for an alternative course of action, and it was on the flight back to Stockholm he remembered that during the Open Championship at Carnoustie the previous year he had shared accommodation with a Swedish chiropractor, Michael Jansche, who was into eastern medicine and yoga.

Raphaël Jacquelin

It was worth a try, and it worked. "When he saw me he pin-pointed the problem straight away," said Pierre. "The vertebrae in my neck and back were in the wrong place and were sending wrong messages to the rest of my body. It wasn't my wrist. It was referred back pain."

By early June, Fulke was back on Tour. By mid-July he had finished seventh in the Open Championship at St. Andrews and by the end of August he was a winner again, less than a year after breaking through in the Trophée Lancôme at Saint-Nom-La-Bretèche.

A bogey-free 70 in the final round in the Scottish PGA Championship over the demanding 7,060 yards Monarch's course at the Gleneagles Hotel for a 17 under par aggregate of 271 saw him home by two shots from his fellow countryman, Henrik Nyström.

It was the first time the 29-year-old Swede had led going into a last round, and he answered all the questions in a resounding manner. His fitness was not in doubt. Neither was his stomach for a battle.

"This proves I am back to where I was after the Lancôme," he said. "I coped with the situation, and the level of my game is back to where it was a year ago, probably even better."

The local fans had been hoping that one of their own, Alastair Forsyth, would be the winner of the 109,495 euro (£66,660) first

The Course

The Jack Nicklaus course was opened for play only seven years ago, and already it is regarded as one of Scotland's finest inland courses - and, at just short of 7,100 yards, the longest. It has taken a little while to mature and establish itself alongside the much-loved King's and Queen's Courses, but, almost to a man, the field for the Scottish PGA Championship voiced their approval. If there is a criticism it is that none of the five par threes is less than 190 yards. But because of the wide choice of tees available this is easily rectified, depending on the wind. Master of Mystery

Henrik Nyström

prize. He had been in joint second place after a 65 on a gloriously warm Friday afternoon and still in contention with 18 holes remaining.

However, a 75 on a Sunday tormented by torrential showers left him in equal seventh place and bitterly disappointed. The fact that on the same afternoon his beloved Rangers had been slaughtered 6-2 by Celtic did nothing to raise his spirits.

Still, by then the spectators probably had decided that if anyone else was going to win it ought to be Fulke. They had watched a round of great quality on the Friday - a 63 - and were further endeared to him when he said he always enjoyed coming to Scotland.

"I love the courses here," he said. "And the food's better in Scotland than in England." At the moment north of the border he is only a notch behind Mel Gibson in the popularity stakes!

Yet Fulke had not been a factor in the opening round, the honours going to Raphaël Jacquelin and to the 1999 Open champion, Paul Lawrie.

Jacquelin had been nowhere to be seen in the betting, having missed eight cuts in a row. But the Frenchman had shown his potential in

Shot of the Week

In most week's Fulke's holed five iron second shot at the 13th would have been a clear winner. But the honour has to go to Paul Lawrie's hole-in-one at the 208 yards tenth hole with a seven iron. It was downhill and downwind, but it was his very first shot of the tournament.

Mark James and Sam Torrance: The 1999 and 2001 Ryder Cup captains respectively

May by finishing 13th in the Volvo PGA Championship at Wentworth Club, thanks to a last round of 65.

He went one better at Gleneagles, lowering the course record by two shots with a round that contained no bogeys and only 23 putts.

By the time Jacquelin was back in the Dormy House, however, Lawrie already had stolen the headlines by starting his round (at the tenth) with a hole-in-one.

Holes-in-one on the European Tour are fairly common, but for a player to begin a tournament with one is a rarity, so rare that a spokesman for the bookmakers, Victor Chandler, described it as "well over a 10,000 - 1 chance."

By comparison, Fulke's 70 was mundane. But his time was nigh. Twenty four hours later he lowered the day-old course record to 63, holing a five iron shot of 190 yards for an eagle two at the 13th.

Indeed, a five under par run of four, two, two, three was the core of his victory over Nyström, whose second place suddenly gave him hope of retaining his Tour card for the following season.

Jock MacVicar

Hennie Otto

GLENEAGLES HOTEL, AUCHTERARDER, SCOTLAND, 24-27 AUGUST 2000, PAR 72, 7060 YARDS, 6456 METRES

Pos.	Name		Rd1	Rd2	Rd3	Rd4	Total	Par	Prize Money Euro	£
1	Pierre FULKE	Swe	70	63	68	70	271	-17	109495.05	66660.00
2	Henrik NYSTROM	Swe	70	66	68	69	273	-15	72996.70	44440.00
3	Raphaël JACQUELIN	Fr	64	71	73	69	277	-11	41130.45	25040.00
4	Benn BARHAM	Eng	65	74	70	69	278	-10	32851.80	20000.00
5	Olle KARLSSON	Swe	71	73	69	66	279	-9	27858.33	16960.00
6	Hennie OTTO	SA	71	71	69	69	280	-8	22996.26	14000.00
7	Grant HAMERTON	Eng	72	70	70	69	281	-7	18068.49	11000.00
	Alastair FORSYTH	Scot	70	65	71	75	281	-7	18068.49	11000.00
9	Jeremy ROBINSON	Eng	73	69	68	72	282	-6	13929.17	8480.00
	Nick LUDWELL	Eng	71	70	71	70	282	-6	13929.17	8480.00
11	Andrew OLDCORN	Scot	74	69	70	70	283	-5	10735.97	6536.00
	John SENDEN	Aus	73	71	68	71	283	-5	10735.97	6536.00
	Henrik STENSON	Swe	77	67	72	67	283	-5	10735.97	6536.00
	Richard BLAND	Eng	70	71	68	74	283	-5	10735.97	6536.00
	Johan SKOLD	Swe	71	71	75	66	283	-5	10735.97	6536.00
16	Sam TORRANCE	Scot	70	71	73	70	284	-4	8689.30	5290.00
	Stephen FIELD	Eng	73	68	70	73	284	-4	8689.30	5290.00
	Jonathan LOMAS	Eng	71	74	72	67	284	-4	8689.30	5290.00
	Paul LAWRIE	Scot	67	74	75	68	284	-4	8689.30	5290.00
20	Ross DRUMMOND	Scot	71	68	72	74	285	-3	7539.49	4590.00
	Andrew MCLARDY	SA	75	71	70	69	285	-3	7539.49	4590.00
	Rolf MUNTZ	Hol	71	69	73	72	285	-3	7539.49	4590.00
	Charles CHALLEN	Eng	73	70	71	71	285	-3	7539.49	4590.00
24	Roger CHAPMAN	Eng	76	72	69	71	286	-2	6734.62	4100.00
	Mark JAMES	Eng	72	70	72	72	286	-2	6734.62	4100.00
	Grant DODD	Aus	71	70	74	71	286	-2	6734.62	4100.00
	Roger WINCHESTER	Eng	71	74	69	72	286	-2	6734.62	4100.00
28	Bill LONGMUIR	Scot	71	73	73	70	287	-1	5847.62	3560.00
	Klas ERIKSSON	Swe	70	67	74	76	287	-1	5847.62	3560.00
	Miles TUNNICLIFF	Eng	77	69	70	71	287	-1	5847.62	3560.00
	Adam MEDNICK	Swe	74	70	72	71	287	-1	5847.62	3560.00
	James HEPWORTH	Eng	72	72	72	71	287	-1	5847.62	3560.00
33	Peter MITCHELL	Eng	76	69	71	72	288	0	5081.08	3093.33
	John CHILLAS	Scot	71	72	72	73	288	0	5081.08	3093.33
	Luis CLAVERIE	Sp	75	70	73	70	288	0	5081.08	3093.33
36	Malcolm MACKENZIE	Eng	74	72	71	72	289	1	4336.44	2640.00
	Gary MURPHY	Ire	75	71	71	72	289	1	4336.44	2640.00
	José Manuel CARRILES	Sp	75	67	74	73	289	1	4336.44	2640.00
	Simon D. HURLEY	Eng	74	69	75	71	289	1	4336.44	2640.00
	Sam LITTLE	Eng	73	69	75	72	289	1	4336.44	2640.00
	Bradley DREDGE	Wal	75	68	75	71	289	1	4336.44	2640.00
	Francisco CEA	Sp	71	73	75	70	289	1	4336.44	2640.00
	Iain PYMAN	Eng	73	74	74	68	289	1	4336.44	2640.00
44	Wayne RILEY	Aus	71	75	71	73	290	2	3416.59	2080.00
	Paul SHERMAN	Eng	76	68	74	72	290	2	3416.59	2080.00
	Justin ROSE	Eng	74	71	72	73	290	2	3416.59	2080.00
	Andrew BEAL	Eng	74	71	73	72	290	2	3416.59	2080.00
	Ignacio GARRIDO	Sp	72	69	73	76	290	2	3416.59	2080.00
	Matthew BLACKEY	Eng	72	72	76	70	290	2	3416.59	2080.00
50	David J RUSSELL	Eng	77	68	69	77	291	3	2562.44	1560.00
	Gary EMERSON	Eng	72	74	72	73	291	3	2562.44	1560.00
	Colin GILLIES	Scot	76	71	71	73	291	3	2562.44	1560.00
	Sebastien BRANGER	Fr	75	71	74	71	291	3	2562.44	1560.00
	Tim SPENCE	Eng	71	76	73	71	291	3	2562.44	1560.00
	Gianluca PIETROBONO	It	72	72	69	78	291	3	2562.44	1560.00
	Ivo GINER	Sp	71	74	76	70	291	3	2562.44	1560.00
57	Robert COLES	Eng	73	72	72	75	292	4	2036.81	1240.00
58	Mark MOULAND	Wal	71	76	75	71	293	5	1609.74	980.00
	Mark DAVIS	Eng	72	75	69	77	293	5	1609.74	980.00
	Philip ARCHER	Eng	74	73	76	70	293	5	1609.74	980.00
	Euan LITTLE	Scot	72	72	76	73	293	5	1609.74	980.00
	Greig HUTCHEON	Scot	75	71	76	71	293	5	1609.74	980.00
	Ian HUTCHINGS	SA	76	70	74	73	293	5	1609.74	980.00
	Fabrice TARNAUD	Fr	74	70	75	74	293	5	1609.74	980.00
	Tomas Jesus MUÑOZ	Sp	73	73	74	73	293	5	1609.74	980.00
	Van PHILLIPS	Eng	73	74	73	73	293	5	1609.74	980.00
	Raymond RUSSELL	Scot	75	70	76	72	293	5	1609.74	980.00
	Frédéric CUPILLARD	Fr	75	72	72	74	293	5	1609.74	980.00
	Fredrik WIDMARK	Swe	75	71	73	74	293	5	1609.74	980.00
70	Tony CAROLAN	Aus	74	73	72	75	294	6	1100.76	670.14
	Brian NELSON	USA	75	72	74	73	294	6	1100.76	670.14
72	David GILFORD	Eng	75	71	75	74	295	7	977.00	594.79
	Paul AFFLECK	Wal	73	75	75	72	295	7	977.00	594.79
	Andrew BARNETT	Wal	72	70	76	77	295	7	977.00	594.79
	Scott HENDERSON	Scot	74	72	75	74	295	7	977.00	594.79
	Thomas NORRET	Den	74	70	76	75	295	7	977.00	594.79
77	Andrew BUTTERFIELD	Eng	73	71	79	73	296	8	966.50	588.40
	Leon STANFORD	Eng	74	70	78	74	296	8	966.50	588.40
79	Daren LEE	Eng	73	74	76	75	298	10	962.00	585.66
80	Donald MCKAY	Scot	72	74	81	75	302	14	959.00	583.83
81	Stephen MCALLISTER	Scot	73	74	81	75	303	15	956.00	582.01
82	Peter MALMGREN	Swe	70	73	79	85	307	19	953.00	580.18

The Prince of Denmark

GOLFCLUB MÜNCHEN NORD-EICHENRIED, MUNICH, GERMANY

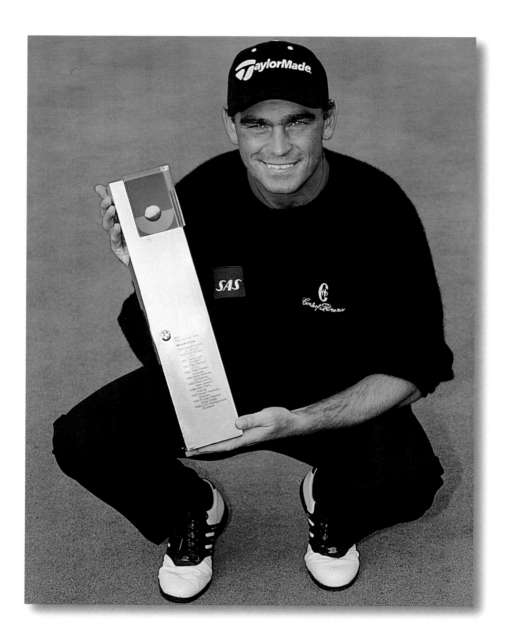

To win or not to win, that was the question. OK, so it has to be admitted that we're talking bowdlerisation here, but only to a limited extent. We ARE, after all, talking about a Prince of Denmark, albeit an uncrowned one, and we ARE, too, talking about a tragic hero. It's just that the first and the second are different people.

With due deference to that bloke who wrote a play or two a while back and got the odd decent write-up, we're shifting the scenario and the dialogue forward by 500 years or so and applying it to golf, which, as we all know, is at once more trivial and yet infinitely more important than anything a sling or arrow of outrageous fortune could ever throw at a man.

We are talking here about a great Dane and a slightly lesser Spaniard who could boast the most confused genealogy of anybody currently playing on the European Tour. We are discussing, in the first instance, Thomas Björn, and in the second, Carl Suneson.

As the BMW International Open got under way under benevolent skies at Golfclub München Nord-Eichenried at the end of August, there were many who had their own agenda that extended far beyond the mere four days of a golf tournament. Björn and Suneson were just two of those who had points to prove, even if they were at the time at different ends of the achievement scale.

To take Björn first: He had finished in a tie for second place in the Open Championship and then finished outright third in the US PGA Championship. He was the form horse, playing as well as anybody in Europe, Lee Westwood, Darren Clarke and Colin Montgomerie (of whom more later) included. But he needed to validate that form with something more tangible. Nothing less than a victory would do that for him.

Thomas Björn

Carl Suneson

As for Suneson, the man with the Swedish father and the English mother, the man who had been brought up in the Canary Islands, had been a naturalised Spaniard since 1996 and was attached to the Royal Golf Club of Las Palmas in Gran Canaria, he had something more basic on his wish-list. Like retaining his playing privileges on the most proudly cosmopolitan Tour in world golf, for instance, after winning the European Challenge Tour Rankings in 1999.

Well, they both succeeded, to a greater or lesser extent. It was the greater for Björn, because he went out and won a tournament that, magnificently, set a benchmark for quality of presentation in Europe, but Suneson, although faltering sadly in the death throes of the tournament, also produced what, when taken as a whole, was the best performance of his life.

The record books will show that Björn won with a total of 268, 20 under par. They will also reveal that Suneson came third and pocketed the biggest pay-cheque of a career that thus far had been notable more for promise than achievement. But in both cases, there was more — much more — to it than that.

For all his deeds of derring-do in the final two major championships of the season, Björn went to Bavaria a hungry man. He was proud of his golf in the previous two months, and so he should have been. But he felt that the only way he could put the final franking stamp on his performances at St Andrews and Valhalla was with a victory, back home in Europe. He was a man on a mission, and it proved far from impossible.

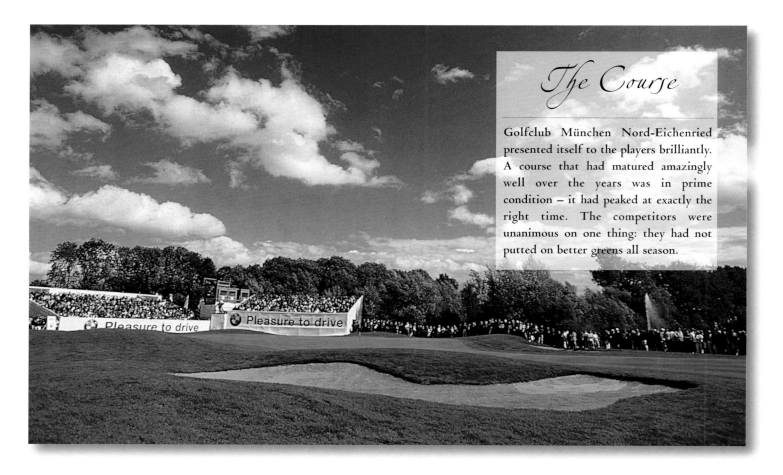

The Course

Golfclub München Nord-Eichenried presented itself to the players brilliantly. A course that had matured amazingly well over the years was in prime condition – it had peaked at exactly the right time. The competitors were unanimous on one thing: they had not putted on better greens all season.

Meanwhile, Suneson, an insulin-dependent diabetic who had also fought and defeated an extra, unwanted, medical problem induced by an over-active thyroid gland, produced the performance of a lifetime. To Björn went the victor's spoils but, in his own way, Suneson was also a winner.

Fact: Björn had a closing 67 to finish three strokes ahead of Bernhard Langer, the ultimate local hero. Fact: Suneson was third and won a great deal of money, but with two holes to go, it looked likely that he was going to tuck the first six-figure pay-cheque of his life into his wallet. That he did not was the result of a cruel confluence of good fortune and bad.

The good was that Langer birdied the 72nd hole of the tournament to leave him in second place all on his own. The bad was that Suneson missed a three-foot par putt on the same hole to reduce him to third. Until the very final act, his had been a part well played.

Björn, on the other hand, made only one mistake in the closing round and even managed a damage-limitation exercise there, too. He was in all sorts of bother on the 16th after a poor drive and equally mediocre second and third shots, but when a double-bogey loomed that might have nudged ajar an almost-closed door, he responded with a nerveless five foot putt to drop only one stroke. His 15 foot birdie putt on the 17th slammed the portal closed again.

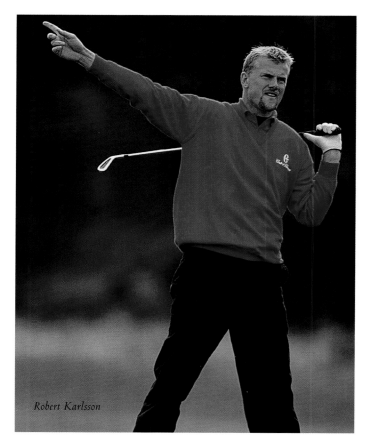

Robert Karlsson

Darin Lee

It was the final, telling act of a wonderfully contested tournament. With a final round of 67, Langer was second after a weekend surge that had taken him from nowhere in particular to somewhere significant. It was just a small shame that Montgomerie had not been around to play his part.

For the first time in his life, Montgomerie was late on the tee for the first round. It was only by a minute, but he still had to take the punishment of a two-stroke penalty, and the after-shock of the minor earthquake led to his missing the halfway cut in a European Tour event for the first time since he had had to go home early from the same tournament in 1998.

Like the big man he is, Montgomerie took full responsibility for his gaffe, committed as it was in total innocence. He had firmly believed that his tee-time was ten minutes later than it was, but there's no relief from even a small error. On the European Tour, punctuality is, rightly, next to godliness. "A rule's a rule," he said ruefully. "There's no excuse."

No, there isn't, unfortunately. Montgomerie missed the cut by five strokes. It left the way clear for Björn to trample on the opposition in the final 36 holes of the tournament. He did, too — he was, truly, the 'nunmer eins' among equals at Nord-Eichenried. Nobody deserved it more.

Mel Webb

Colin Montgomerie having been given the news

Miguel Angel Martin

Shot of the Week

It was only a tiddler. No more than five feet, actually. It was the putt that saved Thomas Björn from a possible double-bogey six on the 16th in the last round. He had been in trouble with his drive and also with his second and third shots. If he had missed, it would have given Carl Suneson and Bernhard Langer hope. There was no chance of that as he stroked it into the heart of the hole – it's not often that a putt for a bogey qualifies for the shot of the week.

GOLFCLUB MÜNCHEN NORD-EICHENRIED, MUNICH, GERMANY, 31 AUGUST - 3 SEPTEMBER 2000, PAR 72, 6914 YARDS, 6321 METRES

Pos.	Name		Rd1	Rd2	Rd3	Rd4	Total	Par	Prize Money Euro	£
1	Thomas BJÖRN	Den	69	63	69	67	268	-20	250000.00	153000.65
2	Bernhard LANGER	Ger	69	69	66	67	271	-17	166660.00	101996.35
3	Carl SUNESON	Sp	67	67	67	71	272	-16	93900.00	57467.04
4	Ignacio GARRIDO	Sp	67	69	71	68	275	-13	75000.00	45900.19
5	Miguel Angel MARTIN	Sp	67	66	73	70	276	-12	43700.00	26744.51
	Emanuele CANONICA	It	70	67	68	71	276	-12	43700.00	26744.51
	Ernie ELS	SA	70	71	69	66	276	-12	43700.00	26744.51
	Gustavo ROJAS	Arg	68	71	66	71	276	-12	43700.00	26744.51
	Greg OWEN	Eng	72	68	68	68	276	-12	43700.00	26744.51
	Daren LEE	Eng	66	70	66	74	276	-12	43700.00	26744.51
11	Barry LANE	Eng	67	69	71	70	277	-11	26700.00	16340.47
	Justin ROSE	Eng	68	69	70	70	277	-11	26700.00	16340.47
13	Thomas GÖGELE	Ger	69	69	67	73	278	-10	23050.00	14106.66
	Ian GARBUTT	Eng	68	71	71	68	278	-10	23050.00	14106.66
	Jarmo SANDELIN	Swe	68	68	69	73	278	-10	23050.00	14106.66
16	Santiago LUNA	Sp	67	72	70	70	279	-9	19837.50	12140.60
	Anthony WALL	Eng	70	68	68	73	279	-9	19837.50	12140.60
	Knud STORGAARD	Den	66	73	71	69	279	-9	19837.50	12140.60
	Christopher HANELL	Swe	67	70	72	70	279	-9	19837.50	12140.60
20	David HOWELL	Eng	68	68	72	72	280	-8	16980.00	10391.80
	Padraig HARRINGTON	Ire	67	66	74	73	280	-8	16980.00	10391.80
	Greg TURNER	NZ	65	72	74	69	280	-8	16980.00	10391.80
	Roger WINCHESTER	Eng	67	70	68	75	280	-8	16980.00	10391.80
	Henrik NYSTROM	Swe	67	71	70	72	280	-8	16980.00	10391.80
25	Gordon BRAND JNR.	Scot	71	68	70	72	281	-7	14250.00	8721.04
	Andrew OLDCORN	Scot	69	69	72	71	281	-7	14250.00	8721.04
	Wayne RILEY	Aus	65	71	72	73	281	-7	14250.00	8721.04
	Brian DAVIS	Eng	71	69	71	70	281	-7	14250.00	8721.04
	Søren HANSEN	Den	67	68	73	73	281	-7	14250.00	8721.04
	Alex CEJKA	Ger	72	68	69	72	281	-7	14250.00	8721.04
	Niclas FASTH	Swe	70	69	71	71	281	-7	14250.00	8721.04
32	Anders FORSBRAND	Swe	67	70	74	71	282	-6	11475.00	7022.73
	Greg NORMAN	Aus	70	70	74	71	282	-6	11475.00	7022.73
	Søren KJELDSEN	Den	69	71	68	74	282	-6	11475.00	7022.73
	Per-Ulrik JOHANSSON	Swe	64	74	74	70	282	-6	11475.00	7022.73
	David LYNN	Eng	68	68	73	73	282	-6	11475.00	7022.73
	Raymond RUSSELL	Scot	67	68	76	71	282	-6	11475.00	7022.73
38	Hennie OTTO	SA	70	70	67	76	283	-5	9300.00	5691.62
	Ian POULTER	Eng	70	69	72	72	283	-5	9300.00	5691.62
	Geoff OGILVY	Aus	67	70	71	75	283	-5	9300.00	5691.62
	Scott ROWE	USA	68	73	70	72	283	-5	9300.00	5691.62
	Robert KARLSSON	Swe	70	68	73	72	283	-5	9300.00	5691.62
	Jorge BERENDT	Arg	72	69	73	69	283	-5	9300.00	5691.62
	Wolfgang HUGET	Ger	68	71	68	76	283	-5	9300.00	5691.62
	Alastair FORSYTH	Scot	71	69	72	71	283	-5	9300.00	5691.62
46	Andrew MCLARDY	SA	71	68	70	75	284	-4	7650.00	4681.82
	Thomas LEVET	Fr	67	67	73	77	284	-4	7650.00	4681.82
	Joakim HAEGGMAN	Swe	69	70	73	72	284	-4	7650.00	4681.82
49	Mark JAMES	Eng	70	70	71	74	285	-3	6300.00	3855.62
	Fredrik LINDGREN	Swe	69	70	72	74	285	-3	6300.00	3855.62
	Mathias GRÖNBERG	Swe	68	72	70	75	285	-3	6300.00	3855.62
	Nicolas VANHOOTEGEM	Bel	68	69	71	77	285	-3	6300.00	3855.62
	Van PHILLIPS	Eng	71	67	76	71	285	-3	6300.00	3855.62
	Bradley DREDGE	Wal	72	68	71	74	285	-3	6300.00	3855.62
55	Tony JOHNSTONE	Zim	71	69	73	73	286	-2	4650.00	2845.81
	Sam TORRANCE	Scot	71	70	69	76	286	-2	4650.00	2845.81
	David GILFORD	Eng	64	73	78	71	286	-2	4650.00	2845.81
	Peter BAKER	Eng	71	69	72	74	286	-2	4650.00	2845.81
	Roger WESSELS	SA	67	69	74	76	286	-2	4650.00	2845.81
	Stephen GALLACHER	Scot	71	69	70	76	286	-2	4650.00	2845.81
61	Jarrod MOSELEY	Aus	68	73	72	74	287	-1	3900.00	2386.81
	David PARK	Wal	68	70	72	77	287	-1	3900.00	2386.81
	Max ANGLERT	Swe	70	70	72	75	287	-1	3900.00	2386.81
64	John SENDEN	Aus	70	65	73	80	288	0	3225.00	1973.71
	Paul EALES	Eng	68	72	76	72	288	0	3225.00	1973.71
	Peter O'MALLEY	Aus	70	71	72	75	288	0	3225.00	1973.71
	John BICKERTON	Eng	67	71	75	75	288	0	3225.00	1973.71
	Benoit TEILLERIA	Fr	70	67	75	76	288	0	3225.00	1973.71
	Tobias DIER	Ger	72	69	69	78	288	0	3225.00	1973.71
70	Simon D. HURLEY	Eng	68	69	74	78	289	1	2495.00	1526.95
	Dean ROBERTSON	Scot	70	69	75	75	289	1	2495.00	1526.95
72	Simon WAKEFIELD	Eng	70	70	76	74	290	2	2247.00	1375.17
73	Olivier EDMOND	Fr	71	70	77	73	291	3	2239.50	1370.58
	Jonathan LOMAS	Eng	71	70	77	73	291	3	2239.50	1370.58
	Fabrice TARNAUD	Fr	69	70	70	82	291	3	2239.50	1370.58
	Johan SKOLD	Swe	71	69	71	80	291	3	2239.50	1370.58
77	Russell CLAYDON	Eng	70	71	73	78	292	4	2232.00	1365.99
78	Peter FOWLER	Aus	69	72	72	80	293	5	2229.00	1364.15
79	Gary MURPHY	Ire	68	73	73	83	297	9	2226.00	1362.32

ESCADA
SPORT

The Year of the Cat

CRANS-SUR-SIERRE, CRANS MONTANA, SWITZERLAND

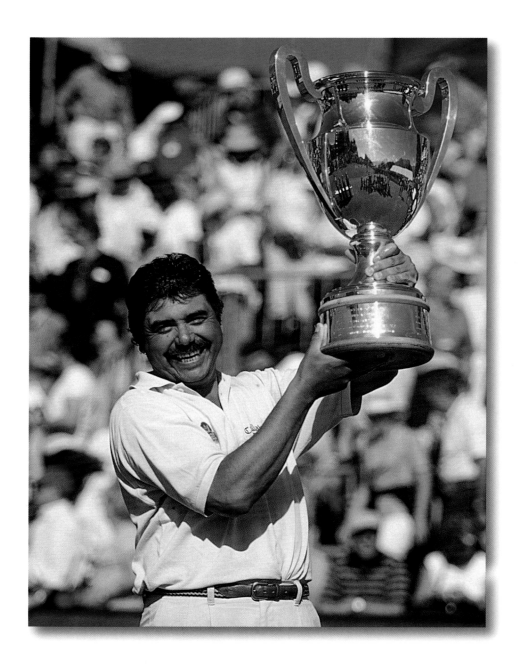

To the Chinese, 2000 was a year of the dragon, but in golfing terms it was definitely the year of the big cat.

Mostly it was a Tiger who prowled around creaming off the top prizes. But Eduardo Romero - whose nickname of El Gato means

The Cat - also got in on the act at the Canon European Masters. Romero led from start to finish and eventually romped home by ten shots from the bang in-form Thomas Björn, with Darren Clarke a further shot in arrears.

Canon
EUROPEAN MASTERS
CRA

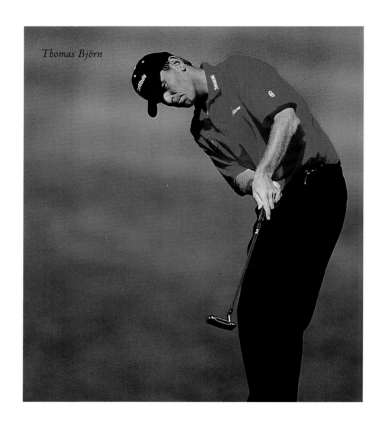

Thomas Björn

It was a highly popular triumph for the likeable Argentinean, who is a regular and welcome visitor to Crans-sur-Sierre - the gloriously situated Alpine resort was also the scene of the last of his six previous European Tour wins six years earlier. Romero - at 46, the oldest winner on Tour in almost a decade - blamed the drought in between those victories on an inability to concentrate fully on his game.

A course in yoga helped as he took the mental disciplines he learned there onto the golf course with him. And there was no doubting that he was fully focused from the moment he launched his title bid with a seven under par 64. That earned him a one stroke lead over Michael Campbell, and at the end of the second round Romero had moved to ten under, three shots clear of Clarke and Lee Westwood.

The men who occupied the first two places in the Volvo Order of Merit at the time were fully expected to turn up the heat over the weekend, especially as this was the first qualifying tournament for the 2001 Ryder Cup. But Westwood in particular wilted in the blazing sunshine which provided the perfect setting for some scorching golf from Romero. He fired a stunning 62 in the third round to move eight clear of Clarke, while defending champion Westwood dropped out of the frame with a three over par 74.

The Course

Crans-sur-Sierre, nestling high in the Swiss Alps, provided a stunning backdrop as always. The course was bathed in sunshine on all four days, so there was plenty of run on the ball. With the added effect of playing at high altitude, drives of 300 yards-plus were commonplace. The sloping greens provoked plenty of comment, as usual, but they held no terrors for Romero.

Shot of the Week

John Mellor earned the biggest prize of his career with a hole in one on the 194 yards 11th hole. The 30-year-old Sheffield golfer won a £21,000 Volvo V70 thanks to his ace in the final round, achieved with a five iron. It was only the second time Mellor had managed a hole in one, but the 25th on the European Tour in 2000.

Romero followed up with four birdies on the front nine on day four, and for a while it seemed he was certain to better or at least equal the Tour record winning margin of 11 shots. Clarke was powerless to prevent that as he surrendered second place with a double bogey at the 16th and another dropped shot at the 17th, and Björn overtook him with a final round of 66 to finish runner-up for the second year in succession.

That meant Romero had to settle for "merely" the biggest margin seen on Tour all year, and he had praise heaped on him from all quarters. Another frequent visitor to Crans, Nick Faldo, gasped in amazement when he saw Romero's winning total. Faldo felt he had played pretty well to secure a share of sixth place on nine under, but said: "What Eduardo has done is just phenomenal.

"I believe this course has become a couple of shots tougher in the past couple of years since Seve Ballesteros re-designed the greens. But Eddie has taken it apart. I reckon his score would have been worth around 35 under on the old course!"

A delighted Romero was in no mood to argue, as he clutched the biggest cheque of his career, for 250,000 euro (£154,000). He said: "My concentration has been terrible, terrible, terrible, in the last few years. But it was wonderful this week, and that was the key. It has completely changed around, and my dream of winning again on the Tour has come true.

"I felt fantastic and I played fantastic. I was using the new Callaway driver and ball, and I was hitting it miles. Maybe it is because I eat plenty of Argentinian beef as well! I hit my best drive of the week on the ninth hole in the last round, 325 yards, and then hit a three wood pin high. Darren Clarke said to me: 'It's unbelievable - you're hitting the ball further than Tiger'. I enjoyed hearing that because it made me feel strong. I felt Tiger-good!"

Romero's winning margin was certainly straight out of the Woods collection. And it was good to see a player nearly twice his age produce golf of such an incredibly high standard.

David Facey

"Pull"! – Mark Mouland aiming for birdies in the Alps

CRANS-SUR-SIERRE, CRANS MONTANA, SWITZERLAND, 7-10 SEPTEMBER 2000, PAR 71, 6846 YARDS, 6226 METRES

Pos.	Name		Rd1	Rd2	Rd3	Rd4	Total	Par	Prize Money Euro	£
1	Eduardo ROMERO	Arg	64	68	62	67	261	-23	250000.00	153937.10
2	Thomas BJÖRN	Den	72	64	69	66	271	-13	166660.00	102620.63
3	Darren CLARKE	N.Ire	68	67	67	70	272	-12	93900.00	57818.77
4	Niclas FASTH	Swe	74	66	69	64	273	-11	75000.00	46181.13
5	Mathias GRÖNBERG	Swe	72	66	67	69	274	-10	63600.00	39161.60
6	Nick FALDO	Eng	69	73	66	67	275	-9	48750.00	30017.73
	Phillip PRICE	Wal	69	68	67	71	275	-9	48750.00	30017.73
8	Jarrod MOSELEY	Aus	68	67	71	70	276	-8	35550.00	21889.85
	Matthew BLACKEY	Eng	71	69	69	67	276	-8	35550.00	21889.85
10	Angel CABRERA	Arg	69	72	69	67	277	-7	27800.00	17117.80
	Dean ROBERTSON	Scot	71	73	63	70	277	-7	27800.00	17117.80
	Michael CAMPBELL	NZ	65	73	71	68	277	-7	27800.00	17117.80
13	Thomas GÖGELE	Ger	73	69	69	67	278	-6	22575.00	13900.52
	Paolo QUIRICI	Swi	67	71	66	74	278	-6	22575.00	13900.52
	Van PHILLIPS	Eng	71	69	69	69	278	-6	22575.00	13900.52
	Markus BRIER	Aut	70	70	68	70	278	-6	22575.00	13900.52
17	Anders FORSBRAND	Swe	71	69	67	72	279	-5	19050.00	11730.01
	Mark MOULAND	Wal	70	69	70	70	279	-5	19050.00	11730.01
	Ian GARBUTT	Eng	71	70	69	69	279	-5	19050.00	11730.01
	Fredrik JACOBSON	Swe	73	72	67	67	279	-5	19050.00	11730.01
21	Miguel Angel JIMÉNEZ	Sp	69	71	69	71	280	-4	17175.00	10575.48
	Lee WESTWOOD	Eng	69	66	74	71	280	-4	17175.00	10575.48
23	Roger CHAPMAN	Eng	68	73	68	72	281	-3	15600.00	9605.67
	Stephen LEANEY	Aus	75	67	70	69	281	-3	15600.00	9605.67
	Soren HANSEN	Den	69	73	69	70	281	-3	15600.00	9605.67
	José COCERES	Arg	71	71	68	71	281	-3	15600.00	9605.67
	Christopher HANELL	Swe	72	67	69	73	281	-3	15600.00	9605.67
28	Peter SENIOR	Aus	72	68	73	69	282	-2	13125.00	8081.70
	Raphaël JACQUELIN	Fr	70	75	68	69	282	-2	13125.00	8081.70
	Fredrik LINDGREN	Swe	74	69	70	69	282	-2	13125.00	8081.70
	Massimo FLORIOLI	It	72	70	72	68	282	-2	13125.00	8081.70
	Nicolas VANHOOTEGEM	Bel	71	70	69	72	282	-2	13125.00	8081.70
	André BOSSERT	Swi	74	67	70	71	282	-2	13125.00	8081.70
34	Mark MCNULTY	Zim	69	72	72	70	283	-1	10500.00	6465.36
	Maarten LAFEBER	Hol	72	73	68	70	283	-1	10500.00	6465.36
	Andrew MCLARDY	SA	71	73	66	73	283	-1	10500.00	6465.36
	Jamie SPENCE	Eng	71	72	70	70	283	-1	10500.00	6465.36
	Gary EMERSON	Eng	69	70	74	70	283	-1	10500.00	6465.36
	Paul LAWRIE	Scot	70	73	69	71	283	-1	10500.00	6465.36
	Alastair FORSYTH	Scot	72	71	70	70	283	-1	10500.00	6465.36
	Brett RUMFORD	Aus	67	72	73	71	283	-1	10500.00	6465.36
42	David HOWELL	Eng	72	70	73	69	284	0	8250.00	5079.92
	Barry LANE	Eng	71	71	70	72	284	0	8250.00	5079.92
	Brian DAVIS	Eng	73	68	69	74	284	0	8250.00	5079.92
	Ian POULTER	Eng	73	68	74	69	284	0	8250.00	5079.92
	Ricardo GONZALEZ	Arg	74	71	72	67	284	0	8250.00	5079.92
	Francis VALERA	Sp	72	72	71	69	284	0	8250.00	5079.92
	Lucas PARSONS	Aus	71	74	70	69	284	0	8250.00	5079.92
49	Gordon BRAND JNR.	Scot	70	75	71	69	285	1	5715.00	3519.00
	Eamonn DARCY	Ire	69	70	73	73	285	1	5715.00	3519.00
	Santiago LUNA	Sp	72	72	69	72	285	1	5715.00	3519.00
	Sam TORRANCE	Scot	75	69	74	67	285	1	5715.00	3519.00
	Gary MURPHY	Ire	74	71	71	69	285	1	5715.00	3519.00
	José Manuel CARRILES	Sp	72	72	69	72	285	1	5715.00	3519.00
	Nick O'HERN	Aus	75	69	72	69	285	1	5715.00	3519.00
	Greg OWEN	Eng	73	69	71	72	285	1	5715.00	3519.00
	Daren LEE	Eng	70	71	71	73	285	1	5715.00	3519.00
	Stephen GALLACHER	Scot	74	70	69	72	285	1	5715.00	3519.00
59	Miguel Angel MARTIN	Sp	73	72	71	70	286	2	4125.00	2539.96
	Hennie OTTO	SA	66	69	75	76	286	2	4125.00	2539.96
	Patrik SJÖLAND	Swe	73	71	69	73	286	2	4125.00	2539.96
	David CARTER	Eng	72	73	68	73	286	2	4125.00	2539.96
63	David GILFORD	Eng	71	73	70	73	287	3	3600.00	2216.69
	Ian HUTCHINGS	SA	71	72	73	71	287	3	3600.00	2216.69
	Michael JONZON	Swe	74	71	71	71	287	3	3600.00	2216.69
66	Seve BALLESTEROS	Sp	74	71	70	73	288	4	3075.00	1893.43
	Malcolm MACKENZIE	Eng	72	72	74	70	288	4	3075.00	1893.43
	Simon D. HURLEY	Eng	75	69	72	72	288	4	3075.00	1893.43
	Diego BORREGO	Sp	73	70	74	71	288	4	3075.00	1893.43
70	Jeremy ROBINSON	Eng	73	72	72	72	289	5	2412.33	1485.39
	Stephen ALLAN	Aus	69	75	72	73	289	5	2412.33	1485.39
	Henrik NYSTROM	Swe	71	71	73	74	289	5	2412.33	1485.39
73	Wayne RILEY	Aus	72	72	74	72	290	6	2242.50	1380.82
	Olle KARLSSON	Swe	70	74	72	74	290	6	2242.50	1380.82
75	John MELLOR	Eng	75	68	73	76	292	8	2238.00	1378.04
76	Scott ROWE	USA	71	73	74	75	293	9	2233.50	1375.27
	Dimitri BIERI	Swi	74	70	75	74	293	9	2233.50	1375.27
78	Stephen FIELD	Eng	69	74	76	75	294	10	2227.50	1371.58
	Iain PYMAN	Eng	70	75	74	75	294	10	2227.50	1371.58
80	Steve REY	Swi	71	73	76	77	297	13	2221.50	1367.89
	Johan SKOLD	Swe	74	71	78	74	297	13	2221.50	1367.89

WORLD'S SMALLEST

AND

LIGHTEST CAMCORDER

A small item of world news from Canon: the new MV3i MC. You won't find a smaller, lighter camcorder anywhere. Weighing just 370 grams, the MV3i MC offers outstanding image quality and features that put larger camcorders to shame: 10x optical and 40x digital zoom, high-resolution LCD screen, DV-out and DV-in for editing and an ergonomically designed metal body. With its removable memory card, the MV3i MC also allows you to take high quality still images and easily transfer them to your computer. And to top up things, the precision lens in front says Canon.

MV3i MC

Canon Europa N.V., P.O. Box 2262, 1180 EG Amstelveen, The Netherlands, www.canon-europa.com

Imaging across networks

Falling in Love Again

SAINT-NOM-LA-BRETÈCHE, PARIS, FRANCE

As Retief Goosen was presented with the 218,400 euro (£133,000) winners' cheque for victory in the 31st Trophée Lancôme, the last tune that would have crossed his mind was Lost in France. Certainly Je t'aime would have been more appropriate.

For of his three previous European Tour victories, two had also been recorded on French soil in the 1997 and 1999 Open de France staged at Le Golf National and Golf du Mèdoc respectively. "It looks like I like playing golf in this country," said the jubilant 31-year-old South African. "We always play on good golf courses here and the crowds are great."

Goosen, though, deserved credit for repaying a 2,000-strong gallery which followed the final threeball over the closing stretch with a cool performance in the face of several strong challenges. Three groups ahead of him Fiji's Vijay Singh, the reigning Masters Champion, and England's Lee Westwood, seeking to intensify his personal battle with Darren Clarke at the top of the Volvo Order of Merit, made late surges.

Goosen could also not ignore his playing partners, Alex Cejka and Clarke. Though they struggled to keep apace with his six birdie assault over nine holes from the fourth, the pair kept the destination of the trophy hanging in the balance until Goosen sank his final three-foot putt at the 18th.

That Goosen should have eyed that putt with deep suspicion was a reflection of the most consistent question posed to the entire field over all four days at Saint-Nom-La-Bretéche. The ability to read the subtle borrows on the fast greens being the key to success. In the sunshine, which presented the course in its best possible light with quick running fairways on the opening day, the formula was unlocked by Goosen's fellow South African, Roger Wessels.

Playing alongside Mats Lanner, who on the old par 70 layout had set the course record of 62 in 1989, Wessels produced an eight under par round of 63 to take the early lead. He, however, was to start day two with a double bogey and shot 81 to miss the cut.

Darren Clarke

There were other similar stories late on Friday afternoon, as a two club wind swept across Versailles and the scoring dropped. Later a heavy rainstorm ensured the course would have more teeth for the final two rounds as it played longer with club-strangling, damp rough.

The young Australian left hander Nick O'Hern led going into the third round, but like Wessels 24 hours earlier and Cejka, who was to hold a two shot lead at the start of the final round, opened with a double bogey which took the edge off his confidence.

It was a casual sidebet, so befitting the genteel and opulent ambience of the Trophée Lancôme, which inspired Goosen to shoot 64, the round of the tournament in the chilling Saturday wind, to move up among the leaders. His playing partner, Michael Campbell, had just purchased a Ferrari and Goosen, possessing a leather protective cover for a similar sports car which he no longer required, suggested they play for it.

Though Campbell was to fire a 65, and eventually banked a 114,000 euro (£69,500) cheque as the joint runner up, he had to forfeit £600 to pay Goosen for the Ferrari cover instead of winning it on merit.

Nick Faldo

The Course

The mature rolling parkland composite layout at Saint-Nom-La-Bretèche featured just one change for the new millennium with the relaying and raising of the green at the par three seventh. However, the course altered its character after the second round. Having greeted the Tour with fast running fairways, they slowed down after a spectacular Friday night rainstorm and this was reflected in the scoring.

Shot of the Week

Retief Goosen's 220 yards four iron out of rough to the eighth green during the final round. The shot gave Goosen a third successive birdie and from that moment he did not relinquish the lead.

With Cejka stumbling early on, though he was to regain some ground with an eagle three at the sixth in the final round, and Clarke, constantly battling with a swing fault that had driven him from the range after hitting only five balls the day before the tournament, Goosen quickly emerged as the tournament favourite.

As the crowds homed in on the excitement - they lined both sides of the fairways for the final six holes - Goosen took a lead which he was never to relinquish with a wonderful recovery from the rough on the right of the par five eighth. His four iron to 18 feet from 220 yards out set up the birdie which was to see him complete the outward nine in 32.

With only four holes to play Goosen was three shots ahead of Cejka with Clarke one further back, but the Ulsterman birdied both the 16th and 17th to reduced the gap to two strokes on the final tee, where the result was by no means a formality.

With the pin at the 209 yards par three set close to water, which had earlier ended Westwood's challenge, and Clarke, having hit first and given himself a long birdie putt, Goosen could not afford a mistake. He responded to the challenge with a seven-iron to the heart of the green - an appropriate way to seal victory for a golfer in love with France.

Graham Otway

Michael Campbell

Study in concentration: Alex Cejka

SAINT-NOM-LA-BRETÈCHE, PARIS, FRANCE, 14-17 SEPTEMBER 2000, PAR 71, 6903 YARDS, 6311 METRES

Pos.	Name		Rd1	Rd2	Rd3	Rd4	Total	Par	Prize Money Euro	£
1	Retief GOOSEN	SA	69	71	64	67	271	-13	218461.21	133330.00
2	Darren CLARKE	N.Ire	67	70	67	68	272	-12	113842.98	69480.00
	Michael CAMPBELL	NZ	72	68	65	67	272	-12	113842.98	69480.00
4	Vijay SINGH	Fiji	67	72	68	66	273	-11	60558.96	36960.00
	Alex CEJKA	Ger	67	69	66	71	273	-11	60558.96	36960.00
6	Phillip PRICE	Wal	70	72	69	63	274	-10	45878.00	28000.00
7	Miguel Angel MARTIN	Sp	64	72	73	66	275	-9	30358.13	18528.00
	Nick O'HERN	Aus	64	69	72	70	275	-9	30358.13	18528.00
	Dean ROBERTSON	Scot	69	65	70	71	275	-9	30358.13	18528.00
	Lee WESTWOOD	Eng	68	68	71	68	275	-9	30358.13	18528.00
	Brett RUMFORD	Aus	68	66	74	67	275	-9	30358.13	18528.00
12	Nick FALDO	Eng	70	67	74	66	277	-7	20743.41	12660.00
	Tony JOHNSTONE	Zim	70	68	68	71	277	-7	20743.41	12660.00
	Anders HANSEN	Den	70	65	71	71	277	-7	20743.41	12660.00
	Paul LAWRIE	Scot	67	68	75	67	277	-7	20743.41	12660.00
16	Sam TORRANCE	Scot	68	71	70	69	278	-6	16712.70	10200.00
	Marc FARRY	Fr	67	72	69	70	278	-6	16712.70	10200.00
	Paul MCGINLEY	Ire	71	71	71	65	278	-6	16712.70	10200.00
	José COCERES	Arg	69	66	72	71	278	-6	16712.70	10200.00
	Thomas BJÖRN	Den	66	75	73	64	278	-6	16712.70	10200.00
	Angel CABRERA	Arg	71	70	67	70	278	-6	16712.70	10200.00
22	Eduardo ROMERO	Arg	69	71	69	70	279	-5	14615.42	8920.00
	Stephen GALLACHER	Scot	68	69	67	75	279	-5	14615.42	8920.00
24	Ian WOOSNAM	Wal	68	70	77	65	280	-4	13042.46	7960.00
	Raphaël JACQUELIN	Fr	74	67	71	68	280	-4	13042.46	7960.00
	Maarten LAFEBER	Hol	66	76	66	72	280	-4	13042.46	7960.00
	John SENDEN	Aus	69	69	73	69	280	-4	13042.46	7960.00
	Miguel Angel JIMÉNEZ	Sp	69	72	70	69	280	-4	13042.46	7960.00
	Ian GARBUTT	Eng	71	72	71	66	280	-4	13042.46	7960.00
30	David GILFORD	Eng	67	72	71	71	281	-3	10388.09	6340.00
	Soren KJELDSEN	Den	69	71	72	69	281	-3	10388.09	6340.00
	Gary EMERSON	Eng	69	71	72	69	281	-3	10388.09	6340.00
	Peter MITCHELL	Eng	70	71	73	67	281	-3	10388.09	6340.00
	Paul EALES	Eng	68	73	70	70	281	-3	10388.09	6340.00
	Ignacio GARRIDO	Sp	73	65	72	71	281	-3	10388.09	6340.00
	Bradley DREDGE	Wal	71	68	73	69	281	-3	10388.09	6340.00
	Fredrik JACOBSON	Swe	68	69	77	67	281	-3	10388.09	6340.00
38	Des SMYTH	Ire	70	72	70	70	282	-2	8126.96	4960.00
	Mark MCNULTY	Zim	70	71	71	70	282	-2	8126.96	4960.00
	José Maria OLAZÁBAL	Sp	65	72	75	70	282	-2	8126.96	4960.00
	Stephen LEANEY	Aus	67	72	74	69	282	-2	8126.96	4960.00
	Gregory HAVRET	Fr	68	72	69	73	282	-2	8126.96	4960.00
	Robert KARLSSON	Swe	73	70	70	69	282	-2	8126.96	4960.00
	David PARK	Wal	70	71	72	69	282	-2	8126.96	4960.00
	Andrew COLTART	Scot	66	72	77	67	282	-2	8126.96	4960.00
46	Brian DAVIS	Eng	74	66	73	70	283	-1	6160.76	3760.00
	Andrew MCLARDY	SA	75	68	72	68	283	-1	6160.76	3760.00
	Colin MONTGOMERIE	Scot	69	72	68	74	283	-1	6160.76	3760.00
	Fredrik LINDGREN	Swe	67	74	70	72	283	-1	6160.76	3760.00
	Carl SUNESON	Sp	71	69	72	71	283	-1	6160.76	3760.00
	Diego BORREGO	Sp	71	68	74	70	283	-1	6160.76	3760.00
	Gary ORR	Scot	72	68	74	69	283	-1	6160.76	3760.00
53	Gary EVANS	Eng	69	73	69	73	284	0	4587.80	2800.00
	Nicolas JOAKIMIDES	Fr	71	72	72	69	284	0	4587.80	2800.00
	John BICKERTON	Eng	72	71	70	71	284	0	4587.80	2800.00
	Lucas PARSONS	Aus	72	70	75	67	284	0	4587.80	2800.00
	Alastair FORSYTH	Scot	67	71	77	69	284	0	4587.80	2800.00
58	Mats LANNER	Swe	68	74	72	71	285	1	3670.24	2240.00
	Santiago LUNA	Sp	65	74	71	75	285	1	3670.24	2240.00
	Jonathan LOMAS	Eng	70	68	76	71	285	1	3670.24	2240.00
	Peter O'MALLEY	Aus	72	71	71	71	285	1	3670.24	2240.00
	Matthew BLACKEY	Eng	68	70	75	72	285	1	3670.24	2240.00
63	Anthony WALL	Eng	69	72	71	74	286	2	3014.84	1840.00
	Thomas LEVET	Fr	70	72	74	70	286	2	3014.84	1840.00
	Jeremy ROBINSON	Eng	73	70	73	70	286	2	3014.84	1840.00
	Van PHILLIPS	Eng	72	69	74	71	286	2	3014.84	1840.00
	Stephen ALLAN	Aus	70	69	75	72	286	2	3014.84	1840.00
68	Markus BRIER	Aut	67	74	74	72	287	3	2621.60	1600.00
69	Rodger DAVIS	Aus	71	71	77	69	288	4	2490.52	1520.00
70	José RIVERO	Sp	71	69	77	72	289	5	2074.40	1266.04
	Peter FOWLER	Aus	69	73	75	72	289	5	2074.40	1266.04
	David HOWELL	Eng	73	68	77	71	289	5	2074.40	1266.04
	Russell CLAYDON	Eng	71	71	75	72	289	5	2074.40	1266.04
74	Jean VAN DE VELDE	Fr	71	72	73	75	291	7	1955.50	1193.47
	Stuart LITTLE	Eng	71	72	72	76	291	7	1955.50	1193.47
76	Emanuele CANONICA	It	70	73	74	75	292	8	1951.00	1190.72
77	Mathias GRÖNBERG	Swe	69	74	76	74	293	9	1948.00	1188.89
78	Per NYMAN	Swe	72	70	78	74	294	10	1945.00	1187.06
79	Pierre FULKE	Swe	71	72	76	79	298	14	1942.00	1185.23

Never-Say-Die

ROYAL ZOUTE, KNOKKE-LE-ZOUTE, BELGIUM

*W*ho wants a diamond when you can have the real thing? At the 16th hole at Royal Zoute, during an absorbing Belgacom Open, there was on offer for a hole-in-one, a heart-shaped diamond. No-one won it, although three players in one day, over the opening round, did make holes in one, disappointingly for them, at the other three par-threes.

If you were looking for real heart, though, the golfing blue-blood

strain, or the never-say-die type, you could have found it.

Lee Westwood re-established himself as Europe's number one in the 2000 Volvo Order of Merit with an exhilarating fifth win of the year. The 27-year-old Englishman was always there or thereabouts and when he produced one of his stunning finishes, this one a 65, no-one could touch him. Then, if Tiger Woods hadn't been able to on the last day in Hamburg, that came as no surprise. Westwood's four-stroke win signalled his intent to be the new peer of European golf...a full-blooded success.

But heart is not all about winning, as poolside spectators at The Olympics in Sydney a few days before, had appreciated when 'Eric the Eel' floundered but crawled on to the finishing line.

Ironically, it was an Australian in Europe who caught the imagination of the knowledgeable in Knokke. Not a novice like the Olympic swimmer, but certainly not an 'Eddie the Birdie'. John Wade came to the Belgian event without a penny in 2000 earnings to his name. The Tasmanian-born player from Victoria could only dream about flying in to the North Sea holiday resort by helicopter, as some did that week. His European Tour career winnings up to the week, might just about have paid for helicopter fuel both ways. Just 3,920 euro (£2,450) had gone into the bank in three previous seasons. And up to Belgium, the 32-year-old Wade had missed every cut.

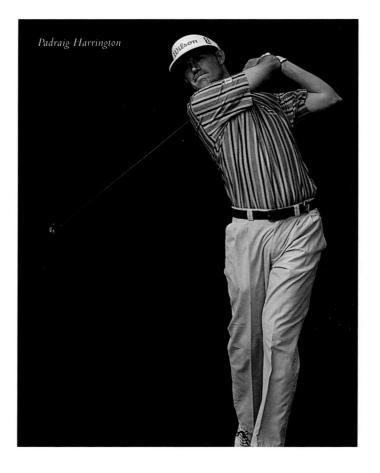

Padraig Harrington

Eduardo Romero gets caught in a sand storm

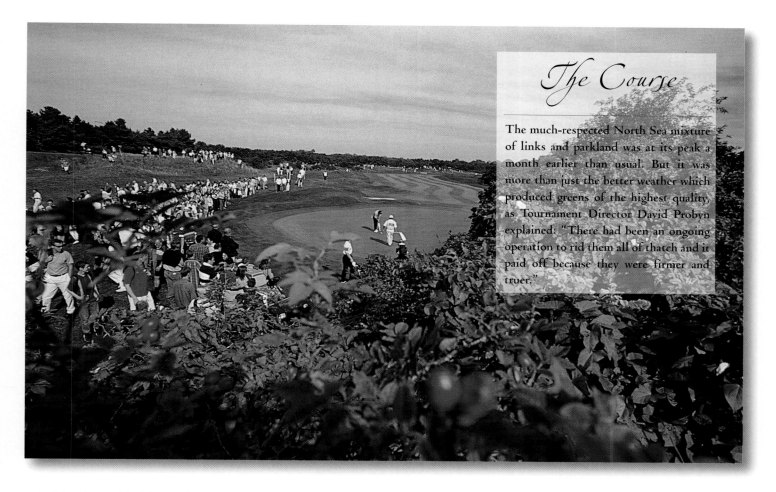

The Course

The much-respected North Sea mixture of links and parkland was at its peak a month earlier than usual. But it was more than just the better weather which produced greens of the highest quality, as Tournament Director David Probyn explained: "There had been an ongoing operation to rid them all of thatch and it paid off because they were firmer and truer."

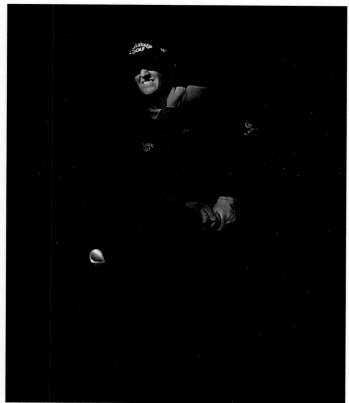

Out of the shadows – Colin Montgomerie

An opening 74 by the Australian did not bode well. The early bath beckoned once again as the South African rookie Hennie Otto rubbed salt into the wound by setting up the chance of a major pay cheque, leading by a stroke following an accomplished 64, seven under par.

Something strange happened next day, though. Something clicked for Wade. And this time there was no debilitating tummy bug to upset his round, no tweak or sprain to hinder the swing. A 65 went on to the card. Wade had reached the promised land. There would be bread on the table at the weekend at last. In fact, the determination that built cities out of bush had taken him three shots better than the cut.

If Wade had shown pluck, then the second round leader, American Tom Gillis, had found plenty of heart, too. Only two years before at Royal Zoute, he had sunk a putt on the 72nd green which kept him his European Tour card by just £200. A 64 set up his chance of going from low to high in two years marred by personal problems.

In this, the third Ryder Cup qualifying event, Padraig Harrington needed a heartening performance. The Irishman, one of the favourite bets for The De Vere Belfry, had not earned a point. Saturday was his day to launch the 2001 Ryder Cup campaign. Harrington erred

Shot of the Week

Paul Affleck, Ivo Giner and Jean-Francois Remesy, who were aces high in the first round, Padraig Harrington with a remarkable blind shot to the 18th on Saturday night, and Lee Westwood, giving himself a two-stroke cushion with an approach to a metre on the ninth in the final round, might all qualify. But Alastair Forsyth's pitch-in for an eagle on the 17th to seal a share of fifth place gets the nod.

Søren Hansen

just once in a round of 68. He bogeyed the last with a hook into the pines. And even though he made a magnificent recovery to drop only one shot, it brought his playing-partner Westwood and the Dane Søren Hansen to his shoulder, just a stroke behind.

Hansen, compiling a 63, the joint-best score of the week with Peter Baker, had taken up cudgels for Denmark after Thomas Björn had retired on Thursday with a sore foot. Hansen could have done Björn a favour by keeping his Volvo Order of Merit rival Westwood away from the winner's enclosure. Westwood was not to be denied, though.

Once Harrington had opened the door with early bogeys, there was only going to be one winner. The 166,660 euro (£102,000) first prize took Westwood back to the top in Europe, replacing Darren Clarke who had missed the halfway cut. Eduardo Romero's concentration-enhancing yoga sessions brought more rich pickings for the 46-year-old Argentine as he pipped Harrington and Gillis for runner-up by a stroke.

Wade, in a share of 22nd place, took away his first wages of the year. His prize of 10,850 euro (£6,640) would not buy many diamonds, but it gave him great heart.

Norman Dabell

ROYAL ZOUTE, KNOKKE-LE-ZOUTE, BELGIUM, 21-24 SEPTEMBER 2000, PAR 71, 6907 YARDS, 6316 METRES

Pos.	Name		Rd1	Rd2	Rd3	Rd4	Total	Par	Prize Money Euro	£
1	Lee WESTWOOD	Eng	65	69	67	65	266	-18	166660.00	102006.97
2	Eduardo ROMERO	Arg	69	67	68	66	270	-14	111110.00	68006.68
3	Padraig HARRINGTON	Ire	65	67	68	71	271	-13	56300.00	34459.33
	Tom GILLIS	USA	67	64	71	69	271	-13	56300.00	34459.33
5	Dean ROBERTSON	Scot	69	67	68	68	272	-12	38700.00	23686.96
	Alastair FORSYTH	Scot	69	69	67	67	272	-12	38700.00	23686.96
7	Marc FARRY	Fr	65	69	71	68	273	-11	23160.00	14175.45
	Jean-Francois REMESY	Fr	66	69	72	66	273	-11	23160.00	14175.45
	Soren HANSEN	Den	67	71	63	72	273	-11	23160.00	14175.45
	Paul MCGINLEY	Ire	68	68	71	66	273	-11	23160.00	14175.45
	David PARK	Wal	68	68	68	69	273	-11	23160.00	14175.45
12	Gary EMERSON	Eng	68	69	66	72	275	-9	15150.00	9272.80
	Paolo QUIRICI	Swi	70	65	70	70	275	-9	15150.00	9272.80
	Olle KARLSSON	Swe	65	71	73	66	275	-9	15150.00	9272.80
	Pierre FULKE	Swe	67	72	67	69	275	-9	15150.00	9272.80
	Andrew RAITT	Eng	66	69	70	70	275	-9	15150.00	9272.80
	Adam SCOTT	Aus	69	70	66	70	275	-9	15150.00	9272.80
18	Philip ARCHER	Eng	69	66	70	71	276	-8	12225.00	7482.51
	Peter BAKER	Eng	70	70	63	73	276	-8	12225.00	7482.51
	Geoff OGILVY	Aus	70	69	72	65	276	-8	12225.00	7482.51
	Roger WINCHESTER	Eng	69	69	70	68	276	-8	12225.00	7482.51
22	Eamonn DARCY	Ire	71	68	68	70	277	-7	10850.00	6640.92
	John WADE	Aus	74	65	68	70	277	-7	10850.00	6640.92
	Hennie OTTO	SA	64	72	67	74	277	-7	10850.00	6640.92
	Roger WESSELS	SA	70	64	72	71	277	-7	10850.00	6640.92
26	Justin ROSE	Eng	69	72	70	67	278	-6	9650.00	5906.44
	Colin MONTGOMERIE	Scot	69	69	70	70	278	-6	9650.00	5906.44
	Gary EVANS	Eng	66	68	74	70	278	-6	9650.00	5906.44
	José COCERES	Arg	68	67	74	69	278	-6	9650.00	5906.44
30	Wayne RILEY	Aus	67	74	67	71	279	-5	7925.00	4850.63
	David GILFORD	Eng	70	72	68	69	279	-5	7925.00	4850.63
	Maarten LAFEBER	Hol	71	69	69	70	279	-5	7925.00	4850.63
	Nick O'HERN	Aus	69	68	73	69	279	-5	7925.00	4850.63
	Jonathan LOMAS	Eng	70	67	72	70	279	-5	7925.00	4850.63
	Jorge BERENDT	Arg	69	68	69	73	279	-5	7925.00	4850.63
	Stephen SCAHILL	NZ	65	73	71	70	279	-5	7925.00	4850.63
	Daren LEE	Eng	70	70	67	72	279	-5	7925.00	4850.63
38	Bernhard LANGER	Ger	69	72	67	72	280	-4	6100.00	3733.60
	Santiago LUNA	Sp	69	70	70	71	280	-4	6100.00	3733.60
	Miguel Angel MARTIN	Sp	69	72	71	68	280	-4	6100.00	3733.60
	Peter FOWLER	Aus	72	68	68	72	280	-4	6100.00	3733.60
	Anders HANSEN	Den	71	70	71	68	280	-4	6100.00	3733.60
	Anthony WALL	Eng	68	69	74	69	280	-4	6100.00	3733.60
	Gary ORR	Scot	71	68	70	71	280	-4	6100.00	3733.60
	Robert COLES	Eng	69	70	72	69	280	-4	6100.00	3733.60
	Raymond RUSSELL	Scot	68	71	75	66	280	-4	6100.00	3733.60
47	Andrew OLDCORN	Scot	69	73	68	71	281	-3	4300.00	2631.88
	Soren KJELDSEN	Den	72	68	71	70	281	-3	4300.00	2631.88
	Thomas LEVET	Fr	69	68	73	71	281	-3	4300.00	2631.88
	Massimo FLORIOLI	It	70	70	71	70	281	-3	4300.00	2631.88
	Stephen FIELD	Eng	71	67	71	72	281	-3	4300.00	2631.88
	Ian HUTCHINGS	SA	69	73	70	69	281	-3	4300.00	2631.88
	Ivo GINER	Sp	69	69	69	74	281	-3	4300.00	2631.88
	Stephen GALLACHER	Scot	68	68	72	73	281	-3	4300.00	2631.88
	Brett RUMFORD	Aus	68	72	69	72	281	-3	4300.00	2631.88
56	Anders FORSBRAND	Swe	68	72	71	71	282	-2	3075.00	1882.10
	Mark MOULAND	Wal	71	70	69	72	282	-2	3075.00	1882.10
	Gary MURPHY	Ire	70	72	68	72	282	-2	3075.00	1882.10
	Jeremy ROBINSON	Eng	71	69	70	72	282	-2	3075.00	1882.10
60	Des SMYTH	Ire	68	74	71	70	283	-1	2400.00	1468.96
	Sven STRÜVER	Ger	68	73	71	71	283	-1	2400.00	1468.96
	Greg TURNER	NZ	70	72	71	70	283	-1	2400.00	1468.96
	Paul EALES	Eng	70	72	69	72	283	-1	2400.00	1468.96
	Richard S JOHNSON	Swe	70	71	72	70	283	-1	2400.00	1468.96
	Jarrod MOSELEY	Aus	75	67	67	74	283	-1	2400.00	1468.96
	Paul AFFLECK	Wal	66	72	75	70	283	-1	2400.00	1468.96
	Robert KARLSSON	Swe	69	73	69	72	283	-1	2400.00	1468.96
	Stephen ALLAN	Aus	70	69	67	77	283	-1	2400.00	1468.96
69	José RIVERO	Sp	70	69	72	73	284	0	1900.00	1162.93
70	Rodger DAVIS	Aus	70	65	76	74	285	1	1609.00	984.81
	Richard GREEN	Aus	71	70	72	72	285	1	1609.00	984.81
	Bradley DREDGE	Wal	72	69	71	73	285	1	1609.00	984.81
73	Ross MCFARLANE	Eng	70	69	74	73	286	2	1492.50	913.51
	Olivier EDMOND	Fr	73	68	74	71	286	2	1492.50	913.51
75	Simon D. HURLEY	Eng	71	71	75	70	287	3	1488.00	910.75
76	Costantino ROCCA	It	70	71	71	76	288	4	1479.00	905.25
	José Maria OLAZABAL	Sp	70	72	72	74	288	4	1479.00	905.25
	José Manuel CARRILES	Sp	70	71	72	75	288	4	1479.00	905.25
	Matthew BLACKEY	Eng	72	70	71	75	288	4	1479.00	905.25
	John MELLOR	Eng	69	73	71	75	288	4	1479.00	905.25
81	Nicolas VANHOOTEGEM	Bel	72	68	77	72	289	5	1468.50	898.82
	Gustavo ROJAS	Arg	72	70	72	75	289	5	1468.50	898.82
83	Ian POULTER	Eng	71	67	79	77	294	10	1464.00	896.07

Long Distance Affair

GUT LÄRCHENHOF, COLOGNE, GERMANY

After firing a third round 66 in the Linde German Masters, boasting record prize money of 2,700,000 euro (£1,600,000), Colin Montgomerie, 15 under par but four strokes behind New Zealand's Michael Campbell, admitted: "I'll need to shoot something silly like 62 tomorrow."

Tomorrow never came for Montgomerie as torrential rain flooded fairways, greens and bunkers, rendering the Gut Lärchenhof course near Cologne unplayable and leaving Tournament Director Mikael Eriksson, after consultation with the sponsor and promoters Erwin and Bernhard Langer, to declare it a 54-hole event.

Padraig Harrington

Campbell, who followed an opening 68 with brilliant rounds of 64 and 65, thus won by a single stroke from Argentina's José Coceres, with Montgomerie and Padraig Harrington joint third three further back and Thomas Björn fifth one stroke behind them.

So exactly 155 years after his great-great-great grandfather Sir Logan Campbell left Edinburgh to seek his fortune on the other side of the world, Campbell returned "home" to harvest riches of his own in the shape of a 450,000 euro (£271,500) jackpot, which nudged his season's official winnings past the £1 million mark.

As Campbell recorded his third European Tour success of the 2000 campaign, having opened up with all guns blazing in the Johnnie Walker Classic in Taiwan and the Heineken Classic in Western Australia, the Cologne Marathon, unhindered by the deluge, was being run through the city streets. Campbell's journey to his first victory on European soil had also been a long distance affair.

It began in fairytale fashion in his rookie season of 1995 when he led the Open Championship back in the land of his forefathers at St Andrews with a round to go, ending in joint third place.

Things went awry as he ran into wrist injury problems and lost his card. But he won it back at the 1997 European Tour Qualifying School and, following the arrival of baby son, Thomas, in 1998, it's been all down hill for the smiling Kiwi.

Mats Lanner with his prize at the 16th hole

Shot of the Week

Mats Lanner's hole in one with a four iron at the 193 yards 16th won him a £26,000 Jaguar, but the shot of the week in that same first round was Nick Faldo's "splash out" with a sand iron over a towering bank to 15 feet to save par when his ball ended in the water beyond the 17th green and he waded in minus shoes and socks. "A career best up and down" declared Faldo.

"It rekindled my motivation and inspired me to go all out to provide the best living I could for my family and I've won five tournaments since then," admitted Campbell, whose first victory on European soil fulfilled a burning ambition.

He explained: "Having had three second place finishes (The Compass Group English Open, Volvo Scandinavian Masters and Trophée Lancôme) I was beginning to get a bit down on myself, even paranoid because my all round game has improved immensely over the last 12 months.

"I've been working out in the gym almost every day and I haven't smoked a cigarette since February and feel very strong physically. Winning one of the biggest tournaments is a great reward.

"Sam Torrance asked me if my family connection with Scotland entitled me to a British passport. Although I'm a tax resident in Britain, and have just moved into a new home in Brighton, I'm in a bit of a grey area. It's a pity because I would have loved to have played in the Ryder Cup."

Campbell, who had words of praise for caddie Michael Waite and close friend Björn, was convinced he would have won over 72 holes and "slightly disappointed" at not having the chance to prove it.

He said: "My last couple of rounds were phenomenal. My 64 on Friday would have been 62 had I not lipped out from 15 feet and ten feet on the last two greens. Mind you my caddie, who is my sternest critic, said I wasn't yet playing as well as when I won at The Vines.

Vijay Singh

"The thing I have going with Thomas helps. One week he's up there, the next it's me. It's healthy rivalry between great pals and brings the best out of both of us."

One of the first to congratulate Campbell, although disappointed to have finished third for the second week running when in with a great chance to win, was Padraig Harrington, who shared the halfway lead with him after two opening 66s.

Back in May, Harrington was disqualified when leading by five strokes on the final morning of the Benson and Hedges International Open at The De Vere Belfry when it came to light he had not signed his card on day one.

The Irishman had been confused when playing partner Campbell mistakenly signed his name in the "player's" space on Harrington's card alongside the marker's signature.

Harrington, who blames no one but himself, explained: "The legacy of The Belfry is that I'm asked about it every week. It's put a lot of pressure on me but I'm getting over it. Hopefully another win will put the incident behind me, but I won't know until it happens."

Bernhard Langer

Gordon Richardson

The Course

It was ironical that an excess of water shrunk the event to 54 holes for water is the key feature of Jack Nicklaus's layout 20 miles from Cologne, coming into play on 12 holes, most notably the ninth, where the lake is on the right, and the 18th when danger lurks left and where so many come to grief, especially when the wind whistles over the flat, exposed terrain.

GUT LÄRCHENHOF, COLOGNE, GERMANY, 28 SEPTEMBER - 1 OCTOBER 2000, PAR 72, 7209 YARDS, 6589 METRES

Pos.	Name		Rd1	Rd2	Rd3	Rd4	Total	Par	Prize Money Euro	£
1	Michael CAMPBELL	NZ	68	64	65		197	-19	450000.00	271612.84
2	José COCERES	Arg	66	67	65		198	-18	300000.00	181075.22
3	Padraig HARRINGTON	Ire	66	66	69		201	-15	152010.00	91750.82
	Colin MONTGOMERIE	Scot	67	68	66		201	-15	152010.00	91750.82
5	Thomas BJÖRN	Den	68	66	68		202	-14	114480.00	69098.31
6	Bernhard LANGER	Ger	67	67	69		203	-13	71496.00	43153.85
	Sam TORRANCE	Scot	70	67	66		203	-13	71496.00	43153.85
	Miguel Angel JIMÉNEZ	Sp	68	70	65		203	-13	71496.00	43153.85
	Ignacio GARRIDO	Sp	69	67	67		203	-13	71496.00	43153.85
	Adam SCOTT	Aus	70	65	68		203	-13	71496.00	43153.85
11	Jean VAN DE VELDE	Fr	71	64	69		204	-12	46530.00	28084.77
	Angel CABRERA	Arg	66	69	69		204	-12	46530.00	28084.77
	Lee WESTWOOD	Eng	70	66	68		204	-12	46530.00	28084.77
14	Roger CHAPMAN	Eng	70	67	68		205	-11	39690.00	23956.25
	Paul MCGINLEY	Ire	71	70	64		205	-11	39690.00	23956.25
	Pierre FULKE	Swe	71	67	67		205	-11	39690.00	23956.25
17	Sergio GARCIA	Sp	72	65	69		206	-10	33696.00	20338.37
	Mark MCNULTY	Zim	71	68	67		206	-10	33696.00	20338.37
	Greg TURNER	NZ	71	65	70		206	-10	33696.00	20338.37
	Paul LAWRIE	Scot	72	66	68		206	-10	33696.00	20338.37
	Patrik SJÖLAND	Swe	66	71	69		206	-10	33696.00	20338.37
22	David HOWELL	Eng	70	68	69		207	-9	27675.00	16704.19
	Peter MITCHELL	Eng	68	70	69		207	-9	27675.00	16704.19
	Jarrod MOSELEY	Aus	70	67	70		207	-9	27675.00	16704.19
	Per-Ulrik JOHANSSON	Swe	68	71	68		207	-9	27675.00	16704.19
	Roger WINCHESTER	Eng	67	71	69		207	-9	27675.00	16704.19
	Alex CEJKA	Ger	69	67	71		207	-9	27675.00	16704.19
	Phillip PRICE	Wal	70	72	65		207	-9	27675.00	16704.19
	John BICKERTON	Eng	68	69	70		207	-9	27675.00	16704.19
30	Nick FALDO	Eng	70	68	70		208	-8	20495.45	12370.73
	Marc FARRY	Fr	71	71	66		208	-8	20495.45	12370.73
	John SENDEN	Aus	68	70	70		208	-8	20495.45	12370.73
	Andrew MCLARDY	SA	68	70	70		208	-8	20495.45	12370.73
	Paul EALES	Eng	72	67	69		208	-8	20495.45	12370.73
	Russell CLAYDON	Eng	68	70	70		208	-8	20495.45	12370.73
	Emanuele CANONICA	It	67	70	71		208	-8	20495.45	12370.73
	Ian GARBUTT	Eng	70	68	70		208	-8	20495.45	12370.73
	Andrew COLTART	Scot	68	70	70		208	-8	20495.45	12370.73
	David CARTER	Eng	67	74	67		208	-8	20495.45	12370.73
	Erol SIMSEK	Ger	72	68	68		208	-8	20495.45	12370.73
41	Santiago LUNA	Sp	69	71	69		209	-7	15120.00	9126.19
	Brian DAVIS	Eng	69	73	67		209	-7	15120.00	9126.19
	Sven STRÜVER	Ger	73	69	67		209	-7	15120.00	9126.19
	Steen TINNING	Den	71	67	71		209	-7	15120.00	9126.19
	Vijay SINGH	Fiji	69	70	70		209	-7	15120.00	9126.19
	Dean ROBERTSON	Scot	69	70	70		209	-7	15120.00	9126.19
	Christopher HANELL	Swe	70	69	70		209	-7	15120.00	9126.19
	Tobias DIER	Ger	72	68	69		209	-7	15120.00	9126.19
49	Gary ORR	Scot	67	72	71		210	-6	12420.00	7496.51
	Greg OWEN	Eng	70	70	70		210	-6	12420.00	7496.51
51	Eamonn DARCY	Ire	73	67	71		211	-5	10530.00	6355.74
	Kalle VAINOLA	Fin	73	66	72		211	-5	10530.00	6355.74
	Anthony WALL	Eng	69	70	72		211	-5	10530.00	6355.74
	Rolf MUNTZ	Hol	72	69	70		211	-5	10530.00	6355.74
	Roger WESSELS	SA	71	70	70		211	-5	10530.00	6355.74
56	Costantino ROCCA	It	74	68	70		212	-4	7868.57	4749.34
	Eduardo ROMERO	Arg	69	70	73		212	-4	7868.57	4749.34
	Stephen LEANEY	Aus	71	70	71		212	-4	7868.57	4749.34
	Paolo QUIRICI	Swi	70	70	72		212	-4	7868.57	4749.34
	Massimo FLORIOLI	It	68	72	72		212	-4	7868.57	4749.34
	David PARK	Wal	72	69	71		212	-4	7868.57	4749.34
	Knut EKJORD	Nor	73	69	70		212	-4	7868.57	4749.34
63	Mats LANNER	Swe	70	72	71		213	-3	6480.00	3911.22
	Gary EVANS	Eng	71	67	75		213	-3	6480.00	3911.22
	Niclas FASTH	Swe	70	71	72		213	-3	6480.00	3911.22
66	Peter BAKER	Eng	73	68	73		214	-2	5535.00	3340.84
	Mathias GRÖNBERG	Swe	69	72	73		214	-2	5535.00	3340.84
	Diego BORREGO	Sp	73	69	72		214	-2	5535.00	3340.84
	Retief GOOSEN	SA	70	71	73		214	-2	5535.00	3340.84
70	Felix LUBENAU	Ger	73	69	73		215	-1	4485.00	2707.07
	Wolfgang HUGET	Ger	68	74	73		215	-1	4485.00	2707.07
72	Francisco CEA	Sp	72	70	74		216	0	4047.00	2442.70
73	Steve WEBSTER	Eng	71	71	77		219	3	4044.00	2440.89
74	Michael JONZON	Swe	71	71	80		222	6	4041.00	2439.08

Clear orientation and commitment – that´s the basis of our success.

As an international enterprise we use our partners' experience and perspectives. We are on the move forward, too. Gaining more understanding and being better understood.

Engineering and Contracting

Material Handling

Refrigeration

Industrial Gases

www.linde.com

Technology works

Linde

The Young Pretender

WENTWORTH CLUB, SURREY, ENGLAND

*G*etting up before dawn to play a Monday morning round of golf is probably one of the last things Lee Westwood would normally think of doing. He is, by his own admission, not the best of early morning risers, and this time he had to rouse himself after ploughing around a sodden Wentworth West Course for 42 marathon holes the day before.

But the lure of winning his sixth title of a remarkable 2000 season, and outgunning his arch-rival Colin Montgomerie in his own backyard, turned the 6.00am alarm call and the 8.00am start on a

bitter October morning into a cheerfully accepted challenge.

In the end all the effort proved worthwhile as Westwood, the young pretender who had threatened all summer to depose Montgomerie as Europe's Volvo Order of Merit king, ended his reign as emperor of Wentworth in the most thrilling of finishes to the Cisco World Match Play Championship. It left Westwood joking that he and best friend Darren Clarke, winner of the WGC - Andersen Consulting Match Play, should get together at their next practice round to have "a unification bout."

Westwood, however, also knew the extent of his achievement. He added: "I had to play my socks off against Sergio Garcia, Ernie Els and Colin. To beat Colin on a course he knows better than anyone gives me real satisfaction. To go head to head with the best players in the world is so exciting."

It was not until the 38th hole of a final that radiated almost unrelenting tension and drama, to equal any in the Match Play's glittering 37 year history, that Montgomerie finally bowed to his conqueror. Until that moment he had looked set to maintain his stranglehold on the Cisco purse strings, having collected 1,368,000 euro (£855,000) in his last five visits to the West Course, including capturing three successive Volvo PGA Championship titles and the 1999 Cisco crown.

He cruised to the final with a 5&3 victory over fast-improving Irishman Padraig Harrington and an equally impressive 5&4 semi-final dismissal of Masters Tournament champion Vijay Singh.

Westwood had a much more rocky route to the final, just seeing off the precociously talented young Spaniard, Garcia 2&1 and then staging a remarkable comeback from two down with three to play against three-times Match Play champion Els before winning at the 36th when Els missed a two foot putt.

Ernie Els

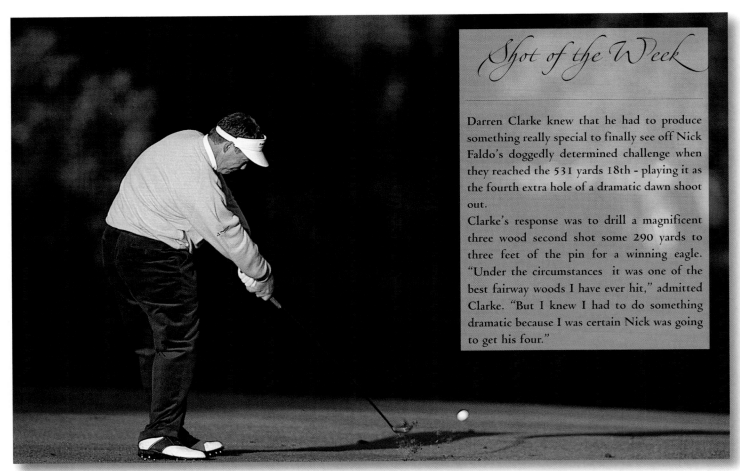

Shot of the Week

Darren Clarke knew that he had to produce something really special to finally see off Nick Faldo's doggedly determined challenge when they reached the 531 yards 18th - playing it as the fourth extra hole of a dramatic dawn shoot out.

Clarke's response was to drill a magnificent three wood second shot some 290 yards to three feet of the pin for a winning eagle. "Under the circumstances it was one of the best fairway woods I have ever hit," admitted Clarke. "But I knew I had to do something dramatic because I was certain Nick was going to get his four."

Colin Montgomerie

Retief Goosen

The first half of the final on the Sunday afternoon saw Westwood wielding his putter like a magician to take a three hole lead going to the 18th where Montgomerie produced his own minor miracle with an eagle putt from 40 feet to reduce the gap to two.

With an almost apocalyptic weather forecast for Monday afternoon, the organisers wisely opted for an 8.00am start but Westwood's putter appeared to have gone almost as cold as the chill morning air, suffering his first bogey in 44 holes at the second, and allowing Montgomerie to turn that two hole deficit into a one hole lead by the eighth.

The match see-sawed again on the closing stretch with Montgomerie bogeying the 13th and 14th and Westwood three putting the 15th, to leave it all square.

The turning point was the long 17th when Montgomerie drilled a magnificent three wood second shot to 35 feet. Westwood, having seen his second fall 40 yards short, chipped too strongly but then showed an ice-cool nerve by holing crucially from 20 feet for a half. "You always have to expect your opponent to do something like that, but even so I must admit it was a surprise," said Montgomerie.

Both players did well to scrape birdie fours at the last and par fours at the first extra hole before Westwood again used his putter like a dagger to hole an 18 footer across the second green before Montgomerie's effort from 14 feet slid agonisingly wide.

Nick Faldo

Westwood, a tremendous 13 under par for 38 holes, was left to collect the splendid silver trophy and the 420,000 euro (£250,000) first prize, while Montgomerie was left with only thoughts of what might have been.

The Cisco World Match Play Championship, as always, had produced drama from the start with the pick of the first round seeing Nick Faldo underline his welcome return to form by taking Darren Clarke to the 40th in a thrilling dawn shoot-out (equalling the longest ever match in Championship history) before bowing to a brilliant eagle.

Padraig Harrington survived an early fright to outgun the lone American Bob May 6&5, while the eagerly awaited clash of the two 20-year-old discoveries, Garcia and Australian Adam Scott ended with Garcia edging through 2&1, while Retief Goosen outgunned Thomas Björn 5&4.

The second round scoring was remarkable even by the Match Play's elevated standards. The eight players were an eclectic 79 under par, scoring 88 birdies and two eagles between them, with Singh and Els overcoming Clarke and Goosen respectively, and once again the spectators were treated to a week of spectacular golf which will live long in the memory.

John Whitbread

The Course

Despite the atrocious conditions the famous Burma Road was in remarkably good condition - a fact underlined by the extraordinarily brilliant scoring - as Wentworth Course Superintendent Chris Kennedy and his staff once again rose to the challenge.

Mark H McCormack (front row, second from left), Chairman and CEO of the International Management Group and the founder of the World Match Play Championship, and William Nuti, President of Cisco Systems EMEA (front row, second from right), gathered on the eve of the 2000 Championship with the players:
Back row (left to right): Darren Clarke, Retief Goosen, Lee Westwood, Thomas Björn, Ernie Els, Nick Faldo, Vijay Singh, Padraig Harrington, Adam Scott
Front row (left to right): Bob May, Colin Montgomerie and Sergio Garcia

A sporting finish to a great final

WENTWORTH CLUB, SURREY, ENGLAND
5-9 OCTOBER 2000, PAR 72, 7047 YARDS 6446 METRES

		Euro	Sterling
FIRST ROUND			
Padraig Harrington (Ire) beat Bob May (USA)	6 & 5	83,665	50,000
Darren Clarke (N Ire) (5) beat Nick Faldo (Eng)	at 40th	83,665	50,000
Sergio Garcia (Sp) (6) beat Adam Scott (Aus)	2 & 1	83,665	50,000
Retief Goosen (SA) beat Thomas Björn (Den) (7)	5 & 4	83,665	50,000
SECOND ROUND			
Colin Montgomerie (Scot) (1) beat Padraig Harrington	5 & 3	108,765	65,000
Vijay Singh (Fiji) (4) beat Darren Clarke	5 & 4	108,765	65,000
Lee Westwood (Eng) (3) beat Sergio Garcia	2 & 1	108,765	65,000
Ernie Els (SA) (2) beat Retief Goosen	2 & 1	108,765	65,000
SEMI-FINALS			
Colin Montgomerie beat Vijay Singh	5 & 4	142,231	85,000
Lee Westwood beat Ernie Els	1 hole	142,231	85,000
FINAL			
Lee Westwood beat Colin Montgomerie	at 38th	418,327	250,000
		200,797	120,000
Total		1,673,310	1,000,000

Heart of a Lion

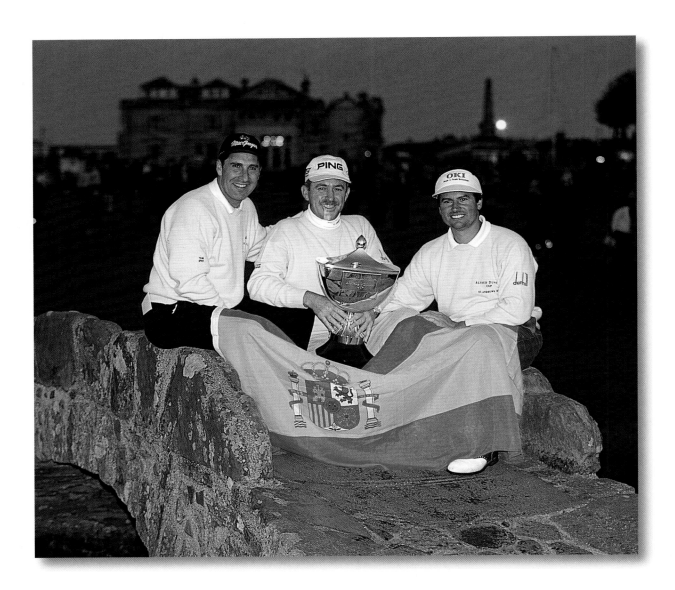

Some old prejudices were corrected and a few suspicions confirmed as the last staging of the Alfred Dunhill Cup at St Andrews in a 16 nation, medal matchplay tournament turned out to be one of the best in the event's history.

Blessed by decent weather and some glorious golf - Ernie Els was 20 under par for his five rounds - Spain held onto the title they'd won for the first time the year before thanks to a nail-biting victory over South Africa in the final.

Those who felt before a ball was teed up that South Africa, winners in 1997 and 1998, and Spain, the holders, would again prove the pick of the bunch, were proved right.

That said, the manner in which the Spaniards earned a 2-1 victory thanks to a courageous fight-back from Miguel Angel Martin in his game with David Frost, was unexpectedly compelling.

After both players were round in 74, it was Martin's par four at the first extra hole against Frost's bogey which demonstrated his courage, secured victory and earned the praise of his captain José Maria Olazábal.

"Miguel may be small in stature but he's a big man and showed the heart of a lion to win his match and help us win the Cup," said Olazábal. "Really, it was astonishing the way he came back after a double bogey at the 17th."

After Els defeated Olazábal and Miguel Angel Jiménez was a shot better than Retief Goosen, the outcome of the final was finely balanced as both Martin and Frost made a hash of the Road Hole, running up double-bogey sixes. Perhaps Frost's course management let him down on this occasion. When he saw Martin's approach finish on the road, Frost should have gone short and right. Instead he went long and right. This meant the South African went up the last with a one stroke lead. He must have felt he was home and dry, mind you, when Martin's second struck the flag and spun away into the Valley of Sin.

There were shades of Costantino Rocca, though, at the 1995 Open Championship when the Spaniard recovered his composure and holed a 50 foot putt for birdie to take the match into extra holes. At the first, Frost three-putted and Martin's par earned 166,417 euro (£100,000) apiece for himself and his team-mates. A late replacement for Sergio Garcia, Martin couldn't hide his joy. "This was a great day for me, the team and Spain," he grinned.

David Frost

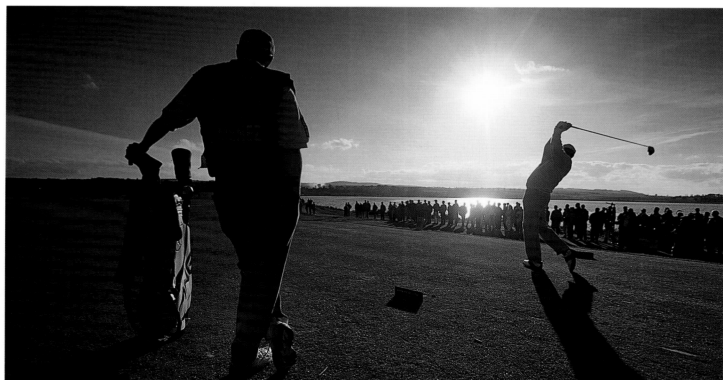

Driving into the setting sun at St Andrews

Shot of the Week

José María Olazábal, the Spanish captain, conjured up a memorable shot onto the green at the Road Hole on Saturday. Having sliced his drive, Olazábal found his ball lying a matter of inches from the wall of the Old Course Hotel. However, Olazábal whacked a nine iron which carried 165 yards to the green.

In the group matches, much attention focused on section one where Scotland and England were drawn together along with Wales and Germany.

The Scottish team of Colin Montgomerie, Andrew Coltart and Gary Orr had a mission to fulfil - it was their last chance to beat England.

As it turned out, Montgomerie followed in the footsteps of the Scottish rugby captain Andy Nicol and football's Colin Hendry by leading the Scots to a 2-1 success. He even played a captain's role, holing a daunting putt of 15 feet for a birdie on the last with nearly two feet of break. It was good enough for 69, one shot better than the 70 carded by Brian Davis. Coltart, the pick of the Scots, then secured victory with a 68 to Jamie Spence's 73.

After Orr and Roger Chapman both fired 69s, the Englishman won his match at the first extra hole. Orr's approach to the first green

spun back into the burn and he could do no better than a bogey. The Helensburgh man was entitled to feel shortchanged since he, too, holed a wonderful birdie putt at the last.

It was the first time since the competition started in 1985 that the Scots had triumphed over their oldest rivals at golf. In five previous meetings, most recently in the 1992 final, England won each time. "Better late than never," quipped Coltart, "but it took us 16 years to do it."

Scotland's pleasure at dispatching England was tempered, however, by defeats from both Germany and Wales. Indeed, the No 1 seeds, never lived up to their pre-tournament billing and it was the Welsh side of Ian Woosnam, Phillip Price and David Park who flew the flag for Britain in the semi-finals.

At that stage they lost 2-0 to South Africa. The former champions won all three of their matches in Group Two where neither Ireland nor New Zealand were quite good enough to live with the Springboks.

The Spaniards carried all before them in Group Three where Zimbabwe were not quite at their best and the Swedes fell just a little short. In Group Four, the Argentine trio of Eduardo Romero, Angel Cabrera and José Coceres beat America for the first time and were fancied by many to run out winners until crossing swords with Spain in the semi-finals. As it turned out, Spain had too much firepower with both Olazábal and Martin helping to secure a 2-1 win.

Nevertheless, Romero took personal satisfaction from his win over Jiménez and was delighted with his side's contribution to the match. "We were really proud to reach the semi-finals for the first time," he said. "It was a great week for us and I felt we did well. It was just a pity that Angel, who started with three birdies against Olazábal, couldn't maintain his good start."

A new tournament, supported by Alfred Dunhill Ltd with US $5 million in prize money will, in 2001, replace the Alfred Dunhill Cup. The Alfred Dunhill Links championship will be a 72 hole strokeplay event with a pro-am format. Two competitions will run concurrently - an individual pro event and team competition for a pro and an amateur. Counting towards official money and Ryder Cup points, the Links Championship will prove an outstanding success if it delivers even half the enjoyment Martin gleaned from being part of a winning team.

Mike Aitken

Ernie Els

The Course

Although the Alfred Dunhill Cup gained a reputation for attracting wild weather over the years, the last staging of the tournament at the Old Course was blessed with mostly bright and mild conditions. The wind blew a little over the weekend but scores were mostly low as the Home of Golf bid a gentle farewell to the nations cup format.

ST ANDREWS, FIFE, SCOTLAND, 12-15 OCTOBER 2000, PAR 72, 7115 YARDS, 6506 METRES

FINAL
Spain beat South Africa 2-1
MA Martin (74) **beat** D Frost (74)*
MA Jiménez (70) **beat** R Goosen (72)
JM Olazábal (70) **lost to** E Els (68)
*Won at 1st extra hole

SEMI FINAL
South Africa beat Wales 2-0
D Frost (70) **beat** I Woosnam (76)
E Els (69) **beat** D Park (77)
P Price (68) **halved with** R Goosen (68)#
Did not conclude play-off

SEMI FINAL
Spain beat Argentina 2-1
JM Olazábal (69) **beat** A Cabrera (71)
MA Jiménez (71) **lost to** E Romero (69)
MA Martin (71) **beat** J Coceres (72)

Day 1

Group One

Scotland lost to Germany 1-2
G Orr (70) lost to B Langer (68)
A Coltart (70) bt T Gögele (71)
C Montgomerie (70) lost to S Strüver (66)

Wales beat England 3-0
I Woosnam (72) bt R Chapman (73)
P Price (70) bt B Davis (73)
D Park (67) bt J Spence (73)

Group Two

South Africa beat France 2-1
D Frost (68) bt J-F Remesy (74)
R Goosen (72) lost to R Jacquelin (70),
E Els (68) bt T Levet (74)

New Zealand lost to Ireland 1-2
G Turner (69)* bt D Smyth (69)
G Waite (71) lost to P Harrington (68)
M Campbell (69) lost to P McGinley (67)
*Won at 1st extra hole

Group Three

Spain beat China 3-0
MA Jiménez (66) bt Wu Xiang Bing (79)
MA Martin (70) bt Zhang Lian-Wei (71)
JM Olazábal (66) bt Laing Wen-chong (71)

Sweden beat Zimbabwe 2-1
P Sjöland (72) lost to M McNulty (67)
P-U Johansson (69) bt T Johnstone (75)
M Grönberg (69) bt N Price (73)

Group Four

Australia beat United States 2-1
S Leaney (67) bt J Daly (70)
N O'Hern (65) bt L Mize (71)
P O'Malley (73) lost to T Lehman (68)

Argentina beat Japan 3-0
E Romero (70) bt T Nishikawa (72)
A Cabrera (70) bt I Aoki (71)
J Coceres (65) bt T Watanabe (71)

Day 2
Group One

Scotland beat England 2-1
C Montgomerie (69) bt B Davis (70)
A Coltart (68) bt J Spence (73)
G Orr (69) lost to R Chapman (69)*
*Won at 1st extra hole

Wales beat Germany 2-1
I Woosnam (70) bt B Langer (72)
D Park (71) bt S Strüver (71)*
P Price (69) lost to T Gögele (70)
*Won at 1st extra hole

Group Two

South Africa beat Ireland 3-0
D Frost (66) bt D Smyth (68)
R Goosen (71)* bt P McGinley (71)
E Els (67) bt P Harrington (69)
*Won at 1st extra hole

New Zealand beat France 3-0
G Turner (73) bt J-F Remesy (74)
G Waite (70) bt R Jacquelin (72)
M Campbell (69) bt T Levet (70)

Day 1

Group Three

Sweden beat China 3-0
P Sjöland (67) bt Liang Wen-Chong (72)
P-U Johansson (72) bt Wu Xiang-Bing (80)
M Gronberg (71) bt Zhang Lian-Wei (72)

Spain beat Zimbabwe 2-1
MA Martin (73) lost to T Johnstone (72)
MA Jimenez (67) bt N Price (68)
JM Olazabal (67) bt M McNulty (71)

Group Four

Australia beat Japan 3-0
N O'Hern (70) bt I Aoki (71)
S Leaney (73) bt T Watanabe (74)
P O'Malley (69) bt T Nishikawa (70)

Argentina beat United States 3-0
E Romero (70) bt L Mize (72)
J Coceres (73) bt J Daly (75)
A Cabrera (68) bt T Lehman (71)

Day 3

Group One

Scotland lost to Wales 0-3
C Montgomerie (73) lost to I Woosnam (73)*
A Coltart (72) lost to D Park (70)
G Orr (72) lost to P Price (69)
*Won at 2nd extra hole

Germany beat England 3-0
B Langer (71) bt J Spence (76)
T Gögele (69) bt R Chapman (72)
S Struver (72) bt B Davis (74)

Day 1

Group Three

South Africa beat New Zealand 2-1
R Goosen (71)* beat G Turner (71)
D Frost (75) lost to G Waite (71)
E Els (68) beat M Campbell (69)
*Won at 1st extra hole

Ireland beat France 3-0
P McGinley (67) bt R Jacquelin (69)
D Smyth (70) bt J-F Remesy (76)
P Harrington (69) bt T Levet (74)

Group Three

Zimbabwe beat China 2-1
T Johnstone (69) bt Wu Xiang-Bing (76)
M McNulty (71) bt Liang Wen-Chong (74)
N Price (71) lost to Zhang Lian-Wei (68)

Spain beat Sweden 2-1
MA Martin (69) bt P Sjöland (71)
MA Jiménez (72) lost to P-U Johansson (71)
JM Olazábal (72) bt M Grönberg (74)

Group Four

Argentina beat Australia 2-1
E Romero (72) lost to N O'Hern (69)
A Cabrera (70) bt S Leaney (75)
J Coceres (74) bt P O'Malley (76)

United States beat Japan 2-1
J Daly (73) lost to I Aoki (73)*
T Lehman (74) bt T Nishikawa (75)
L Mize (70) bt T Watanabe (76)
*Won at 3rd extra hole

PRIZE MONEY

	Matches Won	Individual Games Won	Team Prize Money euro	£	Player Prize Money euro	£	Total Prize Money euro	£
GROUP 1								
Wales (8)	3	8						
Germany	2	6	74,887	45,000	24,962	15,000		
Scotland (1)	1	3	42,436	25,500	14,145	8,500		
England	0	1	32,451	19,500	10,817	6,500	149,774	90,000
GROUP 2								
South Africa (4)	3	7						
Ireland	2	5	74,887	45,000	24,962	15,000		
New Zealand (5)	1	5	42,436	25,500	14,145	8,500		
France	0	1	32,451	19,500	10,817	6,500	149,774	90,000
GROUP 3								
Spain (3)	3	7						
Sweden (6)	2	6	74,887	45,000	24,962	15,000		
Zimbabwe	1	4	42,436	25,500	14,145	8,500		
China	0	1	32,451	19,500	10,817	6,500	149,774	90,000
GROUP 4								
Argentina (2)	3	8						
Australia (7)	2	6	74,887	45,000	24,962	15,000		
United States	1	3	42,436	25,500	14,145	8,500		
Japan	0	1	32,451	19,500	10,817	6,500	149,774	90,000
LOSING SEMI FINALISTS								
Wales			158,096	95,000	52,698	31,666		
Argentina			158,096	95,000	52,698	31,666	316,192	190,000
RUNNERS-UP								
South Africa			249,625	150,000	83,208	50,000	249,625	150,000
WINNERS								
Spain			499,251	300,000	166,417	100,000	499,251	300,000

All Our Yesterdays

CLUB DE CAMPO, MADRID, SPAIN

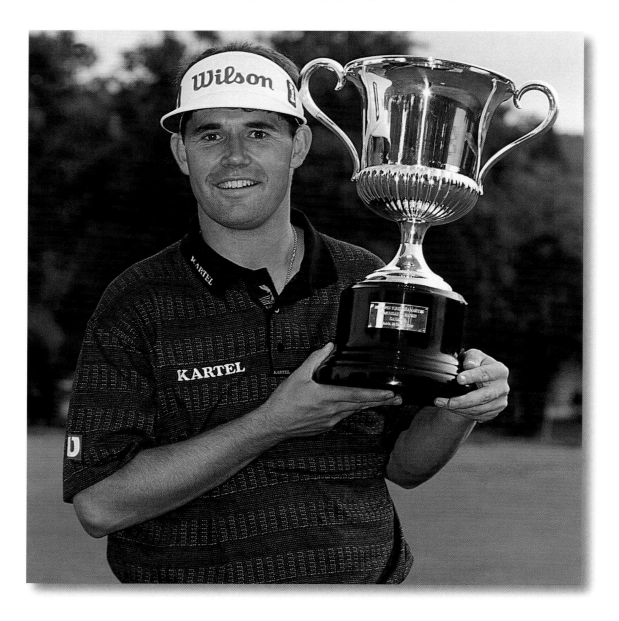

*I*magine the picture. There you are practising intently on the range before going out to try to win your second title of the year, knowing you hold a substantial lead. Then out of the corner of your eye you spot the Tournament Director walking over to you. Pinch yourself. It's the old nightmare again. When will those Belfry demons go away?

But wait. You're wide awake. Trusty caddie Dave McNeilly's alongside offering the usual encouraging words in his Ulster brogue. Surely it can't be happening again?

Wait again, though. He's smiling. The Tournament Director's smiling. Andy McFee's face was white as a sheet at The De Vere Belfry. There can't be a problem this time. Thank goodness for that.

Shot of the Week

Padraig Harrington's double-bogey on 13 reduced his lead to only a stroke and that could have been wiped out after missing the 14th green with his approach. His ball was nestling down the bank by the adjacent course, but he steadied a rocking boat with a pinpoint pitch under the branch of a tree to ten feet and made an important birdie.

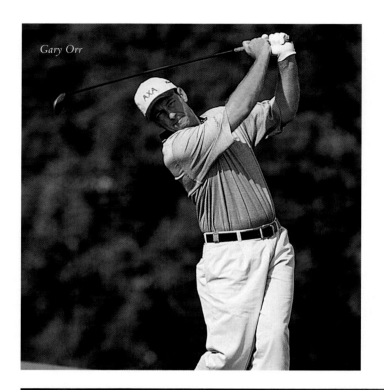

Gary Orr

When Tournament Director Mike Stewart wandered innocently over to the range for a casual look at Padraig Harrington's new irons before the final round of the BBVA Open Turespaña Masters Comunidad de Madrid, the spectre of the 2000 Benson and Hedges International Open came back to haunt the 29-year-old Dubliner. It was not as if he had been able to put it out of his mind, anyway, that horrifying moment when he was told he would be disqualified for not signing a first-round card. Only three weeks before when he had yet another chance to lay his Belfry ghost, Harrington had confessed that the cruel blow which denied him his chance of taking advantage of a five-stroke final-day lead, was still playing on his mind.

This time there was no chilling hand of fate. But it was deja-vu, as Harrington pulled off a deserved third career win and a second of the year by winning at Club de Campo by two strokes. Because of his success there in 1996 when he took the Peugeot Open de España title in only the tenth tournament of his professional career, Harrington had decided to go the extra mile - for the memories, because he relished Madrid, liked the course. His troublesome neck and shoulder were in good enough fettle to stand a fifth week in a row. A wise decision.

Paul McGinley

The Course

Club de Campo is a woodland course on dramatically plunging and swooping country and it was from the club's famous caddie school that players such as José Maria Cañizares, Antonio Garrido and Manuel Piñero emerged.

All the talk beforehand was Darren Clarke's bid to wrest the Volvo Order of Merit top placing from stablemate Lee Westwood. The Ulsterman lurked after round one, only two behind rookie Markus Brier, whose 64 proved he, too, was trying to make it happy returns to Spain. He had been runner-up in the spring at PGA Golf de Catalunya on the outskirts of Barcelona.

Tony Johnstone's role in 'All Our Yesterdays' as the Zimbabwean contended strongly, was to excel with a putter which was in use about the sort of time Arnaud Massy was winning copious Spanish tour events. It was a 1920 George Nichol Pin-Splitter borrowed from an American student at St Andrews the week before.

Harrington's opening 67 was carefully checked and signed twice, his ritual since The De Vere Belfry. The following day's 64 to earn him a one-shot lead over the defending champion Miguel Angel Jiménez, received similar scrutiny. Harrington had reminded everyone clearly of his 1996 glory, with a stunning shot-making action replay of his rookie year.

Jiménez had already repeated history. He was aiming to be only the third player to win a European Tour title three years in succession

Miguel Angel Jiménez

and soon took over from Harrington. When Harrington hit Jiménez with four birdies in five holes coming home, though, the man from Malaga's dream of triple success was over.

For Harrington the agony of unfulfilment was over, but not without a few more worrying moments after a determined bid by Per-Ulrik Johansson in the final round. A player who does not peruse leaderboards, Harrington accidentally saw from the Swede's carry-board at the eighth that Johansson was tracking him. He went on the defensive just as his driving started to betray him. Johansson took off the pressure by missing short putts, though. Harrington's task then was to surpass the target set by Scotland's Gary Orr, who might have won but for three successive bogeys around the turn. Johansson had to settle for third while fourth place was not good enough to take Clarke back to European number one.

When the genial Harrington sat waiting to make his winner's speech the memory of The De Vere Belfry returned. It may never really go away. But this time it was a happy return. This time fate was on his side.

Norman Dabell

Francisco Cea

CLUB DE CAMPO, MADRID, SPAIN, 19-22 OCTOBER 2000, PAR 71, 6957 YARDS, 6362 METRES

Pos.	Name		Rd1	Rd2	Rd3	Rd4	Total	Par	Prize Money Euro	£
1	Padraig HARRINGTON	Ire	67	64	66	70	267	-17	166660.00	97824.68
2	Gary ORR	Scot	67	68	68	66	269	-15	111110.00	65218.41
3	Per-Ulrik JOHANSSON	Swe	72	63	67	68	270	-14	62600.00	36744.42
4	Darren CLARKE	N.Ire	66	70	70	65	271	-13	50000.00	29348.58
5	Paul MCGINLEY	Ire	67	69	68	68	272	-12	38700.00	22715.80
	Francisco CEA	Sp	68	67	70	67	272	-12	38700.00	22715.80
7	Eduardo ROMERO	Arg	72	66	67	68	273	-11	27500.00	16141.72
	Miguel Angel JIMÉNEZ	Sp	66	66	69	72	273	-11	27500.00	16141.72
9	Eamonn DARCY	Ire	69	67	67	71	274	-10	20266.67	11895.96
	Santiago LUNA	Sp	65	70	66	73	274	-10	20266.67	11895.96
	Roger WESSELS	SA	68	65	69	72	274	-10	20266.67	11895.96
12	Raphaël JACQUELIN	Fr	72	65	72	66	275	-9	16200.00	9508.94
	Fredrik LINDGREN	Swe	70	69	68	68	275	-9	16200.00	9508.94
	Angel CABRERA	Arg	72	66	69	68	275	-9	16200.00	9508.94
15	David HOWELL	Eng	70	67	67	72	276	-8	13800.00	8100.21
	Peter BAKER	Eng	68	71	65	72	276	-8	13800.00	8100.21
	Greg OWEN	Eng	70	70	69	67	276	-8	13800.00	8100.21
	Raymond RUSSELL	Scot	69	70	66	71	276	-8	13800.00	8100.21
19	Anthony WALL	Eng	67	69	73	68	277	-7	11500.00	6750.17
	Steen TINNING	Den	69	70	72	66	277	-7	11500.00	6750.17
	Marcel SIEM	Ger	68	67	73	69	277	-7	11500.00	6750.17
	Gary EVANS	Eng	74	65	70	68	277	-7	11500.00	6750.17
	Pierre FULKE	Swe	68	68	71	70	277	-7	11500.00	6750.17
	Stephen GALLACHER	Scot	67	69	68	73	277	-7	11500.00	6750.17
25	Des SMYTH	Ire	70	69	69	70	278	-6	9800.00	5752.32
	Sergio GARCIA	Sp	68	69	71	70	278	-6	9800.00	5752.32
	Gary EMERSON	Eng	67	70	70	71	278	-6	9800.00	5752.32
	Peter MITCHELL	Eng	72	69	68	69	278	-6	9800.00	5752.32
	Markus BRIER	Aut	64	72	72	70	278	-6	9800.00	5752.32
30	Tony JOHNSTONE	Zim	66	70	70	73	279	-5	8300.00	4871.86
	Miguel Angel MARTIN	Sp	70	68	69	72	279	-5	8300.00	4871.86
	Juan QUIROS	Sp	72	70	70	67	279	-5	8300.00	4871.86
	Soren HANSEN	Den	72	68	67	72	279	-5	8300.00	4871.86
	Andrew COLTART	Scot	71	70	70	68	279	-5	8300.00	4871.86
35	Roger CHAPMAN	Eng	70	70	68	72	280	-4	6800.00	3991.41
	José RIVERO	Sp	67	69	73	71	280	-4	6800.00	3991.41

Pos.	Name		Rd1	Rd2	Rd3	Rd4	Total	Par	Prize Money Euro	£
	Richard GREEN	Aus	68	73	71	68	280	-4	6800.00	3991.41
	Carlos RODILES	Sp	68	69	73	70	280	-4	6800.00	3991.41
	Ian GARBUTT	Eng	70	68	70	72	280	-4	6800.00	3991.41
	Gustavo ROJAS	Arg	71	67	72	70	280	-4	6800.00	3991.41
	Michael JONZON	Swe	71	70	69	70	280	-4	6800.00	3991.41
	Christopher HANELL	Swe	71	68	71	70	280	-4	6800.00	3991.41
43	Rodger DAVIS	Aus	70	65	73	73	281	-3	5300.00	3110.95
	David GILFORD	Eng	67	70	71	73	281	-3	5300.00	3110.95
	Carl SUNESON	Sp	71	68	71	71	281	-3	5300.00	3110.95
	Phillip PRICE	Wal	69	67	72	73	281	-3	5300.00	3110.95
	Peter LONARD	Aus	67	72	71	71	281	-3	5300.00	3110.95
	Johan SKOLD	Swe	73	68	68	72	281	-3	5300.00	3110.95
	Niclas FASTH	Swe	71	69	66	75	281	-3	5300.00	3110.95
50	Jarrod MOSELEY	Aus	70	66	74	72	282	-2	4200.00	2465.28
	Mathias GRÖNBERG	Swe	69	71	71	71	282	-2	4200.00	2465.28
	Ignacio GARRIDO	Sp	74	65	70	73	282	-2	4200.00	2465.28
	Patrik SJÖLAND	Swe	71	68	70	73	282	-2	4200.00	2465.28
54	Bernhard LANGER	Ger	72	69	71	71	283	-1	3320.00	1948.75
	Sam TORRANCE	Scot	69	71	72	71	283	-1	3320.00	1948.75
	Soren KJELDSEN	Den	69	71	73	70	283	-1	3320.00	1948.75
	Steve WEBSTER	Eng	71	68	70	74	283	-1	3320.00	1948.75
	Stephen SCAHILL	NZ	72	69	73	283	-1	3320.00	1948.75	
59	Jose Manuel LARA	Sp	70	70	75	69	284	0	2900.00	1702.22
60	Marc FARRY	Fr	70	71	73	71	285	1	2500.00	1467.43
	Juan Carlos AGUERO	Sp	73	67	69	76	285	1	2500.00	1467.43
	Knud STORGAARD	Den	72	69	75	69	285	1	2500.00	1467.43
	Philip GOLDING	Eng	69	71	75	70	285	1	2500.00	1467.43
	Rolf MUNTZ	Hol	71	70	73	71	285	1	2500.00	1467.43
	Iain PYMAN	Eng	72	66	77	70	285	1	2500.00	1467.43
67	Anders HANSEN	Den	69	71	75	71	286	2	2000.00	1173.94
	Paul AFFLECK	Wal	71	70	72	73	286	2	2000.00	1173.94
	John MELLOR	Eng	70	71	72	72	286	2	2000.00	1173.94
70	Per NYMAN	Swe	70	68	76	73	287	3	1830.00	1074.16
71	Maarten LAFEBER	Hol	70	70	74	74	288	4	1500.00	880.46

It's your choice - sit in the clubhouse or go out and play

Avoid disappointment - At No Cost!
Free guaranteed tee off time booking service

Novo Sancti Petri Golf Course

The worst tee off is one that doesn't take place. Avoid the worries and frustration of booking your tee off times overseas. Let Media Marketing Golf Services arrange your guaranteed tee off times while you concentrate on your swing.

Many golfers have learned the hard way that going on a golf trip abroad without confirmed tee off times can be a disaster. If you've tried to book ahead yourself in a foreign country you also know how hard and uncertain it can be to arrange times over the phone or fax in a foreign language and currency.

Before you travel to Spain or Portugal, put your golf trip in the hands of those who specialise in guaranteed tee off times free of charge - Media Marketing Golf Services. No group too big or small. We have many years' experience as exclusive golf agents for top British and German tour operators and major hotel groups throughout Spain and Portugal.

Tournament packages for pro-ams, celeb-ams and celeb-pro-ams. For societies or individuals, we can organise VIP days, corporate golfing days, or whatever you have in mind. With a multinational staff ready to assist you, we will leave nothing to chance.

Mallorca · Ibiza · Costa Blanca · Costa del Sol · Costa Brava · Costa Dorada · Portugal
Pre-book your guaranteed tee off times:
Tel: +34 971 703 070 - 402 907 - Fax: +34 971 401 590
E-mail: eurogolfservice@baleares.com

A Close Shave

IS MOLAS, SARDINIA, ITALY

*I*t was a classic battle between battle-scarred veteran and spruce and sprightly young 'un, past master against eager pupil, eyes that had seen everything against eyes that had everything still to see, feet that had walked a million miles versus infant's strolling gear that were still taking their first, hesitant steps. Oh yes, and one grizzled beard against two rather snazzy sideburns.

And the youthful one, the one with his eyes on the stars and stars in his eyes, the wearer of that pair of impossibly precise whiskers, was the one who prevailed. Ian Poulter must have to get up extremely early in the morning to shave round his facial adornments: the slightest nudge of the razor, the merest twitch, would ruin their perfect, pencil-line symmetry.

Gordon Brand Jnr.

Poulter's main challenger as the final round of what had been a fascinating tournament developed was Gordon Brand Jnr, he of the salt-and-pepper Van Dyke job on his chin. When Brand won his first European Tour event, the 1982 Coral Classic at Royal Porthcawl, Poulter was six years old. Now the toddler was giving the long-distance hiker a run for his money, and more.

Is Molas lies on the south coast of the beautiful island of Sardinia. Inland lie the mountains of Capoterra, while a couple of miles south is the little seaside resort town of Pula, wherein, among other delights, lie not only the Phoenician ruins of Nora but, even more significantly in the life of the European Tour in the year 2000, the Ristorante Acropoli, where the pizzas are delicious and as big as manhole covers. But that is by the by, if the affairs of the inner man can ever be considered irrelevant.

For the purposes of this particular story, a much more significant fact is that this was the first full European Tour event to be held on the course since Vijay Singh took the Volvo Open in 1989, but Poulter had been there much more recently. He had played in the Is Molas Challenge on the European Challenge Tour in 1999, and quite clearly had some memories of it stored away on his hard disk. Brand, on the other hand, had not returned since way back then, but it didn't take him long to re-acquaint himself with the place.

John Bickerton

If he puts as much effort into his golf as he does into preserving hirsute balance on his countenance, he is going to win an awful lot of tournaments. Thankfully, if his performance in the 57th Italian Open Championship is anything to go by, he would appear to know exactly when to stop fine-tuning his face and start doing the same thing to his swing. Need proof? OK — he won the thing with a total of 267, 21 under par.

Shot of the Week

It's so difficult to call that honours will have to be shared between two. The saving grace is that they were both played by the same man, on the same hole, in the same round. First Ian Poulter hit a perfect sand-wedge on the penultimate hole of the tournament, then followed it with a tricky 12 foot putt for birdie. The second would not have been possible without the first and the first would have been useless had the second not come off. Between them, they brought him victory.

It can't have done. Nobody who reaches the 72nd and last hole of a tournament on 21 under par does so any other way but by careful negotiation and a sure and certain knowledge of where and when to attack. As Brand stepped onto the 18th tee for the fourth and last time he was leading Poulter by a shot and looked as safe as the US Federal gold reserve.

He hit his tee shot into the perfect position, but then watched in horror as his second shot thudded with a sickening thwack into the right-hand greenside bunker. He had, by his own admission, been awful from sand all season, and in a desperate, last-ditch attempt to prove his point, could put his trap-shot no closer than 15 feet. Two putts later, he had dropped his only shot of his round.

Just as Brand was having carnage wrought on his soul, Poulter was performing great deeds. He had just got up and down, courageously, on the 16th and now, on the 17th and 71st he was performing heroics of an even greater order. First he put his sand-wedge second shot to 12 feet, then holed the slippery, downhill, right-to-left birdie putt with some aplomb.

In a trice, there had been a two-shot swing. What once had been Brand's was now Poulter's for the taking. Outwardly, he was calmness on legs. Deep inside, he was quivering like Mr Chivers's finest — only he knew for certain, but everybody could make a pretty good guess, and they would not have been far wrong.

Andrew Oldcorn

Thomas Gögele

Nevertheless, he put a good swing on his tee shot and landed it in the perfect position on the fairway. From there, he struck a huge, soaring draw that left the ball 25 feet from the hole, pin-high to the left. He was still in three-putt country, but with nerves that were twanging like a tightly-strung Stradivarius — he admitted as much afterwards, although not in so many words — he rolled the putt to three inches. In holing it he emulated another player who won in his first season in 1999. Now Poulter could be mentioned in the same breath as Sergio Garcia.

Poulter was modesty itself afterwards, as self-effacing in victory as Brand, doughty old war-horse that he is, had been generous a little earlier in defeat. Nobody should really have been surprised about the gallantry or the modesty, though, should they? Golfers are like that. This time, it was Poulter's day, and he carried it off beautifully. Victory was his: but, to return to where we started, it was a mighty close shave.

Mel Webb

The Course

Van Phillips it was who declared that the Is Molas greens were the best he had putted on since the Dubai Desert Classic. Few disagreed; those who did were just having a bad putting week. The rest of the course was in fine fettle, too. Is Molas is a man-made creation, but looks completely natural - no higher compliment can be paid to any golf course, anywhere.

Richard Green

IS MOLAS, SARDINIA, ITALY, 26-29 OCTOBER 2000, PAR 72, 6980 YARDS, 6383 METRES

Pos.	Name		Rd1	Rd2	Rd3	Rd4	Total	Par	Prize Money Euro	£
1	Ian POULTER	Eng	66	67	65	69	267	-21	166660.00	96895.35
2	Gordon BRAND JNR.	Scot	67	69	66	66	268	-20	111110.00	64598.84
3	Richard GREEN	Aus	67	65	70	68	270	-18	56300.00	32732.56
	Francisco CEA	Sp	70	63	68	69	270	-18	56300.00	32732.56
5	Peter BAKER	Eng	68	65	70	68	271	-17	38700.00	22500.00
	Van PHILLIPS	Eng	65	68	68	70	271	-17	38700.00	22500.00
7	Andrew OLDCORN	Scot	67	68	68	69	272	-16	23160.00	13465.12
	Carl SUNESON	Sp	67	69	71	65	272	-16	23160.00	13465.12
	Pierre FULKE	Swe	66	74	70	62	272	-16	23160.00	13465.12
	Roger WESSELS	SA	67	66	68	71	272	-16	23160.00	13465.12
	John BICKERTON	Eng	67	70	67	68	272	-16	23160.00	13465.12
12	Elliot BOULT	NZ	66	66	70	71	273	-15	15480.00	9000.00
	Paul EALES	Eng	69	69	69	66	273	-15	15480.00	9000.00
	Thomas GÖGELE	Ger	69	69	65	70	273	-15	15480.00	9000.00
	Ricardo GONZALEZ	Arg	66	67	68	72	273	-15	15480.00	9000.00
	Lee WESTWOOD	Eng	67	70	70	66	273	-15	15480.00	9000.00
17	Eamonn DARCY	Ire	65	68	70	71	274	-14	12700.00	7383.72
	Jeremy ROBINSON	Eng	66	69	70	69	274	-14	12700.00	7383.72
	Michael JONZON	Swe	69	72	68	65	274	-14	12700.00	7383.72
	Matthew BLACKEY	Eng	72	68	67	67	274	-14	12700.00	7383.72
21	Santiago LUNA	Sp	69	71	66	69	275	-13	11000.00	6395.35
	David HOWELL	Eng	70	65	69	71	275	-13	11000.00	6395.35
	Justin ROSE	Eng	70	69	69	67	275	-13	11000.00	6395.35
	Steen TINNING	Den	66	70	67	72	275	-13	11000.00	6395.35
	Gary EVANS	Eng	70	68	66	71	275	-13	11000.00	6395.35
26	Raphaël JACQUELIN	Fr	67	69	69	71	276	-12	9500.00	5523.26
	Roger WINCHESTER	Eng	68	70	73	65	276	-12	9500.00	5523.26
	Peter LONARD	Aus	70	69	69	68	276	-12	9500.00	5523.26
	Stephen SCAHILL	NZ	69	65	71	71	276	-12	9500.00	5523.26
	Johan SKOLD	Swe	70	67	70	69	276	-12	9500.00	5523.26
31	Sam TORRANCE	Scot	65	70	70	72	277	-11	7675.00	4462.21
	Alessandro NAPOLEONI	It	71	68	70	68	277	-11	7675.00	4462.21
	Anders HANSEN	Den	70	71	67	69	277	-11	7675.00	4462.21
	Greig HUTCHEON	Scot	71	67	71	68	277	-11	7675.00	4462.21
	Fredrik LINDGREN	Swe	67	68	72	70	277	-11	7675.00	4462.21
	Russell CLAYDON	Eng	72	68	66	71	277	-11	7675.00	4462.21
	Jonathan LOMAS	Eng	68	69	71	69	277	-11	7675.00	4462.21
	Robert COLES	Eng	71	67	71	68	277	-11	7675.00	4462.21
39	Richard BOXALL	Eng	70	69	69	70	278	-10	6300.00	3662.79
	Ronan RAFFERTY	N.Ire	70	69	70	69	278	-10	6300.00	3662.79
	José RIVERO	Sp	69	72	68	69	278	-10	6300.00	3662.79
	Maarten LAFEBER	Hol	71	70	67	70	278	-10	6300.00	3662.79
	Ian GARBUTT	Eng	67	72	74	65	278	-10	6300.00	3662.79
44	Steve WEBSTER	Eng	73	66	70	70	279	-9	4900.00	2848.84
	Knud STORGAARD	Den	74	68	72	65	279	-9	4900.00	2848.84
	Massimo FLORIOLI	It	69	71	71	68	279	-9	4900.00	2848.84
	Massimo SCARPA	It	69	72	70	68	279	-9	4900.00	2848.84
	Nicolas VANHOOTEGEM	Bel	70	71	71	67	279	-9	4900.00	2848.84
	Gustavo ROJAS	Arg	68	73	70	68	279	-9	4900.00	2848.84
	Bradley DREDGE	Wal	73	69	67	70	279	-9	4900.00	2848.84
	Iain PYMAN	Eng	69	71	70	69	279	-9	4900.00	2848.84
	Stephen GALLACHER	Scot	67	70	71	71	279	-9	4900.00	2848.84
53	Emanuele CANONICA	It	66	69	72	73	280	-8	3600.00	2093.02
	David PARK	Wal	70	67	73	70	280	-8	3600.00	2093.02
	Raymond RUSSELL	Scot	70	72	67	71	280	-8	3600.00	2093.02
	Dean ROBERTSON	Scot	68	70	73	69	280	-8	3600.00	2093.02
57	Ian WOOSNAM	Wal	69	70	73	69	281	-7	3050.00	1773.26
	Soren HANSEN	Den	70	70	72	69	281	-7	3050.00	1773.26
59	Costantino ROCCA	It	70	69	70	73	282	-6	2700.00	1569.77
	Gary MURPHY	Ire	73	69	72	68	282	-6	2700.00	1569.77
	Soren KJELDSEN	Den	69	72	71	70	282	-6	2700.00	1569.77
	Diego BORREGO	Sp	72	70	69	71	282	-6	2700.00	1569.77
	Daren LEE	Eng	70	72	70	70	282	-6	2700.00	1569.77
64	Mats LANNER	Swe	69	73	68	73	283	-5	2200.00	1279.07
	Philip GOLDING	Eng	71	70	75	67	283	-5	2200.00	1279.07
	Jorge BERENDT	Arg	68	74	68	73	283	-5	2200.00	1279.07
	Markus BRIER	Aut	71	71	71	70	283	-5	2200.00	1279.07
	Marco BERNARDINI	It	71	70	71	71	283	-5	2200.00	1279.07
69	Silvio GRAPPASONNI	It	72	69	74	69	284	-4	1681.75	977.76
	Peter MITCHELL	Eng	69	71	72	72	284	-4	1681.75	977.76
	Didier DE VOOGHT	Bel	73	68	70	73	284	-4	1681.75	977.76
	Grant HAMERTON	Eng	74	68	68	74	284	-4	1681.75	977.76
	Edoardo MOLINARI (AM)	It	72	70	75	67	284	-4		
74	Olivier EDMOND	Fr	73	69	73	70	285	-3	1492.50	867.73
	Francesco GUERMANI	It	70	68	74	73	285	-3	1492.50	867.73
76	Mike HARWOOD	Aus	69	73	69	75	286	-2	1486.50	864.24
	Craig HAINLINE	USA	70	70	74	72	286	-2	1486.50	864.24
78	Marcello SANTI	It	69	70	74	74	287	-1	1477.50	859.01
	David LYNN	Eng	72	70	76	69	287	-1	1477.50	859.01
	Federico BISAZZA	It	70	72	71	74	287	-1	1477.50	859.01
	Benoit TEILLERIA	Fr	65	75	72	75	287	-1	1477.50	859.01
82	Jarrod MOSELEY	Aus	71	70	72	75	288	0	1470.00	854.65

Swedish Rhapsody

*J*ust to qualify for the Volvo Masters at Montecastillo was quite a feat for Pierre Fulke. When Darren Clarke was beating Tiger Woods to win a million dollars and the WGC - Andersen Consulting Match Play title in February, the Swede had still to play his first event of the season because of injury.

And when Clarke added The Compass Group English Open in June, Fulke, by now told that the problem was actually in his back rather than his wrist, remained on the sidelines waiting to hit his opening shot of the campaign.

Pierre Fulke later described it as "the best shot I've hit in my career – especially under the pressure of knowing the title was on the line". After a perfect fairway-splitting drive at the 70th hole of the tournament, the 517 yards par five 16th, Fulke faced a 215 yards approach in a left to right wind with water guarding the green on the right. He hit a perfect five wood to 25 feet and holed the eagle putt which secured the Volvo Masters.

Ricardo Gonzalez

That shot finally came the following week, and, remarkably, six weeks later he tied Clarke for seventh place in the Open Championship. Five weeks later, he won the Scottish PGA Championship and then, after four more top 20 cheques in a row, he arrived in Spain 31st on the Volvo Order of Merit and 15th on the Ryder Cup Points table.

That was all a mere hors-d'oeuvre to what was just to come, though. It would put the 29-year-old 12th on the Volvo Order of Merit, catapult him top of the Ryder Cup race and bring him to everyone's notice.

From the moment he teed off in the first round Fulke, small in size and undemonstrative in character, made it plain that he had the form to challenge for a first prize of 575,654 euro (£333,330) which was double that from a year before and outside of the Open Championship and World Golf Championships the largest ever offered in Europe.

Sure, he had the advantage of the calmer morning conditions, but a bogey-free five under par 67 on a course toughened up from the Tour's previous visit was quality golf in any language. It did not grab

Darren Clarke

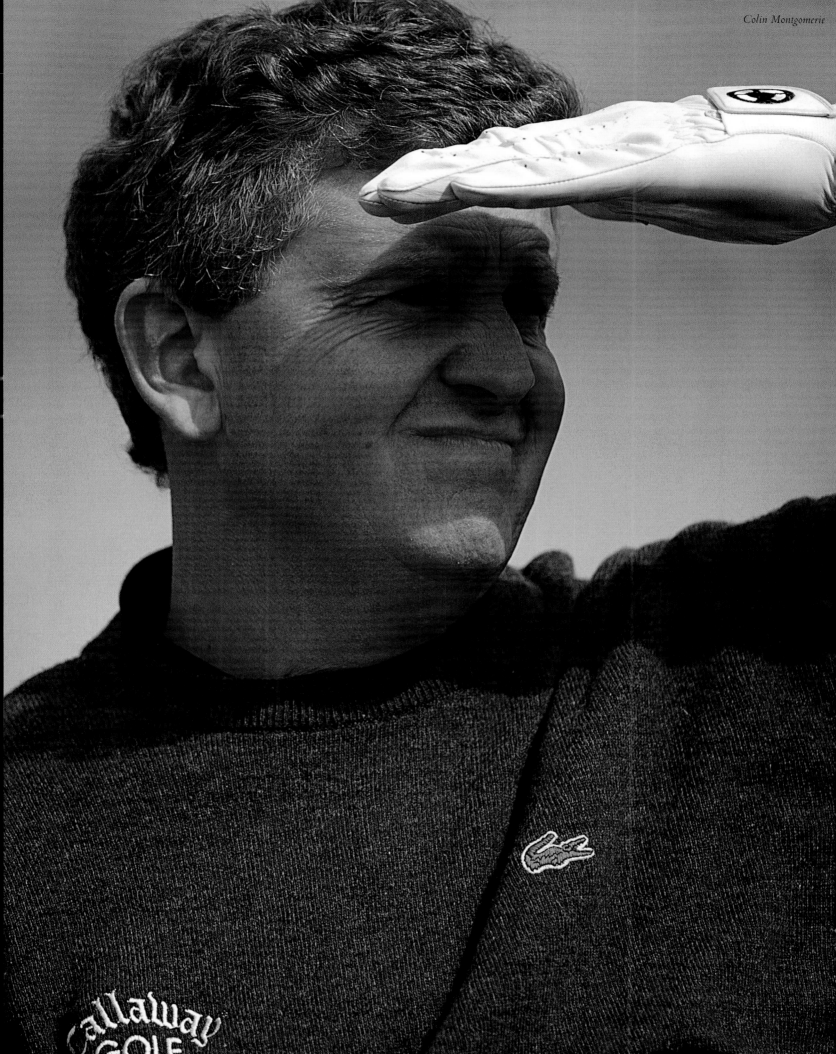

José Maria Olazábal

Sergio Garcia

the local headlines because José Maria Olazábal later defied the strong winds to match the score and, in the battle to be crowned European number one, Clarke tucked in only a single stroke behind and Lee Westwood, bringing an 81,000 euro (£46,900) advantage to Jerez, dropped six shots in four holes from the 14th for a 76 that left him 56th of the 66 starters.

With the leaders out last from the second round onwards there was no hiding place for Fulke. He did not need it. He went head-to-head with double Masters champion Olazábal and returned a 68 to the Spaniard's 69 to lead on his own at halfway at nine under par.

Still, there were reasons to focus not on the former handball player, but on events elsewhere. Colin Montgomerie, having set himself the target of victory in the last two events to make it a staggering eighth successive Volvo Order of Merit title, holed-in-one at the 174 yards 14th and with a second 69 was close behind.

"I'm the face in the rear-view mirror and they don't like it," said Montgomerie. "Never write me off, please." He virtually did it himself, though, after crashing to a third round 75 which felt all the worse because he saw playing companion Clarke, now the man most likely to dethrone him, shoot 68 and take the outright lead.

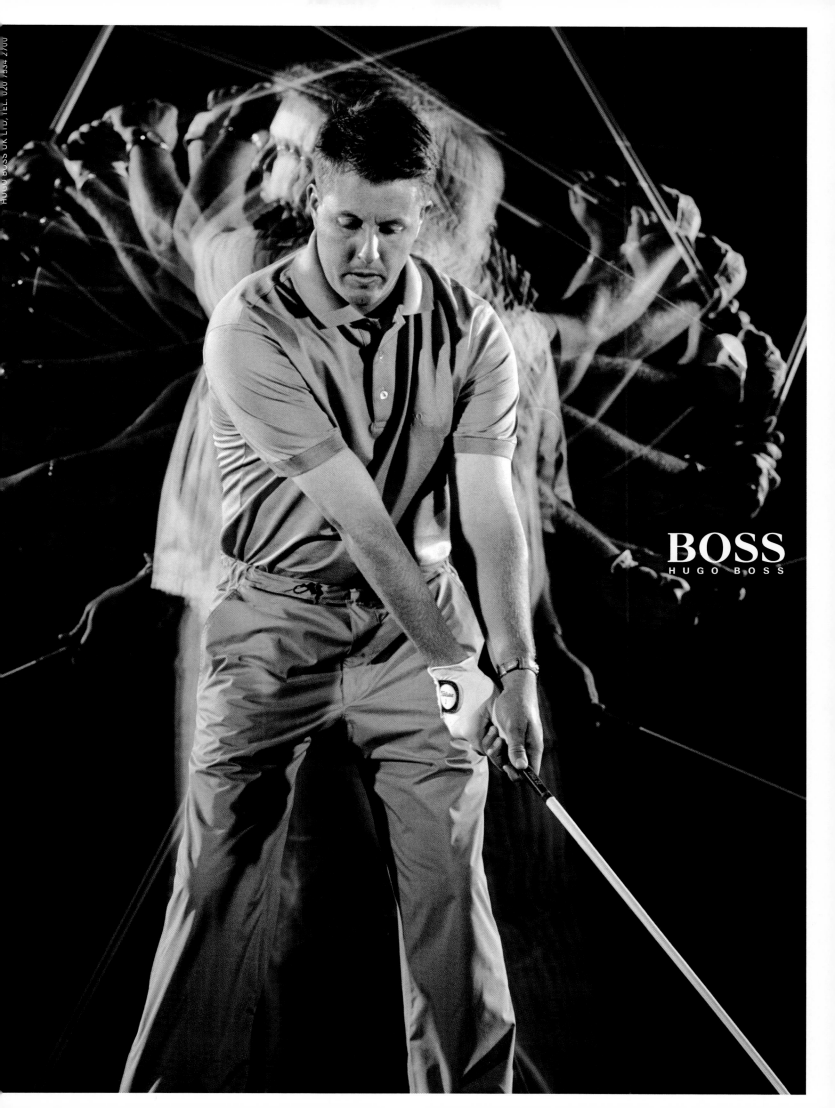

BOSS
HUGO BOSS

Michael Campbell

Nick O'Hern

Correction. Just as that was being written, Fulke birdied the 18th and for the second day running had out-scored Olazábal in the last match. He was level with Clarke as he had been at St Andrews, and now it was becoming clear he was made of stern stuff.

Westwood, meanwhile, had hit back from his first round collapse with rounds of 69 and 65. Could he go on to produce one of the great comeback and win? Could Clarke end Montgomerie's long reign? Or could Fulke, a David amongst the Goliaths, slay them all?

First Montgomerie shot 65. If the reign was to end in Spain, it would not be on this day. It brought the Scot up to ninth place. Then Westwood also shot 65, but that was not enough to win or even finish second. He had to settle for a share of third place with Michael Campbell, whose dazzling 63 equalled the course record and also kept him in the Volvo Order of Merit race.

The battle for the Volvo Masters title, though, had become a duel. Fulke nosed in front twice on the front nine, but a bogey on the tenth and Clarke's birdie at the long 12th turned things round.

Lee Westwood: A Grandstand Finish

Phillip Price

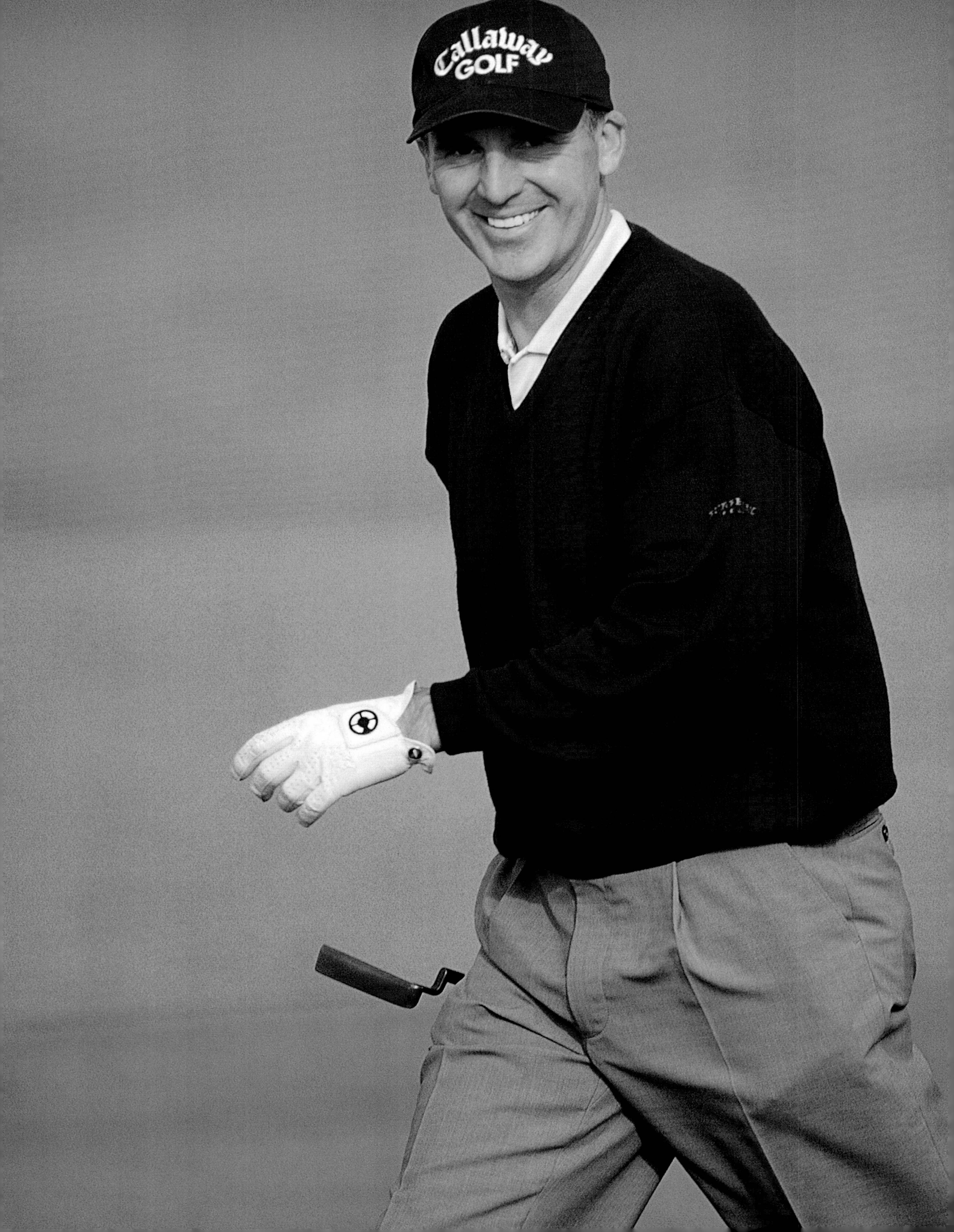

Again Fulke hit back to level, then Clarke went ahead again. But at the 517 yards 16th the Swede hit a glorious five wood to 25 feet and, in fitting style for the man ranked second in putting on Tour behind Westwood, holed for eagle.

Clarke followed him in from 12 feet for birdie to leave them level once more, but a bad hook on the 17th went not just left of the fairway, but left of the crowd as well.

The par he needed to prevent Fulke going in front could not be rescued and when his birdie attempt from 20 feet on the last did not find the hole either, Fulke, impressively solid given the circumstances, tapped in to win. And, after all he had endured earlier in the year and all the attacks he had withstood during the week, how he deserved it.

Mark Garrod

Darren Clarke

The Course

On the outskirts of Jerez, the sherry-producing capital of the world, the Jack Nicklaus-designed Montecastillo provides a test of a player's nerve as well as skill.
With the rough toughened up accuracy became the name of the game. The perils of water are introduced as well on the front nine and then brought back with a vengeance at the last three holes. Add a wind and this is no place for the faint-hearted.

Pierre Fulke: The Sky's the Limit

MONTECASTILLO, JEREZ, SPAIN, 2-5 NOVEMBER 2000, PAR 72, 7069 YARDS, 6453 METRES

Pos.	Name		Rd1	Rd2	Rd3	Rd4	Total	Par	Prize Money Euro	£
1	Pierre FULKE	Swe	67	68	70	67	272	-16	575654.24	333330.00
2	Darren CLARKE	N.Ire	68	69	68	68	273	-15	383769.50	222220.00
3	Lee WESTWOOD	Eng	76	69	65	65	275	-13	194457.95	112600.00
	Michael CAMPBELL	NZ	73	67	72	63	275	-13	194457.95	112600.00
5	José Maria OLAZABAL	Sp	67	69	72	68	276	-12	133668.25	77400.00
	Angel CABRERA	Arg	69	70	69	68	276	-12	133668.25	77400.00
7	Ricardo GONZALEZ	Arg	71	68	69	69	277	-11	94983.90	55000.00
	Roger WESSELS	SA	71	68	72	66	277	-11	94983.90	55000.00
9	Colin MONTGOMERIE	Scot	69	69	75	65	278	-10	77368.70	44800.00
0	Peter SENIOR	Aus	71	71	69	68	279	-9	62977.20	36466.66
	Fredrik JACOBSON	Swe	72	65	71	71	279	-9	62977.20	36466.66
	Andrew COLTART	Scot	73	69	68	69	279	-9	62977.20	36466.66
13	Sergio GARCIA	Sp	73	71	70	66	280	-8	54227.17	31400.00
14	Gordon BRAND JNR.	Scot	69	70	73	69	281	-7	50888.34	29466.66
	Bernhard LANGER	Ger	70	72	68	71	281	-7	50888.34	29466.66
	Padraig HARRINGTON	Ire	72	69	69	71	281	-7	50888.34	29466.66
17	Roger CHAPMAN	Eng	71	72	69	70	282	-6	45246.88	26200.00
	Jean VAN DE VELDE	Fr	74	68	68	72	282	-6	45246.88	26200.00
	Paul LAWRIE	Scot	72	70	68	72	282	-6	45246.88	26200.00
	Greg OWEN	Eng	68	71	72	71	282	-6	45246.88	26200.00
	Patrik SJÖLAND	Swe	71	72	69	70	282	-6	45246.88	26200.00
22	Retief GOOSEN	SA	71	72	69	71	283	-5	41102.12	23800.00
23	Tony JOHNSTONE	Zim	72	72	71	69	284	-4	37371.85	21640.00
	Stephen LEANEY	Aus	71	66	69	78	284	-4	37371.85	21640.00
	Anthony WALL	Eng	75	71	68	70	284	-4	37371.85	21640.00
	Ian POULTER	Eng	74	67	70	73	284	-4	37371.85	21640.00
	Phillip PRICE	Wal	71	70	69	74	284	-4	37371.85	21640.00
28	Nick FALDO	Eng	74	68	73	70	285	-3	31603.73	18300.00
	Miguel Angel MARTIN	Sp	72	70	70	73	285	-3	31603.73	18300.00
	Eduardo ROMERO	Arg	70	72	75	68	285	-3	31603.73	18300.00
	Emanuele CANONICA	It	72	68	70	75	285	-3	31603.73	18300.00
	Thomas BJÖRN	Den	78	71	68	68	285	-3	31603.73	18300.00
	Dean ROBERTSON	Scot	68	74	73	70	285	-3	31603.73	18300.00
34	David HOWELL	Eng	72	71	68	75	286	-2	26422.80	15300.00
	Mark MCNULTY	Zim	71	75	67	73	286	-2	26422.80	15300.00
	Peter O'MALLEY	Aus	72	73	70	71	286	-2	26422.80	15300.00
	Paul MCGINLEY	Ire	73	70	70	73	286	-2	26422.80	15300.00
38	Peter BAKER	Eng	71	72	70	74	287	-1	23314.23	13500.00
	Alex CEJKA	Ger	72	70	74	71	287	-1	23314.23	13500.00
40	Anders HANSEN	Den	76	69	72	71	288	0	21241.86	12300.00
	Richard GREEN	Aus	74	69	71	74	288	0	21241.86	12300.00
42	Miguel Angel JIMÉNEZ	Sp	73	71	73	72	289	1	20032.97	11600.00
43	Ian GARBUTT	Eng	74	74	70	72	290	2	19342.18	11200.00
44	Costantino ROCCA	It	73	74	72	72	291	3	16924.40	9800.00
	Lian-Wei ZHANG	PRC	73	75	76	67	291	3	16924.40	9800.00
	Nick O'HERN	Aus	71	72	75	73	291	3	16924.40	9800.00
	Steen TINNING	Den	73	76	69	73	291	3	16924.40	9800.00
	Per-Ulrik JOHANSSON	Swe	76	70	71	74	291	3	16924.40	9800.00
	Jarmo SANDELIN	Swe	74	72	76	69	291	3	16924.40	9800.00
50	Geoff OGILVY	Aus	80	67	70	75	292	4	14290.76	8275.00
	Lucas PARSONS	Aus	75	71	72	74	292	4	14290.76	8275.00
52	Mathias GRÖNBERG	Swe	75	70	74	74	293	5	13643.14	7900.00
53	Alastair FORSYTH	Scot	75	76	72	71	294	6	13211.40	7650.00
54	José COCERES	Arg	74	73	74	74	295	7	12434.26	7200.00
	Niclas FASTH	Swe	73	72	74	76	295	7	12434.26	7200.00
	Stephen GALLACHER	Scot	75	75	72	73	295	7	12434.26	7200.00
57	Brian DAVIS	Eng	77	74	72	73	296	8	11570.77	6700.00
	Ignacio GARRIDO	Sp	78	76	72	70	296	8	11570.77	6700.00
59	Ronan RAFFERTY	N.Ire	73	74	73	77	297	9	10879.98	6300.00
	Gary ORR	Scot	74	76	73	74	297	9	10879.98	6300.00
61	Seve BALLESTEROS	Sp	80	72	74	74	300	12	10189.18	5900.00
	Ian WOOSNAM	Wal	75	77	73	75	300	12	10189.18	5900.00
63	Rolf MUNTZ	Hol	74	76	75	76	301	13	9757.44	5650.00
64	Mike HARWOOD	Aus	79	73	76	74	302	14	9498.39	5500.00
65	Jonathan LOMAS	Eng	77	74	78	79	308	20	9239.34	5350.00
66	Jamie SPENCE	Eng	76	76	76	W/D	228	12	9066.65	5250.00

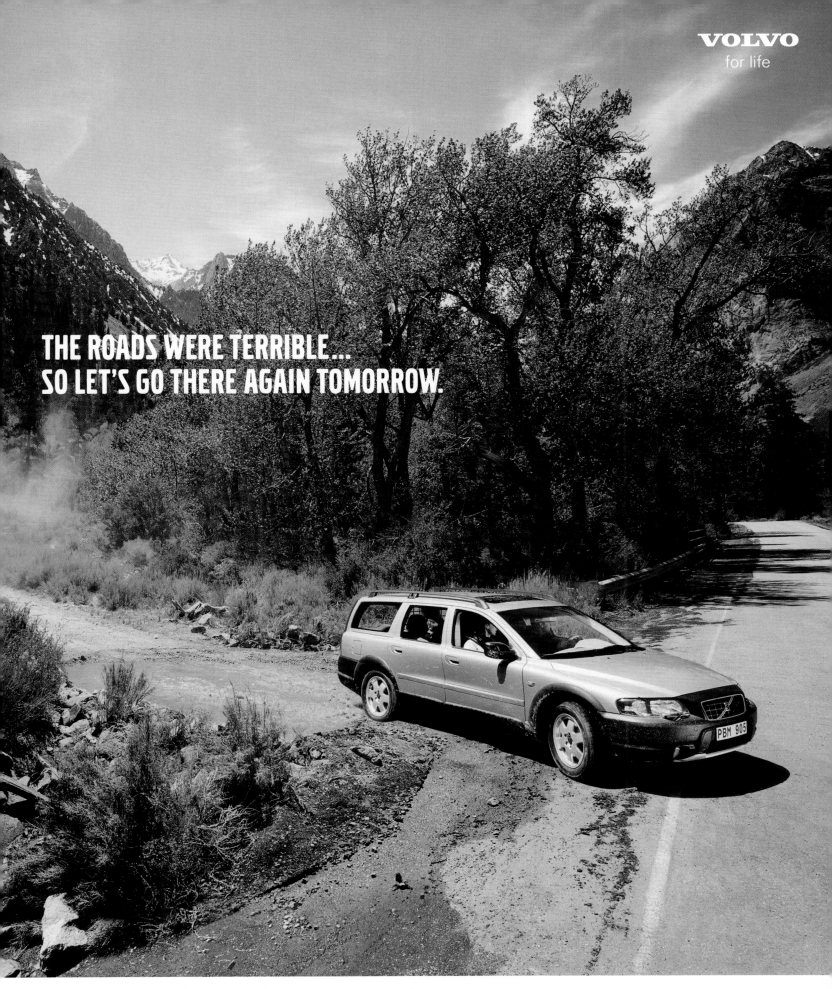

THE ROADS WERE TERRIBLE...
SO LET'S GO THERE AGAIN TOMORROW.

he Volvo Cross Country is designed to be right at home on even the worst roads. Which is quite useful, because the most beautiful places are often at the end of e most rugged roads. Since they're usually miles away, we've added a 200-hp turbo ngine and exceptional handling on tarmac. You travel quietly and comfortably, with- ut a hint of the shake, rattle and roll associated with ordinary 4x4's. Get yourself a good map and come in for a test drive.

VOLVO
for life

THE NEW VOLVO CROSS COUNTRY
GETAWAY.VOLVOCARS.COM

In for a Pound

CLUB DE GOLF, VALDERRAMA, SPAIN

Lee Westwood and Tiger Woods both arrived at Valderrama on Spain's Costa del Sol for the WGC - American Express Championship with an eye on winning the title and creating a slice of history. Westwood was determined to become the new European Number One at the start of a new millennium; Woods was seeking the tenth victory of another special season. That both should come down the stretch with a chance of winning the title increased the drama of the final afternoon on the 2000 European Tour International Schedule.

Louis Martin, Chief Executive, Southern Africa Tour, Ramlan Dato' Harun, Chief Executive Director, Asian PGA, Ken Schofield, Executive Director of The European Tour, Edward L. Moorhouse, Executive Vice President and Chief Legal Officer, US PGA Tour, Kosaku Shimada, Executive Director, Japan Golf Tour, and Arthur Sanderson, Executive Director, PGA Tour of Australasia, at the opening ceremony of the WGC - American Express Championship

Since Westwood had already won five Volvo Order of Merit tournaments in addition to the Cisco World Match Play Championship and Woods, the defending champion, had captured three major championships among his nine wins, it is fair to assume that Victor Chandler, the official Bookmakers of the European Tour, would have laid more than a share of odds-on a player with his surname starting with "W" winning the title. They would have paid out, too, because although neither Westwood nor Woods claimed the American Express Championship, Mike Weir, of Canada, finished the week by celebrating the most important victory of his career.

Weir, aged 30, turned professional in 1992 and, after being a medallist at the 1998 US PGA Tour Qualifying Tournament, he made an immediate impact by winning the Air Canada Championship in his native country on his way to finishing 23rd in the 1999 US Tour money list. By making further progress in 2000, Weir arrived at Valderrama convinced that he could take his game to a new level. That he achieved his aim was a tribute not only to his skill and self-belief, but also his ability to operate under intense pressure.

For the final round of the WGC - American Express Championship was always going to be a test of nerve. Quite simply the popular Hidemichi Tanaka, whose stated ambition was to get the autograph of Tiger Woods, might have been leading the way, and making a name for himself back home in Japan, but at nine under par he was

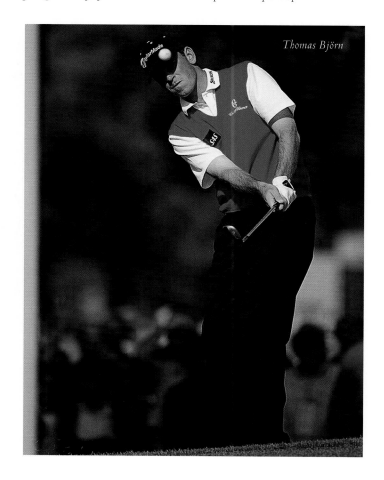

Thomas Björn

Miguel Angel Jiménez

being pursued by Mark Calcavecchia and Weir on eight under, Nick Price and Woods on seven under, Padraig Harrington and Duffy Waldorf on five under and Michael Campbell, Bob May, Vijay Singh and Westwood on four under par.

The scenario had been set following a first day on which Price, whose career was launched on victories in Europe, carded a 63 to lead by three from Harrington and by four from Andrew Coltart and Scott Hoch. Price notched 11 birdies and enjoyed the round all the more because David McNeilly, who once worked for him as a caddie, was in the group alongside Harrington. "Just watching him, sometimes cracks me up," said Price.

The second round was always going to be one in which Price would need to focus following such a fabulous first day. He shot 72 for 135 - one ahead of Tanaka, who followed a 71 with a 68 - and said: "I went and did what I wanted to do which was to shoot around par and not make too many mistakes. It was the kind of day where I really couldn't gain a lot, but I could lose a lot."

It was also a day when Colin Montgomerie, bidding for a win which could yet extend his run of being European Number One to eight successive years, provided a glimmer of hope for himself. Montgomerie had shot 75 on the first day, but his second round of

Shot of the Week

Colin Montgomerie recorded a second hole-in-one in the space of a week, and he did so with a four iron at the difficult 195 yards 12th hole. It pitched six inches short of the hole, took one hop and disappeared. "Amazing," said Montgomerie.

The Course

Robert Trent Jones enhanced the shot making values of Valderrama when in 1975 he remodelled the course which is spectacular for both its beauty and difficulty. The American influence of this steeply undulating panoramic course is clearly visible: long, elevated, tree-framed tees; huge, contoured greens; and cavernous white sand traps that dazzle in the sun.

67, which included two eagles, brought him back into the race. It included a hole-in-one - his second in successive tournaments - when he aced the 12th with a four iron.

That race for Number One place in the Volvo Order of Merit was without question capturing the attention of many observers with Darren Clarke having come into the Championship with a slender lead ahead of Westwood. Ernie Els, Thomas Björn, Campbell and Montgomerie could also finish Number One, although Els took leave early because of a back injury when he withdrew after eight holes.

So by the time the third day dawned, Montgomerie still held high hopes of keeping his run intact. It was not to be. He faltered, scoring 73 to be eight off the pace, as the diminutive Tanaka compiled a superb 70 for a nine under par total of 207. Now Tanaka had good cause to start thinking about how the $1,000,000 first prize and a World Golf Championship title might change his life, but he still joked: "I still want Tiger's autograph."

The final day, with little breeze, seemed certain to bring low scoring, as the early starting Sergio Garcia indicated with a 64, but whereas for Tanaka it was a bad day at the office so Weir took the initiative with four birdies in five holes from the fourth.

Carlos Franco

Nevertheless he still faced a stiff examination as he came down the stretch although, one by one, his rivals found trouble at the 17th with Price, poised to apply the pressure, visiting the water twice and Westwood and Woods among its victims. Weir, by now in control of his own destiny, was through the green in three, but he chipped down close to the hole to make the par that enabled him to enjoy playing the 18th.

"It feels fantastic," said Weir, who became the first Canadian and the first left handed player to win a World Golf Championship event. "There were so many players with a chance to win that you knew there would be a lot of swings back and forth."

Woods had to settle for a share of fifth place but, as the sun set in Spain's Costa del Sol and on the season, so Westwood finished runner-up which enabled him to leapfrog Clarke, end Montgomerie's reign and start the new millennium as Europe's Number One golfer.

Westwood had raided the record books on many occasions to fulfil his dream. He had, for instance, won six titles on the European Tour International Schedule, equalling the number won by Severiano Ballesteros in 1986 and emulated by Nick Faldo and Montgomerie in 1992 and 1999 respectively, and he had set a new target for winnings in the Volvo Order of Merit with 3,125,146 euro (£1,858,602).

Stuart Appleby

Tiger Woods

He also had a special "trophy" to take home and frame - a one pound coin! "Darren and I had a bet in August on who would win the Volvo Order of Merit," explained Westwood. "We wagered one pound. Darren paid up immediately; I said thank you! It's a great honour to be Number One; a reward for all the good golf that I have played in

2000. I've got to say that, having found out how difficult it is to win one, I now realise what Colin has achieved to win seven in a row. That is a colossal achievement, and I don't think it will ever happen again."

Mitchell Platts

CLUB DE GOLF, VALDERRAMA, SPAIN, 9-12 NOVEMBER 2000, PAR 72, 7069 YARDS, 6453 METRES

Pos.	Name		Rd1	Rd2	Rd3	Rd4	Total	Par	Prize Money Euro	£
1	Mike WEIR	Can	68	75	65	69	277	-11	1160901.68	690417.01
2	Lee WESTWOOD	Eng	72	72	68	67	279	-9	580450.85	345208.51
3	Vijay SINGH	Fiji	71	70	71	68	280	-8	333178.78	198149.68
	Duffy WALDORF	USA	70	69	72	69	280	-8	333178.78	198149.68
5	Tiger WOODS	USA	71	69	69	72	281	-7	182842.02	108740.68
	Padraig HARRINGTON	Ire	66	72	73	70	281	-7	182842.02	108740.68
	Sergio GARCIA	Sp	69	74	74	64	281	-7	182842.02	108740.68
	Nick PRICE	Zim	63	72	74	72	281	-7	182842.02	108740.68
9	Michael CAMPBELL	NZ	72	71	69	70	282	-6	133503.70	79397.96
10	Mark CALCAVECCHIA	USA	72	67	69	75	283	-5	21894.68	72493.79
11	Steve FLESCH	USA	71	72	73	68	284	-4	101191.93	60181.35
	Hidemichi TANAKA	Jpn	71	66	70	77	284	-4	101191.93	60181.35
	Bob MAY	USA	71	69	72	72	284	-4	101191.93	60181.35
14	José COCERES	Arg	70	71	74	70	285	-3	79521.77	47293.57
	Kirk TRIPLETT	USA	72	73	71	69	285	-3	79521.77	47293.57
16	Chris PERRY	USA	68	75	71	72	286	-2	74297.71	44186.69
17	José Maria OLAZÁBAL	Sp	70	76	69	73	288	0	65300.72	38835.96
	Phillip PRICE	Wal	73	72	69	74	288	0	65300.72	38835.96
	Scott HOCHUSA	USA	67	76	71	74	288	0	65300.72	38835.96
	Darren CLARKE	N.Ire	74	70	74	70	288	0	65300.72	38835.96
	Angel CABRERA	Arg	74	74	67	73	288	0	65300.72	38835.96
	Andrew COLTART	Scot	67	75	74	72	288	0	65300.72	38835.96
	Nic HENNING	SA	69	74	73	72	288	0	65300.72	38835.96
	Franklin LANGHAM	USA	68	74	76	70	288	0	65300.72	38835.96
25	Eduardo ROMERO	Arg	71	72	74	72	289	1	53981.93	32104.39
	Justin LEONARD	USA	72	74	69	74	289	1	53981.93	32104.39
	Stuart APPLEBY	Aus	72	76	71	70	289	1	53981.93	32104.39
	Colin MONTGOMERIE	Scot	75	67	73	74	289	1	53981.93	32104.39

Pos.	Name		Rd1	Rd2	Rd3	Rd4	Total	Par	Prize Money Euro	£
	Nobuhito SATO	Jpn	73	73	72	71	289	1	53981.93	32104.39
	Miguel Angel JIMÉNEZ	Sp	74	73	70	72	289	1	53981.93	32104.39
	Gary ORR	Scot	71	74	73	71	289	1	53981.93	32104.39
	Robert ALLENBY	Aus	69	76	73	71	289	1	53981.93	32104.39
	David TOMSUSA	USA	70	75	72	72	289	1	53981.93	32104.39
	Chris DIMARCO	USA	74	74	73	68	289	1	53981.93	32104.39
35	Bernhard LANGER	Ger	75	69	76	70	290	2	45855.62	27271.47
	Naomichi "Joe" OZAKI	Jpn	72	76	71	71	290	2	45855.62	27271.47
	Paul MCGINLEY	Ire	70	77	70	73	290	2	45855.62	27271.47
	Retief GOOSEN	SA	69	75	74	72	290	2	45855.62	27271.47
39	Jeff MAGGERT	USA	72	71	75	7	292	4	42953.36	25545.43
40	Darren FICHARDT	SA	76	80	69	68	293	5	41212.02	24509.81
	Thomas BJÖRN	Den	70	77	71	75	293	5	41212.02	24509.81
42	Peter SENIOR	Aus	73	77	72	72	294	6	38309.75	22783.76
	Mathias GRÖNBERG	Swe	74	70	79	71	294	6	38309.75	22783.76
	Pierre FULKE	Swe	75	77	73	69	294	6	38309.75	22783.76
45	Carlos Daniel FRANCO	Par	69	77	71	78	295	7	35020.54	20827.58
	Dennis PAULSON	USA	75	71	72	77	295	7	35020.54	20827.58
	Lucas PARSONS	Aus	78	72	75	70	295	7	35020.54	20827.58
48	Dudley HART	USA	72	76	73	76	297	9	33375.92	19849.49
	Scott VERPLANK	USA	71	80	76	70	297	9	33375.92	19849.49
50	Shigeki MARUYAMA	Jpn	71	77	78	72	298	10	32215.03	19159.08
	Tjaart VAN DER WALT	SA	76	73	75	74	298	10	32215.03	19159.08
52	Kyi Hla HAN	Myan	75	74	77	77	303	15	31344.35	18641.26
53	Jesper PARNEVIK	Swe	72	76	77	W/D	225	9	30183.44	17950.84
54	Rocco MEDIATE	USA	71	78	W/D		149	5	30183.44	17950.84
55	Ernie ELS SA		RETD						30183.44	17950.84

A Cause for Celebration

THE DE VERE BELFRY, SUTTON COLDFIELD, ENGLAND

10th hole from behind the green

When Peter Alliss and Dave Thomas first surveyed the site on which Ryder Cup history would in time be created, they were not filled with the same euphoria which so entranced Bobby Jones when he originally viewed the setting for Augusta National.

Jones instinctively knew on seeing Fruitlands, a 365-acre nursery where the progeny of a number of trees and plants imported from all over the world had been nurtured, that the plunging terrain provided the ideal location for his golf course. "It seemed that the land had been lying there for years just waiting for someone to lay a golf course on it," Jones said.

What Alliss and Thomas said to each other as they cast their eyes on 15 potato fields at Sutton Coldfield, near Birmingham, is most probably unprintable. Yet it was there that they, having by then jettisoned their bag and clubs for pencil and drawing board, created at The Belfry, The Brabazon course on which for the fourth time the Ryder Cup will be played on September 28-30, 2001.

Initially, it would be criticised and maligned, causing some professionals to be so outspoken that they were fined. Now it sits proudly by the Lichfield Road as one of the most famous courses in Europe and part of a magnificent complex where the Professional Golfers' Association also has its home.

The birth of The Belfry can be traced to 1970 when Alan Hunter, the estates director of the Greenall Whitley company, asked Thomas to look at the site (a modest 49 acres that then went with the hotel)

and the adjoining land in other ownerships. Hunter said: "We asked them to tell us the preferred areas required to form an 18 hole championship course plus an 18 hole supporting course. Following this I acquired the necessary land options to purchase and following town-planning approval acquired the land on behalf of The Belfry Company."

In fact it was in 1959 that Jimmy Burns, an entrepreneur, had purchased Moxhull Park, a private house at the time, for £18,500 and turned it into The Belfry. His expansion programme increased the number of bedrooms to 59 and made The Belfry a well known centre for wedding receptions and a place where in the 1960s such groups as Led Zeppelin, the Moody Blues, Slade and Status Quo performed live. In 1969 Burns sold The Belfry to a group called Allied Vintners Investments which in turn was bought by Greenall Whitley. At this time the PGA had their headquarters at the Kennington Oval and it was there, over a pie and a pint, that Colin Snape, then the new Executive Director of the PGA, lunched with Alliss. Snape felt that is was an imposition to be continually apologising for the surroundings as he ushered guests into the confined offices at the rear main stand of the cricket ground.

His dream of the PGA was a new headquarters which were geographically acceptable with two golf courses and modern offices. He had looked at both Royal Birkdale in Lancashire and Foxhills in Surrey, but the then 28-strong PGA Committee felt that his plan was no more than a pipe-dream since at that time in February, 1973, the PGA's assets were a paltry £40,000.

Alliss came to the rescue over lunch. He told Snape of an old hotel on the outskirts of Birmingham known as The Belfry which was being renovated and converted to a sports complex. Thomas and Alliss had originally been asked to design and build a pitch and putt course there.

Snape convinced the committee that expansion was a necessity and he must truly have felt he had the Midas touch. Ellerman Lines, the shipping company, was keen to diversify into leisure whereas Greenall Whitley, owners of The Belfry, lacked funds at that time as they were investing in a new brewery.

Thus Ellerman Lines formed a company called The Belfry (Sutton Coldfield) Ltd, taking 86.7 per cent of the equity with Greenall Whitley retaining 13.3 per cent for providing the hotel and land, and purchased a further 265.5 acres. In 1975 work began on two courses - The Brabazon and the Derby - by Thomas and Alliss. Brian Cash, a jocular but hard-nosed businessman, was brought in to oversee the operation, which included the refurbishment of the hotel. Cash, too, visualised the enormous potential of this triangular area of land near where the Tamworth and Lichfield roads merge at Wishaw. The access was splendid with close proximity to the M1, M5 and M6.

The PGA lacked the funds to become involved but The Belfry

Sam Torrance celebrates the putt with which Europe secured victory in 1985 – in 2001 he returns to The De Vere Belfry as European Team Captain

Company built the new PGA offices, funding the cost of approximately £100,000 as part of the overall deal with the PGA for two Ryder Cups. Meanwhile Accles and Pollock, the sports equipment company, funded the furnishings of the PGA's Headquarters at The Belfry in addition to investing a significant sum over ten years in the PGA's training school.

In 1977 the PGA waved farewell to The Oval to begin a new innings at The Belfry with a peppercorn rent for a 99-year lease. That year, with the existing hotel completely rebuilt, The Brabazon course was officially opened with a challenge match, Severiano Ballesteros and Johnny Miller against Tony Jacklin and Brian Barnes.

The first official tournament to be held on the Brabazon course was the Hennessy Cup, a match between Great Britain and the Continent of Europe. This was played in September, 1978, and if any one player put the course on the map then it was Severiano Ballesteros who performed a feat that the designers had deemed impossible.

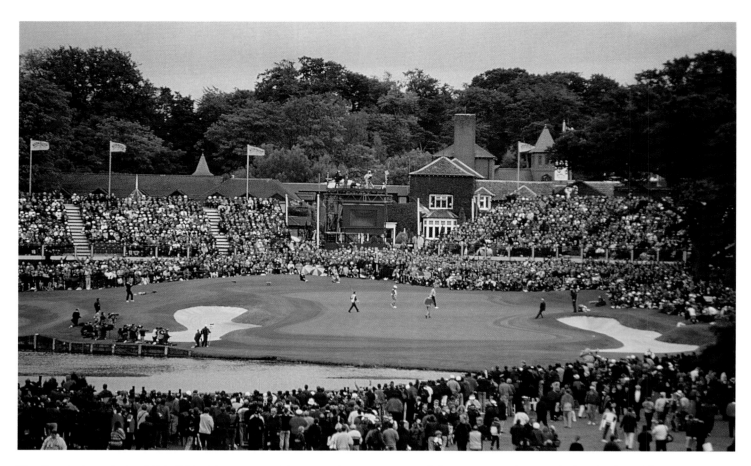

The Spaniard watched as Nick Faldo, his opponent, hit an iron into the perfect position at the tenth from which to pitch over the water onto the green. Ballesteros reached for his driver and launched the ball into orbit. It was an imperious blow, for the ball soared then carried the trees strategically placed to stop such a shot before finishing eight feet from the hole.

The hole then measured 310 yards, and a plaque marks Ballesteros's achievement and remains as evidence of the moment when The Belfry was truly born.

Nevertheless, The Belfry, or more precisely The Brabazon course, had its critics as well as its supporters. The problem was the money supply. It had taken £2.3 million to refurbish the hotel and to build the two courses. Cash said: "We could not fool ourselves. We were aware that we did not have the perfect piece of land and that it would take time to get the course absolutely right."

Thomas quite rightly received praise for his fashioning of The Brabazon course, which was American in style, but there was little he could do now that it was in the hands of owners with, so it seemed, no funds to rectify matters.

In October 1981 Greenall Whitley purchased all Ellerman Lines shares in The Belfry Company, and immediately launched the resurrection of The Brabazon course. This was important because

part of the agreement the PGA had with The Belfry Company was for the Ryder Cup to be played on the course twice in eight years and, following criticism during the English Classic in 1979, the match was switched to Walton Heath in 1981.

The course required the kiss of life and it started with the soil of the fairways being broken to a depth of nine inches so the stones which were causing so many complaints could be removed. Then the fairways were top-dressed with a mixture of fern peat and topsoil. In addition, 100 mature, 20-foot trees, costing £500 each, were planted to increase definition while at the same time strengthening the overall layout. It was coupled with an extensive drainage programme. Much of the work was carried out by floodlight so as not to disturb play during the day.

Off the fairways, Greenall Whitley spent a further £1.3 million on a new accommodation block - Jacklin House - of 48 bedrooms, a covered driving range and also opened a leisure centre. The chalet pub next to the famous tenth green became the Bel Air nightclub.

By now The Belfry had become part of The De Vere Group of hotels. With a further 56-bedroom extension - Trevino House - it was ready to stage the Ryder Cup which would be the ultimate test for The Brabazon course - and it unquestionably passed the examination. There were no complaints in 1985, when for the first time since 1957, the United States were beaten. The match drew

unprecedented crowds of more than 90,000 in comparison to 16,000 at Walton Heath in 1981. That the course itself was presented in superb condition was naturally important, especially as by now investment stood at £8.1 million.

The persuasive tongue of the enterprising Cash led to The De Vere board investing a further £8 million for the 1989 match which ended in a tie with Europe retaining the Cup following their historic 15-13 win at Muirfield Village in 1987 - the first time that the Americans had been beaten on home soil.

For 1989 two new lakes were constructed to control water flow and improve the aesthetics. An electrical irrigation system was installed. More importantly, as far as the spectators were concerned, special mounds were created to improve viewing and accessibility.

By now the management was convinced that from those small potato fields had grown a golf course of which everyone could be proud. Indeed the Ryder Cup returned to The De Vere Belfry in 1993, when the United States retained Samuel Ryder's elegant golden chalice following their win at Kiawah Island in South Carolina in 1991.

For 1993, when The De Vere Belfry made history by hosting the Ryder Cup for a third time, the De Vere Group spent a further

Christy O'Connor Jnr.

£2.5 million remodelling The Brabazon course to enhance spectator viewing and to provide an even tougher test and improving the hotel facilities. No fewer than ten of the holes underwent improvement changes. Thomas said: "It was exciting to go back and do some of the things you would have liked to have done originally."

Stuart Reed, then the Chairman and Chief Executive of De Vere Hotels, pointed out that the "huge success and popularity of The Belfry, De Vere Hotel's flagship golf resort, has played a vital part in shaping the development of the group. The leisure and business guest who wants to play golf is becoming more and more discerning and quite rightly - more demanding. The programme of work at The De Vere Belfry focused on creating the best venue for the Ryder Cup because we wanted to make sure players from both teams, officials and sponsors were as comfortable as possible. But the benefit of that investment will be seen in the coming years by all those who visit The De Vere Belfry, and play the course and enjoy the facilities."

Now, following another eight years of continued refurbishment and building of the hotel and in particular in the remodelling of The Brabazon course, The De Vere Belfry is ready to host the Ryder Cup for a fourth time. There have been many changes since 1993 with an overall investment in excess of £40 million on the complex including 120 significant changes and £3.5 million spent on alterations and improvements to The Brabazon course.

Mike Maloney, the Executive Director of The De Vere Belfry, has seen the complex grow since he first arrived at the hotel in May 1991, but the tremendous progress made in the last eight years have

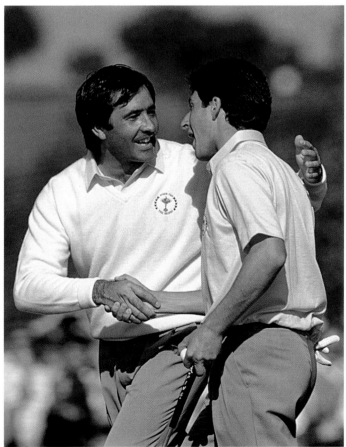

Seve Ballesteros and José Maria Olazábal: For many the finest partnership in Ryder Cup history

provided him and all his staff with a challenge that they have brought to fruition with enormous skill and diligence.

Even so Maloney acknowledged: "Our selection for this prestigious event could not have been achieved without the tremendous help received from the local community. I would particularly like to thank all the people at The De Vere Belfry together with North Warwickshire Borough Council, the Birmingham Marketing Partnership, the NEC Group and Birmingham City Council. We have enjoyed working with them all in the build up to what will be a magnificent week for golf."

The De Vere Belfry, part of the De Vere chain of hotels owned by The De Vere Group plc, also played host to the Benson and Hedges International Open in 2000 and this famous tournament returns to the venue in 2001. De Vere Group Chief Executive Paul Dermody, said: "The Ryder Cup Committee's choice of The De Vere Belfry is a tribute to the management and staff who have done such an excellent job over the previous three Ryder Cup matches. I am absolutely confident that the hotel, the staff and the course will live up to the high expectation entrusted in us by the Committee.

"We have been totally committed to the standards of excellence worthy of this great event and Dave Thomas has spent five years enhancing The Brabazon course in a way that it has never been seen before."

Thomas also designed the PGA National Championship course, which opened in 1997. This further enhances the golf facilities at The De Vere Belfry and provides golfers with three demanding championship courses.

Sandy Jones, Chief Executive of the Professional Golfers' Association said: "No one can deny that The De Vere Belfry has already staged three very successful Ryder Cup Matches. Taking this into consideration together with the superb development and refurbishment of The Brabazon course, and coupled with the fact that in 2001 The PGA, the oldest PGA in the world, celebrates its centenary, makes us believe that The De Vere Belfry is the ideal venue for the staging of the 34th Ryder Cup Match. De Vere, owners of The De Vere Belfry, are loyal and long-standing supporters of the Association and of golf in general, and nothing gives us more pleasure than to be at home during our 100 years celebration."

There can be no doubt, too, that there will be much to celebrate in September, 2001, when the eyes of the sporting world will focus on The De Vere Belfry and once again will come ample evidence that from those small potato fields has grown a course of which all can be proud.

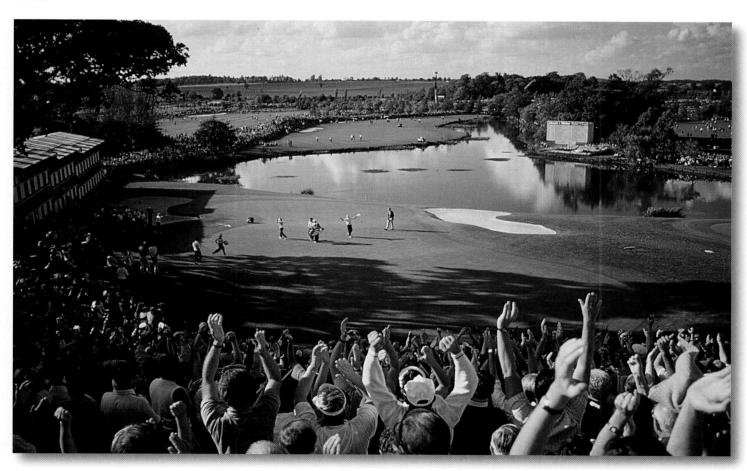

Ireland

A Natural Home for the
RYDER CUP 2005

Aer Lingus

Ireland, a golfer's paradise, with every shape, size and shade of green and the friendliest 19th watering hole on the circuit. Ireland has produced more than her share of Ryder Cup contenders and welcomed many of the greats, including Ballesteros, Langer, Faldo and Montgomerie. The 2005 Ryder Cup. Ireland, a perfect venue, an ideal host.

WATERFORD
CRYSTAL

The Brabazon Course

HOLE 1

The tees have been lowered in a stepped formation to form an amphitheatre. The hole is essentially a straight away par four but alterations to the fairway bunkers and the addition of a further bunker on the right combined with changes in the mowing pattern creates a different effect. The green has remained the same although the greenside bunkers have been enlarged and reshaped.

HOLE 2

The tee formation has been altered and a new back tee has been built to make it play a little longer. The fairway bunker on the right has been removed and two new bunkers have been built in a more aggressive position on the left of the fairway which means the tee shot needs to be played more to the right. The green has been enlarged as have the formation and shape of the greenside bunkers. This makes it a much better hole from the tee where the golfer can appreciate the dramatic mounding which changes the playing characteristics and improves the aesthetic appeal.

HOLE 3

One of the major changes. The long par four has been replaced by a dramatic dog-leg right to left par five. The tees have been raised to give a better view of the existing fairway bunkers which have also been remodelled. A good drive will provide the opportunity to reach the green in two shots but the golfer will have to carry his second shot across a substantial new lake. A new green has been designed with deep bunkers in front and to the right with extensive mounding around it. It is anticipated that this will become a favourite spectator viewing point and should provide dramatic TV shots.

HOLE 4

The second major change. The hole now plays as a long par four with several new features. The drive must negotiate two new bunkers placed to encourage a left to right drive or a straight carry across the newly enlarged pond. The second shot must clear the widened stream to a new sloped green guarded by two greenside bunkers. Viewed from the tee the hole has been enhanced with new earthworks to provide greater interest and visual appeal.

Ready & Waiting

H O L E   5

New tees have been created. The stream which previously crossed the fairway has been culverted but now flows into an enlarged pond on the left hand side. A substantial spectator viewing mound has been constructed which in combination with the change of a bunker from the left side to the right side of the fairway encourages a right to left tee shot. The green has not been altered but the three greenside bunkers have been enlarged and reshaped.

H O L E   6

Anyone who has played The Brabazon in the past will appreciate the dramatic change to this hole. The tees remain the same but the lake on the left has been reshaped and the fairway has been lowered by 1½ metres to give a greater visual role. The bunker on the right of the fairway has been enlarged and repositioned. The green remains unaltered although two new greenside bunkers have been added on the left and the existing right hand bunker has been remodelled.

H O L E   7

New tees have been constructed and a substantial bunker feature covering much of the approach to the green has been added to act as the main design feature of the hole. Interlocking mounds and fingers of grass have enhanced the impression that existed before of an island green surrounded by sand.

H O L E   8

New tees have shortened the hole but the tees have been raised to provide a better view of the hole and the lake on the left. New bunkers have been positioned on the right of the fairway as well as additional mounding to make it a more attractive tee shot. The green is unaltered but the greenside bunkers have been enlarged and deepened.

H O L E   9

New tees have been created and raised to provide a better view of the hole. The left hand bunker has been enlarged. The dramatic green beside the lake in front of the hotel is unaltered.

H O L E   1 0

Little has been done to this world famous hole. The fairway bunkers have been remodelled along with some minor fairway changes. Most interestingly, the green has been extended a few yards further towards the lake providing more flag positions tantalisingly close to the water's edge.

Fully equipped offices, wherever you do business

Wherever in the world you do business, Regus offers total flexibility with fully equipped business centres available in over 300 locations across 47 countries... instantly. So wherever you find yourself doing business, you'll find Regus.

0845 30 10 300   www.regus.com

HOLE 11

New back tees have been created and raised to provide a better view of the hole. The left hand bunker has been remodelled to provide a wider opening for the drive. The fairway mowing pattern has been changed to make the hole look more attractive.

HOLE 12

This is another dramatic change to the original Brabazon design. The par three hole has been shortened by 26 yards and the tees raised substantially to provide a good view of a newly formed lake which has replaced the existing stream which used to run across in front of the green. The green has been altered to provide space to the right to encourage tricky flag positions just behind the newly constructed re-circulating stream and stone feature.

HOLE 13

The tees have been reshaped and extended. The existing fairway bunkers have been enlarged and the fairway mowing changed to encourage a more left to right positional drive. The green has been extended and slopes added for greater interest. A pot bunker added to the rear of the green and the two existing greenside bunkers have been remodelled.

HOLE 14

A new raised back tee provides a view of the newly created tee to green bunker which dominates the left hand side of this par three. The green has not been altered although the greenside bunker has been remodelled and substantial mounding added to the rear of the green and the right side of the fairway to create another amphitheatre for spectators.

HOLE 15

New tees have been constructed and the back tee substantially raised to provide a view down the entire length of the hole. Fairway bunkers have been enlarged and reshaped as has the bunker 100 yards short of the green.

HOLE 16

The fairway and greenside bunkers have been remodelled, but essentially this hole will remain the same except for substantial mounding to the left which gives it a slightly different look.

HOLE 17

New tees have been constructed and realigned to encourage more shots across the fairway bunker at the corner of the dog-leg. The fairway bunkers across the stream have been remodelled.

HOLE 18

Few playing changes have been made to this dramatic world famous finishing hole though substantial mounding has been added to provide better spectator viewing opportunities. All the tees have been raised to give the player a better view across the corner of the lake. The first fairway bunker which rarely troubled the top players has been removed, but the second one further up the fairway has been enlarged and reshaped.

CARD OF THE COURSE			
Hole	Yards	Metres	Par
1	411	376	4
2	379	346	4
3	538	492	5
4	442	404	4
5	408	373	4
6	395	361	4
7	177	162	3
8	428	391	4
9	433	396	4
Out:	**3611**	**3301**	**36**
10	311	284	4
11	419	383	4
12	208	190	3
13	384	351	4
14	190	174	3
15	545	498	5
16	413	378	4
17	564	516	5
18	473	432	4
In:	**3507**	**3206**	**36**
Total:	**7118**	**6507**	**72**

One Irish name is guaranteed for the 2005 Ryder Cup in Ireland.

In 2005 the whole world will be watching the biggest names in golf as the most
prestigious event in the international calendar comes to Ireland for the very first time.
The Ryder Cup 2005, where the finest American players take on the best that
Europe has to offer on the championship course at the K Club.

While we don't know how many Irish players will be on the European team, we can
tell you there will be one name you'll know; AIB Group. Our association with
top quality golf extends to the European Open and the Irish Seniors Open
and that means Ireland's largest financial services group is also one of the
biggest supporters of the game.

AIB Group. Proud Partner to the 2005 Ryder Cup in Ireland.

Sam Torrance MBE

2001 EUROPEAN TEAM CAPTAIN

Sam Torrance's appointment as European Ryder Cup captain at The De Vere Belfry in 2001 was a prefect example of combining nostalgia with common sense. It was at the superb Midlands complex that Torrance, already a household name in Britain through his successful exploits on the European Tour, found global fame as the man who sank the historic putt which saw the Ryder Cup return to European shores for the first time since 1957.

So when a new leader was required to succeed Mark James for the 2001 edition of golf's greatest team event, it was impossible to overlook the claims of a highly popular, universally respected and vastly experienced Ryder Cup campaigner with eight 'tours of duty' under his belt.

Torrance delivered the winning point against Andy North on the final green - and that defining moment for Europe in the glittering history of the competition ensured that Torrance's name would always be written in large neon letters whenever discussions arise surrounding Ryder Cups at The Belfry.

It remains his most cherished moment in a remarkable 30-year career as a playing professional on the European Tour which has seen the popular Scotsman accumulate no fewer than 21 titles on his home Tour and ten others world wide.

"I have many fond memories, but that particular moment in 1985 will stay with me forever. Nothing else comes close, not even my Tour wins," says Torrance.

His golfing passion began in earnest at the age of nine, four years after his father, Bob, the highly respected coach and club professional, introduced him to the game at Rossendale GC, Lancashire, England, before the family moved back to Scotland where Torrance Snr took up the post at Largs Routenburn GC in Ayrshire, on the west coast of Scotland, not far from two of the world's greatest links courses, Royal Troon and Turnberry.

Young Sam proved to be a good pupil and a quick learner. He recalled: "The first time I broke 40 at Rossendale I rushed in to tell my dad and he didn't believe me. We then went back to the course

together and I did it again!" As a youngster, he became hopelessly addicted to golf, playing three rounds a day - "sometimes four," he added - during the long, light summer nights in Scotland.

He left school at 13 and was employed in a variety of odd-jobs, including erecting television aerials and working in a supermarket, until turning professional in 1970 just short of his 17th birthday.

In 1971 he was sponsored by wealthy Sunningdale members, Angus Mackenzie and his sons, Norman and Gerald, to play on the European Tour. He managed to play only one tournament that year, the Agfa Gevaert at Stoke Poges, where he finished 39th and won the princely sum of £35 to be ranked 232nd on the Order of Merit.

The following season he finished 37th on the money list with £1,732 and collected the Sir Henry Cotton Rookie of the Year award on the European Tour. It was the first of 28 consecutive seasons Torrance has played on the Tour, during which time he has accumulated more than £3½ million in official money and approaching £5 million in total.

Torrance had to wait until 1976 to record his first victory in the Piccadilly Medal at Finham Park. Many others followed and he is especially proud of his victories in the 1981 Carrolls Irish Open at Portmarnock and the same title 14 years later in a play-off at Mount Juliet.

Of becoming the latest in a long line of well-respected European captains, he said: "It's a fabulous honour to be the European captain. I've never made a secret of how much I enjoy being part of the Ryder Cup, and to be the captain makes me feel very proud. It has been a privilege to be involved with four wonderful and very different Ryder Cup captains in John Jacobs, Tony Jacklin, Bernard Gallacher and Mark James, and each of them is very special in their own way. Hopefully, I can take a little of what I have learned from all of them to live up to the very high standards set by my peers."

Curtis Strange

2001 UNITED STATES TEAM CAPTAIN

It was Sam Torrance, at the time of being appointed the European Ryder Cup Team captain, who summed up the character of Curtis Strange best of all when he said: "You know where you are with Curtis. It's laid down in front of you. No messing."

Further amplification was barely necessary. Torrance's implication was that, in Strange, the United States had a captain of substance - a man who can cut through a morass of red tape to get exactly what he wants and won't be deflected from his objectives.

The parallels are glaringly obvious. Like Torrance, Strange grew up in a golfing environment, the son of a club professional, Tom, who sadly passed away when young Curtis was a teenager. Like Torrance, he became a prolific winner on Tour and, just like Sam, he enjoyed a long and successful Ryder Cup career.

Torrance said: "He's a dear friend, Curtis. I've known him for almost 30 years. If you'd asked me to pick a Ryder Cup captain in the last 20 years who I would like to be against when it eventually came to me, it would have been Curtis Strange because I love what he stands for in the game."

Strange won the Virginia State Junior Championship at the age of 15 and, in a poignant reminder of his late father, he won the Eastern Amateur in 1975, 18 years after his dad became the inaugural winner of the event.

He progressed quickly and became College Player of the Year in 1974 as a student at Arnold Palmer's alma mater of Wake Forest University and represented the United States in the Walker Cup the following year.

He turned professional in 1976 and earned his card in the US Tour Qualifying School in 1977. Strange's big break came relatively quickly when he captured the 1979 Pensacola Open.

Now 45, Strange enjoyed several Ryder Cup highs and lows - and he crossed swords with Mr Torrance on a couple of occasions, with honours being shared. In 1987 at Muirfield Village Strange and Tom Kite enjoyed a 4 and 2 win over Torrance and Howard Clark in the opening foursomes.

Then two year later, when the Ryder Cup was tied at The De Vere Belfry, Sam and Gordon Brand Jnr took a measure of revenge by beating Strange and Paul Azinger by one hole.

However, Strange's most glorious moments came in 1988-89 when he emulated Ben Hogan's feat of capturing the US Open (1950-51) in successive years. The first victory at The Country Club, Brookline, came after an 18-hole play-off with Nick Faldo.

Twelve months later he defended successfully at Oak Hill, shooting a second round 64 on his way to a one stroke victory over Welshman Ian Woosnam, Chip Beck and Mark McCumber.

It was a superb achievement to follow in the footsteps of Hogan, but his most recent return to Oak Hill was less successful. The Virginian was selected as a wild card by United States captain Lanny Wadkins for the 1995 Ryder Cup Match and lost his three games, including a singles defeat by Faldo who exacted a measure of revenge for his 1988 US Open play-off loss.

Strange came close to collecting a third US Open title in 1994 but he fell one stroke short of the play-off which involved Colin Montgomerie, Loren Roberts and eventual winner Ernie Els.

That first US Open win saw Strange become the first player on the US PGA Tour to pass the $1 million mark for a season, while one of his career highlights came at the Home of Golf, St Andrews, in 1987 when he reduced the Old Course to 62 blows, ten under par and a course record which has yet to be equalled or surpassed.

Married to Sarah, with two sons, Strange has an identical twin brother, Allen, who also played on the US PGA Tour for a time. That 1989 US Open win was to be Curtis's last, and in 1997 he began a full-time assignment as an analyst for ABC Sports - a role which grew rapidly and resulted in his promotion to main analyst for the major US network.

The Tradition Continues

Tiger Woods and Mark O'Meara

𝒯he World Cup of Golf became the fourth event of the World Golf Championships when it was played at the Buenos Aires Golf Club, Argentina, in December 2000. EMC joined World Golf Championships umbrella sponsors, Andersen Consulting, NEC and American Express, by sponsoring the 2000 WGC - EMC World Cup.

The International Golf Association, the organisation which operated the World Cup from 1953, entered into an agreement with the

International Federation of PGA Tours whereby the Federation sanctioned the World Cup of Golf as the fourth World Golf Championships event. As a World Golf Championships event, the Federation will re-stage and promote the World Cup as the team component of this elite series.

Two-man teams representing 24 countries qualified for the 2000 WGC - EMC World Cup with two days of foursomes and two days

Victory for England in 1998: David Carter and Nick Faldo celebrate

Paul McGinley and Padraig Harrington (Ireland, winners 1997)

of fourballs being played in a revised format. The prize fund of $3 million enabled the winning team to share $1million.

"The World Cup of Golf has held an esteemed position within the golf world for decades," PGA Tour Commissioner Tim Finchem said on behalf of the Federation. "It has done as much to promote golf around the world as any event in sport. We were delighted the World Cup joined the World Golf Championships."

At Buenos Aires the United States, following the victory achieved by Mark O'Meara and Tiger Woods in Malaysia in 1999, were bidding to win for the 23rd time.

The World Golf Championships are a series of events launched in February 1999 that feature the game's leading players competing against one another in a variety of formats. The EMC World Cup joined the Andersen Consulting Match Play, NEC Invitational and American Express Championship in the World Golf Championships line-up. The events rotate through a variety of outstanding venues worldwide.

Mitchell Platts

Aussie Rules

Noel Ratcliffe and John Jacobs

Australian Noel Ratcliffe opened a new era for the European Seniors Tour when he was crowned the Tour's Number One after a scintillating 2000 season which came to an incredible climax in the desert in Abu Dhabi. Ratcliffe went into the inaugural Abu Dhabi Seniors Tour Championship with a slender lead at the top of the Order of Merit table but it wasn't until he rammed home a putt of six feet on the final green that his new status was confirmed.

That putt meant that Ratcliffe, the winner of both The Scotsman Scottish Seniors Open and the TEMES Seniors Open in Greece, had pipped America's John Grace by a mere 1,639 euro (£953) for the John Jacobs Trophy, awarded annually to the winner of the European Seniors Tour Order of Merit.

On the Tee: Tommy Horton

It also meant the end of Tommy Horton's long and impressive reign as the Tour's Number One, the Englishman's consolation being that three days later, on his return to the British Isles, he went with, his wife, Helen, and their family to Buckingham Palace where the Queen awarded him a much deserved MBE for services to golf.

The 2000 season started in what once could be described as a predictable fashion when Horton, the winner of 22 Seniors Tour titles, added another to his name when he won the inaugural Royal Westmoreland Barbados Open in spectacular fashion. Horton, who had won the John Jacobs Trophy, awarded to the Number One golfer on the Order of Merit, for the previous four seasons, started the final round four shots in arrears of the leader, but went on to finish two shots ahead of America's Jerry Bruner after a final round of 68, four under par.

Horton had won the opening event in three out of the previous four seasons, but anyone who anticipated that he would go on to dominate the Tour schedule as he had done in past seasons was in for something of a surprise because he was to go the rest of the season without recording another victory. He did do well enough to finish in fourth place on the Order of Merit with 147,767 euro (£85,911) but that can have been but scant consolation for a man who had recorded 11 victories in his previous three seasons on the Tour. What is more, he was also to go on to miss his first ever cut

Brian Huggett

in nine years of competing on the European Seniors Tour, missing out on the final round at the AIB Irish Seniors Open at the new Tulfarris course south of Dublin.

With Horton in less dominant form than he had been in previous seasons, the first nine events of the 2000 season were all won by different golfers. Brian Huggett was the next man to enter the winner's circle, recording his tenth win of his European Seniors Tour career after defeating Australia's Bob Shearer on the first hole of a sudden-death play-off at the Beko Classic at the Gloria Golf Resort in Turkey.

America's Bruce Fleisher, making a welcome debut on the Seniors Tour on this side of the Atlantic, was the next to record a victory, at the aforementioned AIB Irish Seniors Open at Tulfarris and he was followed by the evergreen Neil Coles who won The Microlease Jersey Seniors Open at La Moye. Coles, 65, turned the clock back in spectacular fashion at La Moye, registering rounds of 66, 71 and 70 to finish three shots ahead of the luckless Bruner, who had now been the bridesmaid on six occasions without registering a maiden Seniors Tour win. It was an impressive performance but what made the victory so special was that it not only meant he had beaten his own record as the oldest winner in European Seniors Tour history, but also that it made him the first professional golfer to win an individual event in six separate decades. That run started when he won the Gor-Ray tournament in England in 1956. Such was his form during the 2000 season, that it is difficult to imagine that it won't continue for some time to come.

Coles won for the 45th time in a long and illustrious career when he emerged victorious in Jersey and he almost made it 46 a week later when he battled his way into a play-off against David Huish and John Fourie in the Lawrence Batley Seniors at Huddersfield Golf Club. This time, however, Huish won his third European Seniors Tour title at the first extra hole and five tournaments later he was to become the first double winner of the 2000 season when he equalled the Seniors Tour 18 hole record of 62 on his way to winning the Bad Ragaz PGA Seniors Open in Switzerland.

Bruce Fleisher

The impressive Fleisher had been the first, debut winner on the 2000 Tour and in successive weeks at the end of June and the start of July he was joined by two more when Australia's Ian Stanley won the Coca-Cola Kaiser Karl European Trophy at Haus Kambach Golf Club in Germany and England's Nick Job produced a flawless final round of 67 in dreadful weather conditions to win the TotalFina Elf Seniors Open at Le Golf de Joyenval in France.

Rain had caused difficulties at almost all of the opening seven events of the 2000 European Seniors Tour season and it also proved to be a problem when play had to be suspended for a while at the Senior British Open, presented by MasterCard, at Royal County Down Golf Club. However, the suspension did little to upset Ireland's Christy O'Connor Jnr who became only the second man in history to successfully defend this prestigious title when he overcame a one shot overnight deficit to defeat South Africa's John Bland by two shots. O'Connor's win was worth 102,758 euro (£63,300) and catapulted him to the top of the Order of Merit where he was to remain for several months.

Horton, who finished tied for sixth place, won rather less, but his cheque for 20,291 euro (£12,500) took him through the one million euro career earnings barrier on the European and European Seniors Tour.

Neil Coles

Seniors Tour Guide 2001

Neil Coles is one of the greatest talents ever to grace the game of golf and in the year 2000 he created history when he became the first player to win a professional tournament in six successive decades. Time and again Coles proved that age is no obstacle during a glorious season and the 2001 European Seniors Tour Guide gives the full story.

Tommy Horton had dominated the European Seniors Tour as number one since 1996 and his attempt to remain at the top is chronicled in a classic summer when John Grace, David Oakley, Noel Ratcliffe, Ian Stanley and Coles challenged his supremacy.

Renowned for the friendly yet intensely competitive nature of tournaments the European Seniors Tour is enjoyed by increasing galleries and wider TV audiences. The figures and facts behind the winning of every tournament throughout the millennium year can be found in the 2001 European Seniors Tour Guide plus biographies, statistics, records and notable achievements. It is a must for all students of the game.

Ordering a copy of the 2001 European Seniors Tour Guide is simple: send a cheque for £12.50 UK and Europe (includes postage and packaging) or £17.50 for Overseas (which includes postage and packaging), made payable to the PGA European Tour to Emily Doughty, Communications Division, European Tour, Wentworth Drive, Virginia Water, Surrey GU25 4LX or call +44 1344 840442 with credit card details.

Nick Job

The early part of the season had been dominated by golfers from Britain and Ireland and that was to continue when David Creamer became the fourth first-time winner of the season when he won the Energis Senior Masters over the Edinburgh course at Wentworth Club. But then, after that success and Huish's second victory of the season in Switzerland, it was the turn of the overseas challengers to take over, winning the next eight events in succession.

During the summer months, Ratcliffe was to emerge as a potential winner of the Order of Merit title, winning both The Scotsman Scottish Seniors Open at Marriott Dalmahoy Hotel & Country Club and the TEMES Seniors Open at Glyfada Golf Club, in Greece. Ratcliffe, a former winner of two events on the European Tour, including the 1987 Benson and Hedges International Open at Fulford, also finished second at the De Vere Hotels Senior Classic at Ferndown Golf Club and the Tui Golf Championship Fleesensee at Fleesensee Golf and Country Resorts in Germany, finally usurping O'Connor at the top of the Order of Merit as the season entered its final two months.

Ratcliffe's form did a great deal to shape the second half of the season and so, too, did the emergence of a group of American golfers who confirmed their talent while winning five events in August, September and October. David Oakley set the ball rolling when he won the De Vere Hotels Senior Classic at Ferndown Golf Club and

Ian Stanley

David Huish

what made his second European Seniors Tour victory even more impressive was that he registered rounds of 67, 64 and 65, for a 17 under par total of 196, a mere two shots outside the 54-hole record set by Brian Waites at the 1998 Elf Seniors Open at Pau. It also meant that he had also become just the third man in Seniors Tour history to post a 54 hole aggregate of below 200, joining Waites and Ireland's Denis O'Sullivan, who both achieved that feat at Pau in 1998.

Jeff Van Wagenen was another American to enter the winner's circle, emerging as the winner at the Tui Golf Championship Fleesensee at the impressive new Fleesensee Golf and Country Resorts in what used to be East Germany, but that victory, popular though it was, was somewhat overshadowed by the form of his compatriot, John Grace. He was to win three times in five starts, a run of form that, ultimately, was to lift him to second place on the Order of Merit. Grace had registered his first triumph when he captured The Belfry PGA Seniors Open over the PGA National course at The De Vere Belfry. He missed the cut at the subsequent Scotsman Scottish Seniors Open at Marriott Dalmahoy Hotel & Country Club but then made it two out of three at the Ordina Legends in Golf event at Crayestein Golf Club in The Netherlands.

The American, a career amateur, who represented his country in the 1975 Walker Cup match at St Andrews, and who did not turn pro until he reached 50, had started the season hoping to earn a place in

Jeff Van Wagenen

it was the impressive South American who was to go on to lift the 26,626 euro (£16,000) first prize, firing six birdies in 16 holes to defeat his rival 3 & 2.

Diniz was the seventh first-time winner of the 2000 season and more evidence of the improved strength in depth on the Seniors Tour was supplied the following week when O'Sullivan, a former Irish Amateur Stroke Play and Match Play champion, won his maiden professional victory at the Dan Technology Senior Tournament of Champions at the Buckinghamshire Golf Club.

Once more the golf was sparkling with O'Sullivan registering three birdies over his final three holes to snatch a one shot victory from Ross Metherell, Nick Job and Maurice Bembridge. Earlier, Bembridge, making a determined effort to win his third Seniors Tour title, and his first since 1998, had closed with a seven under par 65 that until O'Sullivan's late birdie blitz seemed certain to give the Englishman a place in a play-off. Later, Job kept the excitement bubbling right to the end, almost holing a bunker shot at the last that would have meant that extra holes would have been required to settle who was to win the 34,073 euro (£20,000) first prize.

O'Sullivan's victory catapulted the Irishman into 13th place in the Order of Merit and seven days later he moved up to third when he also won the Abu Dhabi Seniors Tour Championship over the

John Grace

the Tour's top-50. He adjusted his sights after his first two victories and then, all of a sudden, emerged as a realistic challenger for the Order of Merit title when he won for a third time at the Big 3 Records Monte Carlo Invitational.

That win, confirmed with a flawless round of 65 in the company of Hollywood actor, Kevin Costner, took his earnings for the season to 144,517 euro (£86,840), less than 7,200 euro (£4,500)behind Ratcliffe. The scene was set for a tantalising end to the season and so it was to prove with the winner of the John Jacobs Trophy not being decided until the last round of the season's final tournament.

After Monte Carlo, the European Seniors Tour moved on to Le Meridien Penina Golf & Resort, where the inaugural Daily Telegraph European Seniors Match Play Championship, presented by SSL and Sodexho, was contested under cloudless skies. Throughout the season there had been a perceptible improvement in scoring and this was confirmed over the testing Penina course - designed by Sir Henry Cotton - where the standard of golf would not have been out of place on the regular European Tour.

After a series of surprises, including victories over Horton and Scotland's Bernard Gallacher, Brazil's Priscillo Diniz, a rookie from San Paulo, fought his way through to the final to face Stanley and

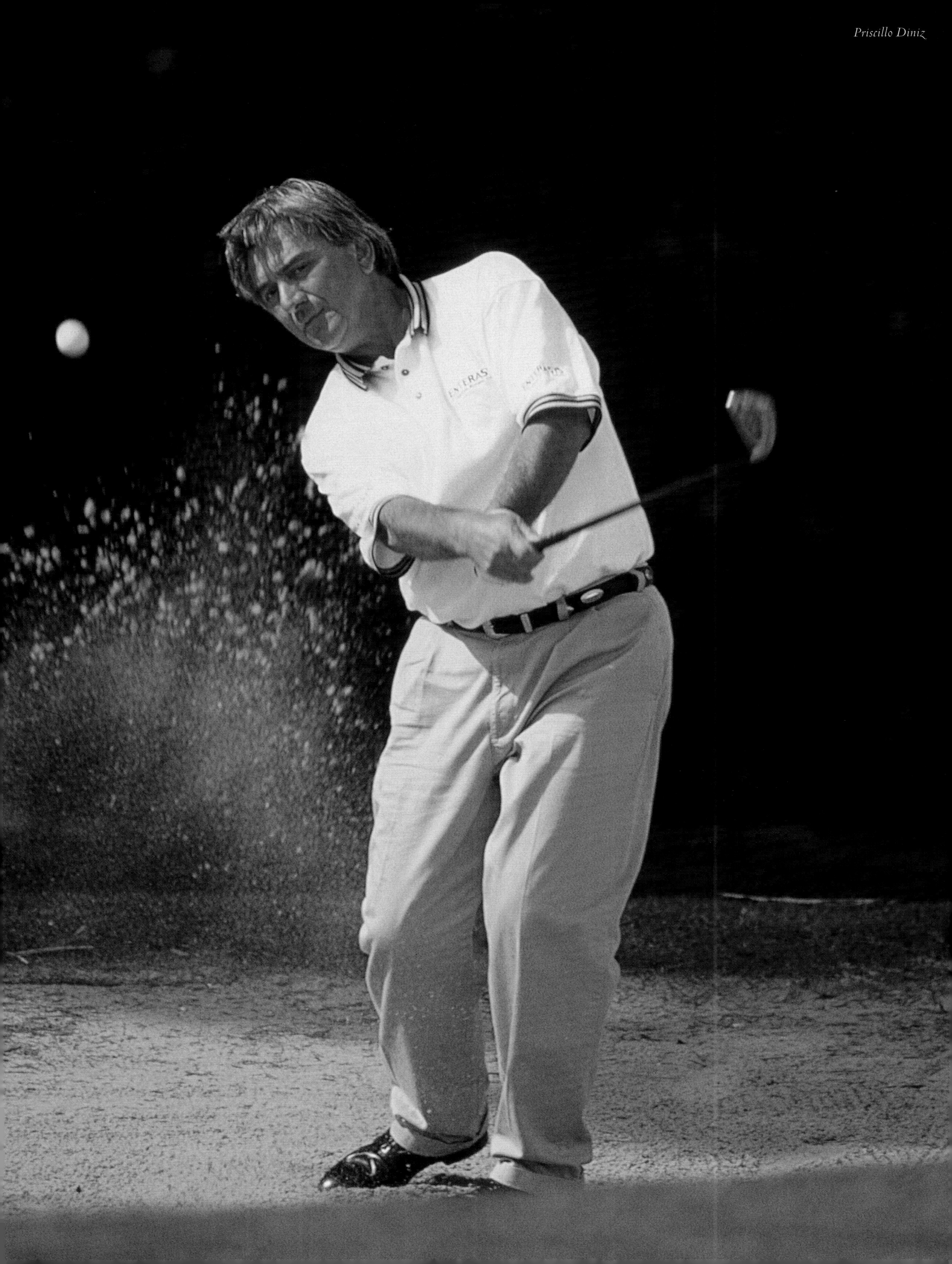
Priscillo Diniz

impressive new National course at the Abu Dhabi Golf Club by Sheraton. As befits the Tour's finale, the golf in the desert was almost as hot as the weather, O'Sullivan closing with nine birdies in a 65 that gave him a one shot victory over Diniz, whose consolation was that the 39,678 euro (£23,068) he won was enough to vault him over Japan's Seiji Ebihara and win the 2000 European Seniors Tour Rookie of the Year Award.

O'Sullivan won the title, worth 59,523 euro (£34,606) but he wasn't the sole winner because in finishing in a tie for 18th place Ratcliffe pipped John Grace for the Order of Merit title.

In fact, the race for the money title was just as exciting as the tournament itself, with Ratcliffe holing from six feet on the last and then having to wait for over half an hour to see if Grace could work his way into a top-four place. In the end, he fell one tantalising shot short, finishing tied for eighth, earning 1,639 euro (£953) less than he needed to wrest the John Jacobs Trophy from his rival's grasp. Horton also made a late challenge to perpetuate his reign as Number One. Going into the Abu Dhabi tournament, he knew that he had to win to move from third to first on the Order of Merit and, in the end, he came so very near, closing with a battling 68 for third place on his own.

Noel Ratcliffe and Nick Job

Denis O'Sullivan

"It was fitting that the season should finish in such dramatic circumstances because, all season long, we were entertained by some wonderful golf," said Andy Stubbs, Managing Director of the European Seniors Tour. "I have no doubt that the standard of golf played on the Seniors Tour in 2000 was better than ever before and that was certainly borne out in Abu Dhabi where the golf was as good as I've ever seen.

"I congratulate Noel for winning the Order of Merit title and commiserate with John Grace for coming so close. I'd also like to pay a special tribute to Tommy Horton. He might have lost his Number One position, after four years at the top, but the manner in which he fought to the end to retain the title, suggests to me that the race for the 2001 title will be just as closely contested."

Colin Callander

Eddie Polland: All smiles on the European Seniors Tour

EUROPEAN SENIORS TOUR ORDER OF MERIT

Pos	Name			Euro	Sterling Equivalent	Pos	Name			Euro	Sterling Equivalent
1	Noel RATCLIFFE	(Aus)	(19)	163,164.73	94,863.22	51	Norman WOOD	(Scot)	(17)	27,624.66	16,060.85
2	John GRACE	(USA)	(17)	161,525.45	93,910.15	52	Joe MCDERMOTT	(Ire)	(18)	27,340.59	15,895.69
3	Denis O'SULLIVAN	(Ire)	(20)	156,966.21	91,259.42	53	Paul LEONARD	(N.Ire)	(15)	26,438.31	15,371.11
4	Tommy HORTON	(Eng)	(20)	147,767.34	85,911.24	54	Bobby VERWEY	(SA)	(16)	26,078.34	15,161.83
5	Ian STANLEY	(Aus)	(19)	137,679.47	80,046.20	55	Barry SANDRY	(Eng)	(15)	24,842.38	14,443.24
6	Priscillo DINIZ	(Bra)	(20)	128,136.42	74,497.92	56	Toshiaki NAMIKI	(Jpn)	(12)	20,981.98	12,198.83
7	David HUISH	(Scot)	(20)	126,960.71	73,814.37	57	Shoichi SATO	(Jpn)	(13)	19,562.43	11,373.51
8	David OAKLEY	(USA)	(19)	121,609.29	70,703.08	58	Steve WILD	(Eng)	(14)	19,467.98	11,318.59
9	Neil COLES	(Eng)	(13)	119,803.42	69,653.15	59	John GARNER	(Eng)	(13)	19,439.26	11,301.90
10	David CREAMER	(Eng)	(20)	114,433.20	66,530.93	60	Pat KAYLOR	(USA)	(11)	19,109.78	11,110.34
11	Jim RHODES	(Eng)	(20)	112,963.31	65,676.34	61	Jay DOLAN III	(USA)	(14)	18,634.56	10,834.05
12	Bob SHEARER	(Aus)	(14)	112,441.63	65,373.04	62	Tomas PERSSON	(Swe)	(13)	17,866.29	10,387.38
13	Christy O'CONNOR JNR	(Ire)	(4)	111,099.71	64,592.85	63	TR JONES	(USA)	(8)	17,770.98	10,331.97
14	Maurice BEMBRIDGE	(Eng)	(19)	100,954.14	58,694.27	64	John IRWIN	(Can)	(13)	17,126.98	9,957.55
15	Seiji EBIHARA	(Jpn)	(13)	96,907.12	56,341.35	65	Gordon MACDONALD	(Scot)	(14)	15,878.29	9,231.56
16	Nick JOB	(Eng)	(19)	95,452.85	55,495.84	66	Snell LANCASTER	(USA)	(12)	15,061.42	8,756.64
17	Jeff VAN WAGENEN	(USA)	(18)	92,585.49	53,828.77	67	Hugh INGGS	(SA)	(11)	14,673.28	8,530.98
18	Jerry BRUNER	(USA)	(21)	89,663.25	52,129.80	*68	Keith R MACDONALD	(Scot)	(3)	14,589.47	8,482.25
19	Brian HUGGETT	(Wal)	(10)	86,467.58	50,271.85	69	Fritz GAMBETTA	(USA)	(17)	12,687.49	7,376.45
20	Peter DAWSON	(Eng)	(18)	83,521.46	48,558.99	70	Ian RICHARDSON	(Eng)	(11)	11,585.36	6,735.67
21	David JONES	(N.Ire)	(15)	79,807.18	46,399.52	71	Skip PRATT	(USA)	(10)	10,908.82	6,342.34
22	Eddie POLLAND	(N.Ire)	(21)	78,341.89	45,547.61	72	David OJALA	(USA)	(7)	10,543.86	6,130.15
23	Malcolm GREGSON	(Eng)	(17)	78,148.23	45,435.02	73	Renato CAMPAGNOLI	(It)	(13)	10,374.06	6,031.43
24	Ross METHERELL	(Aus)	(20)	72,802.44	42,327.00	74	Raymond KANE	(Ire)	(14)	9,197.17	5,347.19
25	David GOOD	(Aus)	(17)	69,707.88	40,527.84	75	Art RUSSELL	(USA)	(7)	9,093.77	5,287.08
26	Terry GALE	(Aus)	(13)	69,029.97	40,133.70	76	John BENDA	(USA)	(5)	8,402.48	4,885.16
27	Alan TAPIE	(USA)	(19)	66,604.20	38,723.37	77	Jan BJÖRNSSON	(Swe)	(7)	8,335.96	4,846.49
28	Kurt COX	(USA)	(16)	59,125.01	34,375.01	78	Manuel SANCHEZ	(Sp)	(12)	7,624.37	4,432.77
29	Alberto CROCE	(It)	(18)	56,520.61	32,860.82	79	José CABO	(Sp)	(7)	7,255.30	4,218.20
30	Bill HARDWICK	(Can)	(18)	55,440.62	32,232.92	80	Kenny STEVENSON	(N.Ire)	(12)	7,163.89	4,165.05
31	Liam HIGGINS	(Ire)	(16)	52,816.43	30,707.23	81	Gordon PARKHILL	(N.Ire)	(14)	6,864.75	3,991.13
32	John TOLHURST	(Aus)	(17)	50,459.77	29,337.08	82	J.R. DELICH	(USA)	(8)	6,679.32	3,883.33
33	Bernard GALLACHER	(Scot)	(19)	49,611.74	28,844.03	83	Gordon BROWN	(Scot)	(14)	5,960.65	3,465.49
34	Craig DEFOY	(Wal)	(20)	47,929.06	27,865.73	84	David SNELL	(Eng)	(6)	5,881.19	3,419.30
35	Manuel BALLESTEROS	(Sp)	(16)	47,375.56	27,543.93	85	Sid DENHAM	(Eng)	(11)	5,864.51	3,409.60
36	Tony PETERSON	(USA)	(15)	45,927.22	26,701.87	86	John HUDSON	(Eng)	(12)	5,376.28	3,125.74
37	Antonio GARRIDO	(Sp)	(20)	45,241.70	26,303.31	87	Bill LOCKIE	(Scot)	(4)	5,347.68	3,109.12
38	Jay HORTON	(USA)	(20)	41,575.75	24,171.95	88	Ian J SMITH	(SA)	(13)	5,158.93	2,999.38
39	Trevor DOWNING	(Aus)	(12)	41,236.77	23,974.87	89	Doug ROBB	(Can)	(8)	4,912.02	2,855.83
40	Brian WAITES	(Eng)	(18)	40,301.56	23,431.14	90	Paddy MCGUIRK	(Ire)	(8)	4,744.00	2,758.14
41	John FOURIE	(SA)	(18)	38,269.90	22,249.94	91	Hiro TAHARA	(Jpn)	(13)	4,405.94	2,561.59
42	George BURNS	(USA)	(14)	37,468.35	21,783.92	92	Tienie BRITZ	(SA)	(14)	4,373.82	2,542.92
43	Agim BARDHA	(Alb)	(14)	34,761.73	20,210.31	93	Joe CARR	(USA)	(6)	4,136.15	2,404.74
44	Tommy PRICE	(USA)	(12)	33,355.56	19,392.77	94	Glenn MACDONALD	(Can)	(4)	4,107.11	2,387.85
45	Geoff PARSLOW	(Aus)	(16)	32,194.47	18,717.72	95	Chick EVANS	(USA)	(6)	4,038.44	2,347.93
46	Peter TOWNSEND	(Eng)	(17)	31,218.99	18,150.58	96	Michael MURPHY	(Ire)	(12)	3,551.24	2,064.67
47	Denis DURNIAN	(Eng)	(12)	31,091.02	18,076.17	97	Glenn MALM	(USA)	(5)	3,512.61	2,042.22
48	John MORGAN	(Eng)	(4)	30,843.61	17,932.35	98	Roger FIDLER	(Eng)	(9)	3,332.13	1,937.28
49	Ray CARRASCO	(USA)	(11)	30,533.13	17,751.82	99	Andrew BROOKS	(Scot)	(2)	3,116.83	1,812.11
50	John MCTEAR	(Scot)	(17)	28,424.14	16,525.66	100	Michael STEADMAN	(Eng)	(4)	2,938.96	1,708.70

• *Figures in parentheses indicate number of events played*

No Short Cut to the Top

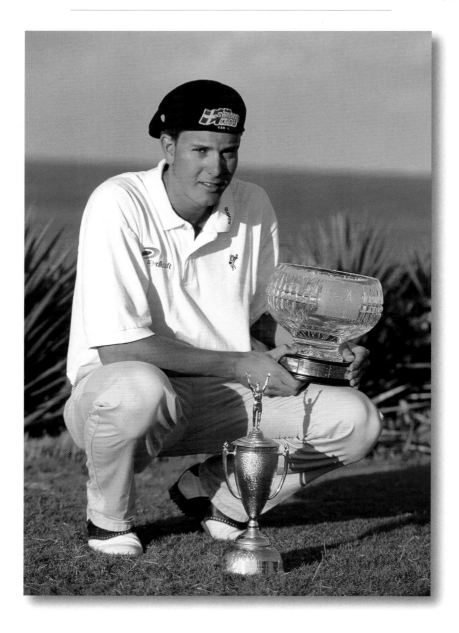

They are calling him the next Jesper Parnevik. Only time will tell, but Henrik Stenson possesses all the right ingredients to become Sweden's next golfing superstar and could eclipse anything Parnevik has achieved.

The world is at Stenson's feet and, on current form, there seems little that he cannot accomplish. Having topped the European Challenge Tour Rankings with seemingly the minimum of effort, he looks destined to become a household name as far as European golf is concerned.

Following an impressive amateur career, Stenson has been a professional for little more than two years, which makes his progress through the rankings little short of meteoric. He played just six tournaments in 1999, never finished worse than 15th and had five top-tens. He came close to winning the Grand Final in Cuba, ending just two strokes behind the winner, Stephen Scahill from New Zealand.

Johan Ryström

Here was a champion in the making and this year he has proved it, being in a class of his own. The only puzzling feature was that it took him so long to secure that maiden victory. He was knocking on the door from the start of the year but it took until June before he managed to prise it open. Runner-up in the Tusker Kenya Open, Stenson was then beaten in a play-off by fellow Swede Johan Ryström for The Costa Blanca Challenge in Spain. Third at the Muermans Real Estate Challenge Open in The Netherlands, it seemed that the 24-year-old from Malmo was destined to be the bridesmaid but never the bride.

But we were deluding ourselves. That first triumph was just around the corner and it came in the BIL Luxembourg Open when he rolled in a birdie putt from 15 feet at the second extra hole. What made it all the more impressive was that he also secured a birdie at the 72nd hole when he needed it to get into the play-off with Nils Rorbaek, from Denmark, and Belgian teenage amateur Nicolas Colsaerts, all three finishing on 18 under par 270.

"It feels like I deserve this," he said. "I haven't won anything big for three years but I have been up there and if you are up there often enough you are going to have the chance of winning."

The top prize of almost 13,000 euro (£8,000) took him to the top of the European Challenge Tour Rankings and secured his card for the main tour in 2001. But he had no intention of throttling back. "I will keep on going because I want to finish number one," he said, although his season has been punctuated by crucial breaks so not to become over-golfed.

Stephen Scahill

Carlos Rodiles

In the end he played just 14 of the 23 tournaments, securing nine top-tens including three victories, two seconds and two third places. And he only missed two cuts. If there was any doubt over his credentials to finish top of the class in 2000 Stenson erased it by winning the Grand Final in Cuba by a massive five shots.

That he was given such a close fight for the Order of Merit by runner-up David Higgins speaks volumes for the Irishman, who emerged as a force after securing his first victory in the NCC Open in Sweden in June.

Speaking at the time, Higgins said: "I'm thrilled to bits. It's been a long time coming but all the hard work I put in over the winter in America is beginning to pay off. This shows I can win and if I can do so again I can finish in the top 15 at the end of the year to regain my card for the main Tour."

He didn't have to wait long. Just over a month later Higgins was back in the winner's circle after edging out Spain's Carlos Rodiles in a play-off for the Günther Hamburg Classic in Germany. The biggest first prize of the year, outside of the double-badge Buzzgolf.com North West of Ireland Open, 38,962 euro, (£24,402) hoisted the 27-year-old from Waterville top of the Rankings and confirmed his place on the main Tour.

Although Stenson took over again by winning the Gula Sidorna Grand Prix near his Malmo home in September ahead of Higgins, the two took their rivalry to the Grand Final in Cuba in November.

David Higgins

Dennis Edlu

The Perfect Drive

(Has a Beazer Home at the end of it.)

We've been building homes of outstanding quality throughout the UK for many years.

In that time we've earned a reputation for creating homes that sympathetically

reflect local character.

If you'd like to see more, visit our website at www.beazer.co.uk,

or call us on freephone 0800 413 869.

Beazer
HOMES

José Manuel Lara

Eric Carlberg

Following in the illustrious footsteps of a famous father is never easy. The offspring of such as Jack Nicklaus, Gary Player and Tony Jacklin, to name just three, have tried yet failed to hit the same dizzy heights. The expectations are huge, which is why it will be interesting to see whether Higgins can buck the trend.

Higgins's father, Liam, is not a major champion like those listed but he is still a tough act to follow. Liam has etched his name into Irish golf and been a title-winner on the European Seniors Tour. But Higgins junior has upstaged his father in one respect. He won three times on this year's European Challenge Tour, the final leg of the treble coming with the Rolex Trophy in Geneva in August.

There has been a similarity between the top two this year, and there is a parallel in their approach to the game. Both go about their golf in a quiet and clinical fashion, there are no histrionics on the course no matter what occurs, and both are keenly focused on what they want to achieve.

Stenson and Higgins apart, the 2000 European Challenge Tour was notable for the emergence of another promising Spaniard in Rodiles, the number of Swedish winners, the comeback men as well as the first time champions.

Christian Cévaër

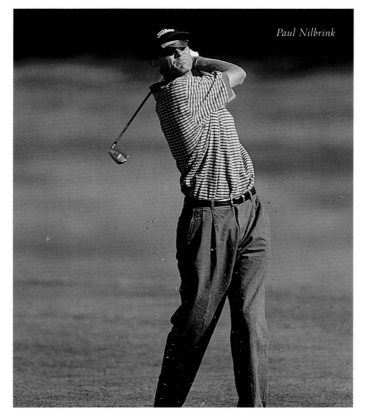

Paul Nilbrink

Rodiles, 25, from Malaga, could easily extend the line of famous Spanish golfers now that he is destined for the top level. He is basically self-taught, practises at Guadalhorce, alongside the likes of Miguel Angel Jiménez, and he underlined his potential by finishing tied seventh in both the Spanish and French Opens.

His third place on the European Challenge Tour Rankings, the highest position gained by a non-winner, was impressive with three runners-up positions, including two play-off defeats, and a fourth in 14 starts. The son of a scratch player, Carlos spent over four years at college in Florida, hence his good English, and rates the Challenge Tour as the hardest tour in the world because of the quality of play, the fact that only 50 players make the cut, and the amount of prize money. He will be a welcome addition to the European Tour.

Nine titles went to Swedes, one more than in 1999, among them Dennis Edlund, who took the San Paolo Vita Open with a closing 63, his first success in four years. But fellow countryman, Fredrik Andersson eclipsed that with the seven-year itch, his Le Touquet Challenge de France triumph being his first since 1993.

Eric Carlberg also ended a lengthy wait for another victory when he got the season underway in February with success in the Challenge

Shaun Webster of England with the Beazer Homes Challenge Tour Championship Trophy

de España at Badajoz. The young Swede had won before, back in 1994 as an amateur, so this was another notable first.

Fredrik Henge gained his first triumph in three years with victory in the Danish Open 2000 in June and followed it by taking the Formby Hall Challenge in Lancashire in September. But Alvaro Salto from Spain didn't have to wait quite so long for his return to the frame in the Credit Suisse Private Banking Open in Switzerland, his first win for two years, as were those of Christian Cévaër of France in the Finnish Masters in Helsinki, and Johan Ryström in The Costa Blanca Challenge.

Another Swede, Paul Nilbrink, was the only champion to win in successive years when he followed up his victory in the 1999 Volvo Finnish Open by taking the Norwegian Open in August.

As with most years, there were a number of players securing maiden victories, Stenson and Higgins included. Trevor Immelman, the promising young South African, won the Tusker Kenya Open in March, Richard Gillot from France took the Muermans Real Estate Challenge Open in May, fellow Frenchman Pascal Edmond triumphed in June's Aa 4th Open de Saint Omer, and yet a third Frenchman, Renaud Guillard, took the Open des Volcans in July.

And it didn't end there. Another Springbok, Jean Hugo, came out on top in the Volvo Finnish Open, England's Shaun Webster took the

Beazer Homes Challenge Tour Championship at Bowood Golf and Country Club in August, Marco Bernardini from Italy the BMW Russian Open in Moscow, while another Englishman, Kenneth Ferrie burst upon the Challenge Tour scene with a vengeance in September.

The young man from Northumberland, who spent a couple of years at college in the United States, played nine tournaments, missing five cuts, until he arrived at the Tessali Open del Sud in Italy in September. That week he found his Challenge Tour feet and claimed his first victory. To underline it wasn't a fluke, the 22-year-old from Ashington finished joint runner-up to Stenson the following week in the Gula Sidorna Grand Prix at Ljunghusens. The two performances lifted him from 105th to 18th on the rankings, underlining what can be achieved in a short space of time on the Challenge Tour.

And that is the nub of life on the Challenge Tour. Application brings success yet there are no easy answers, no short cut to the top. Everything comes through hard work and the standards continue to rise. But the European Challenge Tour is still the best way to the top and it continues to produce champions with the right credentials to boost Europe on golf's world stage.

David Hamilton

Erol Simsek

Challenge Tour Guide 2001

The European Challenge Tour is the toughest of proving grounds for new talent and each year hundreds of aspiring champions put their ambitions to the test.

It demands skill, determination, dedication and the ability to handle disappointment on the way to success but the rewards are enormous. Thomas Björn, Ignacio Garrido and Costantino Rocca have paved the way by graduating from the Challenge Tour to earn Ryder Cup honours.

Last year Lucas Parsons, a graduate from the class of 1999, burst on to the European Tour scene by winning the Greg Norman Holden International in Sydney. The Challenge Tour is without doubt a breeding ground for champions of the future.

In the year 2000 the Challenge Tour comprised of 24 tournaments visiting 15 countries from Kenya to Cuba, Russia to Spain. The leading 15 players at the end of the season gained promotion to the European Tour where they joined the likes of Darren Clarke, Colin Montgomerie, Thomas Björn, Lee Westwood, Michael Campbell and Ernie Els on the 2001 European Tour International Schedule.

The tremendous progress of the European Challenge Tour, notable achievements, updated biographies, records, and statistics are all meticulously chronicled in the illustrated 2001 European Challenge Tour Guide. It's a must for the library of every golf enthusiast.

Ordering a copy of the 2001 European Challenge Tour Guide is simple: send a cheque for £12.50 UK and Europe (which includes postage and packaging) or £17.50 for Overseas (inc postage and packaging), made payable to the PGA European Tour to Emily Doughty, Communications Division, European Tour, Wentworth Drive, Virginia Water, Surrey GU25 4LX or call +44 1344 840442 with credit card details.

EUROPEAN CHALLENGE TOUR RANKINGS

Pos	Name			Euro	Sterling Equivalent	Pos	Name			Euro	Sterling Equivalent
1	Henrik STENSON	(Swe)	(14)	108,710.95	62,948.59	51	Mark FOSTER	(Eng)	(11)	17,051.63	9,873.67
2	David HIGGINS	(Ire)	(16)	81,040.53	46,926.15	52	Mattias ELIASSON	(Swe)	(12)	16,187.32	9,373.19
3	Carlos RODILES	(Sp)	(15)	71,679.80"	41,505.87	53	Stuart LITTLE	(Eng)	(12)	15,967.05	9,245.65
4	Mikael LUNDBERG	(Swe)	(19)	71,607.84	41,464.20	54	Andrew BUTTERFIELD	(Eng)	(7)	15,812.38	9,156.09
5	Michele REALE	(It)	(19)	52,978.99"	30,677.25	55	Luis CLAVERIE	(Sp)	(15)	15,375.35	8,903.03
6	Tobias DIER	(Ger)	(14)	51,477.15	29,807.61	56	Simon KHAN	(Eng)	(9)	15,355.60	8,891.59
7	Fredrik HENGE	(Swe)	(19)	48,320.42	27,979.72	57	Scott DRUMMOND	(Scot)	(10)	15,286.38	8,851.51
8	Christian CÉVAER	(Fr)	(15)	47,653.67	27,593.64	58	Lee S JAMES	(Eng)	(19)	14,609.93	8,459.81
9	Johan RYSTRÖM	(Swe)	(17)	46,392.47	26,863.35	59	Ulrik GUSTAFSSON	(Swe)	(18)	12,694.86	7,350.90
10	Trevor IMMELMAN	(SA)	(20)	44,662.67	25,861.72	60	Graeme STORM	(Eng)	(9)	12,568.83	7,277.92
11	Jose Manuel LARA	(Sp)	(19)	43,446.03	25,157.23	61	Gianluca BARUFFALDI	(It)	(18)	12,420.51	7,192.04
12	Erol SIMSEK	(Ger)	(18)	41,152.04	23,828.90	62	Jean-François LUCQUIN	(Fr)	(19)	12,308.69	7,127.29
13	Jean HUGO	(SA)	(19)	39,241.85	22,722.82	63	Peter HANSON	(Swe)	(8)	12,162.49	7,042.64
14	Andrew RAITT	(Eng)	(12)	38,610.86	22,357.44	64	Marcello SANTI	(It)	(20)	11,924.40	6,904.77
15	Marco BERNARDINI	(It)	(17)	37,336.37	21,619.46	65	Henrik BJORNSTAD	(Nor)	(15)	11,766.36	6,813.26
16	Graham RANKIN	(Scot)	(20)	36,852.66	21,339.37	66	Richard BLAND	(Eng)	(18)	11,593.67	6,713.26
17	Shaun P WEBSTER	(Eng)	(19)	36,781.46	21,298.14	67	Miles TUNNICLIFF	(Eng)	(6)	11,239.91	6,508.42
18	Simon HURD	(Eng)	(22)	34,959.23	20,242.98	68	Marc PENDARIES	(Fr)	(19)	11,123.66	6,441.11
19	Kenneth FERRIE	(Eng)	(14)	33,047.86	19,136.21	69	Simon WAKEFIELD	(Eng)	(9)	11,062.56	6,405.73
20	Christophe POTTIER	(Fr)	(21)	32,082.72	18,577.35	70	Franck AUMONIER	(Fr)	(8)	10,969.76	6,351.99
21	Dennis EDLUND	(Swe)	(16)	31,545.07	18,266.03	71	Paul SHERMAN	(Eng)	(16)	10,323.99	5,978.06
22	Garry HOUSTON	(Wal)	(20)	31,213.50	18,074.04	72	Patrik GOTTFRIDSON	(Swe)	(18)	10,270.41	5,947.03
23	Mark PILKINGTON	(Wal)	(22)	30,812.54	17,841.86	73	Euan LITTLE	(Scot)	(13)	10,211.68	5,913.03
24	Fredrik ANDERSSON	(Swe)	(19)	30,056.25	17,403.94	74	Bjorn PETTERSSON	(Swe)	(18)	10,190.41	5,900.71
25	Adam MEDNICK	(Swe)	(19)	29,980.84	17,360.27	75	Thomas NORRET	(Den)	(19)	9,703.07	5,618.52
26	Alvaro SALTO	(Sp)	(18)	29,939.17	17,336.14	76	James HEPWORTH	(Eng)	(16)	9,686.08	5,608.68
27	Nils RORBAEK	(Den)	(21)	28,763.63	16,655.45	77	Fredrik WIDMARK	(Swe)	(17)	9,616.36	5,568.31
28	Eric CARLBERG	(Swe)	(21)	28,701.05	16,619.21	78	Francesco GUERMANI	(It)	(20)	9,495.74	5,498.47
29	Pehr MAGNEBRANT	(Swe)	(17)	27,971.66	16,196.86	79	Peter LAWRIE	(Ire)	(17)	9,097.17	5,267.68
30	Alberto BINAGHI	(It)	(15)	27,165.10	15,729.83	80	Tony EDLUND	(Swe)	(13)	8,892.02	5,148.88
31	Raimo SJÖBERG	(Swe)	(18)	26,941.55	15,600.38	81	Neil CHEETHAM	(Eng)	(10)	8,725.06	5,052.21
32	Stephen DODD	(Wal)	(19)	26,886.84	15,568.70	82	Peter HEDBLOM	(Swe)	(16)	8,652.32	5,010.09
33	Richard GILLOT	(Fr)	(16)	25,989.48	15,049.09	83	Hennie WALTERS	(SA)	(7)	8,603.11	4,981.59
34	Carlos LARRAIN	(Ven)	(17)	25,681.91	14,870.99	84	Daniel WESTERMARK	(Swe)	(9)	8,508.87	4,927.02
35	Gregory HAVRET	(Fr)	(18)	25,679.63	14,869.67	85	Francis VALERA	(Sp)	(10)	8,094.84	4,687.28
36	Pascal EDMOND	(Fr)	(20)	25,326.60	14,665.25	86	Tony CAROLAN	(Aus)	(10)	7,904.66	4,577.16
37	Federico BISAZZA	(It)	(20)	25,270.66	14,632.86	87	Chris GANE	(Eng)	(10)	7,870.23	4,557.22
38	Andrew BEAL	(Eng)	(6)	25,137.84	14,555.95	88	Grant DODD	(Aus)	(6)	7,745.88	4,485.22
39	Mårten OLANDER	(Swe)	(18)	24,805.18	14,363.33	89	Charles CHALLEN	(Eng)	(15)	7,553.31	4,373.71
40	Jesus Maria ARRUTI	(Sp)	(17)	24,396.70	14,126.80	90	Knut EKJORD	(Nor)	(13)	7,393.67	4,281.27
41	Paul NILBRINK	(Swe)	(15)	22,271.45	12,896.18	91	Francis HOWLEY	(Ire)	(7)	7,367.22	4,265.96
42	Renaud GUILLARD	(Fr)	(15)	22,182.65	12,844.76	92	Carl WATTS	(Eng)	(11)	7,340.63	4,250.56
43	Kalle BRINK	(Swe)	(17)	21,483.02	12,439.65	93	Dominique NOUAILHAC	(Fr)	(15)	7,196.71	4,167.22
44	Joakim RASK	(Swe)	(10)	21,319.06	12,344.71	94	Andreas LJUNGGREN	(Swe)	(6)	7,165.71	4,149.22
45	Mattias NILSSON	(Swe)	(17)	20,749.09	12,014.67	95	Simon D. HURLEY	(Eng)	(7)	7,089.77	4,105.30
46	Martin ERLANDSSON	(Swe)	(17)	18,813.29	10,893.75	96	Nicolas JOAKIMIDES	(Fr)	(7)	7,088.22	4,104.40
47	Robert Jan DERKSEN	(Hol)	(14)	18,598.62	10,769.45	97	Peter GUSTAFSSON	(Swe)	(17)	7,011.16	4,059.78
48	Gary CLARK	(Eng)	(18)	18,494.99	10,709.44	98	John HAWKSWORTH	(Eng)	(6)	6,905.24	3,998.45
49	Morten BACKHAUSEN	(Den)	(20)	18,392.59	10,650.15	99	Mikael PILTZ	(Fin)	(12)	6,629.88	3,839.00
50	Magnus PERSSON	(Swe)	(14)	18,092.25	10,476.24	100	Thomas HAVEMANN	(Den)	(15)	6,490.34	3,758.20

• Figures in parentheses indicate number of events played

Flirting with Danger

Pierre Fulke knew instinctively that he had just hit the shot of his life when the ball flew sweetly off the face of his five wood, travelled 215 yards to the left portion of the green and nestled softly on the surface 25 feet from the pin.

The 29-year-old Swede duly rolled in his eagle putt at the 517 yards 16th hole at Montecastillo Hotel and Golf Resort. At that precise moment, Fulke effectively won the 2000 Volvo Masters title. On the tee he had been one stroke behind Darren Clarke with three holes remaining. When he left the green the pair were level, and Clarke's bogey at the 71st hole left Fulke holding the sparkling Waterford Crystal trophy.

But for that shot of supreme precision and courage, Fulke might not have won the Volvo Masters. He might not, in consequence, have earned a place in the following week's World Golf Championships-American Express Championship. He would most certainly not have accelerated to the head of the European Ryder Cup points table.

In the event, the stocky Swede, who had missed the first six months of the 2000 campaign due to a persistent wrist injury sustained shortly after his breakthrough victory on the European Tour in the 1999 Trophée Lancôme, prevailed on the strength of that towering stroke which won Fulke the Canon Shot of the Year Award.

"It was, without question, the best shot I've hit in my career - especially under the pressure of knowing the title was on the line," he said, recalling the satisfying moment he laid one eager hand on the trophy and the other on the piece of paper made out for the amount of 575,654 euro (£333,330).

He continued: "I split the fairway with my drive and as I walked towards my ball I thought the wind was pretty much in my face and I reckoned I would need a three wood to reach the green. However I got there and realised the wind was off the left, blowing towards the water guarding the green to the right. Darren played first and laid up just short of the green. I expected him to make a birdie four from there - as he did - so I knew the worst I could afford was a birdie to match him. I wasn't really thinking 'eagle' at that stage.

"I had the perfect yardage for my five wood so I grabbed the club, and hit the shot just where I aimed, about six yards to the left of the pin. It was a dangerous shot and I knew it. I had to aim to the left because anything off-line to the right would flirt with the water, especially with the left to right wind. If I had gone in the water that would have been that.

"My mouth was dry but I knew as soon as I made contact that it was a good strike and I was on the move straight away, still watching my ball in flight but knowing it was good. It landed softly on exactly the place on the green that I wanted to hit, and the eagle putt was a bonus."

Indeed, a worthy winner of the Canon Shot of the Year and following in a long line of exquisite strokes, such as Nick Faldo's Ryder Cup-winning wedge at Oak Hill in 1995; Colin Montgomerie's driver off the fairway at the 72nd hole in the Dubai Desert Classic in 1996, Montgomerie's 18th hole tee shot in the 1997 Ryder Cup; Miguel Angel Jiménez's chip-in at the Trophée Lancôme in 1998 and Sergio Garcia's bravura six iron shot in the 1999 US PGA Championship.

Asprey & Garrard
Golfer of the Month Awards 2000

Padraig Harrington, Asprey & Garrard Golfer of the Month in October, receives a silver salver from Edward Asprey, Corporate Director of Asprey & Garrard

The Asprey & Garrard Golfer of the Month Awards are presented throughout the year followed by an annual award.
Previous winners have been:

1999 Colin Montgomerie	*1994 Ernie Els*	*1989 Nick Faldo*
1998 Lee Westwood	*1993 Bernhard Langer*	*1988 Severiano Ballesteros*
1997 Colin Montgomerie	*1992 Nick Faldo*	*1987 Ian Woosnam*
1996 Colin Montgomerie	*1991 Severiano Ballesteros*	*1986 Severiano Ballesteros*
1995 Colin Montgomerie	*1990 Nick Faldo*	*1985 Bernhard Langer*

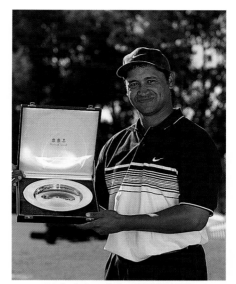

Michael Campbell – **JANUARY**

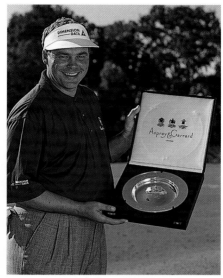

Darren Clarke – **FEBRUARY**

Roger Chapman – **MARCH**

Seve Ballesteros – **APRIL**

Colin Montgomerie – **MAY**

Lee Westwood – **JUNE**

Ernie Els – **JULY**

Thomas Björn – **AUGUST**

Eduardo Romero – **SEPTEMBER**

Meeting the Challenge

The Marquess Course 12th hole

The Marquess Course is a spectacular new addition to the renowned Woburn Golf and Country Club and joins the existing Duke's and Duchess courses to create a 54-hole complex recognised by many to be unrivalled anywhere in the United Kingdom. Designed by Peter Alliss, Clive Clark, European Golf Design (Ross McMurray) and Alex Hay, The Marquess, named after the Marquess of Tavistock, is the result of a joint venture between PGA European Tour Courses PLC, and The Bedford Estate. Constructed to international tournament standards, the course was officially opened on June 5, 2000.

At 7,200 yards, The Marquess has been designed to test the best golfers in the world and in 2001 it will host the Victor Chandler British Masters on May 31-June 3. It lies within 200 acres of mixed woodlands, overlapping the county boundary dividing Bedfordshire and Buckinghamshire. Lofty pine, beech, spruce, sweet chestnut and oak tower sentinel above a variety of testing holes which form a superb challenge as The Marquess Course moves through deep valleys and across high grounds offering glorious golfing vistas.

The history of The Marquess Course is already long and varied since, although first dreamt of in the late 1980s, it has taken more than ten years for the project to come to fruition. Some observers who have walked the course regard The Marquess as the "Augusta National of England", and there can be no question that PGA European Tour Courses have seriously added to their portfolio with the growth of Woburn Golf and Country Club in addition to the arrival of PGA Golf de Catalunya in Spain.

PGA European Tour Courses PLC

The Sarazen World Open provided a wonderful start for PGA Golf de Catalunya as a venue for European Tour events when it unfolded there in October, 1999, with Denmark's Thomas Björn taking the title and in the year 2000 Brian Davis rose to the challenge by winning the Peugeot Open de España on this outstanding course.

PGA Golf de Catalunya, lying 45 minutes north east of Barcelona in the La Selva region, close to Girona, was designed by Neil Coles and Angel Gallardo, in association with European Golf Design, two men with illustrious playing careers on the European Tour and with equally illustrious credentials as golf course architects. Between them they have created a very special golfers' haven on land dense with cork, oak and pine trees, with the mountains of Montseny to the west and vistas of the Pyrenees to the north. Overall, the course measures 7,204 yards from the back tees.

The Marquess Course 9th hole

PGA Golf de Catalunya is destined to take its place as one of the finest golf resorts in Europe. It has full clubhouse facilities, bar and restaurant, a driving range, putting greens and a golf academy. The opening marked the completion of the first stage of the plan which incorporates a second golf course, a 200-room hotel, and residential villas.

Meanwhile, PGA European Tour Courses continues to expand and is in discussion with a number of UK and European projects. The latest of these to come to fruition was the opening of a new resort in Germany in May 2000, "Fleesensee Golf and Country Club", also designed by European Golf Design, where the American Jeff Van Wagenen won the Tui Golf Championship Fleesensee on the European Seniors Tour in September.

PGA European Tour Courses is uniquely placed for the ownership, development and management of golf courses that can host professional tournaments under the auspices of the European Tour.

The aim of the Company is to expand and develop golf facilities throughout Europe that not only provide a championship test for professionals but also offer outstanding amenities for the visiting golfer. This philosophy is implemented at their five flagship courses. Kungsängen in Sweden, Quinta do Lago in Portugal, Woburn Golf and Country Club and PGA Golf de Catalunya.

The Marquess Course 6th hole

The policy of expansion and development that underlines PGA European Tour Courses's approach has been further emphasised by Ken Schofield, Executive Director of the European Tour. He summarises: "The development of European Tour Courses signifies our desire on entering the 21st Century to build a strong portfolio of courses and also to design and refine our own courses for Tour competition. This will support our policy to provide the best possible courses for play on the European Tour, the European Seniors Tour and the European Challenge Tour. PGA Golf de Catalunya is a case in point; the newest course in the portfolio, designed by Neil Coles, Angel Gallardo and European Golf Design, and set on undulating land. We feel confident it challenges the best players in the world and we feel the same about The Marquess Course at Woburn Golf and Country Club."

Mitchell Platts

The Marquess Course 15th hole

PGA GOLF DE CATALUNYA

Quinta do Lago

AXA
PERFORMANCE DATA℠

FOR THE 2000 EUROPEAN TOUR SEASON

STROKE AVERAGE

1	Lee WESTWOOD (Eng)	(85)	69.62
2	Ernie ELS (SA)	(36)	69.67
3	Michael CAMPBELL (NZ)	(73)	70.25
4	Colin MONTGOMERIE (Scot)	(85)	70.26
5	Darren CLARKE (N.Ire)	(82)	70.29
6	Padraig HARRINGTON (Ire)	(81)	70.33
7	Pierre FULKE (Swe)	(57)	70.51
8	Eduardo ROMERO (Arg)	(87)	70.69
9	Thomas BJÖRN (Den)	(93)	70.74
10	Gary ORR (Scot)	(94)	70.76
11	Phillip PRICE (Wal)	(94)	70.79
12	Angel CABRERA (Arg)	(89)	70.88
	José COCERES (Arg)	(75)	70.88
14	Sergio GARCIA (Sp)	(47)	70.89
15	Adam SCOTT (Aus)	(37)	70.92
16	Bernhard LANGER (Ger)	(76)	70.95
17	Paul MCGINLEY (Ire)	(94)	70.97
18	José Maria OLAZÁBAL (Sp)	(74)	71.00
19	Carlos RODILES (Sp)	(24)	71.08
20	Retief GOOSEN (SA)	(82)	71.11
21	Steen TINNING (Den)	(89)	71.17
22	Fredrik JACOBSON (Swe)	(72)	71.22
23	Miguel Angel MARTIN (Sp)	(78)	71.24
24	Des TERBLANCHE (SA)	(47)	71.26
	Nick O'HERN (Aus)	(82)	71.26
26	Andrew COLTART (Scot)	(97)	71.32
	Per-Ulrik JOHANSSON (Swe)	(65)	71.32
28	Paul LAWRIE (Scot)	(60)	71.33
29	Patrik SJÖLAND (Swe)	(74)	71.34
30	Mark MCNULTY (Zim)	(62)	71.37
31	Miguel Angel JIMÉNEZ (Sp)	(63)	71.40
32	Anders HANSEN (Den)	(97)	71.41
33	Dean ROBERTSON (Scot)	(78)	71.44
34	Roger CHAPMAN (Eng)	(96)	71.45
	Ricardo GONZALEZ (Arg)	(87)	71.45
	Steve WEBSTER (Eng)	(77)	71.45
37	Peter O'MALLEY (Aus)	(76)	71.47
38	Stephen LEANEY (Aus)	(73)	71.49
39	Ross DRUMMOND (Scot)	(24)	71.50
40	Greg OWEN (Eng)	(93)	71.52
41	Ian WOOSNAM (Wal)	(83)	71.53
42	Anthony WALL (Eng)	(73)	71.55
43	Mathias GRÖNBERG (Swe)	(98)	71.58
44	Santiago LUNA (Sp)	(87)	71.60
	Paolo QUIRICI (Swi)	(75)	71.60
	Ian GARBUTT (Eng)	(95)	71.60
47	Soren HANSEN (Den)	(93)	71.61
	Peter MITCHELL (Eng)	(83)	71.61
49	Brian DAVIS (Eng)	(87)	71.63
50	Joakim HAEGGMAN (Swe)	(67)	71.64
	Olle KARLSSON (Swe)	(42)	71.64
52	Roger WESSELS (SA)	(91)	71.65
53	Jamie SPENCE (Eng)	(64)	71.66
54	Alastair FORSYTH (Scot)	(101)	71.71
	Roger WINCHESTER (Eng)	(91)	71.71
56	Niclas FASTH (Swe)	(72)	71.72
57	John BICKERTON (Eng)	(96)	71.73
	Jarmo SANDELIN (Swe)	(89)	71.73
	Robert KARLSSON (Swe)	(56)	71.73
60	Ignacio GARRIDO (Sp)	(78)	71.76
	Christopher HANELL (Swe)	(89)	71.76
62	Ian POULTER (Eng)	(92)	71.78
63	Alex CEJKA (Ger)	(61)	71.79
	Jean VAN DE VELDE (Fr)	(47)	71.79
65	Mark MOULAND (Wal)	(55)	71.82
66	Brett RUMFORD (Aus)	(36)	71.83
67	Carl SUNESON (Sp)	(80)	71.84
68	Henrik NYSTROM (Swe)	(50)	71.86
69	Alberto BINAGHI (It)	(34)	71.88
70	Soren KJELDSEN (Den)	(106)	71.90
	David LYNN (Eng)	(91)	71.90
	Jorge BERENDT (Arg)	(72)	71.90
73	Stephen GALLACHER (Scot)	(95)	71.92
74	Jarrod MOSELEY (Aus)	(80)	71.93
	Thomas GÖGELE (Ger)	(94)	71.93
76	Nicolas VANHOOTEGEM (Bel)	(84)	71.94
77	Emanuele CANONICA (It)	(67)	71.96
78	David PARK (Wal)	(101)	71.99
79	Andrew OLDCORN (Scot)	(62)	72.00
80	David CARTER (Eng)	(79)	72.01
81	Peter BAKER (Eng)	(96)	72.03
82	Sam TORRANCE (Scot)	(65)	72.06
83	Greg TURNER (NZ)	(58)	72.07
	Tony JOHNSTONE (Zim)	(70)	72.07
85	David HOWELL (Eng)	(92)	72.09
86	Geoff OGILVY (Aus)	(62)	72.10
87	Gary EVANS (Eng)	(83)	72.12
88	Andrew MCLARDY (SA)	(95)	72.13
89	Des SMYTH (Ire)	(73)	72.14
90	Raphaël JACQUELIN (Fr)	(87)	72.15
	José RIVERO (Sp)	(72)	72.15
	Lian-Wei ZHANG (PRC)	(26)	72.15
93	Olivier EDMOND (Fr)	(63)	72.16
	Peter LONARD (Aus)	(73)	72.16
95	Tom GILLIS (USA)	(75)	72.17
96	Richard GREEN (Aus)	(76)	72.18
97	Gordon BRAND JNR. (Scot)	(72)	72.22
98	Stephen ALLAN (Aus)	(75)	72.23
	David GILFORD (Eng)	(64)	72.23
100	Sven STRÜVER (Ger)	(79)	72.24

( ) = rounds played

DRIVING ACCURACY (%)

1	Richard GREEN (Aus)	(76)	79.5
2	José COCERES (Arg)	(71)	78.7
3	John BICKERTON (Eng)	(96)	78.0
4	Gary ORR (Scot)	(90)	76.3
5	Pierre FULKE (Swe)	(53)	75.6
6	Andrew OLDCORN (Scot)	(62)	73.4
7	Peter O'MALLEY (Aus)	(76)	73.1
8	Mark MCNULTY (Zim)	(62)	72.5
9	Anders HANSEN (Den)	(97)	72.3
10	Miguel Angel JIMÉNEZ (Sp)	(59)	72.0
11	Simon WAKEFIELD (Eng)	(50)	71.8
12	Jean-Francois REMESY (Fr)	(73)	71.5
13	John SENDEN (Aus)	(76)	71.5
14	Paul EALES (Eng)	(84)	71.0
15	Jorge BERENDT (Arg)	(72)	70.4
16	Nick O'HERN (Aus)	(82)	70.2
17	Greg OWEN (Eng)	(93)	69.9
18	Ian GARBUTT (Eng)	(95)	69.7
19	Colin MONTGOMERIE (Scot)	(81)	69.7
20	Gary MURPHY (Ire)	(86)	69.6

DRIVING DISTANCE (YARDS)

1	Emanuele CANONICA (It)	(67)	295.3
2	Angel CABRERA (Arg)	(85)	293.5
3	Adam SCOTT (Aus)	(37)	292.4
4	Ricardo GONZALEZ (Arg)	(87)	291.4
5	Stephen ALLAN (Aus)	(75)	290.5
6	Alberto BINAGHI (It)	(34)	290.2
7	Sergio GARCIA (Sp)	(43)	287.9
8	Paolo QUIRICI (Swi)	(75)	287.0
9	Mattias ELIASSON (Swe)	(28)	286.0
10	Carl SUNESON (Sp)	(80)	285.8
11	Des TERBLANCHE (SA)	(47)	285.1
12	Geoff OGILVY (Aus)	(62)	285.0
13	Stephen GALLACHER (Scot)	(95)	284.9
14	Ivo GINER (Sp)	(62)	283.9
15	Mathias GRÖNBERG (Swe)	(94)	283.5
16	Ignacio GARRIDO (Sp)	(78)	283.4
	Lee WESTWOOD (Eng)	(81)	283.4
18	Kevin CARISSIMI (USA)	(38)	283.2
19	Greg OWEN (Eng)	(93)	282.4
	Thomas GÖGELE (Ger)	(94)	282.4

SAND SAVES (%)

1	Tony JOHNSTONE (Zim)	(70)	78.9
2	Ian HUTCHINGS (SA)	(67)	77.9
3	Mark MOULAND (Wal)	(55)	77.8
4	John SENDEN (Aus)	(76)	71.2
5	Bernhard LANGER (Ger)	(72)	70.6
6	Gustavo ROJAS (Arg)	(68)	70.1
7	José Maria OLAZÁBAL (Sp)	(70)	69.8
8	Miguel Angel MARTIN (Sp)	(78)	68.2
9	David PARK (Wal)	(101)	67.5
10	Pierre FULKE (Swe)	(53)	66.2
11	Seve BALLESTEROS (Sp)	(43)	65.2
12	Alberto BINAGHI (It)	(34)	64.3
13	Nick O'HERN (Aus)	(82)	63.3
	Jorge BERENDT (Arg)	(72)	63.3
15	Sergio GARCIA (Sp)	(43)	63.0
16	Raymond RUSSELL (Scot)	(85)	62.2
17	Jean VAN DE VELDE (Fr)	(47)	61.7
	Daniel CHOPRA (Swe)	(32)	61.7
19	Ian POULTER (Eng)	(92)	61.5
	Paolo QUIRICI (Swi)	(75)	61.5

GREENS IN REGULATION (%)

1	Gary ORR (Scot)	(90)	77.8
2	Colin MONTGOMERIE (Scot)	(81)	77.1
3	José COCERES (Arg)	(71)	76.4
4	Ian GARBUTT (Eng)	(95)	74.4
5	Greg OWEN (Eng)	(93)	74.3
6	Padraig HARRINGTON (Ire)	(77)	74.0
7	John SENDEN (Aus)	(76)	73.6
8	Angel CABRERA (Arg)	(85)	73.3
9	Miguel Angel JIMÉNEZ (Sp)	(59)	73.1
10	Andrew COLTART (Scot)	(93)	73.0
	Retief GOOSEN (SA)	(78)	73.0
12	Gary MURPHY (Ire)	(86)	72.2
	Thomas LEVET (Fr)	(94)	72.2
14	Bernhard LANGER (Ger)	(72)	72.1
15	Peter O'MALLEY (Aus)	(76)	71.7
	Peter BAKER (Eng)	(96)	71.7
17	Sergio GARCIA (Sp)	(43)	71.6
18	John BICKERTON (Eng)	(96)	71.4
	Eduardo ROMERO (Arg)	(83)	71.4
20	Mats LANNER (Swe)	(67)	71.3

Lee Westwood

Richard Green

Emanuele Canonica

Tony Johnstone

Gary Orr

AVERAGE PUTTS PER ROUND

1	Lee WESTWOOD (Eng)	(81)	28.4
2	Daniel CHOPRA (Swe)	(32)	28.5
	Pierre FULKE (Swe)	(53)	28.5
	Jamie SPENCE (Eng)	(64)	28.5
5	Michael CAMPBELL (NZ)	(69)	28.6
6	Paul LAWRIE (Scot)	(60)	28.7
	Peter SENIOR (Aus)	(40)	28.7
8	Jeev Milkha SINGH (Ind)	(32)	28.8
	Dean ROBERTSON (Scot)	(78)	28.8
	Brian Davis (Eng)	(87)	28.8
	Phillip PRICE (Wal)	(90)	28.8
	Sam TORRANCE (Scot)	(65)	28.8
	Raymond RUSSELL (Scot)	(85)	28.8
	Russell CLAYDON (Eng)	(71)	28.8
15	Des TERBLANCHE (SA)	(47)	28.9
	Fredrik JACOBSON (Swe)	(72)	28.9
	Nick O'HERN (Aus)	(82)	28.9
18	Jean VAN DE VELDE (Fr)	(47)	29.0
	Derrick COOPER (Eng)	(28)	29.0
	Joakim HAEGGMAN (Swe)	(67)	29.0

PUTTS PER GREEN IN REGULATION

1	Lee WESTWOOD (Eng)	(81)	1.718
2	Michael CAMPBELL (NZ)	(69)	1.719
3	Pierre FULKE (Swe)	(53)	1.726
4	Jamie SPENCE (Eng)	(64)	1.741
5	Phillip PRICE (Wal)	(90)	1.743
6	Padraig HARRINGTON (Ire)	(77)	1.746
7	Des TERBLANCHE (SA)	(47)	1.753
	Jarmo SANDELIN (Swe)	(89)	1.753
9	Brian DAVIS (Eng)	(87)	1.755
	Fredrik JACOBSON (Swe)	(72)	1.755
11	Darren CLARKE (N.Ire)	(78)	1.756
12	Jean VAN DE VELDE (Fr)	(47)	1.762
13	Paul LAWRIE (Scot)	(60)	1.763
14	Dean ROBERTSON (Scot)	(78)	1.767
	José Maria OLAZÁBAL (Sp)	(70)	1.767
16	Olle KARLSSON (Swe)	(42)	1.769
17	Daniel CHOPRA (Swe)	(32)	1.770
	Raymond RUSSELL (Scot)	(85)	1.770
	Paul MCGINLEY (Ire)	(90)	1.770
20	Nick O'HERN (Aus)	(82)	1.771

Volvo Order of Merit

2000

Pos	Name & Country		Total Prize Money		Pos	Name & Country		Total Prize Money	
			€	£				€	£
1	Lee WESTWOOD (Eng)	(23)	3,125,146.81	1,858,602.30	26	Paul LAWRIE (Scot)	(19)	512,054.65	304,531.59
2	Darren CLARKE (N.Ire)	(22)	2,717,965.21	1,616,441.33	27	Emanuele CANONICA (It)	(21)	507,191.56	301,639.39
3	Ernie ELS (SA)	(11)	2,017,247.51	1,199,707.10	28	Stephen LEANEY (Aus)	(21)	483,127.60	287,327.96
4	Michael CAMPBELL (NZ)	(21)	1,993,550.31	1,185,613.80	29	Brian DAVIS (Eng)	(26)	465,335.91	276,746.80
5	Thomas BJÖRN (Den)	(27)	1,929,656.91	1,147,614.81	30	Steen TINNING (Den)	(26)	455,588.49	270,949.77
6	Colin MONTGOMERIE (Scot)	(23)	1,740,916.72	1,035,366.33	# 31	Ian POULTER (Eng)	(28)	447,506.65	266,143.30
7	Padraig HARRINGTON (Ire)	(24)	1,350,920.92	803,426.16	32	Jean VAN DE VELDE (Fr)	(13)	419,318.22	249,378.94
8	Phillip PRICE (Wal)	(26)	1,331,590.88	791,930.11	# 33	Roger CHAPMAN (Eng)	(28)	389,821.97	231,836.79
9	José Maria OLAZABAL (Sp)	(21)	1,174,564.39	698,542.56	34	Ricardo GONZALEZ (Arg)	(26)	386,107.45	229,627.67
10	Gary ORR (Scot)	(26)	1,009,472.91	600,358.57	35	Roger WESSELS (SA)	(31)	385,724.95	229,400.19
11	Miguel Angel JIMÉNEZ (Sp)	(19)	1,004,467.45	597,381.69	36	Jamie SPENCE (Eng)	(20)	375,755.30	223,470.99
12	Pierre FULKE (Swe)	(16)	983,078.26	584,661.01	~ 37	Lucas PARSONS (Aus)	(22)	368,367.30	219,077.17
13	José COCERES (Arg)	(21)	939,807.28	558,926.69	38	Jarmo SANDELIN (Swe)	(26)	366,178.36	217,775.35
14	Angel CABRERA (Arg)	(26)	934,349.05	555,680.54	39	Greg OWEN (Eng)	(28)	364,877.91	217,001.94
15	Retief GOOSEN (SA)	(24)	892,759.15	530,946.00	40	David HOWELL (Eng)	(30)	344,312.34	204,771.08
16	Eduardo ROMERO (Arg)	(23)	816,440.44	485,557.37	41	Peter SENIOR (Aus)	(13)	341,862.03	203,313.82
17	Andrew COLTART (Scot)	(28)	800,990.24	476,368.75	42	Nick O'HERN (Aus)	(22)	337,438.74	200,683.18
18	Paul MCGINLEY (Ire)	(26)	769,088.46	457,395.97	43	Ignacio GARRIDO (Sp)	(24)	336,249.00	199,975.62
19	Bernhard LANGER (Ger)	(22)	759,902.62	451,932.93	# 44	Anthony WALL (Eng)	(24)	330,458.60	196,531.92
20	Mathias GRÖNBERG (Swe)	(29)	620,697.13	369,143.97	# 45	Niclas FASTH (Swe)	(22)	322,756.87	191,951.51
21	Sergio GARCIA (Sp)	(13)	599,240.94	356,383.44	46	Alastair FORSYTH (Scot)	(30)	317,562.65	188,862.38
22	Per-Ulrik JOHANSSON (Swe)	(20)	576,022.89	342,575.09	47	Peter O'MALLEY (Aus)	(22)	317,192.72	188,642.37
23	Patrik SJOLAND (Swe)	(24)	573,743.94	341,219.74	48	Geoff OGILVY (Aus)	(20)	313,183.40	186,257.93
24	Ian WOOSNAM (Wal)	(24)	556,004.28	330,669.53	49	Mark MCNULTY (Zim)	(19)	309,770.10	184,227.96
# 25	Fredrik JACOBSON (Swe)	(23)	541,505.80	322,046.92	50	Dean ROBERTSON (Scot)	(23)	302,522.62	179,917.70

Dean Robertson

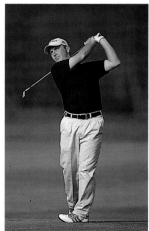

Ian Garbutt

Mark McNulty

Paul Lawrie

Peter O'Malley

Ricardo Gonzalez

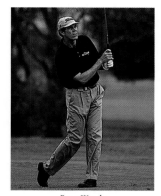

Roger Wessels

Stephen Gallacher

Pos	Name & Country		Total Prize Money	
			€	£
51	Gordon BRAND JNR. (Scot)	(24)	290,209.33	172,594.68
52	Miguel Angel MARTIN (Sp)	(23)	285,810.40	169,978.53
53	Anders HANSEN (Den)	(28)	283,770.45	168,765.32
54	Richard GREEN (Aus)	(26)	274,896.99	163,488.05
55	Ian GARBUTT (Eng)	(31)	272,589.03	162,115.45
56	Stephen GALLACHER (Scot)	(28)	267,154.69	158,883.52
57	Peter BAKER (Eng)	(29)	259,086.24	154,085.01
58	Rolf MUNTZ (Hol)	(21)	256,966.46	152,824.32
59	Jonathan LOMAS (Eng)	(31)	254,902.06	151,596.57
~ 60	Carl SUNESON (Sp)	(25)	232,535.07	138,294.37
61	Stephen ALLAN (Aus)	(24)	230,937.48	137,344.24
62	John BICKERTON (Eng)	(29)	230,391.01	137,019.25
# 63	David LYNN (Eng)	(26)	228,224.75	135,730.92
64	Raymond RUSSELL (Scot)	(26)	227,736.63	135,440.62
65	Christopher HANELL (Swe)	(27)	226,932.88	134,962.61
66	Soren KJELDSEN (Den)	(32)	221,699.44	131,850.15
~ 67	Markus BRIER (Aut)	(27)	216,317.80	128,649.56
68	David PARK (Wal)	(31)	214,782.70	127,736.60
69	Steve WEBSTER (Eng)	(23)	212,930.28	126,634.92
70	Alex CEJKA (Ger)	(18)	211,117.01	125,556.52
71	John SENDEN (Aus)	(25)	208,023.59	123,716.79
72	Peter MITCHELL (Eng)	(26)	206,846.09	123,016.50
73	Soren HANSEN (Den)	(28)	204,727.95	121,756.79
74	Tony JOHNSTONE (Zim)	(22)	200,199.66	119,063.70
75	Van PHILLIPS (Eng)	(29)	198,297.00	117,932.14
76	David CARTER (Eng)	(24)	196,764.69	117,020.84
77	Jarrod MOSELEY (Aus)	(24)	196,081.90	116,614.77
78	Paolo QUIRICI (Swi)	(25)	194,128.33	115,452.93
79	Santiago LUNA (Sp)	(26)	193,101.46	114,842.23
80	Raphaël JACQUELIN (Fr)	(30)	192,568.18	114,525.07
81	Thomas GÖGELE (Ger)	(30)	188,840.54	112,308.15
82	Roger WINCHESTER (Eng)	(29)	188,361.76	112,023.41
# 83	Tom GILLIS (USA)	(25)	187,425.63	111,466.67
84	Greg TURNER (NZ)	(20)	187,239.38	111,355.90
~ 85	Maarten LAFEBER (Hol)	(30)	186,601.88	110,976.76
86	Gary EVANS (Eng)	(29)	185,983.20	110,608.82
87	Sam TORRANCE (Scot)	(19)	180,602.75	107,408.93
88	Thomas LEVET (Fr)	(30)	179,659.31	106,847.85
89	Jean-Francois REMESY (Fr)	(24)	178,388.56	106,092.10
90	Mark JAMES (Eng)	(15)	178,139.56	105,944.01
91	Andrew MCLARDY (SA)	(30)	174,207.03	103,605.24
92	Andrew OLDCORN (Scot)	(22)	165,571.95	98,469.74
93	Marc FARRY (Fr)	(26)	158,744.88	94,409.52
94	Peter LONARD (Aus)	(23)	155,404.45	92,422.88
95	Wayne RILEY (Aus)	(30)	154,853.75	92,095.36
# 96	Richard S JOHNSON (Swe)	(24)	154,758.23	92,038.56
97	Gary EMERSON (Eng)	(30)	150,274.17	89,371.77
# 98	Nicolas VANHOOTEGEM (Bel)	(25)	149,505.02	88,914.34
99	Sven STRÜVER (Ger)	(25)	149,073.54	88,657.73
✱ 100	Des TERBLANCHE (SA)	(14)	148,386.75	88,249.28

Pos	Name & Country		Total Prize Money	
			€	£
101	Wei-Tze YEH (Taiwan)	(11)	147,138.90	87,507.15
✱ 102	Adam SCOTT (Aus)	(11	146,119.39	86,900.82
103	Barry LANE (Eng)	(22)	145,450.35	86,502.93
104	Joakim HAEGGMAN (Swe)	(21)	144,104.98	85,702.80
105	Francisco CEA (Sp)	(27)	143,695.54	85,459.30
106	Diego BORREGO (Sp)	(28)	142,274.94	84,614.43
~ 107	Bradley DREDGE (Wal)	(28)	141,202.93	83,976.88
# 108	Henrik NYSTROM (Swe)	(16)	140,746.36	83,705.35
109	Olivier EDMOND (Fr)	(20)	135,744.81	80,730.80
110	Massimo SCARPA (It)	(27)	135,001.25	80,288.59
111	Des SMYTH (Ire)	(25)	133,402.29	79,337.65
112	Paul EALES (Eng)	(27)	132,905.54	79,042.22
113	José RIVERO (Sp)	(23)	123,821.36	73,639.63
114	Robert KARLSSON (Swe)	(18)	122,944.93	73,118.40
#~ 115	Daren LEE (Eng)	(25)	122,327.06	72,750.94
116	Mark DAVIS (Eng)	(24)	120,604.00	71,726.19
117	Rodger DAVIS (Aus)	(20)	118,046.63	70,205.26
118	Jorge BERENDT (Arg)	(24)	116,257.50	69,141.22
119	David GILFORD (Eng)	(19)	116,059.54	69,023.49
~ 120	Johan SKOLD (Swe)	(32)	112,749.91	67,055.17
~ 121	Gustavo ROJAS (Arg)	(23)	110,539.64	65,740.66
# 122	Justin ROSE (Eng)	(29)	108,821.96	64,719.12
# 123	Robert COLES (Eng)	(26)	107,383.68	63,863.74
124	Craig HAINLINE (USA)	(22)	101,261.12	60,222.50
125	Russell CLAYDON (Eng)	(26)	101,189.96	60,180.18
# 126	Matthew BLACKEY (Eng)	(23)	101,189.33	60,179.80
~ 127	Iain PYMAN (Eng)	(30)	101,019.60	60,078.86
# 128	Malcolm MACKENZIE (Eng)	(29)	100,199.72	59,591.26
129	Jeremy ROBINSON (Eng)	(31)	98,431.91	58,539.90
130	Olle KARLSSON (Swe)	(13)	98,123.89	58,356.71
131	Fredrik LINDGREN (Swe)	(28)	97,446.49	57,953.84
# 132	Massimo FLORIOLI (It)	(27)	94,285.45	56,073.89
133	Nic HENNING (SA)	(11)	92,200.39	54,833.86
134	Mark MOULAND (Wal)	(17)	92,178.86	54,821.05
~ 135	Hennie OTTO (SA)	(30)	92,106.21	54,777.85
# 136	Gary MURPHY (Ire)	(28)	89,011.82	52,937.54
137	Eamonn DARCY (Ire)	(24)	88,911.05	52,877.61
$ 138	Carlos RODILES (Sp)	(6)	86,436.13	51,405.71
✱ 139	Lian-Wei ZHANG (PRC)	(7)	84,469.70	50,236.22
~ 140	Benoit TEILLERIA (Fr)	(29)	81,865.17	48,687.25
141	Paul AFFLECK (Wal)	(26)	80,610.96	47,941.34
# 142	Peter FOWLER (Aus)	(29)	77,423.92	46,045.92
✱ 143	Brett RUMFORD (Aus)	(11)	76,992.59	45,789.40
~ 144	Knud STORGAARD (Den)	(29)	71,888.54	42,753.90
145	Jeev Milkha SINGH (Ind)	(13)	68,199.26	40,559.79
# 146	Scott ROWE (USA)	(22)	68,152.30	40,531.86
147	Robin BYRD (USA)	(28)	67,873.67	40,366.15
# 148	Elliot BOULT (NZ)	(23)	67,567.18	40,183.88
✱ 149	Kyi Hla HAN (Myan)	(10)	66,515.86	39,558.63
150	Per NYMAN (Swe)	(31)	66,027.51	39,268.20

$ = 2000 Challenge Tour Members   ✱ = Affiliated Member

= Qualifying School Graduates   ~ = Challenge Graduates

 Figures in parentheses indicate number of events played

The European Tour

(A COMPANY LIMITED BY GUARANTEE)

BOARD OF DIRECTORS

N C Coles, MBE *Chairman*

A Gallardo, *Vice Chairman*	M H James (alternate K J Brown)	J E O'Leary
D Cooper	D Jones	R Rafferty
B Gallacher, OBE	T A Horton, MBE	D J Russell

Sir Michael F Bonallack, Kt, OBE *(non Executive Director)*

P A T Davidson *(non Executive Director)*

K S Owen *(non Executive Director)*

TOURNAMENT COMMITTEE

M H James (Eng), *Chairman*

M Lanner (Swe), *Vice Chairman*

A Binaghi (It)

R Chapman (Eng)

R Claydon (Eng)

D Cooper (Eng)

P Eales (Eng)

A Forsbrand (Swe)

B Langer (Ger)

R Lee (Eng)

C Montgomerie MBE (Scot)

O Sellberg (Swe)

J Spence (Eng)

S Torrance, MBE (Scot)

J Van de Velde (Fr)

EXECUTIVE MANAGEMENT

Executive Director	K D Schofield CBE
Deputy Executive Director	G C O'Grady
General Counsel	M D Friend
Assistant to Executive Director and Ryder Cup Director	R G Hills
Group Marketing Director	S F Kelly
Director of Communications and Public Relations	M S Platts
Director of Tour Operations	D W Garland
Assistant Director of Tour Operations	D A Probyn
Chief Referee	J N Paramor
Senior Referee and Qualifying School Director	A N McFee
Managing Director, European Seniors Tour	K A Stubbs
Deputy Managing Director, European Seniors Tour	P Adams
Director of International Policy	K Waters
European Challenge Tour Director	A de Soultrait
Group Company Secretary	M Bray
Senior Tournament Director	M R Stewart
Director of Tournament Services	E Kitson
Director of Tournament Development	J Birkmyre
Group Finance Planner	J Orr
Director/Player Liaison	M MacDiarmid
Director of IT and New Media	M Lichtenhein

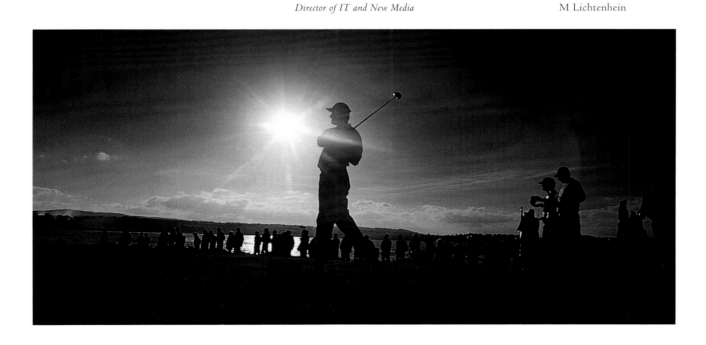

The Contributors

Mike Aitken *(The Scotsman)*
Standard Life Loch Lomond
Alfred Dunhill Cup

Colin Callander
European Seniors Tour

Jeremy Chapman *(Racing Post)*
Victor Chandler British Masters

Bruce Critchley *(Sky Sports)*
The Eurobet Seve Ballesteros Trophy

Norman Dabell
Novotel Perrier Open de France
Belgacom Open
BBVA Open Turespaña Masters Comunidad de
Madrid

Bill Elliott *(The Observer/Today's Golfer)*
The Compass Group English Open
Volvo Order of Merit Winner

David Facey *(The Sun)*
Canon European Masters

Andy Farrell *(The Independent)*
US Open Championship

Alan Fraser *(Daily Mail)*
US PGA Championship

Mark Garrod *(Press Association)*
Volvo Masters

Tim Glover *(Independent on Sunday)*
The Celtic Manor Resort Wales Open

David Hamilton
European Challenge Tour

Martin Hardy *(Daily Express)*
Dubai Desert Classic

Alan Hedley *(The Journal)*
Compaq European Grand Prix

John Hopkins *(The Times)*
WGC - NEC Invitational

John Huggan *(Golf World US)*
Deutsche Bank - SAP Open TPC of Europe

Renton Laidlaw *(The Golf Channel)*
Heineken Classic
Greg Norman Holden International

Jock MacVicar *(Scottish Daily Express)*
Scottish PGA Championship

Lewine Mair *(Daily Telegraph)*
Benson and Hedges International Open

Michael McDonnell
The Year in Retrospect
Volvo PGA Championship
Murphy's Irish Open
129th Open Golf Championship

Charlie Mulqueen *(Irish Examiner)*
Buzzgolf.com North West of Ireland Open

Graham Otway *(Sunday Business)*
Trophée Lancôme

Mitchell Platts *(European Tour)*
Johnnie Walker Classic
Masters Tournament
WGC - American Express Championship
WGC - EMC World Cup
The Ryder Cup 2001
European Tour Courses

Gordon Richardson
TNT Dutch Open
Linde German Masters

Gordon Simpson *(European Tour)*
Alfred Dunhill Championship
Mercedes-Benz - SA Open Championship
Benson and Hedges Malaysian Open
WGC - Andersen Consulting Match Play
Brazil Sao Paulo 500 Years Open
Moroccan Open Méditel
Canon Shot of the Year

Colm Smith *(Irish Independent)*
Smurfit European Open

Mel Webb *(The Times)*
Qatar Masters
Brazil Rio de Janeiro 500 Years Open
Peugeot Open de España
Volvo Scandinavian Masters
BMW International Open
Italian Open

John Whitbread *(Surrey Herald)*
Cisco World Match Play Championship

Roddy Williams *(European Tour)*
Algarve Portuguese Open
Madeira Island Open

The Photographers

Scott Barbour/Allsport
38 top, 43 top, 44

Simon Bruty/Allsport
316

David Cannon/Allsport
8 bottom, 10 top, 13 bottom, 15 top,
16 top, 18-23, 66-67, 68 top, 69 top,
70 top, 96, 99-100, 103 bottom, 104
bottom, 105 top, 129 top, 130, 140
top, 141 top, 162, 163 bottom, 164,
165 top, 166, 192-193, 198 bottom,
220, 222, 224-225, 246-250, 276, 278
bottom, 280, 312-313, 320-324, 327,
328, 348, 366, Back cover

Phil Cole/Allsport
343 bottom, 349 top

Michael Cooper/Allsport
175, 176 bottom, 178 top, 179, 331
bottom, 335, 341

Jon Ferrey/Allsport
165 bottom, 167

Stuart Hannagan/Allsport
36, 37, 39, 40

Harry How/Allsport
12, 21 top, 60, 61 bottom, 62 top, 223
top, 231-234

Phil Inglis Photography
2, 330, 331 top, 332, 334, 336-337,
338 top, 340, 360-361

Craig Jones/Allsport
61 top, 62 bottom, 63, 97-98, 367

Ross Kinnaird/Allsport
144 bottom

Warren Little/Allsport
69 bottom

Andy Lyons/Allsport
221

Bob Martin/Allsport
317

Donald Miralle/Allsport
64, 223 bottom, 230

Stephen Munday/Allsport
1, 9 bottom, 11, bottom, 54-58, 78-82,
102, 103 top, 104 top, 114-118, 128,
129 bottom, 138,140 bottom, 141
bottom, 146-147, 150-154, 180-184,
198 top, 214-218 236-239, 288-289,
290 top, 291 top, 292, 293, 301, 314,
329 top, 339, 342, 344, 350-351, 368

Terry O'Neill/Golf World
Front cover

Dave Pillinger/Allsport
38 bottom

Adam Pretty/Allsport
42, 43 bottom, 45-47

Andrew Redington/Allsport
6-7, 8 bottom, 17 top, 68 bottom, 70
bottom, 71, 72-76, 120-24, 126-127,
174, 176-177, 178 bottom, 211
bottom, 226-229, 142 top, 144 top,
145, 187 bottom, 188 bottom, 189 top,
190, 194, 196 bottom, 197, 199
bottom, 258-263, 270-273, 274
bottom, 275, 277, 278 top, 279, 294-
300, 302-304, 306-311, 326, 329
bottom, 343 top, 345 top, 346, 349
bottom, 352, 358-359, 368

Dave Rogers/Allsport
11 top, 202-207

Paul Severn/Allsport
9 top, 10 bottom, 13 top, 14, 15
bottom, 16 bottom, 17 bottom, 24-28,
30-35, 48-52, 84-88, 90-94, 105
bottom, 106, 108-113, 132-136, 139,
142 bottom, 148, 156-160, 168-173,
186, 187 top, 188 top, 189 bottom,
196 top, 199 top, 200, 208-213, 240-
244, 252-257, 264-268, 274 top, 282-
286, 290 bottom, 291 bottom, 338
bottom, 342, 345 bottom, 354, 355

Jamie Squire/Allsport
163 left

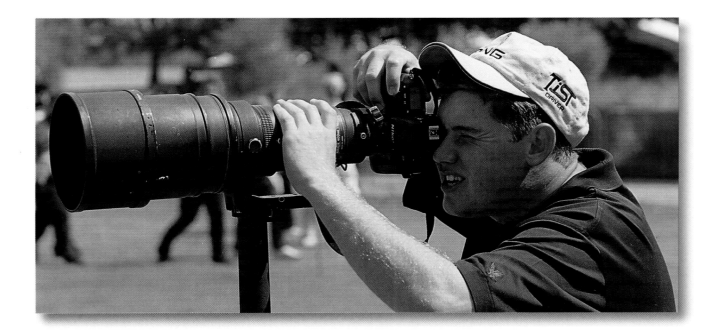